THE FACTS ON FILE GUIDE TO STYLE

THE FACTS ON FILE GUIDE TO STYLE

MARTIN H. MANSER

STEPHEN CURTIS, Associate Editor

☑Checkmark Books
An imprint of Infobase Publishing

THE FACTS ON FILE GUIDE TO STYLE

Checkmark Books
An imprint of Infobase Publishing
132 West 31st Street
New York NY 10001

Library of Congress Cataloging-in-Publication Data

Manser, Martin H.
    The Facts On File guide to style / Martin H. Manser ; associate editor, Stephen Curtis.
        p. cm.
    Includes index.
    ISBN 0-8160-6041-X (acid-free paper)
    ISBN 0-8160-6042-8 (pbk.: acid-free paper)
    1. English language—Style—Handbooks, manuals, etc. 2. Report writing—Handbooks, manuals, etc. I. Title: Guide to style. II. Curtis, Stephen. III. Title.
    PE1421.M36 2006
    808'.042—dc22   2005023169

Checkmark Books are available at special discounts when purchased in bulk quantities for businesses, associations, institutions, or sales promotions. Please call our Special Sales Department in New York at (212) 967-8800 or (800) 322-8755.

You can find Facts On File on the World Wide Web at http://www.factsonfile.com
Martin Manser's Web site is http://www.martinmanser.com

Text design by Erika K. Arroyo
Cover design by Cathy Rincon

Printed in the United States of America

MP Hermitage 10 9 8 7 6 5 4 3 2 1

This book is printed on acid-free paper.

This book is dedicated to all those who want to improve their writing style.

CONTENTS

Introduction   **xi**

PART I. WRITING WITH STYLE

Introduction   **3**

1. What Is Style?   **5**
- The Concept of Style   5
- What Is Style? An Overview   19

2. Beyond Correctness   **21**
- Introduction   21
- Style and Grammatical Correctness   22
- A Feeling for Language   26
- Aesthetic Values   33
- Beyond Correctness: An Overview   35

3. The Qualities of Style   **37**
- Introduction   37
- Clarity   38
- Simplicity   52
- Elegance   53
- Vigor   55
- Variety   63
- The Qualities of Style: An Overview   69

4. Choosing Words   **71**
- Introduction   71
- Use Words You Know   71

➡ The Origins of English Vocabulary 74
➡ Simple versus Complex 76
➡ Use Fewer Nouns 82
➡ Use Longer Words Carefully 87
➡ Enlarging Your Vocabulary 88
➡ Choosing Words: An Overview 91

5. Constructing Sentences 93
➡ Introduction 93
➡ Sentences—the Basics 93
➡ The Logic of the Sentence 105
➡ The Rhythm of the Sentence 115
➡ Constructing Sentences: An Overview 121

6. Constructing Paragraphs 123
➡ Introduction 123
➡ Paragraphs—the Basics 124
➡ Making Paragraphs 133
➡ Unifying Paragraphs 141
➡ Connecting Paragraphs 149
➡ Constructing Paragraphs: An Overview 152

7. Using Figurative Language 153
➡ Introduction 153
➡ The Nature of Figurative Language 154
➡ The Function of Figurative Language 155
➡ Using Figurative Language 156
➡ Figurative Devices 157
➡ The Place for Figurative Language 158
➡ Comic Imagery 160
➡ The Perils of Figurative Language 161
➡ Using Figurative Language: An Overview 163

8. Choosing a Style 165
➡ Introduction 165
➡ Finding the Appropriate Tone 169
➡ Choosing a Style: An Overview 183

9. Expressing Tone through Words 185
➡ Introduction 185
➡ The Power of Language 185

➡	Language and Pictures	186
➡	Formality and Informality	189
➡	Informal English	190
➡	Formal English	195
➡	Neutrality	197
➡	Register	199
➡	Emotiveness and Objectivity	204
➡	Expressing Tone through Words: An Overview	210

PART II. STYLE IN PRACTICE

Introduction		**213**
10. Letters and E-mails		**215**
➡	Introduction	215
➡	The Structure and Conventions of a Business Letter or Formal E-mail	217
➡	Letter-Writing Tactics	223
➡	Delivering Bad News	231
➡	Cover Letters	233
➡	Job Applications	236
➡	Letters of Recommendation	239
➡	Informal E-mails	242
➡	Letters and E-mails: An Overview	243
11. Memorandums and Résumés		**245**
➡	Memorandums	245
➡	Résumés	247
➡	Memorandums and Résumés: An Overview	249
12. Essays and Theses		**251**
➡	Introduction	251
➡	Essays	252
➡	Theses	265
➡	Essays and Theses: An Overview	268
13. Business Reports and Presentations		**269**
➡	Business Reports	269
➡	Presentations	271
➡	Business Reports and Presentations: An Overview	277

14. Promotional Writing   279

- Introduction   279
- Effective Promotion   279
- Emphasizing the Positive   281
- Promotional Writing: An Overview   283

15. Keeping to Style   285

- Introduction   285
- Style and Publishing   285
- Fonts   291
- Numbers   295
- Quotations   299
- Lists and Tables   302
- Illustrations   306
- Keeping to Style: An Overview   308

Index   309

INTRODUCTION

*S**tyle* is a common enough word, but it occurs in so many different contexts and has so many different shades of meaning that when a book puts itself forward as a guide to style, as this one does, the reader may legitimately ask precisely what kind of style he or she is to be guided toward.

Most readers who have reached the point of picking up this book and opening it will doubtless be aware that it is about writing. Writing is, after all, one of the first activities that is likely to spring to mind when the word *style* is mentioned. If anyone who happens to be reading these words hopes to receive some advice on how to dress, decorate a home, or live stylishly, then he or she is, alas, going to be disappointed. Before returning this book to its place on the shelf, however, that person might perhaps take a moment to consider whether he or she may not, even so, find something useful in it.

Writing is not a particularly specialized or uncommon task. Comparatively few people earn the whole of their living by writing, but even fewer, perhaps, earn their living or live their lives in such a way that they are never called upon to write a few words on some subject or other. Modern technology has revolutionized the way we communicate, but it has not done away with the need to put words on paper or into a word-processing program. Writing remains a task that most people have to do, most days if not every day. For some it is a pleasure, but for a good many writing is probably at best a routine task and at worst a chore.

Writing need not be a chore, however. The most effective way of converting almost anything that seems a chore into a worthwhile and even pleasurable activity is to become better at it. To recast the old saying, a job becomes worth doing when you can do it well. If writing becomes a task that you can perform with confidence and, dare it be said, with style, then you will find that you derive a good deal of satisfaction from it. Skill with words is a source of pleasure, pride, and even power, for those who can express themselves fluently and effectively are certainly empowered beyond those who lack that ability. It is not too much to hope that by learning how to use language to best advantage, you will profit both in terms of personal growth and of your value to others who appreciate any job well done.

The purpose of this book is to enable you to do just that. It is not aimed primarily at the established professional writer. Nor is it aimed, in the first instance, at the person who has never before tried to come to grips with the English language and understand the basics of how it works and how it is used. The basic learner should look first at the companion to this volume, *The Facts On File Guide to Good Writing*. That book sets out the fundamentals of the writing process, with suggestions on how to research, plan, compose, and revise a document. It also deals exhaustively with the rules of grammar, punctuation, and usage. It provides a solid foundation on which users of this book can build.

The present volume starts out from the point at which its companion volume ends. While everyone, including professional writers and basic learners, will find much of value in *The Facts On File Guide to Style,* the reader for whom it is chiefly intended is one who, having mastered the basics, wishes to go beyond them and to begin to write not only correctly, but also fluently, effectively, and elegantly—someone, in other words, who will benefit from learning about the craft of writing in order to enhance his or her performance and enjoyment of an everyday task. It is also eminently suited to someone who may be thinking of taking up writing as a hobby or profession in the future.

This book is in two parts, as we consider several different senses of the word *style*. Part I, "Writing with Style," contains chapters on the elements of style, a judicious choice of words, effective sentence and paragraph construction, the crucial relationship between writer and reader, and how language can be adapted to suit a variety of purposes and audiences. Part II, "Style in Practice," considers the techniques to be employed when writing a particular kind of document, for example, a letter, report, essay, or thesis, and reflects on what publishers usually mean by *style*.

As everyone knows, experience gained from life and from living is more valuable than experience gained from books. Nevertheless, the authors and publisher hope that the experience of reading this book will be worthwhile. Its success will be best measured by the number of you, its readers, who feel more confident in dealing with the writing tasks you already have and in preparing you to embark on new projects. We hope that whatever writing tasks you undertake, you will be able to complete them with style, and we wish you "good writing" for the future.

Martin H. Manser
Stephen Curtis

Part I

WRITING WITH STYLE

INTRODUCTION

Any book that aims to give its readers advice on self-improvement or on the right and wrong ways to approach a particular task is under a particularly strong obligation to practice what it preaches. At various points in this work, readers will be urged to plan their work carefully and to make sure that anything they write has a clear and coherent structure. Readers may therefore reasonably expect this book to show the results of careful planning, to possess an intelligible structure, and to lead them on a clearly defined path through the complicated process of understanding what style is, how language can be used stylishly, and how specific writing tasks can be accomplished with style. They will not be disappointed. This, in outline, is the plan.

The book works from the general to the particular. Part I, "Writing with Style," provides the foundation first by dealing with the general nature of style and then by detailing how writers can impart the qualities identified as being essential to style to their writing. Part II, "Style in Practice," is mainly concerned with specific types of document. Part II has its own separate introduction, so for the time being let us look more closely at the structure of part I.

The first few chapters of part I deal with style in the abstract. Chapter 1 attempts to define the concept of style. Chapter 2 begins with a discussion of the relationship between style and grammar, which leads to a consideration of aesthetic values and their place in the assessment of good writing. Chapter 3 considers in detail the qualities that are considered to be characteristic of all good style: clarity, simplicity, elegance, vigor, and variety.

Chapters 4 to 7 deal with the basic skills that all writers who aspire to write with style have to master: how to choose and make the most of words, how to construct sentences, how to link sentences together to form paragraphs, and how to use figurative language.

The final chapters of part I, chapters 8 and 9, show you how to adapt the way you write to suit particular purposes, circumstances, and recipients by varying the tone of what you write. These chapters will explain what is meant by tone and, just as crucially, indicate how writers can use different tones to express their attitude toward their subject matter and their readers.

That, then, is the plan. But there is, of course, a larger plan, set out in the book's introduction, which is to give you, the individual reader, more confidence and skill in dealing with writing tasks. The first step is to know what you are talking about, beginning with analyzing the concept of style and the essential qualities that distinguish stylish writing from that of a more mundane or less accomplished kind.

What Is Style?

THE CONCEPT OF STYLE
Defining the Term

Style is one of those words that resists easy definition. If you were asked to say, off the cuff and without consulting a dictionary, what *style* means, you might very well find yourself having to think fairly hard, even if you were not restricting yourself to the literary senses of the word.

First of all, you would probably want to distinguish between *a style* and *style* in the abstract. *A style*, you might suggest, is roughly the same as *a fashion, a manner,* or even *a form* or *a type.* Each of those words, however, has as many meanings as *style* itself, if not more, and none of them is an exact match. A particular style of dress, for example, may be in fashion or out of fashion. Domestic architecture is one type of architecture, but homes can be built in any number of styles. *Style* in the abstract is equally hard to pin down. Is it the same as *elegance,* or *grace,* or *beauty*? Again, those words come close, but none of them on its own exactly fits what is meant here by *style.*

Style is easier to recognize than it is to define. When someone dresses, serves a meal, handles a situation, dances, or even skateboards with style, most of us are quick to appreciate the fact. We are well aware too that, in using the phrase *with style,* we are expressing admiration. What we are admiring is not so much what is done but the way in which something is done. The manner in which a particular action is performed strikes us as having a certain something that lifts it above the ordinary. And at this point we are again faced with the problem of trying to say what that certain something is.

If we cannot find another single word that exactly reproduces what is meant by *style,* perhaps we should try to put together a group of words that mean the same thing. *Elegance* is likely to be one of them, as well as *grace* and *beauty,* as suggested before, but *self-confidence* perhaps belongs in the group as well. Style in the wider world has a lot to do with presentation. It is possible, for instance, to wear clothes that are in themselves stylish and yet to make a distinctly unstylish impression, not simply by being ungainly but also

5

by being shy or timid. A word such as *pizzazz* might even suggest itself, too. There is often an element of energy or dynamism in things that strike us as stylish. Quiet elegance and classic beauty are definitely not the be-all and end-all of style.

We may argue about precisely which words belong in the group, but once we have decided that the word *style,* in the abstract, denotes a combination of admirable and attractive qualities rather than a quality that can be represented by another single word, we have made considerable progress. We have also made it easier for ourselves to link *style* in the abstract with what we usually mean by *a style.*

If you set out to describe to someone what a ranch-style home is like, you would probably end up listing the characteristics that distinguish a ranch house and make it different from other types of dwelling. You would say that it has only one story, it has a low-pitched roof, its interior is likely an open plan, and so on. You would probably follow the same procedure if we were describing the Gothic style of architecture. Gothic buildings, you would say, have pointed arches and windows; they have high ceilings supported on slender columns; they also tend to be richly decorated inside and outside. In fact, whatever kind of style you are attempting to describe—in apparel, cooking, or even behavior—you would probably go about the task in the same way, listing the characteristics that make it recognizable. A *style,* in other words, is a combination of distinctive and recognizable qualities or features, just as *style* in the abstract is a combination of admirable and attractive qualities. The qualities or features that characterize a particular style will differ in each case and differ again from the qualities that constitute *style* in general, but since each is a combination or mixture of different elements, there is common ground.

Let us now turn our attention to the kind of style that particularly interests us here—writing style—and see how these preliminary observations relate to it.

Writing Styles and Style

When we use the word *style* in relation to writing, we need to make the same primary distinction that we made before. We can speak of *a style* in writing; indeed, if we pay any attention to what we read, we soon notice that there are as many different styles of writing as there are styles of dress or architecture or even types of books or documents. We can also speak of writing *style* in the abstract and mean something that varies rather less. In both instances, the word denotes a combination of qualities or features.

STYLES

Let us think first of particular styles. We know that many famous writers have a style that is distinctively their own. Ernest Hemingway, for example, did not write in the same style as Charles Dickens did. This was partly, of course, because the former was American and the latter British, and partly because they were dealing with different types of subject matter in their novels and approached their subjects in different ways. It was also because they wrote in different centuries, and both writers and readers thought differently and used English differently in the 20th century from the way they did in the 19th century. Even style in the abstract changes somewhat from century to century. But the difference in these authors' styles stems principally from the simple fact that they were different people with something in common: They were both extremely gifted and original writers. This served to ensure that each of them would find a new way of expressing himself. As a result, few readers who know the works of both writers are likely to mistake a passage of Hemingway for a passage of Dickens, or vice versa, and most great writers, even those who were writing the same kind of book during the same period of history, have equally individual and recognizable styles.

However, we do not have to remain in the realms of great literature to notice similar differences in writing technique. Different kinds of book demand different approaches and therefore different styles. Even if you cannot tell a Dickens from a Hemingway, you would probably be able to tell a thriller from a science fiction novel, or a western from a bodice ripper, even without looking at the title and the cover, simply by reading a representative section of the text. Most kinds of popular fiction have certain stylistic conventions, and most of their writers observe them, which is not to imply that popular writers lack individuality, for they most certainly do not.

On this subject we need not confine ourselves to books either. A person who writes for a tabloid newspaper is likely to write in a different style from a person who writes for a highbrow magazine or a learned journal. Similarly, a person who produces advertising copy for a computer manufacturer will probably set about the task in a different manner from a copywriter whose brief is to assist in marketing a new brand of hairspray. Nor do we even need to restrict the discussion to professional writers. A lawyer drawing up a contract or other legal document will employ a different style from the one he or she uses in a letter to a client explaining what has been done. And that same lawyer would probably adopt a different style again if writing on everyday subjects to a personal friend. What the lawyer does, we all do as the occasion demands. Whether speaking or writing, we suit the language we use and the way we use it to the purpose and the audience we have to address. In other words, we all have more than one style at our disposal and often switch from one to another by instinct in response to the demands of the situation confronting us. As socially competent and sensitive beings, we can do no less.

Furthermore, as has been implied more than once already, variation in style is not entirely dependent on external circumstances. Two people can be faced with the same situation and respond to it in two different ways, because of who they are. Likewise, two people can set out to write the same kind of text under the same circumstances and produce different results, because of who they are. From great writers and popular novelists to journalists and copywriters, from politicians, lawyers, academics, preachers, and the many others whose professional success depends to a greater or lesser extent on skill with words, right down to the ordinary man and woman in the street, all of us are individuals.

By virtue of that simple fact, each of us possesses an individual style that cannot be taken away from us. We can try to disguise it, we can choose to ignore it, but if we write at any length, this personal style will almost inevitably show itself. It can mark us out as clearly as our handwriting does so that if we happen to leave a letter unsigned, people who know us will usually still have a good idea of where they should send the reply.

So, a multiplicity of styles appears in writing. They may be personal, professional, genre related, or purpose oriented, and lists could be drawn up detailing their particular characteristics. But the fact that they are many and various should not obscure the fact that there is also another specific combination of characteristics that constitutes style as such. Let us change from a quantitative to a qualitative approach and briefly consider what they are.

Whatever you happen to be writing and in whatever style, you may write well or you may write badly. Like the stylishness that distinguishes some clothes and some of their wearers, there is a stylishness that some writing and some writers possess and others do not. It is, in fact, a combination of admirable and desirable qualities that all writing ought to aspire to. What are those qualities? In this instance, there is little argument among the experts. The qualities that constitute good writing and style for the purposes of this book are clarity, simplicity, elegance, vigor, and variety. Although, as has been said, the prevailing style changes from century to century, for the past 300 years or so there has been general agreement on the basic principles. What an 18th-century writer considered to be elegant or vigorous differs somewhat from a 21st-century writer's concept of the same qualities, but if either had to make a list of the characteristics that make a piece of writing easy and pleasurable to read, then clarity, simplicity, elegance, vigor, and variety would be sure to figure prominently on it.

The Treatment of Style in This Book

As was mentioned in the introduction, this book will deal with style in several different senses of the word. In the preceding subsection, several different aspects of writing style were mentioned. It is now time to sort out which aspects of style are most relevant to our purposes and to set out in greater detail the procedure that will be adopted in dealing with them.

Of the points discussed above, the following are crucial to the argument of the book as a whole:

- There are very many different writing styles that can be used.
- Each person has his or her own writing style.
- Every writer, far from being limited by personal characteristics, can adopt any one of the many different styles available in order to fulfill a particular purpose (that is, adapt his or her own style in such a way as to make it suitable for the purpose in view).
- There are certain qualities common to all good style: clarity, simplicity, elegance, vigor, and variety.

Now, it will be immediately apparent that it is impossible in a book of this size to discuss every particular kind of writing style that the reader may decide to use or be called upon to use. It is likewise impracticable to discuss the individual aspects of every reader's personal style. The basic procedure adopted in this book will therefore be to work from the general to the particular.

We have arrived at a basic definition of what *style* means in general and in writing, but that definition does not tell us all we need to know about style: where it comes from, how it relates to content, how we put style into our writing. Some very interesting questions have been raised but have so far been left unanswered. In particular, alert readers may have noted a certain tension between the statement that style is a distinctly and unavoidably personal trait in a writer and the equally valid statement that writers can and do write in a variety of different styles. Can that tension be resolved, and if so, how?

To What Extent Is Style Personal?

Our personalities, our upbringings, and our experiences all inevitably contribute to shaping how we express ourselves. As a result, each of us has his or her own individual style in speech or writing. In fact, the great French novelist Gustave Flaubert—writing, incidentally, in the days before avoiding sexism became a major concern for writers—went so far as to say that "Style is the man himself."

There is a great deal of truth in that observation. It is said that Sir Winston Churchill, the great British statesman who was also an extremely popular author, especially of large-scale historical works, would rely on a team of researchers to do most of the information gathering for him. His main task, instead, was to unify the finished product and give it the unique Churchillian stamp, which he did by recasting the material that his researchers had provided into the sonorous rolling prose for which he was famous and which his readers expected. Churchill's readers may have wanted to learn history, but they also wanted to feel the presence of the great man in his work. And he was present in the work—through his style.

Few of us possess such an instantly recognizable and reproducible personal style as Churchill's, but equally, few, if any of us, can remain anonymous. It was emphasized earlier that you do not have to be a great writer in order to have an identifiable personal style. We know from common experience that most people when speaking or writing tend to favor particular words or phrases and to put words and phrases together in particular ways. We all know someone who, when confronted by a particular situation, always says the same thing. Most of us find that we remember people from our past not only by how they looked, what they did, and the sound of their voices but by the way in which they habitually used words. How often do we hear people preface a comment with the phrase: "As my grandmother [father/teacher/friend Michael etc.] used to say . . ."? When they do so, they are implicitly bearing witness to the fact that individuals have their own distinctive way with language.

The personal element in writing is very valuable. Teachers certainly think so. They constantly urge students to express their own opinions in their own words. Given the choice, most people would rather read or hear a firsthand impression couched in firsthand words than be offered secondhand thoughts in borrowed language. Given a stack of assignments to grade, teachers especially appreciate anything that shows a fresh approach and speaks to them in a distinctive voice. The same applies outside the education system. People, generally speaking, would rather read a letter or report that appears to have been produced by a living, breathing individual than something that sounds as if it had been issued from a machine. Individuality is to be prized, and if, as has been suggested previously, your personality is bound to show through when you write at any length, then this is something that generally works in your favor. One of the main reasons why people pick up a pen or sit down at the keyboard is to express themselves. You should not be afraid to allow your personal style some scope.

In some respects, however, this is easier said than done—at least, easier said than consciously done. Although we each have our own individual style, most people probably find it harder to describe or even recognize their own style than to define style in general. Other people are usually much better able to spot our characteristic behaviors or quirks in everyday life than we are ourselves, and the same is usually true in writing. There is little point in undertaking a lengthy analysis of your own writings to try to ascertain what precisely it is that makes them yours and nobody else's. So, how do you preserve your individuality? The answer was implied in what was said in the previous paragraph about firsthand and secondhand language. To maintain your individuality, avoid, as far as possible, following standard patterns of thought and using stock phrases. Write about what you know or what you have discovered in the words that come naturally to you. And, as a specific means of achieving this aim, try to keep in touch with your speaking voice when you are composing on screen or on paper.

FINDING YOUR OWN VOICE

If individuality is so valuable, some might ask, what is the point of books like this one? Why should writers not simply do what comes naturally, especially if they are being advised to "write as they talk"?

The nature of the relationship between a person's speaking voice and the way in which he or she writes will be dealt with shortly. Suffice it to say for the moment that first a sense of proportion must be kept. Unfettered individualism is a somewhat dubious commodity in any sphere. The basic rules of good writing apply to everybody, and everybody's writing is likely to be improved by following them. Second, far from diminishing the personal quality of your writing, working in accordance with the advice offered in a book like this one may actually enhance it.

In book reviews you often find the critic saying that an author has found, or is beginning to find, "his or her own voice" in a particular work. This is a cliché of book reviewing, but, for our purposes, a rather interesting one. What do reviewers mean when they use it?

They are saying that the author has now arrived at an original and distinctive manner of putting his or her ideas across and thereby implying that in his or her earlier works the author either showed a general lack of originality or was experimenting unsuccessfully with style, or had been unduly influenced by other books on similar subjects or of a similar nature. Writers are, after all, continually being urged to check out what book or magazine publishers want before submitting their own material, and a beginner author will often feel that the easiest way to get published is to give publishers more of the kind of thing they have published before.

Everyone at some time or other, wittingly or unwittingly, copies what others have done before. The previous references to firsthand and second-hand thought and language imply as much. Imitating others—which is subtly different from simply copying their words or ideas—can be a valuable learning and confidence-building exercise. The first time a person has to write a business letter, say, or a letter to a newspaper, he or she is very likely to look at the way other people usually write the one or the other for fear of sounding like an ignorant beginner who does not know the standard conventions. There is no disgrace in that; almost everyone does it. It is useful to know what the standard forms and courtesies are. This book contains numerous illustrations of how, in the authors' opinion, certain tasks should be tackled and certain kinds of document should be written. The user of this book is welcome to take inspiration from them if they serve his or her purpose; in fact, their very purpose is to offer examples that the user can learn from rather than borrow so that he or she can find personal solutions to the problems and ways of approaching writing tasks—just as the more experienced novelist eventually finds his or her own voice.

Only with practice, and with the increase in skill that comes with practice, do writers acquire the ability and the confidence to say new things in a fresh and distinctive way. The confidence to use your own voice comes from knowing what you are doing and knowing that you are able to do it well. Nothing, perhaps, surpasses practice as a builder of confidence, but understanding the essential principles of style as set forth in a guidebook like this one certainly helps.

Can Style Be Learned?

Yes. That much should be evident from what was said in the previous subsection. Some people are born with a special gift for language and self-expression, just as some people are born with a special aptitude for playing the piano or playing baseball. Even child prodigies and other exceptionally talented people, however, have to learn the standard techniques; they simply learn them much faster and are ready to strike out on their own much sooner than ordinary mortals. People of less staggering ability can at least approach the standard of the precociously gifted by proceeding at their own pace. People of ordinary ability who want to write, play the piano, play baseball, or master any other skill can go a long way by following good advice and practicing.

The basics of a good style in writing are not rocket science. You can learn them from this book. You can learn more by reading other books, fiction or nonfiction, and by careful attention to not only what the authors say but how they say it. Copy what they do or say only if you have to, but remember that to reproduce another writer's words without quotation marks and without an acknowledgment or, in the case of longer borrowings, without permission from the author or publisher is plagiarism. Above all, write as much as you can on any subject that interests you. The best way of learning is always by doing.

How Does Style Relate to Content?

Style is sometimes spoken and written of as if it were a kind of optional extra. There is a view of the writing process that suggests that it operates as follows: You have an idea, you put that idea into ordinary words, then you translate those ordinary words into grander or more stylish words if the words you first thought of were not impressive enough.

This bears some relation to how writers usually proceed, but it is a highly simplified account and based on a false notion of style. It is, in fact, rather difficult to explain the relationship between ideas and words or to explain the process by which a piece of writing gets written. To get around the problem, writers frequently resort to metaphor, and a favorite metaphor from the 18th century onward has compared thought to the human body and language to its clothes. "Style is the dress of thought," according to organist and composer Samuel Wesley, the son and nephew of the founders of Methodism; in other words, a writer "clothes" his or her thoughts in suitable language.

Unfortunately, this metaphor has probably helped promote a false notion of style and its relation to content. Just as a person might have one set of clothes for everyday purposes and another more stylish set for going out or evenings, so, it is reckoned, a writer or speaker may use one kind of language if he or she is not being style-conscious and another kind of language when he or she wants to impress. Style, therefore, becomes a kind of dressing up. Worse still, if we took the metaphor to its logical conclusion, we would have to conclude that language or style covers or conceals thought, for the basic function of clothing is to cover or conceal the human body. If language really were like clothing, then you would have to strip off that clothing to see the idea clearly. That, surely, is not a very positive or helpful starting point for a discussion of this very important relationship.

Style is the expression of thought rather than its dress. The relationship between what you want to communicate and the way in which you actually communicate it ought to be as close as possible. After all, when you write something, what you intend to communicate to the person you are writing to or for are ideas, rather than words as such. Words are simply the means you use to get the ideas across. On that basis, the most important matter is that the words you use should not get in the way of, obscure, or detract from the ideas that constitute your message to your reader. The best style is that which is one with the thought it expresses, which encapsulates that thought in such a way that the hearer or reader understands perfectly and with little effort what the writer or speaker is trying to say.

LANGUAGE AND THOUGHT

For most purposes it is convenient to consider thought and language as if they were separate and distinct, thereby giving meaning to the concept of putting one's thoughts into words. Yet neither this separation nor the familiar phrase that derives from it entirely corresponds to the nature of thought as we usually experience it. Further investigation into this relationship can clarify and reinforce the statements about style made in the previous paragraph.

Thought does not usually exist apart from language. Some people perhaps think in images most of the time. All of us sometimes see things in our mind in the form of a picture or have an idea in the form of a feeling about something. When that happens, we have to divide our consciousness so that one part of our mind can consider the vision or feeling experienced by another part and attempt to find words to describe it. Most of us, however, for most of the time think in words. We think "Those flowers would look better in a blue vase" or "Harold is a perfect saint." We do not generally see an image of the spray of flowers in a blue vase or conjure up a picture of Harold in white robes with a halo around his head. The ideas, rather, present themselves to us already verbalized.

In a great many cases, then, it is difficult to separate an idea from the words in which it enters our minds. Content, therefore, does not usually change its essential form in the process of becoming a finished written document. It does not make sense to speak of "putting words into words," so what are we actually doing when we write?

As has already been said, what we set out to communicate are ideas, not words as such. Thus, when we say to someone "Harold is a perfect saint," our intention is not to make our listeners envision Harold in robes or halo, nor, in the first instance, to imprint the particular manner in which we have expressed our thoughts on their minds. It is rather to impress upon them the fact that Harold is, at least in our opinion, an exceptionally good or exceptionally patient and forbearing person. Our essential purpose is to express our opinion of Harold and/or to change or reinforce other people's opinion of him. The words we use to do this are important inasmuch as the idea does not exist, or at least cannot be communicated, without them, but there their importance really begins and ends.

Thought may most often come to us in verbal form, but the same thought can be expressed in different ways. The previous paragraph illustrates as much. We might say,

Harold is a perfect saint.

or we might equally say,

Harold is an exceptionally patient and forbearing person.

Which of these two—or of all the other possible variants of this particular statement—we actually say during a conversation will probably depend on which of them comes into our head first at the time. Which of them we write may likewise be determined on a "first-come-first-served"—or, in this case, "first used"—basis. But, when we are writing, we are not held captive to the inspiration of the moment. We have time to reflect, to ask ourselves, Is there a better way of putting this? or Of the various ways of expressing this idea, which is the best *or* which best suits the context and/or my purpose in writing? It is at that point, during that moment of reflection, that considerations of style come into play. We then have to decide, in this particular instance, whether a metaphor—*Harold is a perfect saint*—or a more straightforward expression better fulfills our aim. (For more on the possibilities and drawbacks of metaphor use, *see* chapter 7, USING FIGURATIVE LANGUAGE, page 153.)

The criteria we should use in making such decisions are the subject matter of this book. For the moment, we are simply concerned with the type of decision that is involved. It is less often a decision as to how to put something abstract into words and more often a decision as to whether to accept, reject, or modify the wording in which a particular idea presents itself to us. And that, in a nutshell, is the style-conscious writer's basic task.

SUMMING UP

In summing up the relationship between style and content, let us try to get away once and for all from the old clothing metaphor and find a newer one. Language, and therefore style, relates to content roughly as the computer or television screen relates to the image displayed on it. The screen is not the same thing as the image, but you cannot view the image without it. Language is not the same thing as the idea, but you cannot, as a writer, express the idea without it. The screen may need to be adjusted to give the clearest and sharpest picture possible. Your language may need to be adjusted likewise. But just as, in most instances, you do not want your screen image to appear in unnaturally bright colors, so you will not generally want to add extraneous color to your writing. All you want is for the ideas to shine through.

Metaphors apart, most ideas will present themselves to you already formulated, or at least partly formulated, in language. Your job then is to accept, reject, or modify that formulation. Your first formulation may or may not be the best. Paradoxical as it may sound, your first formulation may not even be the one that is most personal to you, since ideas can easily present themselves first in secondhand terms. What is certain is that the more active your imagination, the more language you have at your immediate disposal, and the greater your skill in manipulating language, the more interesting will be both your initial formulations and the modifications you will be able to make if your initial formulation seems in any way unsatisfactory.

In the interval between having the initial inspiration and writing down the idea, you have the opportunity to reflect and make decisions. There are several questions you may ask yourself in the process of making this decision: Is this the best way of putting this? Is this clear? Is this sufficiently distinct from what I have said before? and so forth. But among those questions—just to link this discussion back to another of our main concerns—may be the following: Is this a fresh way of putting it? Is this what I want to say? Is this how I would naturally say it? Is this me? Style as such and your own personal style both come into consideration at this moment, and the best answer to the question will usually be one that reconciles the two.

At What Point in the Writing Process Should the Writer Be Most Concerned about Style?

For a full account and analysis of the writing process, the reader is referred to part I of *The Facts On File Guide to Good Writing*. A brief summary will suffice here.

The writing process has four stages: thinking and researching, planning, writing, and revising. Considerations of style actually enter the process at the very beginning, since when you decide what kind of work you intend to write you are more or less bound to decide at the same time what style you intend to write it in. Even if you do not make a conscious choice between, say, an informal or formal style, an academic or a journalistic style, but merely decide to go ahead and "write it as it comes," you have implicitly opted for your own "default" personal style. Nevertheless, in the nature of things, considerations of style are likely to loom largest in the latter two stages of the writing process, when you are composing and when you are revising.

METHODS OF COMPOSITION

People set about the task of composition in different ways. Some people rush off a first draft, looking neither right nor left, as it were, and trying not to stop for anybody or anything. What is important for them is to get something down on paper in whatever form. What they write may be ungrammatical, may lack punctuation, may not be divided into paragraphs—none of that matters to them. What they are writing is simply a draft: correctness and style can be dealt with later. Other people feel painfully exposed if they are aware that they are leaving a lot of errors and infelicities in their wake. They prefer to proceed from a solid foundation, not to erect a temporary structure that has to be shored up and fitted out later. They proceed slowly and carefully and do their best to get it right the first time. Such people are likely to be more intensely aware of style matters while composing than the members of the get-it-all-down-as-quickly-as-possible school.

The practice of most people will probably lie somewhere between these two extremes. There will be times when ideas come thick and fast and their writing seems to flow. There will be other times when the words only come like blood from a stone, or when the writer becomes absorbed in some key passage and works away at it until he or she is able to fix it in something like a final form.

Every writer should feel free to work at his or her own pace—so far as deadlines will allow—and to adopt the method that suits him or her best. The method advocated in *The Facts On File Guide to Good Writing* is simply intended as a guide to the most logical approach. If any individual's method necessitates ignoring matters of style at any interim stage in the writing process, then so be it. The one stage at which considerations of style cannot be ignored, however, is the final one, the revision stage.

REVISING FOR STYLE

The style-conscious writer's basic task is to accept, reject, or modify the wording in which a particular idea is presented. The writer is likely to perform this sort of operation many times in any writing session, except when consciously suppressing the urge to correct in order to speed ahead. During revision, however, this is the writer's sole task. He or she should work through the entire text checking each and every sentence for its relevance to the work as a whole and using the criteria set forth in this book to assess whether the sentence is stylistically as near perfect as it can be made.

At any point up through the final draft, a writer may get a better idea or may reject whole paragraphs or even whole sections as they stand and decide to rewrite them. Everyone gets last-minute second thoughts at some time or other. But these too, once they are written down, should be submitted to the same rigorous process of revision. Style, as has been suggested, may well be among your first thoughts when you begin. It should definitely be among your final thoughts as you prepare to produce a clean version of the finished text.

ADDING AND SUBTRACTING

Style tends to be thought of as something added on, as in the traditional clothing metaphor; however, in order to arrive at the best and most stylish way of expressing a particular idea, writers as often have to remove unnecessary or inappropriate words as they have to insert more elegant or telling ones. Gardeners have to prune their plants to keep them in shape and in a healthy condition. Writers frequently have to carry out similar operations on their text. The more elegant, simple, and vigorous version of what you have to say may be hidden under a mass of words struggling to get out. Be flexible and open-minded when you are revising your work. Do not automatically assume that improving it means adding to it. Remember the old adage Less is more. It is frequently cited in regard to short-story writing, but it equally applies to other types of writing.

Do not, on the other hand, take too much to heart the equally old advice to Kill your darlings. The British scholar and author Dr. Samuel Johnson was given the following advice by his college tutor: "Read over your compositions, and where ever you meet with a passage which you think is particularly fine, strike it out." Since Johnson's own work is full of fine, high-sounding passages, however, we can safely assume that he did not himself follow this instruction to the letter. Nonetheless, never fall in love with your own compositions to the extent that you feel they are beyond criticism. Always try to distance yourself from them—especially from the "particularly fine passages"—and read them as an uninvolved outsider would. If, at the end, you are satisfied that they are bold and imaginative rather than inflated and overwrought, leave them as they are.

CRITICISM AND SELF-CRITICISM

When you are trying to decide whether you need to add to or subtract from your text in order to perfect it, it is useful to know whether you are by nature a wordy or a laconic writer. As has been said before, identifying the characteristic strengths and weaknesses of your personal style is difficult. But all criticism is difficult—especially self-criticism. Identifying the shortcomings of a particular piece of work may be an extremely unwelcome task for any author; after all, the writer has struggled through to the final period, become rather attached to the way he or she has formulated particular ideas, and has an ego to protect and nurture just like anyone else. You can stare and stare at a piece of your own writing, sometimes knowing instinctively that there is something wrong with it, yet be unable to conjure up any ideas for making it better. At this point, you need help if you can get it.

Self-criticism is the handiest form of criticism because the critic does not have to be summoned away from some other activity to offer an opinion. Self-criticism, however, usually only develops with experience and demands a certain kind of temperament. Besides, if we are honest with ourselves, self-criticism often takes it cue from criticism offered by outsiders. It is often they who first point out what we are doing wrong. If we are wise, we internalize what they have to say and apply it to our own work, without prompting, the next time around.

The aspiring writer should be grateful for criticism from any source. Gratitude is not, of course, the usual emotion that we feel when someone takes a piece that we have labored long and hard to bring to completion and rips it to shreds. Nevertheless, it is an unfortunate truth that we usually learn more from having our faults pointed out than from having our virtues commended. If you can find someone who is able to mix appreciation of your good points into a candid appraisal of your weaknesses, then you will have found the best possible kind of help. But it is better to bite the bullet and offer your work to someone who will deal harshly with it (sometimes in order to enhance his or her own ego at the expense of yours) so long as that person offers specific and fairly detailed comments. Nothing is more frustrating for a writer than to be told, after a cursory inspection, "It looks fine to me." So, try to find someone, preferably a knowledgeable person, who has the time to read through your work and will give an honest and detailed opinion of it. Treasure anything that person says, even though you may have difficulty accepting it with grace at the time, and even though you think he or she may be wrong. You retain the final decision as to whether to act on the criticism or not. If you find the same criticism being offered by several different people or with respect to several different pieces of work, then the chances are that a characteristic weakness of your way of writing has come to light. This knowledge gives you a chance to amend it.

What Should the Relationship Be between the Way You Speak and the Way You Write?

It was suggested earlier in this chapter that one way of preserving the valuable personal element in your writing is to endeavor to stay in touch with your speaking voice. There is yet another old adage that advises writers to Write as you talk. Will the golden age of writing therefore arrive once everyone possesses voice-recognition software and can speak to a computer without the need for such irritating intermediaries as the keyboard and in the certain knowledge that what eventually appears on the screen will be good style? No.

The write-as-you-talk injunction is a useful reminder not to try to be too pretentious when writing. In earlier times, critics sometimes complained that a writer's work "smelled too much of the inkhorn," by which they meant that the work seemed to have been produced by a cloistered individual who had little contact with everyday life and language and was writing simply for a select band of equally erudite or pedantic readers. The modern-day equivalent would perhaps be the kind of prose that is sometimes found in learned journals or official documents and is full of specialist polysyllabic words and unexplained acronyms.

While nobody appreciates writing that is self-consciously arty, there are dangers in going too far in the other direction. Some modern novelists write long passages in the slang or jargon of the streets, and these can be just as difficult to follow as the most formidably academic writing. But these writers, perhaps, write as someone else talks, rather than as they talk themselves.

In reality, few people write precisely as they talk. Most people probably feel they do not speak well enough—that is, fluently, eloquently, and correctly enough—to want their conversational style recorded and passed on, potentially, to posterity. When they sit down to write, they automatically set their sights a little higher and consequently use language more carefully and more formally than they would do if they were addressing a listener across the room rather than an invisible reader. It is right that they should do so. The main advantage that writing has over talking is that it is a delayed-action medium. The writer has time to reflect on what he or she is saying, to have second thoughts, to go through a revision stage before submitting a work for inspection. As has been said before, the moment of reflection is the moment of decision, the crucial moment for considerations of style. Even writers of slang take the opportunity to polish it. The talker usually has to think on his or her feet and has a limited time in which to get a point across. Talk is often full of stops and starts and repetitions and digressions and apologies, and is backed up by hand gestures and eye contact (or lack of it) and body language in general. With the best will in the world, you can hardly reproduce all of these on paper, even if you wish to, even if you are writing dialogue. Nor, in fact, is there any need to try to do so.

That said, however, language does seem to live a fuller life somehow when it is being used in speech. It does need to come out into the open air and be traded between people. Spoken language may often be imperfect, ungrammatical, or disjointed, but equally often it is lively, inventive, and colorful. It arises on the spur of the moment out of immediate contact with situations, as the vast majority of writing does not. Writing almost always is, in the phrase William Wordsworth used to define poetry, "emotion recollected in tranquillity." There are distinct advantages in that, but the danger is that the tranquillity may get the better of the emotion. The text of a play or a poem only comes completely to life when it is spoken by a living actor or reciter. Certain of the finer points of style, similarly, can only be appreciated if you are aware of the spoken value of the words on the page (*see*, in particular, THE RHYTHM OF THE SENTENCE, page 115). If it were possible to get the best of both worlds, that would surely be the ideal solution.

To some extent it is possible. Instead of trying to write exactly as you talk, rather make sure that what you write is speakable in your own voice. To do this you do not necessarily have to read your text to yourself aloud. You may well find yourself unconsciously saying the words "in your mind's voice" as you write them down. If you do not do this automatically, try making a conscious effort to do so. Listen to your text. Listen, especially, to anything you have written that looks long or complicated on paper. Say it over to yourself internally, and if it does not roll off the mind's "tongue," say it again aloud. If it does not lend itself to being spoken in your normal speaking voice, then this fact should immediately put you on your guard. If it does not sound "right" or does not sound "like you," it is advisable to make changes. Work on the sentence or paragraph in question until it becomes speakable with little effort. Thus you not only follow the spirit of the injunction to write as you talk; you also keep in touch with your own style.

Imagination is, obviously, an extremely valuable faculty in a writer. We are more or less conditioned to think of imagination as a kind of visual faculty operating through the mind's eye. From much that has been said in this chapter, however, it should be apparent that "the mind's voice" is, if anything, a more important part of the writer's equipment. It formulates ideas, it checks for readability, and it can help to keep you in touch with the greater world outside. Use it.

WHAT IS STYLE? AN OVERVIEW

- The word *style* denotes both a concrete and an abstract thing, and in both cases it refers to a combination of recognizable and usually admirable qualities.
- The qualities that distinguish good style in writing are clarity, simplicity, elegance, vigor, and variety.
- Each writer has his or her own personal style.
- Each writer has the capacity to adopt different styles or adapt his or her own style to different purposes.
- By learning and following the basic rules of good style, each writer is able to perfect his or her own personal style.
- Style is not the dress of thought, but its expression.
- Thought usually comes ready formulated in language.
- The writer's basic task is usually to accept, reject, or modify the words in which thought presents itself to him or her.
- The writer should listen to the mind's voice.

Beyond Correctness

INTRODUCTION

The title of this chapter may cause some readers to pause and ask themselves, perhaps with a degree of puzzlement, what kind of correctness is being referred to and why anyone should wish to discuss the subject. Surely something is either correct or incorrect, and that is that. If you venture to the other side of correctness, where can you possibly end up except in hypercorrectness, a state of painfully nitpicking pedantry, or back in incorrectness?

The correctness in question is grammatical correctness. As was said in the introduction, this book is a companion volume to *The Facts On File Guide to Good Writing*. The present book, it was claimed, begins from the point at which its companion leaves off; it builds on the foundations provided by its predecessor. Much of the *Guide to Good Writing* is devoted to an exposition of the basic rules of grammar and usage. It describes and exemplifies what is generally considered to be the correct use of English. In order to go further, we must necessarily go beyond correctness in that sense or run the risk of repeating what has been said elsewhere.

But that is not the end of the matter. If style were simply a matter of following grammatical rules, then grammarians and pedagogues would elbow William Shakespeare, John Milton, Charles Dickens, Herman Melville, Henry James, and others out of the pantheon of literature and set themselves up as the only masters and models of good writing. This will never happen, thankfully, because grammarians and pedagogues themselves acknowledge that writing is more of an art than a science, and art has its own rules. Indeed, it sometimes seems that, among artists, rules are "more honored in the breach than the observance." You cannot, it is sometimes suggested, obey rules and expect to produce anything original. Rules, grammar, correctness—all that is for fuddy-duddies. The truly creative mind scorns such restraints.

So, this chapter will attempt to explore the relationship between style and grammar. It will also open a discussion of artistic matters. In doing so, it will not overlook the fact that in tackling questions that deal, in however broad a sense, with art, artistry, and indeed style, we are not on entirely solid ground.

When we are discussing correctness, of the grammatical or any other kind, we can usually do so in full confidence that we can say something is either correct or incorrect, and there is no argument. There are objective, or at least solid, grounds for making the judgment. If you add 12 and 15 and come to a total of 28, you can easily be proved wrong. If necessary someone can produce 12 objects, and then another 15, and ask you to count the total. If you say or write *I are teaching English since twelve years,* someone can easily produce a grammar book and open it to the chapter on subject-verb agreement and open it again to the chapter on prepositions and point out to you that this is not correct. But if you write *When I taught English, I opened my students' starving eyes to a wonderful world of sound and expression,* and someone tells you that this is the most awful twaddle, what is that person to use to back up the judgment?

It is not that there are no criteria for judgment. A book such as this one could not possibly be written if there were none. It is simply that the criteria are, to some degree, subjective. Solidity is relative, and the degree of solidity in aesthetic judgments is less than in many other fields. We have been speaking of grammar as if it were, shall we say, science based. But, of course, not all experts agree on how language works or whether traditional grammar—the kind of grammar set out in *The Facts On File Guide to Good Writing* and the kind of grammar you were probably taught at school—is the best method of describing the way in which it works or of teaching languages to students. Be that as it may, the rules of grammar are sanctioned by tradition and the work of many scholars. They may not be absolutely absolute or absolutely objective, but we do not seriously compromise our intellectual integrity by treating them as if they were. The situation with regard to style is far less clear-cut. Clarity, elegance, and vigor exist in the eye of the beholder, perhaps, to a greater degree than we feel entirely safe with.

So the title "Beyond Correctness" is also intended as an acknowledgment that in dealing with matters of style we have to make value judgments on less than objectively verifiable grounds. In order to be able to discuss style matters, we have, to some degree, to be able to function as literary critics. This chapter, besides discussing the relationship between grammatical correctness and style, also aims to show that on the far side of correctness is something other than a void.

STYLE AND GRAMMATICAL CORRECTNESS

Grammar

The bad news for those who dislike grammar or believe that they do not know any grammar is that, for better or worse, nobody who wishes to write and be understood, let alone write and be considered something of a stylist, can be wholly unconcerned with grammar and usage. Grammar provides the logical framework without which communication in any language would be well nigh impossible. You might think that grammar was a product of more sophisticated ages, and that older and "more primitive" languages would be grammatically simpler. This is not the case. In fact, the very opposite is true of the grammar of at least one modern European language, which has become progressively less complex over the centuries. That language is English. The users of the earliest form of our language—Old English, or Anglo-Saxon—had to cope with a system of different cases for nouns and complicated suffixes to show the tenses and persons of verbs that later ages have entirely dispensed with.

It is worth considering for a moment why people who were living a life that was far simpler and more primitive than ours, and had far narrower intellectual horizons, should have developed methods of communication that were complicated and subtle and demanded considerable powers of memory—or so it would seem to anyone who has tried to learn a heavily inflected language, whether an ancient one such as Latin or a modern one like German. We can only guess at what the reasons were. It seems reasonable to suppose that they were very eager to establish what precisely the relations were between the different words that they used and thus between the different people and things that they talked about in their everyday conversation. It seems equally reasonable to suppose that, for them, as native speakers of the languages in question, the efforts of memory involved were less than they are for us as outsiders when we attempt to learn those same languages.

NO GRAMMAR, NO COMMUNICATION

We can draw two lessons from these assumptions. The first is that we ought to be equally concerned about making absolutely clear the relationships between the words we use and between the people and things we talk about. If we do not know any grammar, we cannot do so. This fact can be easily demonstrated.

The sequence of words *gone fishing back soon love Ted* scrawled on a piece of paper would be immediately understandable to the person for whom the note was intended or to any English-speaking person who happened to pick it up and read it. It looks ungrammatical and it is unpunctuated, but the person who wrote it had a basic grasp of English grammar and expected the reader to have a similar grasp and to understand that he was merely omitting certain words and punctuation marks for the sake of brevity. On the basis of that shared knowledge, everything the writer omitted, the reader could immediately supply. If the note had read *fishing gone soon love Ted back,* however, the link with basic grammar would have been broken. In the first instance the missing elements are obvious *[I have] gone fishing[. I will be] back soon[. L]ove[,] Ted.* In the second, there is no implicit grammatical structure and it is not at all obvious what the relationships between the words are supposed to be, so it is impossible to fill in the gaps.

What is true of the second "note" cited in the previous paragraph is equally true of the even simpler sequence *Ted Nigel hit.* In a language such as Latin it would be immediately clear who had hit whom because one of the names would be in the nominative case (and therefore the subject of the verb) and one of the names would be in the accusative case (and therefore the object of the verb) and no matter the order in which you wrote down the three words, it would always be clear who was the aggressor and who was the victim. In English the word order for a standard sentence is subject followed by verb followed by object: *Ted hit Nigel* or *Nigel hit Ted*. Every English speaker knows this whether the previous sentence with its references to subjects and objects makes any sense to him or her. That is the point and the second lesson to be learned from the assumptions made above about the relationship of the earliest speakers of English to their language. Just as the Anglo-Saxons probably imbibed the complexities of their language with their mothers' milk, so we internalize the comparatively simple grammatical patterns of modern English as part and parcel of the childhood process of learning to speak. A very small child will say *want cookie* rather than *cookie want*. In doing so, the child goes through essentially the same procedure as the adult who says *gone fishing* and not *fishing gone*—and demonstrates just as certainly that he or she, at some level, knows basic grammar.

We need to know grammar in order to speak and to communicate the simplest needs, let alone to write stylishly. There is no question about that. The real questions, perhaps, are Do we need to know the refinements of grammar and usage? and Do we need to know the standard vocabulary that writers use to describe the operations that we carry out instinctively in our everyday use of English?

The Tools of the Trade

The answer to both the questions posed at the end of the previous paragraph is a slightly qualified yes. The qualifications arise from the fact that it is perfectly possible that someone would be able to write adequately, or even take the literary world by storm, without being able to explain the difference between an adverb and an adjective. Just as it is possible to be a gifted musician without being able to read music, so it is possible for someone to be hailed as a literary genius simply on the basis of the use that he or she makes of English that has been assimilated purely by listening and reading.

That said, wild untutored geniuses who stagger the critics and put their expensively educated contemporaries to shame are comparatively rare. They are the exceptions that prove the general rule. Shakespeare—"warbl[ing] his native woodnotes wild," according to John Milton, and knowing "small Latin and less Greek," according to Ben Jonson—is sometimes presented as the prime example in English literature of the simple country boy who came to town and beat the city slickers at their own game. This, however, is a myth. Shakespeare was well educated, even though he did not attend university, and was certainly canny enough to learn from his university-educated contemporaries before he tried to surpass them. More to the point perhaps, wild untutored geniuses who are asked to produce company reports or make presentations to important clients are probably even rarer. Fewer allowances are made for ordinary people with more average talents. They are expected to possess basic knowledge to make up for their lack of exceptional gifts.

We all can get so far on our native wit, but there usually comes a time when we sense that something we have written feels wrong and want to know what is wrong and how we can rectify it. Or maybe someone else criticizes a sentence that we have written and asks us to justify the use of a certain word in a certain place. It makes it much easier to enter into a discussion on language matters either with ourselves or with other people if we know the ins and outs of the subject.

Let us approach this topic from a slightly different angle. You would expect a carpenter to be familiar with the kinds of wood that are suitable for various tasks, with the tools of the trade, and with the names of the various joints, supports, surfaces, and so on that he or she might need to build a structure. Some of the vocabulary used by the carpenter in the course of his or her work might be unfamiliar to the ordinary layperson but is essential to the conduct of the business. A writer uses language most of the time as the carpenter uses wood. Language is the writer's basic construction material. At the same time, there is an array of linguistic and literary technical language that constitutes the writer's terms of art. This specialized language is crucial to the conduct of the writer's business, too, if he or she takes the business at all seriously. A writer who cannot tell an adverb from an adjective, the subject of a verb from its object, or a colon from a semicolon perhaps does not know the proper use of any of them and is a bit like a carpenter who cannot tell a hammer from a chisel. Would you buy a table from such a person?

In immediate practical terms, it will make it much easier to understand some of the analysis undertaken later in this book, if you are familiar with the basic terminology of grammar. Although the rules of grammar are not part of the subject matter, grammatical issues crop up from time to time when matters of style are being discussed, and the relevant technical vocabulary is used. So, as the reader will have noted, the slightly qualified yes given at the beginning of this subsection is in reality an unqualified yes.

Artist's License

Traditionally, artists have been allowed to bend the rules somewhat in order to achieve some special effect or capture some impression or sensation that refuses to be kept within normal bounds—"to snatch a grace beyond the reach of art," as the poet Alexander Pope put it in "An Essay on Criticism" (1711). Indeed they have.

Artist's license, or artistic license, seems to take us immediately into the area beyond correctness that is the stomping ground for this chapter. Most critics would agree that it is justifiable to ignore the normal rules of grammar and usage in the pursuit of a higher objective. But what constitutes a higher objective and how far does the license extend?

In the first canto, stanza XCIII of his epic *Don Juan* (1819–24), Lord Byron wrote:

If you think 'twas philosophy that this did;
I can't help thinking puberty assisted.

We allow the distortion of normal word order (and the hobbledehoy rhythm) in the interests of rhyme and humor. Poets, especially rhyming poets, are allowed a lot of scope. Prose writers, however, are generally expected to be less wayward.

A writer talks about pictures in the newspaper of union bosses attending a meeting abroad that showed them living the high life and generally looking "pretty decadent," and then adds the comment: "Evidentially they didn't know they were being photographed." The same writer, a little later, reports that a woman artist was arrested for breaking and entering and concludes the anecdote by saying: "Her defense was that she was an artist and that the act was performance art and, incredulously, the charges against her were dropped." Housebreaker artists are obviously afforded even greater license than poets, but our first instinct would surely be to query the writer. Shouldn't the first sentence read "Evidently they didn't know . . ." and the second "and, incredibly, the charges . . ."? When you learn that the writer in question is Bob Dylan in his book *Chronicles* (New York: Simon & Schuster, 2004, p. 66), you may pause again and think: "This man is a great artist; it's more likely that I'm wrong, and he's using these words in an interesting new way."

If Bob Dylan takes liberties with English in his songs, few people are likely to complain. If he takes liberties with English in his prose autobiography, few people are likely to complain either, for few are likely to be reading it for the purity of his style. But there are, we might say, more grounds for complaint in the latter case. (In fairness to Dylan it should be pointed out that the *Merriam-Webster's Collegiate Dictionary* gives "incredible" as one sense of *incredulous,* but not everyone would approve of this usage.)

The upshot is that literary artist's license is more likely to be granted to a writer of poetry than of prose, is more likely to be granted to an artist with an established reputation than to a beginner, and may have a place in creative writing sometimes, but has no place at all in writing of the ordinary workday kind. If you depart from established practice, it is far more likely that people will think you have made a mistake than that you are pushing the boundaries of the expressible. If clarity is your aim—and, ordinarily, it should be your primary aim—then stick to what will be understood by other people. Take heart from the fact that almost everything that needs to be said and is worth saying can be said in a way that does not need a special dispensation from the normal rules.

A FEELING FOR LANGUAGE

It may appear that, up to this point, any attempt to move beyond correctness has been met with a stern admonition. Let us at last leave grammar behind and consider something more intangible, what the Germans call Sprachgefühl, a term so useful that it has made its way into English and is defined in *Merriam-Webster's Collegiate Dictionary* (11th edition, 2003) as "an intuitive sense of what is linguistically appropriate."

It is immediately obvious how useful such a faculty is to a writer. If you possess an instinctive sense of how words function (or can acquire it), in particular of how they fit together to form appropriate—that is to say, clear, correct, and expressive—phrases and sentences, then the work of composition and checking ought to become far less laborious. You will know intuitively what makes particular combinations of words felicitous or infelicitous. You will also be aware of the full value of words, which encompasses both their range of meanings and what we might call their aesthetic potential, the way they sound when spoken and their rhythm.

The Wit and the Crossword Solver

When discussing any kind of skill or special faculty, we always come up against the ineluctable fact that some people are born with it and some are not. Those who are lucky enough to possess the language gene (if there is such a thing) or whose brains are hard wired to process linguistic information have an obvious advantage. They are likely to shine in English classes and to be able to learn foreign languages much more quickly than their fellow students. Others have to work much harder in order to achieve the same standard. Among the various categories of people who seem to possess a highly developed feeling for language, there are two that perhaps illustrate the difference between those in whom the talent is inborn and those who have acquired their skills over time, though both, in order to exercise their talents, must possess an above-average capacity for language. Step forward then on the one hand the witty person and on the other hand the person who, when handed a newspaper or magazine, immediately looks for the page where the crossword puzzle is printed.

WIT

Wit relies on the ability to understand in a flash the humorous potential of what somebody says or of the situation and to respond in no time with an amusing commentary on it. You cannot be witty unless you have an exceptional sensitivity to language because, without it, you would be unlikely to realize the possibility of other meanings in what was said to you, and you certainly would not be able to exploit those possibilities in your reply. When someone says to Groucho Marx, "There's a man outside with a big black mustache," he immediately interprets this not as a descriptive statement about the man waiting at the door but as an announcement of the arrival of a door-to-door salesman and replies, "Tell him I've got one." It is possible that this exchange was laboriously worked out during a series of scriptwriting sessions, but it is very difficult to imagine that it was not either improvised on the set of *Horse Feathers* or came to Groucho, in a flash, while the script was being written.

   Neither Groucho Marx nor any other great wit actually needs a stooge to deliver a feed. Oscar Wilde died, impoverished and in disgrace, in a seedy lodging house in Paris. His last words were "Either that wallpaper goes, or I do." What makes this witty (and full of pathos) is not simply the pun on the word *go*—"to be removed, die"—nor the allusion to the stock phrase familiar from household disputes either in real life or at least as represented on stage. In addition, it recalls Wilde's whole image—and self-image—as a man of extreme refinement and sensitivity, the decadent aesthete, the lover of art, the wearer of silk and velvet, the last person to put up with awful wallpaper if he had any choice in the matter. All this is hinted at in that final remark.

All this contributes to the sense, too, that wit does not simply play with or on words but also plays with or on our broader knowledge and experience of life, and may be used to make a serious point. "The grave's a fine and private place," observed Marvell in summing up his argument against his mistress's coyness, "But none I think do there embrace" (Andrew Marvell [1621–78], "To his Coy Mistress").

Marvell's is a studied kind of wit, but wit in general is spontaneous. Most people would agree that it is a gift, doubly a gift, in fact, for you not only have to be born with the feeling for words and the mental quickness that enable you to make the connections but also have to be in the right frame of mind to be able to perform to the best of your ability. Not even the wittiest person in the world can be absolutely certain that he or she will be "on form" on any particular occasion—or, for that matter, be presented with an opportunity to display his or her talents. In that respect, wit has a good deal in common with inspiration. It is not so much that it comes and it goes; it either comes, or it does not. Inspiration, as all writers have discovered at one time or another, sometimes comes and sometimes resolutely refuses to put in an appearance, but you cannot will it into existence. By the same token, you cannot will yourself to be witty, nor can you really learn to be witty. There are no textbooks on the subject. Everyone should learn to appreciate wit, however, because if you can get the point of a witty remark, you are beginning to develop a feeling for language and its subtleties.

CROSSWORDS

The ability to solve a crossword puzzle is a different kind of skill. "Brevity is the soul of wit," as Shakespeare says in *Hamlet* (2.2.90), but crossword solving requires you to apply your mind to the problem for some length of time. There are some people, admittedly, who can take a crossword and solve it in five or 10 minutes, but the majority of crossword enthusiasts, though they might envy such ability, would not necessarily covet it, because a good deal of their pleasure comes from a prolonged battle of wits with the compiler.

A simple crossword tests your general knowledge—College town near Bangor (5 letters); Author of *Breakfast at Tiffany's* (6 letters)—and, more particularly, your ability to find a term that fits the description given—Writing material (3 letters)—or that is a synonym for the word given in the clue—Speed (8 letters). If you already know a lot of words, you have an advantage, but in attempting to work out the answer, you may learn more words or at least bring the words that you already know to the forefront of your mind.

The words that each individual knows fall into two categories: the words that you know the meaning of and can understand, and the words that you actually know how to use. The words in the former category are your "passive vocabulary"; the words in the latter constitute your "active vocabulary." A writer needs a large active vocabulary, and anything you can do to enhance it, including searching for the solution to a crossword clue and entering it in the grid, is useful. (For advice on how to achieve this, *see* ENLARGING YOUR VOCABULARY, page 88.)

As crossword clues become less straightforward, they begin to test your language resources more. The clue "Speed (8 letters)" is likely to tax you only until you remember various possibilities: *rapidity* or *velocity* or perhaps even *celerity*. But if the clue were "Speed (4 letters)," you might have to think a little harder. If neither *pace* nor *rate* fitted, then you would have to recall that the word *speed* is not only a noun, it is also a verb. Consequently, four-letter words such as *race, dash, dart, rush,* and *bolt* could also come into consideration. As the clues become more cryptic, so they start to call into play something like the sensitivity to words that wit requires. If the clue is, for example, "Man of war (7 letters)," you have to ask yourself whether the answer is the word *warship*—which is what the term means in the first instance—or a word for a particular type of warship—say, *cruiser*—or whether the crossword compiler is actually setting a trap for the literal minded. Perhaps he or she is making a pun and in an oblique way is referring to a man whose business is war, by analogy with a man of God whose business is a religious ministry. The correct answer might therefore be *soldier* or *warrior.*

Taking this approach even further, some crossword setters attempt to write clues that make sense (or more or less make sense) as literal statements but are to be understood by the solver as containing both a direct indication of the solution and a set of coded instructions for extracting the solution from the surrounding context. On that basis "Operator takes head of tuna fish, producing caviar (8 letters)" generates the solution *sturgeon.* Readers who are not familiar with the crooked thinking and subtle wordplay of crossword compilers may be slightly mystified by the procedure that enables the solver to arrive at this solution, but the procedure is quite logical. The clue proper is "fish producing caviar"—the comma is, if the reader will excuse the pun, a red herring. The compiler wishes the solver, on first reading the clue, to imagine a worker in a magical fish-canning factory. But *operator* is a pun and, in this instance, refers to a person who performs operations, that is, a "surgeon"; the word *surgeon* "takes," that is, incorporates, the "head of tuna," that is, the first letter of the word *tuna,* "t": hence, *sturgeon.*

It is no part of the purpose of this book to explain in detail the art of crossword solving or list all the well-established codes employed by crossword compilers. There are already plenty of books on the market and sites on the World Wide Web that do just that. Nor can it be claimed that crossword solvers necessarily are better stylists than the average person. The brief account given above is merely intended to show how a sense of the possibilities of language is involved in the setting and solution of crosswords, just as it is in wit. Crucially, however, it is eminently possible to learn the art of solving crosswords, whereas it is next to impossible to acquire a capacity for wit if you do not happen to be born with it. By beginning with the easy puzzles and gradually working your way up to the more challenging ones; by learning how to use that extremely useful tool for writers, a thesaurus; by remembering that the same word can function as several different parts of speech and can have radically different meanings depending on whether it is being used in ordinary discourse, informally, or as slang; and, finally, by skewing your approach to the words you see printed as a clue so that you start expecting to encounter puns, code words, and other kinds of verbal trickery, you too can acquire a certain amount of expertise as a crossword solver.

And if you can do that, then, by setting about the task in the right way, you can acquire a feeling for language as well.

Acquiring a Feeling for Language
TYPES OF AWARENESS
Let us first consider once again what it is that we are trying to acquire. Words, especially the words of a highly developed and slowly matured language such as English, carry a lot of baggage. If each word in the dictionary had one sense and was only ever used as one part of speech, life would be a lot simpler for speakers and writers, but also a lot less interesting. The numeral *1* can only ever refer to a single quantity; the word *one,* by contrast, has three separate entries in *Merriam-Webster's Collegiate Dictionary,* and each of those entries defines several different senses. So, the first item on our list of desirable acquisitions is an awareness that any individual word can have multiple meanings and be used in a variety of different ways.

The second item is an awareness that the other meanings of a word do not simply vanish when we choose to use that word in a particular sense. If they did, then it would be impossible to make puns. Those other senses are always latent in the word. We can never absolutely rely on another person understanding a word in precisely the sense that we intended. Our readers and hearers may approach what we say rather in the way that an experienced crossword solver approaches a cryptic clue, unless we do our best to prevent them.

What usually pins down a word to a particular sense—or, to put it another way, releases a particular sense from a given word—is the context in which it appears. Take a simple statement such as "It is not done." Those four words on their own do not supply sufficient information for us to be able to understand what *done* means in this instance. Something is needed to supply a context. If we replace *It* with *The meat,* we know immediately what the statement means, likewise if we extend the statement so that it reads "It is not done to behave like that in public." So the third item on the list is an awareness that words are context sensitive, and that fitting words to their context and the context to words is all important if we are to communicate our intended meaning effectively.

The fourth is an awareness of this other dimension that words possess, their implicit emotional charge. In addition to their regular meanings, many words have what are called "connotations." When we say that a particular word has connotations of this or that, we mean that it is generally associated with this or that emotion, mood, or phenomenon and that its meaning is colored by that association. The word *angelic,* for example, has entirely positive connotations: It has an aura of benignity, sweetness, and beauty, the qualities we traditionally associate with angels. The word *expedient,* on the other hand, has generally rather negative connotations; it suggests, without quite making it explicit, that a person is acting out of self-interest. We may recall, perhaps, the saying attributed to the high priest Caiaphas in the Gospel of John in the Bible that it was "expedient that one man should die for the people" (John 18:14). If we take a pair of common words that are opposite in meaning, such as *broad* and *narrow,* for example, we often find that they have different connotations as well. Generally speaking—and this time leaving aside the Gospel where the wide gate and the broad way lead to destruction, while the strait gate and the narrow way lead to eternal life—the connotations of *broad* are more positive than those of *narrow.* Broadness suggests comfort, expansiveness, freedom; narrowness suggests discomfort, tightness, and restriction. You are unlikely to use *narrow* if you intend to pay a compliment to someone or something. When Emily Dickinson (1830–86) begins her poem about a snake with the lines "A narrow fellow in the grass / Occasionally rides," she chooses the adjective *narrow* perhaps not simply because it aptly describes the body of a snake but also because it suggests the automatic distrust you would feel toward a "narrow fellow" belonging to the human family—a person who looked cunning or sharp or secretive and might be quick to do you harm if you gave him or her the opportunity.

The fifth item takes us away from the area of meaning altogether. Although the primary function of words is to be carriers of meaning, that is not their only function. They are also carriers of sound. It is easy to forget this if you are working with words principally on paper or on screen. But the sound that words make when spoken is not irrelevant to the act of writing. It has already been suggested that you should listen to "your mind's voice"; that recommendation is worth repeating here. In putting words down on paper, you should not be consigning them to silence evermore. On the contrary, you should think of the words you put down on paper as being akin to the musical notes that the composer marks on the stave.

The sixth and final item follows from the fifth. You should know how the words you use are pronounced. Unless you know how to pronounce words correctly, you cannot truly appreciate their sound value, and unless you know on which of their syllables the accent falls in ordinary speech, you cannot appreciate their rhythm. Both sound and rhythm are relevant to style (*see* THE RHYTHM OF THE SENTENCE, page 115). Above and beyond that, however, a love of words develops mainly from their life off the page. Nobody loves the word *serendipity* because it has five syllables or because the upstrokes of *d* and *t* balance the downstrokes of *p* and *y.* It is loved firstly because it denotes a nice idea and secondly because it is a nice word to say. Not all words have sound qualities that reflect their sense, but some do. The long moaning vowel sounds in *lugubrious,* for example, seem to reinforce the melancholy associations of that word, whereas the short, bright vowels of *scintillating* convey something of the brilliance that the word denotes. There are two possible pronunciations of the word *flaccid:* "flassid" and "flacksid." The former, with a longer vowel sound and the long breathy sound of *ss* in the middle, seems to represent the meaning of the word—limp and droopily relaxed—far better than the latter, which has a shorter vowel and a crack or snap in the middle. We should savor these qualities in the words that possess them and do our best to utilize those same qualities in our prose when the opportunity presents itself.

BECOMING AWARE

To know what sensitivities you wish to acquire is probably more than half the battle in this particular case. Once you know what you are seeking—in this case, the kinds of awareness detailed in the previous subsection—you will soon realize that you do not really need to go far in order to find it. The basic handbooks of the writer's craft are reference works on language, particularly dictionaries. Dictionaries not only give all the senses of words and all their parts of speech, they also show how words are pronounced, how they are divided up into syllables, and on which syllable or syllables the stress falls. They also give brief accounts of the history and development of the modern forms of English words, which can sometimes illuminate aspects of the meaning of those words that are not immediately apparent.

But any book, particularly any book by a good writer, can be a potential source of information and inspiration. With respect to the particular qualities of language that we have been discussing, books of poetry are an especially useful resource. Poets do not, it should be emphasized, have a monopoly on rhythmic language or mellifluous sound. At the same time, however, rhythm and sound quality are central to the writing of poetry, whereas they are of lesser importance to most writers of prose. If we wish to be sensitized to them, then it is a good idea to consult the experts. Ezra Pound, in a letter, suggested that "poetry must be as well written as prose." Prose writers can learn as much from poetry, however, and if we can appreciate why lines such as the following work as poetry, we shall gain a greater understanding of the rhythmic and acoustic possibilities of language:

> "I do not know much about gods; but I think that the river
> Is a strong brown god . . ."
>> (T. S. Eliot, "The Dry Salvages," in *Four Quartets* [1941]).

> "Complacencies of the peignoir and late
> Coffee and oranges in a sunny chair
> And the green freedom of a cockatoo
> Upon a rug . . ."
>> (Wallace Stevens, "Sunday Morning," in *Harmonium* [1923]).

> "For Godsake hold your tongue, and let me love . . ."
>> (John Donne [1572–1631], "The Canonization.")

These are the opening lines of poems by T. S. Eliot, Wallace Stevens, and John Donne, respectively. None of them departs far, if at all, from the word order or the rhythms of ordinary prose, but if you prefer your poetry to have a more pronounced and regular rhythm and a set rhyme scheme, you will still be able to learn the same basic lesson from it. Language is a form of energy compressed into sounds and syllables, and that energy is there for you to exploit.

So, consult dictionaries, read prose and poetry, and listen to the language that is being used around you. There is a kind of caricature of the writer that suggests that, while everyone else is merrily engaged in conversation, he or she is sitting on the sidelines, not joining in but carefully noting down what is said in a notebook. George Bernard Shaw wrote an amusing little play, *The Dark Lady of the Sonnets,* in which he depicts William Shakespeare picking up his best lines from, among others, a beefeater on guard outside the Tower of London. It is a caricature, but there is an element of truth in it. All writers do, and in fact should, eavesdrop on the people with whom they come into contact. (On a practical level, however, it is usually advisable to carry any pearls home in your memory, rather than to pull out your notebook on the spot!) If you happen to be writing something that contains direct speech or is in dialogue, you may be able to use your gleanings in their original form. More important, however, you will learn new words, new ways of using the words and phrases that you already know, and something of the rhythms of ordinary speech. All of these you can use to benefit your own writing.

AESTHETIC VALUES
The Elusiveness of the Beautiful

E. B. White, in a chapter that he added to the famous style manual of his mentor William Strunk, Jr., contends that "style is something of a mystery" and that we can never "confidently say what ignites a certain combination of words, causing them to explode in the mind" (*The Elements of Style,* 4th ed. [New York: Longman, 2000], pp. 66–67).

There is a certain amount of truth in what White says, but, on the other hand, a good many people make a living from distinguishing good art from bad art or from attempting to tell students why some authors deserve to be honored and remembered long after they are dead and others deserve to be consigned to oblivion. Literary fame depends not only on what an author says but also on the way in which he or she says it. Neither a synopsis of the plot of *Hamlet* nor a detailed explanation of Shakespeare's intentions or the play's meaning is the same as *Hamlet* itself.

At the same time, we cannot rest content forever with saying, "*Hamlet* must be a good play because lots of people still read it or go to see it performed 400 years after it was written" or even that "the words of Hamlet's soliloquies 'explode in the mind.'" There have to be grounds on which we can justify our good opinion of certain literary works. Preferably, those grounds should be as objective as possible, but if, in the final analysis, there has to be an element of subjectivity in them, so be it. After all, in the final analysis, the criteria by which we judge the style of works of literature are going to be essentially the same criteria by which we judge the success or otherwise of our own efforts, whether or not these have an artistic purpose.

Much can be done by analysis. As an example of powerful, but ultimately undefinable style White takes Thomas Paine's famous statement "These are the times that try men's souls." He then offers four alternative versions of the statement and concludes, not surprisingly, that although none of the alternatives can be faulted for grammar or clarity, none of them measures up to the original. He takes this as proof of the mystery that is at the heart of inspired writing and comments: "We could, of course, talk about 'rhythm' and 'cadence,' but the talk would be vague and unconvincing" (ibid.). But we may feel that White gives up too easily. Such talk need not be altogether vague and unconvincing. Paine's statement sticks in the mind partly at least because it contains subtle alliteration ("*The*se are *the* *t*imes *th*at *t*ry men's souls") and because it has a clear rhythm (/UU/U///, where / represents a stressed and U an unstressed syllable). In particular, it ends with three strongly stressed syllables. If we said they were like three drumbeats, we might be heading into the realms of the fanciful, but the simile is not entirely inappropriate. Using three stressed syllables is undoubtedly an effective way of concluding a statement, for one of the extracts from poems that were quoted earlier ends in exactly the same way:

> "I do not know much about gods; but I think that the river
> Is a strong brown god. . . ."

"Try men's souls" / "strong brown god": the rhythm is exactly the same in both cases and in both instances brings the statement to a powerful close.

Now, it would be perfectly possible to write an utterly unremarkable statement in the same rhythm that Paine employs:

> *Give me a pound of good strong cheese.*

or

> *Such are the sighs from sore men's bowels.*

But the fact that you can extract the rhythm from a great saying and reuse it to write nonsense, does not mean that the rhythm contributes nothing to the greatness of the saying in the first place. To construct his great heroic statement, Paine uses simple resonant words full of meaning with a powerful rhythm and some unobtrusive alliteration to bind them together. Whether the statement was pure inspiration or the result of careful thought and revision may be a mystery, but the statement itself is not wholly beyond analysis.

The Use of Analysis

In order to progress further in our discussion of style, we have to believe that the aesthetic qualities—for they are, principally, aesthetic qualities—are not figments of the imagination or purely subjective. Clarity, elegance, beauty, and similar concepts are not too difficult to define in dictionary terms, but they can be difficult to grasp and difficult to relate to your own writing. To the extent that they exist in the eye of the beholder, the beholder's eye has to be opened to their existence and their nature. If you can develop a feeling for language, as described above, you will be well on the way to appreciating the subtler qualities of writing. To the extent that the definition of these qualities rests on consensus, you will have to read widely among writers on style and writers whose style is generally regarded as admirable. To the extent that they have an objectively verifiable basis, you will have to learn how to perform and use literary analysis.

The brief exercise conducted in the previous subsection is intended, firstly, to show that analysis is possible and can go some way toward explaining why some pieces of writing work well and others do not and, secondly, to prepare the way for further similarly analytical passages later in the book. It is not sufficient to state that this or that example of style is faulty or faultless; some effort has to be made, and will be made, to prove the point. Some people draw back from analysis on the basis that if something is lovely, its loveliness should be left untouched. They perhaps recall Wordsworth's line "We murder to dissect" ("The Tables Turned," first published in *Lyrical Ballads* [1800]) and feel that it applies to literary criticism as much as to 18th-century science. Anyone is entitled to feel that about great literature, and it is no concern of this book to conduct lengthy analyses of great works of the past or present in any event. No one, though, is entitled to feel that way about his or her own productions, which should always be subjected to careful scrutiny, dissected when necessary, and even murdered if they do not come up to expectations.

It is not to be expected that everyone should conduct a full-scale analysis of every sentence that he or she writes. It is advisable that everyone should be in a position to analyze any particular sentence or paragraph that he or she is not happy with and to use aesthetic as well as practical criteria to determine the reason for dissatisfaction and to find a remedy. That is what this book exists to assist you with.

BEYOND CORRECTNESS: AN OVERVIEW

- A knowledge of basic grammar is essential to communication, and every writer should have an extensive knowledge of the rules of grammar and usage and of the technical vocabulary used in discussing them.
- Good writing is grammatically correct.
- Writers should develop a feeling for language.
- A feeling for language involves an awareness of the shades of meaning, possibilities of different meaning, and acoustic and rhythmic qualities that words possess.
- Writers can develop a feeling for language by careful reading and listening.
- Aesthetic judgments are not entirely subjective.
- Literary and linguistic analysis is a useful tool for reinforcing aesthetic judgments.

The Qualities of Style

INTRODUCTION

To proceed further in our investigation of what style is and how to achieve style, we now need to consider carefully each of the individual qualities that, as was suggested earlier, are combined in almost all writing that merits the epithet "stylish." Those qualities are clarity, simplicity, elegance, vigor, and variety.

Readers will probably note the use of the phrase *almost all writing* and correctly conclude that it is possible at least to imagine a piece of writing from which one or more of those qualities might be absent but that still possessed literary merit. Undoubtedly such a thing is imaginable, because, as the previous chapter of this book attempted to point out, there is always scope for a genuinely creative writer to break any rule and still produce work that critics and general readers will praise (*see* ARTIST'S LICENSE, page 25). A novelist might choose to tell a story from the point of view of a character who was entirely uneducated, illiterate, or mentally deficient in some way, in which case he or she might put as much art into reproducing the incoherencies of such a character as another novelist might put into rendering the subtly nuanced observations of an aesthete. But while exceptions need to be acknowledged, they do in the main prove the general rules. Explaining a complex situation might require complex sentence construction, bringing an inelegant person to life might best be achieved by adopting an inelegant style, describing a languid scene might necessitate ignoring everything that will be said in this book about the virtues of vigorous prose, but it is impossible to imagine that a piece of writing that was, at one and the same time, unclear, complicated, inelegant, lackluster, and monotonous would have anything at all to recommend it. Under normal circumstances, the five virtues listed at the end of the first paragraph are essential to successful writing, and a writer needs a very good reason to neglect any one of them.

Where a number of items are described as "essential," it is almost a misuse of language to suggest that any one of them might be more vital than the others. However, most writers on writing would agree that the least dispensable of all the listed qualities is clarity. Be complex or inelegant if you must, be slack or monotonous if you cannot help it, they say, but at all costs be clear. No other rank ordering is necessary, but clarity heads everyone's list. So, let us begin by discussing this first among equals.

CLARITY

It should be immediately obvious why clarity is foremost among the stylistic virtues. Its importance derives from the very nature of communication, "a process," to quote the 11th edition of *Merriam-Webster's Collegiate Dictionary,* "by which information is exchanged between individuals through a common system of symbols, signs, or behavior." If your aim is to exchange information with another individual or to convey information to another individual, and you and the person you are communicating with possess a common system of symbols, then only a lack of clarity in the information that is conveyed or in the way the relevant system of symbols (in this case, the English language) is used to convey it can prevent communication from taking place. If you want your reader or hearer to understand what you are saying, be clear. If you have important information to put across, be clear. Since the system of symbols you are using is a shared one, you have a reasonable right to expect the recipient of your message to be able to understand it. Nevertheless, the onus is first and foremost on you, the creator and deliverer of the message, to ensure that it is received correctly, so, again, be clear.

The importance of clarity may be obvious, but, as is generally the case, achieving clarity is not an entirely simple process. To begin with, there are three aspects to clear communication. The first is that you should be clear about what you want to say. The second is that you should be clear in the way that you say it. The third, as was indicated in the final sentence of the previous paragraph, is that you should take care that what appears clear to you will be equally clear to the person who receives the message.

At the Battle of Balaclava during the Crimean War of 1853–56, the commander of the British forces, Lord Raglan, from his position on a hilltop, could see that the Russians had captured some cannons and were in the process of removing them from the battlefield. He sent an order to his cavalry, who were drawn up in the valley below, to attack the Russian raiding party and prevent them from removing the guns. Lord Raglan was quite clear about what he wanted to say, and, making allowances for battlefield conditions, his order probably stated quite clearly what he wanted to be done. Unfortunately, he failed to take into account that, down in the valley, the cavalry commander could not see the guns that the raiding party was removing. The only guns that the cavalry commander could see were the Russian batteries massed at the farther end of the valley. Those were the guns he charged, and the result was one of the most famous disasters in military history. Fortunately, a similar lack of empathy on the part of the ordinary writer is unlikely to lead to a catastrophe as spectacular as the Charge of the Light Brigade, but the incident is worth remembering. Clarity, we might say, is sometimes in the eye of the beholder.

Being Clear about What You Want to Say

The effort to achieve clarity, like several of the other procedures involved in the pursuit of style, should begin well before you arrive at the point of picking up a pen or switching on the computer. To write clearly, you have to be able to think clearly. It stands to reason that if you are not clear in your own mind about what you want to say, you will likely be unable to convey a clear message to your reader.

Unfortunately, not everyone's thoughts flow as clear as a crystal spring. It is all very well to instruct somebody to think clearly, but, in the end, you might just as well instruct that person from the outset to write brilliantly. Neither clear thinking nor brilliant writing is automatically within the power of any given person on any given day, so arrangements have to be made to deal with human frailty and to cover those periods when your thoughts do not present themselves in a logical sequence.

The keys to achieving clarity about what you want to say are (1) to recognize that thinking is an integral part of the writing process, (2) to give yourself time to think, (3) to know the purpose for which you are writing, (4) to organize in a logical way the material that you intend to use in writing your piece, and (5) to make a plan. The final point is perhaps the most important of the five.

A fuller account of the preliminary stages of the writing process is given in *The Facts On File Guide to Good Writing*. They will, therefore, be dealt with only briefly here, but the summary treatment should not be taken as an indication that the preliminaries are not important. On the contrary, you can save yourself a great deal of time and effort by making adequate preparations in writing as in any other activity. Readers who are interested in style, of course, may be expected to focus their attention on the act of writing and to derive most of their enjoyment from the creative task of assembling a well-written text. However, efficiency is as important to a writer as to anyone else who is not blessed with unlimited time. Professional writers know only too well that deadlines have to be met and that it is rare for them to have the luxury of spending a whole day on crafting one sentence, as some famous writers of the past are said to have done (in most cases, no doubt, after they were already famous and were assured of a reasonable income from their writing or from some other source). If you can deal efficiently, with the basic aspects of your task, you will gain precious time that you can spend on the more pleasurable or sophisticated aspects. Moreover, and more important, it is a mistake to believe that you are only being creative when you are actually putting down words on paper. The novelist or dramatist is being as creative when he or she is working out the plot of the story and deciding which character to introduce when and where, as when writing dialogue for that character. Construction is a creative activity, and the basic work of construction needs to be done in most cases before actual writing commences.

PREPARING TO WRITE

Allow yourself time to think, and if you are working on an overall writing schedule, be sure to incorporate some thinking time into it. Allow yourself space to think, as well as to write. It is much easier to accomplish these tasks if you can free yourself, however temporarily, from other distractions—and other distractions, first and foremost, means other people. Every writer needs a den.

Once you have acquired time and space to think, you first need to think about what precisely you are setting out to write. Before you can know what you are going to say, you have to know what you are trying to do. It is often recommended that a writer provide himself or herself with a "mission statement," a sentence or two setting out very succinctly what he or she intends to achieve. If you think a mission statement would help you, then imagine perhaps that you are intending to sell your writing to a very impatient publisher who will allow you no more than three sentences to state what type of book it is, what it is about, and who you expect to want to read it. Write down those three sentences and keep them beside you as you progress, so as to ensure that you stay on track.

Whether or not you write an actual mission statement, you will need to devote some time and effort to clarifying your purpose. If you intend to write a piece of any length, you will almost inevitably need to collect material from outside sources; indeed, you may need to do extensive research. The more precise your purpose, the more goal oriented you can be in assembling your material. In practice, of course, it often happens that you begin with a general or even only vague idea of what you want to write: A title for an assignment, for instance, may lend itself to treatment in a variety of ways, and you may not immediately be able to fix on precisely the treatment that you wish to give it or are best able to give it. It may be that only as you begin to collect material, or to read up on a subject, do you suddenly hit upon the best method of tackling your assignment. If that happens you may have to reorient your approach, perhaps discarding some of the work you have already done. But this is a small price to pay for the supreme benefit of knowing where you are going so that you can begin to plan how to get there.

In accordance with the general aim of keeping both your internal and external environments in the best possible state to promote clear thinking, it pays to take clear notes and to keep your notes in good order. (For more specific advice on note taking, refer to *The Facts On File Guide to Good Writing*.) Ideally you will start to form a rough plan of the work you are going to write once you conceive the basic purpose of the written work. As you collect your material, therefore, you will organize it not simply in alphabetical order or by subject categories, say, but in a manner that fits in with your plan, allocating evidence or backup to the points you know you are going to make in process of fulfilling your overall purpose.

As has been said before, not everyone's thoughts flow clearly, and likewise, not everyone is sufficiently well-organized to sort and allocate notes as they are made, but there comes a time when, if you are to achieve clarity in the final product, you have to bring some clarity into your thoughts. And if you have been unable to do this earlier, then you should make an all-out attempt to do it when you make your plan.

PLANNING

A good builder does not attempt to construct a home by piling one brick or stone on top of another in a vaguely vertical direction. Because words do not crumble and fall in on their users' heads, however, some writers feel no compunction about beginning their work of construction with only the vaguest notion of how the final edifice ought to look or of what will hold it up. To change the metaphor, they take a very approximate compass bearing and head off into the unknown. Sometimes they get where they want to go; sometimes they do not and end up stumbling and cursing in the wilderness, having to return to their starting point. If you are the essentially optimistic kind of person who hopes that a work will find its own direction, that it will grow organically as you write it, that what is unclear will become clear through the process of being written down, then you will probably become impatient with books or mentors that urge you to plan, plan, plan. But that is what most writers do, indeed have to do, in order to meet their schedules and to get their message across clearly.

It is not, incidentally, complete folly to let a piece of writing, especially a piece of creative writing, "go its own way." A writer, for instance, will sometimes create a scene or a character that takes on a life of its own and demands more space and a fuller treatment than the writer had ever intended to give it; indeed, an incident or personage, originally intended for a minor role, can finish up by shaping the whole book or play. The story—or the writer's subconscious—takes over, and the results can be very exciting.

That said, however, the "hands-off" method of writing is not a particularly efficient one, and it is likely to be downright counterproductive if you intend to put across any kind of reasoned argument. So in most circumstances you should make a plan, specifically an outline that proceeds point by point from your introduction to your conclusion. You should make the plan as detailed as you can, if possible working from paragraph to paragraph or topic sentence to topic sentence (*see* chapter 6, CONSTRUCTING PARAGRAPHS, page 123). Each point you have to make should fill roughly one paragraph, and to each point can be allocated, even at the planning stage, the evidential material that will make that point valid.

If your work is clear in outline, chances are it will be clear when you write it out. An incidental benefit of working from a plan is that you are not necessarily compelled to begin at the beginning. You can select the easiest point of entry and still be confident in the knowledge that what comes before is a known and not an unknown quantity.

Being Clear in the Way That You Say It

If you wish what you say to be clear, then it must be not only clearly stated but also clearly organized. This topic will therefore be broken down into two headings, clarity of organization and clarity of expression.

CLARITY OF ORGANIZATION

As was said in the previous subsection, if your work is clear in outline, then it will remain so when you put it into written form. Making a plan has various practical advantages for you, as a writer, but perhaps the main purpose of a plan is to ensure that what you write is clearly and logically organized. You need to know where you are going and how you are going to get there. The reader also needs to know where he or she is going and, while perhaps not wanting to see too much of the way ahead, will usually feel more comfortable for being able to remember the route by which he or she arrived at any particular point. To keep your readers with you, you need to give them a sense that they are progressing logically, and you probably need to provide them with a few signposts, too, to reassure them that you and they are still on track.

Traditional Structures

There are various tried-and-tested structural formulas that are intended to keep writers and their readers or listeners abreast of one another. Public speakers, for instance, are frequently advised to do the following: Say what you're going to say, say it, and then say that you've said it. This is, in effect, a more down-to-earth version of the usual structure for an essay: introduction, development, and conclusion.

A person who is able to write a good speech or lecture for public delivery has something to teach all writers. The members of an audience in a hall or lecture theater are not usually provided with a script. If they lose the thread, they cannot refer to the previous page or chapter, nor can they, usually, interrupt the speaker to ask for clarification. No self-respecting speaker would, in any case, wish to be either interrupted or confronted with rows of blank, uncomprehending faces. Consequently, a good speechwriter takes account of the fact that the listeners will hear the speech only once, in real time, and makes certain that they can keep up with the argument by arranging his or her argument in a simple and logical fashion and by allowing the audience to hear the vital points in the speech more than once. A writer who writes to be read rather than heard has less need of obvious repetition but still needs to show the same awareness of the needs and the possible frailties of the people whom he or she is addressing.

Another type of writer for whom a clear structure is vitally important is the dramatist—and for basically the same reason: the theater audience also has to assimilate the material in real time. It is not surprising, therefore, that there is a tried-and-trusted sequence of stages through which most dramatic plots proceed. Again the basic pattern of introduction, development, and conclusion is followed, but playwrights have elaborated the structure and given the various sections different names. Most plays begin with an "exposition," during which the audience is given the information it requires to understand the situation in which the characters find themselves. The art of the exposition is to reveal information that many of the characters on stage already know but the audience does not without making it appear that the characters are talking mainly for the audience's benefit and not engaging in a natural conversation. The exposition is followed by the unfolding of the main action, which generally involves embroiling the main characters in a series of conflicts or complications. The final section is known as the "denouement," a word from French that literally means "untying" or "unknotting." In the denouement, the conflicts that have hopefully kept the spectators on the edge of their seats or pleasantly amused during the bulk of the play are resolved, happily or unhappily, and the final fate of the characters is made known.

As is clear from the preceding paragraphs, most written work is based on a three-part structure: a beginning, a middle, and an end. This is what most readers and listeners expect, it works, it makes for clarity, and writers should stick to the formula unless they have a good reason not to and are able to devise an alternative arrangement that is equally effective. Clarity works from the inside out: Clear thinking leads to clear expression; a clear and simple underlying structure generally helps to ensure clarity throughout the work.

Ordering the Body of the Work
The three basic parts into which a standard written work is divided are not of equal length. Beginnings and endings are generally short in comparison with the central section, in which the bulk of the material is contained and where the essential work of communication is done. It should be easy to remember that a work needs an introduction and a conclusion. It is not always easy to decide on a clear and workable principle of organization for the all-important central body of the text.

The principle that you choose will depend on what you are writing. It is important that there should be a principle and, barring some overriding reason to do otherwise, that principle should be kept fairly simple.

Linear Organization
One method of organizing material is what we might call the "linear" method. The simplest type of linear organization is chronological ordering. What was done first or happened first is described first. As events unfold in time, so you recount them. This is the obvious method of telling a story, whether a fictional piece or an account of an actual event. The reader will have no difficulty in relating to it and, indeed, is likely to expect the writer to begin at the beginning and end at the end. This expectation is so natural and so strong that many writers feel that it is boring both for them and the reader to conform to it. Instead, they start at some significant point in the story, such as the discovery of a dead body or an angry exchange between two people, and fill in the events that led up to this incident at some later point in the narrative.

This latter technique is not new; it is, in fact, so ancient that there is a Latin term for it. Writers of epic poems were advised to begin in medias res (in the middle of things), because that is where Homer began the earliest great poem in Western literature, the *Iliad,* the story of the siege and capture of Troy. Homer did not start with the abduction of Helen of Troy and then proceed to describe how the Greek princes and heroes decided to join together to help her husband, Menelaus, win her back. Instead, his poem begins during the siege itself at a point where the greatest warrior among the Greeks, Achilles, feels so angry and insulted that he refuses to take any further part in the fighting. The relevant events from the earlier part of the story are recounted as the poem proceeds.

If this technique has been in use since the very beginnings of Western literature, and is still a favorite with authors today, it must be a very effective one. Indeed it is. But it remains, essentially, a variant on chronological order. The significant event acts as a kind of introduction. The body of the work generally recounts events as they unfold from that point onward but incorporates flashbacks. So long as the writer is clear in his or her own mind about when events took place in the story as a whole and can ensure that the reader possesses the same kind of certainty, no confusion need arise.

Other linear methods that deserve mention are the "journey" and the "process" in which you start at point A and eventually arrive at point D via points B and C. Each point represents a step or stage rather than individual events. You may be describing a literal journey or a literal process, not necessarily an industrial one, perhaps a legal or administrative or biological one. In that case, since both journeys and processes progress in stages, you can easily derive a plan for your written work from the material that you are writing about. But even if you are not actually describing a journey or process, it may help to imagine that you are. If you were writing an account of somebody's career, for example, it might be fruitful to think of that person's development as a "journey"—he or she reached this point and then decided to head for that objective—or as a "process"—he or she underwent this experience and as a result developed that particular skill or character trait or was enabled to grasp that opportunity—rather than as a simple sequence of events in time. In either case, you would be imparting a simple logical structure to your account that would help you to show a clear progression.

Argument Structure

The purpose of a great deal of writing is to discuss a topic or to make a case for something. Here, too, a clear structure is a prerequisite for success. As a writer—in fact, as a human being—you will usually have a point of view on the subject in question. If you have no point of view—if you do not know why Hamlet delays or whether city hall should extend its recycling scheme, and do not really care—then you probably ought not to be writing on the topic in the first place. Your own input, as has been said before, is valuable for its freshness and firsthand quality, but it is also vital as an animating factor. If you are not personally engaged on any level, there will no vitality in your argument. Your point of view might simply be one of fascination or disgust at the fact that other people expend so much time and energy debating such a trivial question. That is still a point of view, and your main aim must be to convince the reader, ultimately, of the rightness of your attitude, whatever it may happen to be. Otherwise, you are like a person who takes part in a game or sport with no desire to win or do well and so derives no enjoyment from it nor provides any enjoyment for the other participants.

A written argument is always and necessarily one sided insofar as there is usually only one writer and he or she has control of the game, so to speak. Nevertheless an astute writer will generally take account of the fact that an astute reader, who does not necessarily share the writer's point of view at the outset, may object to being bludgeoned into submission by a relentless presentation of only one point of view. A true argument is a form of dialogue. One participant makes a point and presents evidence to support it; the other attempts to counter the first point, again backing up the counterargument with evidence; the first participant replies with a counter to the counterargument; and so on. A clear pattern emerges from the normal conduct of an argument or debate between live participants, which the writer can use to organize his or her discussion of a topic. This entails an effort on the part of the writer to collect material representing the opposing point or points of view to his or her own and to present the opposition's view fairly. It may seem tempting to present counterarguments to your own as weak and unconvincing (they may indeed be so), but as in any contest, there is more satisfaction to be gained from beating a strong opponent by fair means than from overcoming a weak one by foul.

If you cannot find material to represent the opposing side or are working on a subject where there is no such material available, then it is always open to you to use your imagination, not to conjure facts out of nothing, but to create a discussion partner who happens to hold opinions that differ radically from your own. Imagine what such a person—skeptical if you are a believer, liberal if you happen to be a conservative—would be likely to say to try to refute your arguments. Build up a case for that person to make, and, again, try not to make it one that is entirely easy for you to knock down.

There are occasions when it is appropriate to present one side of the argument in its entirety, followed by the complete case for the other side, followed by your conclusion. There are no objections to this method of organization from the point of view of clarity of structure, but it perhaps works best if your own contribution is not to endorse either viewpoint wholeheartedly but to suggest a compromise between, or a synthesis of, the two opposing views in the concluding section. If you are personally involved in one side of the argument, then it is probably better to proceed point by point. This is a more dynamic approach. It brings the opposing viewpoints into more dramatic contrast and lets the reader share something of the excitement of an ongoing debate while, at the same time, enabling him or her to follow the process by which the weight of the evidence gradually but clearly begins to favor the winning side, your side.

Signposting

Whatever organizational principle you adopt, it is usually wise to let the reader know what you are doing. There are more and less subtle ways of doing this, and how subtle you need to be will largely depend on what kind of piece you are writing. A novelist is not ordinarily going to write,

> *I introduced this character in Chapter 4, and then he seemed like a pretty nice fellow. I am now going to reintroduce him and show you precisely what kind of a swine he really is.*

On the other hand, it would be perfectly in order for the author of a nonfiction work to write,

I referred in Chapter 4 to the violent opposition of certain members of the Democratic Party to the reforms proposed by the president. I should now like to discuss in more detail the reasons for their opposition.

The conventions of nonfiction writing generally allow an author to intervene and give the reader explicit guidance. The conventions of fiction generally do not. Nevertheless, if we are, say, now in chapter 7 of a novel and the character in question has not played any part in the plot since chapter 4, it may well be useful to jog the reader's memory:

There was a call from James on her answering machine. Rebecca had not heard from him since the evening of Abigail's party and wondered why he should call now, but she remembered the impression she had formed of him then. He had seemed a pretty nice fellow. In fact, he had shown a good deal of interest in her, and she had thought him not unattractive. She pressed the button to play the message once again.

If we want to find examples of really prominent signposting, then the best place to look is often in academic writing:

This article is divided into three sections. In the first section I shall briefly recount the history of the garment-making industry in Mexico. In the second section I shall describe the effect of the North American Free Trade Agreement (NAFTA) on this industry. In the third section . . .

Having dealt with the history of the Mexican apparel industry, I shall now consider the impact of NAFTA on that industry and its workers. . . .

It may seem slightly odd that high-powered intellectuals writing principally for other high-powered intellectuals should need to spell out so distinctly what they are doing. Are memories and attention spans in academia really so short? The more likely explanation is that today's journal article was yesterday's lecture or the paper delivered to an international conference last month. Academics are used to presenting information orally to large gatherings of students or scholars. They are public speakers: They say what they are going to say, say it, then say that they have said it. As has been noted previously, people who write to be listened to need to take extra care that their audience is following the argument, hence the proliferation of explicit statements of intention and of performance.

If we assume that most public speakers and academic writers occupy a position at one end of the scale of explicitness in giving guidance to the reader, and most creative writers of fiction occupy a position at the other end, then, obviously, there is a large expanse of middle ground for writers engaged in other kinds of tasks to occupy. You may not wish to dot all the i's and cross all the t's for your readers' benefit, but you ought nevertheless to provide them with a certain amount of assistance in finding their way through your text. If you are going to intervene in your own text, however, it is worth considering under what guise you ought to do so. When you step out from behind your text, so to speak, in order to give the reader directions, how should you refer to yourself and what form of words should you use?

Authorial Pronouns

If you are the sole author of any text, from a letter to a report or a nonfiction book of a thousand pages, the most natural way to refer to yourself is as *I*:

> *I shall now endeavor to explain why I think this particular course of action would be counterproductive.*

If you are a coauthor of a book or article or are writing on behalf of a group of people who are assumed to speak with one voice, then the correct pronoun to use is *we*:

> *Our research has produced new evidence that, we feel, casts serious doubt on the theory, and we shall now set forth our findings.*

People sometimes feel that it is inappropriate to use *I*. They perhaps feel that they may come across to the reader as pushy or self-absorbed. This, however, will be the case only if they adopt a hectoring tone and appear to be drawing excessive attention to themselves. In conversation it is perfectly legitimate to state your own point of view or describe your own experiences, and it is possible to do this without attempting to dominate the discussion. The same applies to writing. It is not a good idea to use the plural pronoun *we*, for instance, as a substitute for *I* if you are a sole author. That is an outmoded convention and is likely to cause confusion. You may nonetheless wish to use *we*, *us*, and so on, to refer to yourself and the reader, if you imagine that the two of you are engaged in a joint endeavor:

> *Let us now consider the usual arguments against such a policy.*

or to refer to people in general:

> *We are always more eager to demand our rights than to accept our responsibilities.*

You should always be clear in your own mind, of course, precisely to whom *we* refers, and if you are using *we* to denote an authorial team, you should be very cautious about using it in any other sense.

   If you really prefer to avoid using *I*, then the best policy is to adopt impersonal formulas:

> *This particular course of action would be counterproductive for the following reasons: . . .*

*Research has produced new evidence that casts serious doubt on the the-
ory, as appears from the findings set forth below.*

The usual arguments against such a policy ought now to be considered.

The only problems with this method are that it can lead occasionally to awkwardness and to an overreliance on the passive forms of verbs (*see* VIGOR,
page 55).

Some Useful Guidance Formulas
The following are more examples of the kinds of sentences or phrases that
can be used to help the reader along.

Personal

As I/we shall now show/demonstrate/prove . . .

As I/we pointed out in the previous paragraph/section/chapter . . .

I/we shall now move on to discuss . . .

I/we shall now turn my/our attention to . . .

*I/we shall have more to say on this point in a later paragraph/
section/chapter . . .*

I/we can best illustrate this point by means of an example . . .

I/we have shown by these examples how . . .

Impersonal

As will now be shown/demonstrated/proved . . .

As was pointed out in the preceding paragraph/section/chapter . . .

The next point to be discussed is . . .

*This point will be discussed further in a later paragraph/section/
chapter . . .*

This point can best be illustrated by means of an example . . .

As these examples have shown . . .

(For a discussion of related issues and further examples of phrases of this kind,
see LINKERS, page 149.)

It is ultimately your choice whether to intervene in a personal or impersonal style. It is best to maintain consistency throughout a text, however, so having made a choice, you should endeavor to stick to it.

There are two final points that need to be made about signposting. The first is that it is a useful element in most texts, so you should not hesitate to use it when the occasion demands. The second is that it is not a substitute for clear organization and planning. The reader ought to be able to find his or her way through your work adequately without any guidance. Signposting should be a welcome extra, a courtesy. Clarity of structure is of the essence.

CLARITY OF EXPRESSION

According to the poet and essayist Matthew Arnold, the whole secret of style is to "have something to say and say it as clearly as you can" (cited by G. W. E. Russell in *Collection and Recollections* [1903]). When he made this remark, Arnold was reacting brusquely to people who asked him to teach them style and implying that there was no secret recipe for success. Style is simply clear expression.

There is a good deal of truth in what Arnold said, but, to repeat a point made earlier, not everyone's thoughts and words flow clearly on all occasions. Clarity is often a quality that has to be striven for; it is not a natural result of a person's having something interesting to say. The basis of a good style is clear expression, we might say, but expressing yourself clearly is not always simple.

In one way or another, therefore, a great deal of this book is about how to attain clarity of expression. The various methods that should be used to ensure clarity in your choice of words and your construction of sentences and paragraphs are outlined in the chapters that deal with those procedures (chapters 4–6). It would be superfluous to repeat here what is said there, but this account of clarity would be incomplete without a brief discussion of the main points.

The Bases of Clear Expression

The foundations of clarity of expression are correctness and simplicity. It is vital not to put unnecessary obstacles in the way of the reader's understanding of your text. Do not depart from the usual norms for grammar, spelling, and punctuation. The point has been made before and will be made again: Grammar is a shared resource that is the basis of all intelligible communication; spelling and pronunciation should be viewed in the same way, as shared resources. Respect all three to ensure that you start on an equal footing with your reader and that the reader, above all, shares your understanding of what you mean to say. Consider the following example:

> Not much has changed here over 50 years—those who can leave, and those who cannot stay.

A simple error of punctuation makes this statement unintelligible. However, insert two commas and immediately sense returns:

Not much has changed here over 50 years—those who can, leave, and those who cannot, stay.

Likewise, do not choose a complex word, a complicated sentence structure, or an intricate structure for your work as a whole, when a simple one will do the job equally well. Readers do not usually thank writers for making them perform mental gymnastics; they do thank writers for making reading an easy and pleasant task. (For further discussion of the virtue of simplicity, *see* page 52.)

Avoiding Vagueness

Vagueness and obscurity in expression can be avoided, in the first instance, by having something definite to say and by clear thinking. If you do not know precisely what you want to say to the reader or what kind of response you want to evoke in him or her, then you may well find yourself becoming vague and woolly, or even evasive. Assuming that you have not sat down to write purely to pass the time and to help other people pass their time, you will have a point to make. Keep reminding yourself of that fact, and keep your eye on that point. Anything that does not assist in making that point is possibly irrelevant and may need to be moved to another position in the text or removed altogether (*see* PARAGRAPHS—THE BASICS, page 124).

To counteract any tendency toward vagueness and obscurity, you should also choose active words and constructions where possible. Use simple, concrete nouns and verbs to do the main work in your sentences (*see* SIMPLE V. COMPLEX, page 76; USE FEWER NOUNS, page 82; and VIGOR, page 55).

Avoiding Ambiguity

The fact that many words have more than one meaning has already been noted (*see* A FEELING FOR LANGUAGE, page 26). Where a word has several meanings, there is always potential for ambiguity. In order to achieve clarity in expression, you should be aware of this potential and counteract it by ensuring that the context in which you set a word with several meanings makes it absolutely clear which meaning is intended. Consider the example that follows:

Conversations with union representatives revealed changes in the nature of labor that midwives have had to deal with over the last decades.

The presence of the term *union representatives* in this sentence suggests that *labor* means "work" or "working practices," but as the workers involved are midwives, *labor* could equally apply to childbirth. The sentence is therefore ambiguous and must be changed:

Conversations with union representatives revealed that, over the last decades, midwives have had to deal with changes in the nature of their work.

The comic potential in ambiguities is another consideration:

Try our fantastic health program—you won't get better!

But unless your primary aim is to make your readers laugh, be alert and be careful.

Incorrect or sloppy grammar can also lead to ambiguity, as in the following:

Introduce a friend to the club, and they can choose a free gift. They include a sports bag, a coffeemaker, and a digital alarm clock.

Place the contents of the can in a saucepan. Do not allow the saucepan to boil, or it could spoil the flavor.

The pronouns in the second sentence of each pair have a very loose relationship with the words in the first sentence. It is obvious enough in the first example that *They* in the second sentence refers to the *free gift* mentioned at the end of the first. But *they* is a plural pronoun and *gift* is a singular noun, and in any case the writer has already used *they* to refer to *a friend* (another usage that many people frown on). This is poor and potentially confusing writing. Think carefully, think grammatically, and change the second sentence:

Introduce a friend to the club, and he or she can choose a free gift. Gifts include a sports bag, a coffeemaker, and a digital alarm clock.

In the second example, meanwhile, it is unclear what *it* is that will spoil the flavor. Logically and grammatically *it* refers to the *saucepan*. Obviously, however, the saucepan itself will not spoil the flavor; the damage is done by allowing the contents of the can to boil. We need to make this clear and also get rid of the careless phrase *boil a saucepan:*

Place the contents of the can in a saucepan. Do not allow the contents to boil; this could spoil the flavor.

A third common cause of ambiguity is the poor organization of sentences. It is easy, when you have something fairly complex to announce or describe, to allow phrases to drift so that it becomes unclear to which other element in the sentence they are supposed to relate:

A plane tree, said to be more than 200 years old, shades the road as it passes the church with wide-spreading branches.

It is a rather delightful idea that an old tree should spread its branches as it passes the church, but it is not the idea that the writer intended to convey. There is a problem here with *it* again. *It* should refer to the road but can be read to refer to the tree. And the branches, of course, need to be firmly attached to the tree. That final phrase needs to be repositioned, but rearrangement can be difficult. For example,

> *A plane tree with wide-spreading branches, said to be more than 200 years old . . .*

creates a new possibility for ambiguity (What is more than 200 years old? The tree or its branches?), so a more thorough recasting of the sentence is required:

> *A plane tree, with wide-spreading branches and said to be more than 200 years old, shades the road where it passes the church.*

or, to avoid any lingering possibility of confusion with respect to *it*:

> *The wide-spreading branches of a plane tree, said to be more than 200 years old, shade the road as it passes the church.*

(For more on the importance of the position of elements within a sentence, *see* POSITIONING, page 112.)

CONCLUSION

Clarity is a quality that should inform the whole of your work. Think clearly, organize clearly, and express yourself clearly. Always respect the norms of grammar, spelling, and punctuation, and wherever possible, keep it simple.

SIMPLICITY

Simplicity deserves to be highlighted as one of the defining characteristics of a good style. It also deserves, and will receive, simple treatment, for once the importance of simplicity has been stated, we are almost ready to move on.

The advantages of simplicity are implicit in almost all that was said in the previous section about the need for clarity. In order to keep your structure clear, adopt a simple, logical structure. In order to keep your sentences clear, write simple sentences. In order to keep your meaning clear, choose simple everyday words in preference to long, complicated, or technical ones. The principles that should govern word choice are dealt with fully in chapter 4, and the essential principles of sentence construction are dealt with in chapter 5, so there is no need for an extended discussion of either topic here.

In the context of our present discussion, simplicity is a kind of bridge between two neighboring qualities. If it is a requisite for clarity, it is equally a requisite for elegance. Visual elegance, as we know from the worlds of fashion, architecture, and interior design, is not usually ornate or complicated. A gown with several rows of frills or extravagantly trimmed with diamanté is less likely to be elegant than one that is plain but well cut and tailored to the wearer. A skyscraper in a geometric shape with sheer walls of glass is possibly more elegant than one with an Art Deco cap and gargoyles. This is not to say that ornate buildings, clothes, and objects are uninteresting or inartistic. But elegance generally requires sleekness of outline and simplicity.

It is not always easy to be simple. Most work seems to involve developing a complex end product from simpler materials. When the work in question is writing, however, that process sometimes has to be put into reverse (*see* ADDING AND SUBTRACTING, page 16). First formulations and first drafts are frequently wordier and more complicated than they need to be. Simplifying them usually makes them clearer and more elegant. This requires effort, often more effort than it would take to produce a version that might appear more impressive but does not hit the nail on the head quite so squarely. For example, you may have written,

> *In the process of researching this paper we undertook an extensive study of the meteorological conditions generally obtained in western China in order to better understand their possible effects on the economy of that region.*

But consider whether the following would not convey the same idea more economically and less pretentiously:

> *As part of the research for this paper we studied the weather in western China in order to find out what effect it had on the region's economy.*

As another example, imagine you describe a character like this:

> *Mr. Jackson's nature was such that one could easily conceive of him as having it within himself to commit acts of the most ferocious cruelty.*

Consider whether he would not be equally well described like this:

> *Mr. Jackson seemed the sort of man who could be ferociously cruel if he wanted to be.*

Simplicity need not be bland or drab or uninteresting. It should be sharp, to the point, and elegant.

ELEGANCE

Of all the qualities that have been attributed to style, elegance is perhaps the one that is hardest to describe. It has been said that elegance is based on simplicity. That is true. But not everything that is simple is elegant. Elegance is a kind of refined and beautiful simplicity, even, we might say, a sophisticated simplicity, although that may sound like a contradiction in terms. A block of rough granite is simple, but not elegant; a block of polished marble is likewise simple, but it is probably not elegant because of its square shape. It is not difficult, however, to imagine how a simple shape, say, a triangle, or a sphere, or an oval, made of polished black or white marble, could be extremely elegant.

Refinement, beauty, sophistication, shapeliness, polish, fluency, all these qualities seem to be different aspects of elegance, but it is easier, perhaps, to visualize them embodied in physical objects than to exemplify them in writing, let alone to impart them to a piece of writing of your own. Let us, nevertheless, try to see how these qualities can be captured in words.

> *It snowed during the night. By morning the street was covered to an even depth. Until the traffic got going again, everything was pure, clean white.*

> *It snowed thickly, heavily, determinedly all night through, covering everything thickly, heavily, determinedly, as if God was weary of this street, this town, this country, and simply wanted to blot it out.*

> *It snowed heavily overnight, and for a short time in the morning the street, its dirt, and its ordinariness were hidden by a sheet of pure, clean white.*

Our judgment of what is elegant and what is not is bound to be somewhat subjective, but of the three examples given above, only the third has any real claim to elegance. This is not to say that the first two examples represent bad writing. The first example is a simple, no-nonsense account of the scene. It sounds almost as though the writer was determined not to wax lyrical about the transfiguring effect of the snow. That sort of restraint is often admirable and can be very effective in some contexts. By contrast, the second writer is obviously striving for effect and has an emotional response to the snow, indeed wishes to moralize it. But while the threefold repetitions may be powerful, they are too heavy handed, we might say, to be considered elegant. Elegance demands a certain lightness of touch. It is difficult to communicate raw emotion elegantly. In fact, it would in most cases seem out of place to strive for elegance if you were trying to communicate passion or express spontaneous emotion. The third example uses simple language and basically unpretentious image—we are to think of the snow as being like a dust cover thrown over furniture in an unoccupied house rather than a sheet spread over a bed, perhaps—but it has neatness and flow and a more musical rhythm then the heavily accented second example. These qualities entitle it to be called elegant.

Let us consider some further examples:

> *I loathe and detest hypocrisy in any shape or form, but most of all I abominate any person who treats you as if you were his friend, when, in his heart, he would be extremely glad to see you dead.*

> *Mrs. Van Donk has an extraordinary capacity for friendship, which extends even to her very worst enemies.*

In contrast, in this essay, we argue for a broader understanding of what it is to engage in struggle and of what people of our persuasion are, in fact, struggling for.

We, by contrast, would argue that we struggle more effectively when we do so as members of a broadly based coalition.

Again, none of these sentences is badly written, but most readers would probably consider the second and fourth examples to be more elegant than the first and third. If you read these sentences over to yourself, you will find that the second and fourth roll off the tongue more smoothly than the others. Sentence three, in particular, is rather awkward to say, not because it contains any long or difficult words, but because it contains a lot of short, simple ones that are not organized in such a way as to make them flow together. In fact, the sentence seems designed almost deliberately to trip up anybody who tried to read it aloud. It is not, of course, intended to be read aloud. If it had been, the writer would perhaps have taken greater pains to smooth out some of its roughness.

This takes us some distance toward understanding the place of elegance in the overall scheme of style. In the final analysis, elegance has to be rated as less important than clarity and simplicity. Every sentence should be clear, most sentences should be kept simple, but a succession of carefully crafted, seamlessly flowing sentences might in the end prove slightly wearisome for the reader. Elegance, as has been said, is not a quality that coexists well with passion and power. Most people would be willing to sacrifice a beautiful and sophisticated phrase for a really powerful and compelling one.

However, most writing is not necessarily intended to seize the reader by the throat. Page after page of raw power would probably be even more wearisome to read than page after page of studied elegance. It is better that writing should flow than that it should stutter. It is better that simplicity should be combined with refinement than that it should be combined with awkwardness. It is better, usually, to describe a mouse as *a small furry rodent with a pointed snout and a long, slender tail* than as *a little animal that has fur and a pointed nose and a thin, long tail,* because the former is a neat, compact, and agreeable-sounding combination of words, while the latter, though made up of simpler terms, is less neat and less satisfying. A degree of elegance is worth striving for in ordinary prose, because ordinary prose should be neat, economical, simple, and flowing most of the time.

In order to achieve elegance, you should be simple, be as economical as you can with words, and do your best to keep your sentence smooth and flowing. Your best ally in the latter endeavor is, again, your "mind's voice." Listen as you write. Read it out loud. If it sounds balanced and smooth to you, it will create the same impression on the page for the sensitive reader.

VIGOR

Probably the most damning criticism that anyone can express about a piece of writing—apart from condemning it as completely illiterate—is that it is lifeless and boring. The two remaining qualities that make up style, vigor and variety, should preserve your prose from any such criticism.

What gives vigor to words on a page? Let us start by dealing with some of the more obvious sources of energy available to the writer.

Forceful Language

There are words that denote vigorous or forceful action, as those chosen by Robert Browning (1812–89) for his poem "How They Brought the Good News from Ghent to Aix":

> "I sprang to the stirrup, and Joris, and he;
> I gallop'd, Dirck gallop'd, we gallop'd all three."

The use of such language is, of course, not confined to verse:

> *Martha slammed the door, raced down the corridor, jumped into her car, and sped away with a squeal of tires.*

> *A torrent of water rushed down the mountainside carrying away rocks, trees, bushes, bridges, cabins, everything that lay in its path.*

> *The air was forced out of my lungs in a tremendous gush by the shock of hitting the cold water.*

It will come as no surprise to most readers of this book that the English language is full of words with great dramatic potential—*slam, race, jump, leap, spring, torrent, rush, gush, force, strike, hit*—and most writers will not hesitate to use such words if they have something exciting to describe. But what if there is nothing particularly exciting to describe? You might write a report of what happened at a meeting as follows:

> *The chairman rapped on the table with his gavel and asked the people in the hall to be quiet so that he could proceed with the business on the agenda.*

You might then think to yourself that this sounds pretty tame and decide to spice up the sentence a little:

> *The chairman pounded the table repeatedly with his gavel, yelling at the riotous mob in the hall to shut up so that he could finish his agenda.*

There is no doubt that the second sentence makes rather more exciting reading, and if you were writing a novel or a story, you might decide that a meeting at which the people in the hall ran riot suited your purpose better than one at which they were simply a little noisy. But if you were describing an actual meeting, the chairman and the other participants would probably take exception to your suggestion that there was uproar in the hall rather than a mild disturbance. In other words, you should not overdramatize, or even dramatize, an event, if that event was not in itself particularly dramatic. And even when an incident might seem to warrant the use of dramatic language, understatement sometimes works better than overstatement:

> *My fingers slipped, and I dropped the cup, making a vain attempt to catch it as it fell. It broke. It lay on the floor in small, white, guilty fragments.*

> *The cup fell from my nerveless fingers, and, though I grasped and grabbed at it as it fell, it crashed to the floor and shattered in a thousand irredeemable fragments.*

It is debatable whether the more obviously dramatic language of the second sentence—*nerveless fingers, grasped and grabbed, crashed, shattered, a thousand irredeemable fragments*—represents an improvement on the first, where the only concession to drama, we might say, is the use of the word *guilty* to describe the fragments. (This is what is known, technically, as a "transferred epithet." The fragments are not guilty, but the narrator feels guilty for dropping the presumably precious cup and expresses this by applying the word to the result of his or her "crime." Transferred epithets are useful in poetry and imaginative prose but should be avoided in everyday writing.) Despite this, however, in its own quiet way, the first sentence conveys at least as much of the emotion of this small incident as the second. It is often more effective to allow the reader to imagine what you are not saying—to dramatize the silence that follows a period, as it were—than to try to galvanize him or her through the use of words that are highly charged with emotion or action.

The chances are that you will only occasionally find yourself describing events that are very dramatic and exciting. Even if you specialize in writing thrillers, there are bound to be long stretches of text where you relax the tension and allow your characters ordinary, peaceful, everyday activities. Furthermore, the law of diminishing returns can easily come into play if you overindulge in the language of speed and violence. If you start with a volcano erupting, what do you do for a climax? Something other than vigorous terms, useful and attractive as these are, is needed to keep up the energy levels of your prose. Let us turn our attention, then, to another source of energy.

Colloquial Vigor

As noted earlier in this book, spoken language is often particularly "lively, inventive, and colorful," especially in comparison to written language. It is, therefore, quite refreshing to come across sentences like the following in, say, the pages of an academic journal:

> *It is a privilege of reviewers to dump on others from a great height.*

> *There is nothing in the Internet chat room format to prevent academic specialists from competitively boring the pants off one another, but it does usually give them an incentive to express themselves in a more accessible way.*

There is a raciness and often an irreverence about slang and colloquial language that can come like a shot in the arm, especially in a passage of otherwise fairly routine serious prose. Unfortunately, we face the same problem with informal language that we faced with dramatic language: It is not generally suited to the long haul or the average task. It is possible to write whole books in vigorous, colloquial, regional English: Mark Twain's *Huckleberry Finn* is a shining example. But we cannot endlessly rewrite *Huck,* and most of what we have to write will need to be couched in a more neutral tone. It would be altogether inappropriate to set out to write a serious article, assignment, or report in informal language, however refreshing an occasional lapse into slang might be. Although colloquial language is vigorous, it is not the solution to the problem. We still need to find methods to prevent our prose from being slack and lifeless, even when it is dealing with serious subjects and needs to remain respectable.

Vigor for the Long Haul

Let us first revisit some of the places we have been to already. Strangely enough, perhaps, several of the qualities that were put forward as basic constituents of elegance—simplicity, compactness, flow—make writing vigorous as well. It stands to reason that a sentence that is loaded down with too many words will be less vigorous than one that is sparing with them and says what it has to say quickly and neatly. In addition, most of the words that were referred to as "forceful" earlier are in fact short, simple words. If you base your style of writing on the use of basic verbs, concrete nouns, and simple but evocative adjectives and adverbs put together to form uncluttered sentences, then the chances of its becoming tired or flabby are immediately reduced. (*See* AVOIDING UNNECESSARY ADJECTIVES AND ADVERBS, page 59.)

Although a wholesale use of colloquial language is usually inappropriate, the advice given earlier in the book that you should endeavor to keep in touch with the spoken language, especially language as you speak it, should be repeated here. But your verbal resources are not the only resources that you need to draw on. Most of the qualities that we have identified as being hallmarks of good style are achieved through intellectual effort and critical judgment. To be clear, to be elegant, to vary the way in which you write, and even to keep simple what you write usually involve making a conscious choice of selecting the clearest, simplest, or most elegant expression or deliberately differentiating one word, sentence, or paragraph from another. Now, you may apply the same kind of mental effort to being vigorous, but you can also channel vigor directly into your written work from within yourself much more easily than you could channel elegance or variety, for example.

The best way of ensuring that your work possesses and retains vigor is for you to have a positive attitude toward it. Your personality transmits itself almost unconsciously into your writing. This was suggested in the opening chapters of this book that dealt with the personal aspects of style. Likewise, your state of mind when you sit down to write and your attitude toward the subject that you are writing about color the way in which you use language.

Your input into a text will be emotional and even visceral as well as intellectual. If you feel tired or despondent when you sit down to write, you are unlikely to write with much energy. If you feel that the subject you have set yourself to write about is boring nonsense, your lack of conviction will surely communicate itself to the reader. Anything that you can do to put yourself into a positive frame of mind will bring enormous benefits. If you write with the attitude "I have something to say to you, reader, that you will want to hear because it is really interesting and important," you are far more likely to write vigorously than if your attitude at the outset is "I haven't really got anything to say, and I'm only writing this because I have to." When there is nothing that you want to say, the best policy is to say nothing. But when your interest is awakened and you believe in what you are doing, then your positive engagement with the task in hand will lend an equally positive energy to everything you write.

Most writers have to develop strategies to cope with the times when they have to write but are not in the mood to write. Here are two strategies that will assist in keeping your writing vigorous even when you are not at the peak of your form.

Avoiding Unnecessary Adjectives and Adverbs

You will reduce the amount of clutter in your sentences and keep your writing strong and vigorous if you use adjectives and adverbs to make your descriptions more precise rather than more emphatic. There is a class of words that grammarians refer to as "intensifiers"—words such as *very*, *dreadful* and *dreadfully*, *serious* and *seriously*, *terrible* and *terribly*, *total* and *totally*, *utter* and *utterly*, and so on—whose purpose is to increase the force of what you say, but which, if used too often—and that generally means too instinctively, with too little thought—can actually have the opposite effect. This is especially so when they are linked to nouns that are intrinsically "forceful."

A word such as *catastrophe*, for instance, denotes a terrible event. To call an event *a terrible catastrophe, a dreadful catastrophe*, or, worse, *a serious catastrophe* adds nothing. It may, on the other hand, be relevant to specify what kind of catastrophe you are talking about, for example, *a political catastrophe, a financial catastrophe*, or *a domestic catastrophe*. The adjectives in these latter phrases are used to make the statements more precise; in the former phrases they are used simply in an attempt to add emphasis. If you are speaking to somebody face to face, you may feel it necessary to say,

> *I'm terribly sorry. I know you must be feeling completely heartbroken, and it was extremely thoughtless of me to make such an utterly uncalled-for remark.*

Each of the intensifiers—*terribly, completely, extremely,* and *utterly*—is like a shamefaced bow of the head or bend of the knee to pacify the person you have offended. Writing a similar sentence, however, is another matter:

> *He was terribly sorry, for he knew that she must be feeling completely heartbroken and that it had been extremely thoughtless of him to make such an utterly uncalled-for remark.*

Consider whether it would not be more effective without those adverbs:

> *He was sorry, for he knew that she must be feeling heartbroken and that it had been thoughtless of him to make such an uncalled-for remark.*

If that does not seem to convey effectively the person's remorse, recast the sentence using more forceful language but still avoiding intensifiers:

> *He was devastated. What had possessed him, knowing how heartbroken she was, to make such a thoughtless and uncalled-for remark?*

In general, you should try to avoid overloading your sentence with adjectives and adverbs, even when they are genuinely descriptive ones. Take the following example:

> *It was only a small, derelict, uninhabited cabin on top of a low, round-topped hill, but in that flat, sparse country it stood out conspicuously, and to Julia, as a child, it had always marked the farthest boundary of her world.*

Reducing the amount of adjectival and adverbial detail produces a less cluttered and therefore more vigorous and more elegant effect:

> *It was only a small, derelict cabin on top of a low hill, but in that flat country it stood out, and to Julia, as a child, it marked the boundary of her world.*

Vigorous Verbs

Verbs can be used in two ways: actively or passively. In this section entitled "Vigor," the judgment is that we will prefer the active to the passive form.

Let us remind ourselves of the difference between the two. In the "active voice," as it is technically known, the subject of the verb performs the action of the verb. In the following simple sentences the verbs are in the active voice:

> *Our cat killed the mouse.*

> *A team of legal experts will undertake the work.*

In the passive, the subject does not perform an action but is acted upon by something or somebody else. It is very easy to convert simple sentences from the active to the passive voice, or vice versa. The object of a sentence in the active voice (*the mouse* and *the work* in the examples above) becomes the subject of an equivalent sentence in the passive voice. The passive is formed by combining the past participle of the verb with the relevant form of the verb *to be*:

The mouse was killed by our cat.

The work will be undertaken by a team of legal experts.

Some verbs take both a direct and an indirect object:

Juanita gave me [indirect object] *the book* [direct object].

In such cases, either the direct or the indirect object can be made the subject if the verb is put into the passive:

The book was given to me by Juanita.

I was given the book by Juanita.

(For more on the grammar of verbs, see *The Facts On File Guide to Good Writing*.)

In any extended piece of writing, you will inevitably need to use verbs in both the active and the passive voice. Which form you choose will depend on what you wish to emphasize, because, in most cases, the subject of the verb is what any sentence is about. For example, if you say,

The building was destroyed by fire in 2002.

your sentence is essentially about the building in question. But if you say,

Fire destroyed the building in 2002.

the emphasis switches to the means of the building's destruction.

It stands to reason, therefore, that in certain instances, the passive voice is the better form of the verb to use. These include

- when your attention is focused on the person or thing that feels the effects of an action:

  Why was Maggie selected for the basketball team, when Angela is obviously a much better player?

  The whole neighborhood was shaken by the blast.

- when you do not know, or wish to avoid mentioning, the person or thing that performed a particular action:

He was robbed on his way back to the hotel.

The file was shredded. Nobody can now remember how it came to be shredded.

It is regretted that the mail was delayed.

- when you wish to highlight an action by means of a noun coupled with a relatively unemphatic verb:

The decision was taken only after long and serious thought.

Savage cuts were made in spending.

In these last two sentences, the actions involved are "deciding" and "cutting" and the verbs "take" and "make" simply serve to show that those actions took place; they do not add significantly to the meaning.

Although the passive voice has these important functions, writers should not overuse it. A sentence containing a passive verb will inevitably be longer than an equivalent sentence containing an active verb:

A mouse ate the cheese.

The cheese was eaten by a mouse.

Moreover, if you write a long passage in the passive voice, you not only slow down the tempo by adding extra words, you often give the impression that events simply happen without anyone being responsible for making them happen:

The building had been allowed to fall into decay and had eventually been declared unfit for human habitation. It was, however, occupied by squatters before the order for its demolition could be put into effect. The squatters were supported by an action group that had been formed by members of the local community to resist the gentrification of the area. The process of gentrification had been started several years earlier when several former warehouses had been converted into loft apartments by developers. Rents in neighboring buildings had immediately been raised by landlords, and poorer inhabitants felt that they were being priced out of the neighborhood in which they had been born and bred.

If we recast this passage mainly using verbs in the active voice, we have to allocate responsibility for what takes place to different people and organizations:

The authorities had allowed the building to fall into decay and had eventually declared it unfit for human habitation. Squatters occupied it, however, before the authorities could put the order for its demolition into effect. An action group, formed by members of the local community to resist the gentrification of the area, supported the squatters. The process of gentrification had begun several years earlier when developers converted several former warehouses into loft apartments. Landlords immediately raised rents in neighboring buildings, and poorer inhabitants felt that they were being priced out of the neighborhood in which they had been born and bred.

The result is not only shorter and more vigorous, it also gives the reader more and clearer information. So, where you have a choice between using the active or the passive voice to make a statement, choose the active voice unless there is some compelling reason to choose the passive.

VARIETY

Variety is the spice of life, according to the old saying. Let us take up again a theme announced briefly at the beginning of the section on vigor. If the first rule of successful writing is "be clear," the second rule, perhaps, is "be lively" or "do not be boring." In order to get your message across to your reader, you must communicate it clearly. At the same time, however, you must ensure that the reader remains awake, alert, and involved, for if his or her attention starts to wander, even the clearest, most correct, and most elegant exposition of your ideas may fail to achieve its purpose. In the first instance, you should be able to rely on the interesting nature of the subject matter to hold the reader's attention. But anything that you can do to make the way that you write more interesting and more entertaining will help. If you can mix up things a little, put in light and shade, provide occasional comic relief, in short, if you can add variety to the presentation of your material, then you will spice it agreeably and make it that much more palatable for your reader.

What to Vary

Almost any element in a text can be varied and will benefit from variety. You can vary your vocabulary, your sentences, and your paragraphs. You can also vary length, tempo, and tone as well as the way in which you approach your topic. It is often quite refreshing to arrive at a "signpost" in a text that says: "Let us now look at this question from a completely different angle," or: "A fresh approach sheds an entirely new light on this problem," or "This discussion also has its lighter side." The more imaginatively you can ring the changes, the more interesting the text will be.

As always, however, there are limits. Although you do not want your writing to be completely predictable, at the same time you do not want it to be completely unpredictable. It may seem by now that what this book gives with one hand, in terms of allowing the writer liberty and scope, it often takes away with the other. (Give your writing variety, but not too much variety. Add spice to your writing, but do not deliberately spice it up. Do not, for example, distort reality by making it appear more thrilling, threatening, or hilarious than it is in fact. Use your imagination, but do not let your imagination get out of control.) For better or worse, this is the nature of style. Variety is important, but consistency, for example, of tone is important, too (*see* chapter 8, CHOOSING A STYLE, page 165). Creativity needs to be allied with judgment. Even repetition, which might seem the very antithesis of variety, has its place in the writer's repertoire. But this is merely a note of caution. Where you have the opportunity to vary your writing you should do so.

Creating Variety

Consider this example:

> *People think that winning is the only thing that counts. It is not the only important thing, in life or in sports. Fair play is just as important, if we understand the situation correctly. A person who takes illegal drugs to enhance his or her performance cannot claim to be a worthy winner. A person who cheats at cards is actually stealing from the other players. A person who bribes a judge is undermining the whole justice system. Preserving your integrity is just as important as gaining success. We ignore the rules of fair play because we cannot bear to fail. It takes a special kind of courage to fail. You can fail and not be defeated. You are never truly defeated if you have tried your best and behaved honorably. That gives you the strength to try just as hard again. That is what really counts.*

The writer has an interesting point of view, and the passage is sound in respect of grammar and style. But it seems to be very much all on one note. All the sentences are of roughly the same length. All the sentences are constructed on the same pattern, the standard pattern: The subject comes first, followed by the verb and the predicate. Varying the length and pattern of the sentences would improve the passage considerably and give it a lot more impact.

Take the first three sentences, for example:

> *People think that winning is the only thing that counts. It is not the only important thing, in life or in sports. Fair play is just as important, if we understand the situation correctly.*

and compare them with this version:

> *People think that winning is the only thing that counts. It is not. In life or in sports, fair play is just as important, if we understand the situation correctly.*

The short three-word sentence set between two longer sentences is arresting and emphatic. Taking the final phrase from the original second sentence and placing it at the beginning of the third sentence not only breaks the subject-verb-predicate pattern, it also avoids the unnecessary repetition of *the only . . . thing.*

Look then at the next three sentences:

A person who takes illegal drugs to enhance his or her performance cannot claim to be a worthy winner. A person who cheats at cards is actually stealing from the other players. A person who bribes a judge is undermining the whole justice system.

The repetition of the same pattern here is not in itself a fault. But you could recast the passage like this, for example:

An athlete who takes illegal drugs to enhance his or her performance cannot claim to be a worthy winner. To cheat at cards is actually to steal from the other players. When you bribe a judge, you are, in fact, undermining the whole justice system.

You could also retain the repetition but use a rather more interesting sentence pattern. Making a point in the form of a question, for instance, can often liven up a passage:

If you take illegal drugs to enhance your performance, can you claim to be a worthy winner? If you cheat at cards, are you not actually stealing from the other players? If you bribe a judge, do you not undermine the whole justice system?

Either of these solutions has the advantage of removing the rather colorless phrase *A person who . . .* from its very prominent position in the original set of sentences.

Finally, let us see if we can rework the original ending:

It takes a special kind of courage to fail. You can fail and not be defeated. You are never truly defeated if you have tried your best and behaved honorably. That gives you the strength to try just as hard again. That is what really counts.

There are too many sentences here, and the writer seems to be advancing by small and rather tentative steps instead of proceeding boldly to a conclusion. If we vary the length of the sentences, which means running some of them together, perhaps we can improve the effect. We should also, perhaps, try to be clearer about what is meant by *fail* and *defeat*:

It takes a special kind of courage to be defeated without feeling that you have failed. If you have tried your best and behaved honorably, you may have lost the game, but you have not failed so long as you have the strength to try just as hard again. That is what really counts.

So the whole passage in the new and more varied version might look something like this:

People think that winning is the only thing that counts. It is not. In life or in sports, fair play is just as important, if we understand the situation correctly. An athlete who takes illegal drugs to enhance his or her performance cannot claim to be a worthy winner. To cheat at cards is actually to steal from the other players. When you bribe a judge, you are, in fact, undermining the whole justice system. Preserving your integrity is just as important as success, yet we ignore the rules of fair play because we cannot bear to fail. It takes a special kind of courage to be defeated without feeling that you have failed. If you have tried your best and behaved honorably, you may have lost the game, but you have not failed so long as you have the strength to try just as hard again. That is what really counts.

Look out for sameness; look out for repetition. Vary the length of your sentences (and your paragraphs), and vary their construction. That will keep your readers' minds on what they are reading.

A Note on Repetition

It might appear at first sight that repetition was the enemy of variety and therefore had no place in stylish writing at all. This is not always the case:

Behind the sofa, there was a curtain. Behind the curtain, there was a little door. Behind the little door, there was a narrow passage. And at the end of the narrow passage, there was a deep dark hole.

There is a place for repetition in writing that is aimed primarily at children. There is equally a place for repetition in writing that is aimed at adults. Repetition forms the basis of almost all structural organization in writing and most rhetoric (*see* STRUCTURAL ORGANIZATION, page 198):

Give us bread, and we will thank you. Give us the means to make our own bread, and we will bless your name for ever.

Repetition is preferable to ambiguity:

She asked her sister to accompany her to the railroad station. She was rather reluctant to do so, because it was an extremely hot day.

Who is reluctant to do what? One or other element from the first sentence needs to be repeated in order to make the meaning clear:

She asked her sister to accompany her to the railroad station. Her sister was rather reluctant to go, because it was an extremely hot day.

She asked her sister to accompany her to the railroad station. She asked her rather reluctantly, because it was an extremely hot day.

Similarly, consider the following example:

> *A euphemism is a word or phrase that replaces others that might be thought offensive.*

The word *others* is plural and so does not match up exactly with *a word or phrase*. Repetition makes for a better and clearer sentence:

> *A euphemism is a word or phrase that replaces another word or phrase that might be thought offensive.*

There is a difference, however, between repetition for the sake of clarity or for effect and repetition that is simply the result of careless writing:

> *The constellation Orion is one of the most striking constellations in the northern skies.*

> *This new way of seasoning wood is, in many ways, superior to the old way.*

> *Developed in the 1940s, the jet engine represented a major development in the history of powered flight.*

> *These diverse approaches, which vary considerably in their approaches and emphases, have contributed substantially to our understanding of the problem.*

It is all too easy, unfortunately, to make such mistakes. As long as you take the trouble to look through your work when you have completed it and to revise it thoroughly, they can usually be eliminated. Often the easiest remedy is to delete the repeated terms:

> *Orion is one of the most striking constellations in the northern skies.*

or

> *The constellation Orion is one of the most striking in the northern skies.*

> *This new way of seasoning wood is superior to the old in many respects.*

Alternatively, you will have either to replace one of the repetitious elements with an alternative word with a similar meaning or to recast the sentence. Consider the following sentence:

> *Developed in the 1940s, the jet engine represented a major development in the history of powered flight.*

The obvious solution is to try to find another word to replace either *developed* or *development*.

> *Developed in the 1940s, the jet engine represented a major advance* [or *step forward*] *in the history of powered flight.*

This is a reasonably satisfactory outcome. But although the English language is comparatively rich in synonyms, a synonym is not always easy to find. You can make up for the limitations of your personal vocabulary by making use of a thesaurus, but thesauri often promise more than they can actually fulfill. A relatively simple list of synonyms, for instance, offers the following alternatives for the word *develop* in the sense in which it is used in this sentence: *begin, start, set in motion, found, institute, establish, invent, design, generate, produce.* Since the object in question is a machine, only three of those words—*invent, design,* and *produce*—are at all relevant, and none of them is exactly right in this case. A machine may be invented or designed in a primitive form long before it is developed, that is, before it is brought to a state in which it can be used. Leonardo da Vinci designed several sorts of flying machine, but he was not able to develop any of them. It is possible that the jet engine was both invented and developed during the 1940s, but you would need to recheck your facts before you substituted *invented* for *developed* as the first word of the sentence. *First produced in the 1940s* is probably the nearest and safest equivalent. Fortunately, finding a substitute for the noun *development* presents fewer problems.

By all means, use a straightforward replacement word if one comes easily into your mind:

> *Beginning a new relationship was not entirely easy; indeed, it was beginning to seem almost impossible.*

> *Starting a new relationship was not entirely easy; indeed, it was beginning to seem almost impossible.*

> *She decided to break the news to her friends during the afternoon coffee break.*

> *She decided to tell her friends* [or *share the news with her friends*] *during the afternoon coffee break.*

> *He crashed his car into a tree and was lucky to walk away from the crash with a few bruises.*

> *He crashed his car into a tree and was lucky to walk away from the wreck with a few bruises.*

If you cannot immediately think of a substitute, however, think about recasting the sentence before you reach for the thesaurus. Let us revisit an earlier example:

> *These diverse approaches, which vary considerably in their approaches and emphases, have contributed substantially to our understanding of the problem.*

This sentence suffers not only from the repetition of the word *approach,* but also from the fact that the idea conveyed by the adjective *diverse* is virtually repeated in the word *vary.* It also contains two adverbs, *considerably* and *substantially,* that are used to add emphasis rather than specificity. Worst of all, it is very difficult to work out what the writer is trying to say.

If you should happen to write such a sentence, you should first retrace your steps and do your best to disentangle the basic idea you wish to communicate from the words in which the idea first presented itself to you. In this instance, we shall assume that the writer intended to say that different people had approached the problem in different ways. The differences in their approaches highlighted different aspects of the problems, thus contributing to our understanding of it. This unpicking of the original sentence is as awkward and repetitive as the original, but it gives us a starting point for a rewritten version:

> *These approaches, with their different points of view and emphases, have contributed substantially to our understanding of the problem.*

THE QUALITIES OF STYLE: AN OVERVIEW

- The qualities of style are clarity, simplicity, elegance, vigor, and variety.
- Clarity is the one indispensable quality for all writing.
- Clarity is required in every aspect of written work; clear expression depends on clear thinking and should be accompanied by clear organization.
- The best means of achieving clarity and elegance is to aim for simplicity.
- Elegance is a combination of simplicity and refinement.
- Vigor depends partly on your positive attitude toward your writing and your subject.
- Use active rather than passive verbs to keep your writing vigorous.
- Put as much variety into your writing as you can, especially into the length and structure of your sentences.
- Repetition can be a useful device and an aid to clarity, but careless repetition should always be corrected.

Choosing Words

INTRODUCTION

One of the chief glories of the English language is its wide and expressive vocabulary. When you feel the weight of *Webster's Third New International Dictionary* or see the volumes of the *Oxford English Dictionary* arrayed along a library shelf, you cannot help being aware that this is a language that has substance. It contains many words, and over the last three centuries, scholars have labored to establish the correct forms of those words and to pinpoint their precise meanings. This work is ongoing. New words are continually entering the language, new usage of existing words is constantly emerging, and lexicographers are always busy sifting, sorting, and defining to ensure that we all can continue to share this wealth of words and keep communication flourishing. With this vast vocabulary at our disposal, organized and clarified by all these experts, surely there must always be a word that expresses our meaning exactly—and, if possible, elegantly and vigorously—on every occasion. There is. The only problem is finding it—or choosing it from among a number of alternatives. The purpose of this chapter is to help you with that particular problem.

USE WORDS YOU KNOW

Let us begin with a very simple and obvious rule. When you are writing or speaking, always use words that you know how to use.

Knowing what a word means is not necessarily the same as being able to use that word confidently and correctly in a real-life sentence. As was mentioned in chapter 2, "Beyond Correctness," everybody has what is known as an active vocabulary and a passive vocabulary. Your active vocabulary consists of the words that you use in everyday speech and writing. They come to your mind without great effort; you know how to pronounce them, how to spell them and how to make sentences with them. Your passive vocabulary consists of words that you recognize and understand when you hear them or read them, but that do not normally spring to your lips. You may, for instance, have no difficulty in understanding a word such as *reaffirmation.* Even if you have never encountered it before but know the verb *affirm,* you can, in any case, easily work out what it means from the way that it is constructed. You might not, however, feel at all confident about where and when to use *reaffirmation* effectively. The occasions on which anyone needs to use it are relatively rare, and the contexts into which it naturally fits are relatively formal and intellectual, so you may never have had occasion to say it or write it down. If this is the case, *reaffirmation* belongs to your passive vocabulary.

Your active vocabulary is much larger than your passive one, and the former is what you should rely on. Do not be tempted to use words that you know only passively in order to spice up your writing, in case you misuse them in some way. It is better to use words you know than to spoil the impression you are trying to make by an error of grammar, spelling, or usage. For example, an article on reconstruction work in run-down areas of large cities in a recent issue of a scholarly magazine contained the phrase *well-healed gentrifiers.* The writer had no problem with the rare word *gentrifiers*—people who renovate old buildings or run-down districts in order to provide accommodations for new, more affluent residents—but had obviously never seen the much more common word *well-heeled* in written form or had no sense of how it came to have its current meaning. He or she no doubt thought that *well-heeled* was part of his or her active vocabulary but was mistaken, having no notion of how the word evolved and consequently how it was spelled.

It is no disgrace not to know any particular word, especially a hard, long, or technical one. It is, however, a disgrace to misuse a word, especially when recasting what you want to say and using more familiar vocabulary would avoid the mistake. It is good to try to enlarge your vocabulary: the more words you know, the more precisely and subtly you will be able to express yourself. It is bad, however, to overreach yourself in your choice of words. The keynote of this chapter, as of most of this book, is Keep things simple. There will be times when you want to try out new words. Choose appropriate times and contexts, that is, occasions, when your credibility as a writer is not at stake. (For further advice on this issue, *see* ENLARGING YOUR VOCABULARY, page 88.)

With this basic principle established, let us now return to our discussion of the nature of English vocabulary and the considerations that should guide our search for the best word to fit the circumstances.

Pairings

A particular feature of the English language is that it frequently offers a choice between a simple word and a longer and more complex word that mean virtually, and in some cases exactly, the same thing. One such pair of synonymous terms is the ordinary word *sneeze* and the very learned word *sternutation,* which means both "a sneeze" and "sneezing." The French word for a "sneeze" is *éternuement* and the Spanish word is *estornudo.* The French and Spanish terms look rather similar and are, in fact, linguistically related to each other: They both derive from the Latin word *sternutatio*. At some time in the 16th century, the scholarly or more pretentious classes in England decided that they needed a grander word for the humble sneeze. They turned, as they usually did in such cases, to Latin, to the same Latin word, in fact, that had evolved into the ordinary words for a sneeze in French and Spanish. The word *sternutation* was adopted into the English vocabulary, and it remains there to this day.

Similarly, the French word for a "storm" is *tempête* and the Spanish word is *tempestad*. English has precisely the same word: *tempest*. All three go back to the Latin word *tempesta*. Neither French nor Spanish, however, has a word for a period of violent weather that is linguistically akin to the basic English word *storm*. Similarly, neither of these languages has a word that looks or sounds like *sneeze*.

A full list of pairings in English would be very long indeed. Here are but a few examples. All the words in the right-hand column come either directly from Latin or, more usually, from Latin via Old French. They also tend to be longer and more formal than the words in the left-hand column, which have Germanic roots.

ask	request	motherly	maternal
brotherly	fraternal	name	nominate
buy	purchase	odd	strange
cat	feline	prick	pierce
dry	arid	quick	rapid
earthly	terrestrial	reach	attain
fight	battle	sad	miserable
give	donate	top	summit
hard	difficult	udder	teat
icy	glacial	weak	feeble
king	sovereign	yield	produce
light	illumination		

This does not mean that English is full of words that are superfluous because they have the same meanings as other, generally older and simpler, words. Where a new word was introduced alongside an existing one, it usually developed a slightly different meaning or other differing senses over time. We now, for example, speak of "a miserable hovel," but not "a sad hovel," and "a feeble joke," but not "a weak joke." The scope we have for differentiation in the way we describe things is much greater because English contains words of both types.

The fact that English can offer us these options is a direct result of its history. Although modern speakers and writers of English are unlikely to be often in a dilemma over whether to choose *tempest* in preference to *storm*, let alone whether to describe a *sneeze* as a *sternutation*, many of the everyday decisions that confront them when they sift through English's vast vocabulary for the right word to suit the occasion are bound up with that history. A very brief account of it is, therefore, in order here.

THE ORIGINS OF ENGLISH VOCABULARY

The earliest form of English is known either as Old English or as Anglo-Saxon. It was a Germanic language, brought to England by the various peoples from northwestern Europe, particularly from present-day Netherlands, northern Germany, and Denmark, who invaded the country after the fall of the Roman Empire. Because English in its earliest form was a Germanic language, the English word *man* is very similar to the modern German *Mann*, but altogether different from the Latin word *homo* or its modern French and Spanish derivatives, *homme* and *hombre*. Similarly, the English word *God* is recognizably akin to the German *Gott*, but not to the Latin *deus*, French *Dieu*, or Spanish *Dios*.

In 1066 England was invaded, conquered, and settled again, this time by Normans from northern France. They came not so much to settle the country as to rule over it. Their language, Norman-French, became the language of the ruling and the educated classes. Anyone of Anglo-Saxon origin who wished to rise in society had to become proficient in Norman-French. For 200 years, English was the language of uneducated peasants. During this period English was greatly simplified. It ceased, for example, to classify nouns as masculine, feminine, or neuter or to show the grammatical function of words by adding a different ending to the root form.

Beginning in the 13th century, the century that produced the Magna Carta, English began to reassert itself. By the time that Geoffrey Chaucer wrote his *Canterbury Tales* (around 1390), it was truly a national language, used by all social classes. But it was no longer a Germanic language; it was a blend of Germanic and French or Latinate elements. It retained, for example, the words for domesticated animals, such as *cow, calf, ox,* and *sheep,* which are mainly Anglo-Saxon in origin, and incorporated different words for the corresponding types of meat, *beef, veal,* and *mutton,* which come from French. Reflecting the social divisions of the period after the Norman Conquest, it had simple words with Germanic roots for the humbler living quarters of the native English—*hut, house, home,* and *dwelling*—but it had also acquired the grander words *castle, mansion, palace, domicile,* and *residence* from French and Latin, along with a host of other words, covering every aspect of intellectual inquiry then known.

The average modern dictionary of English now contains more words that derive from the French and Latin connection than it does words that can be traced back through Old English to Germanic roots. This is partly because English adopted not only French and Latin words but also the mechanisms that the Romance languages (languages that derive from Latin) use to construct new words from already existing ones. Some sense of the range and nature of the Romance contribution to English may be gained by considering that the prefixes *ab-, anti-, co-, de-, dis-, ex-, inter-, mis-, pre-, post-, pro-, re-, sub-, super-,* and *trans-* and the suffixes *-able, -ant, -ent, -ize, -ment,* and *-tion* all entered our language by this route. So did most of the words of which they form part. In the Middle Ages, French was the language of the court, and Latin was the language of the church. The capacity that English acquired from French to assimilate Latin terms gave us much of the language of abstract concepts, science, and technology.

Anglo-Saxon versus Latin

Because of the way it developed, people sometimes talk about English as if it were a two-level language, as if it had a solid Anglo-Saxon foundation with an ornate French and Latin superstructure built on top or, to change the metaphor, a sturdy Anglo-Saxon body and fancy Latinate clothes. Indeed, it has often been suggested that any writer's prose style would benefit if he or she stripped away the fancy dress and concentrated on using good, plain Anglo-Saxon English.

In the opening chapter of his 1819 novel *Ivanhoe*, Sir Walter Scott introduces two minor characters, a jester and a swineherd, who comment on how the language they use reflects the different social statuses of Norman lords and Anglo-Saxon peasants. Speaking in his own authorial voice, Scott also compares the French and Anglo-Saxon languages in terms that have set the tone for this particular debate:

> French was the language of honour, of chivalry, and even of justice, while the far more manly and expressive Anglo-Saxon was abandoned to the use of rustics and hinds, who knew no other.

Although he goes on to describe "our present English language" as one "in which the speech of the victors and the vanquished have been so happily blended together; and which has been so richly improved by importations from the classical languages," some later writers continued to maintain that the Anglo-Saxon should, wherever possible, be preferred to the Latin because of its greater vigor, simplicity, and earthiness.

This debate touches on an important question of style. It is unhelpful, however, to present the issue as if it were wholly or mainly concerned with the historical origins of the words that writers have at their disposal. It sometimes appears, in fact, that earlier advocates of "manly" Anglo-Saxon had a national if not racial ax to grind when they argued in its favor. Although most of the abstract vocabulary in English comes from Latin via French, not all the words that came into the language by that route are abstract, let alone rarefied or pretentious. The word *beef* is no less expressive than the word *ox*. The words *cap, car,* and *dozen,* all of which come originally from Latin, are no more complex than the words *hat, wheel,* and *twelve* that have impeccably Germanic origins. *Likely* is Germanic and *probable* is French, but there is no justification for always preferring the former to the latter on those grounds or any other. *Sternutation* is a pretentious word, but there are plenty of other Latin imports ending in -*ation*—*conversation, identification,* and *justification,* for example—that are part of everyday vocabulary.

Words that come from Anglo-Saxon do sometimes have "warmer" connotations than their counterparts derived from Latin. The pairings *motherly* and *maternal, fatherly* and *paternal,* and *brotherly* and *fraternal* are the most obvious examples. There is a sense that "brotherly love" is something that people feel, whereas "fraternal love" is something that psychologists analyze and write about. Meanwhile, the Latin equivalent for *sisterly, sororal,* has not become as current in ordinary usage as the other terms.

It would take a conscious effort—and, for most people, frequent consultation of the etymologies given in dictionaries—to produce a passage of prose consisting of words with a purely Anglo-Saxon origin. And, despite the fact that these words are sometimes characterized by greater warmth and concreteness, the effort would not be worthwhile.

Nevertheless, the argument over Anglo-Saxon and Latin, which occasionally resurfaces, even in the 21st century, does lead in to the broader question of what sort of word one should choose, if offered a choice. As we have seen, when English vocabulary does offer alternatives, the choice, as often as not, is between a simple word and a more complex one. That is where the discussion should begin.

SIMPLE VERSUS COMPLEX

It follows from everything that has been said in this book about the general rules for good style that the best words to choose in any circumstance are those that most clearly, appropriately, and effectively convey your meaning. On this basis, simpler and shorter words generally express an idea not only more concisely but with less chance of ambiguity than longer and more complicated words. Simpler words, to return to the rule cited earlier in this chapter, are also likely to be the ones you know best; indeed, they are the words that everyone knows best.

So, it is generally better to use *ask* rather than *request, need* rather than *require, want* rather than *desire, use* rather than *utilize.* It is certainly better to use *start* rather then *commence, complete* or *finish* rather than *finalize, end* rather than *terminate,* and *change* rather than *modify.* There is no need to say or write *remuneration* or *recompense* when *pay* will express your meaning equally well. Remember the character of Mr. Micawber from Charles Dickens's *David Copperfield* (1849–50) who, when speaking of his job selling corn on commission, remarked: "It is not an avocation of a remunerative description—in other words, it does *not* pay." It was not in Mr. Micawber's nature to be plain at the outset, but he usually had the grace to provide a short and simple translation at the end.

It may seem unlikely that anyone but a rather pompous person would say,

I have come to request your assistance.

instead of

I have come to ask for your help.

or

Kindly provide me with a schedule of your requirements.

rather than

Please give me a list of the things you need.

or

Current extravagance may lead to future deprivation.

rather than

Waste not, want not.

The operative word at the beginning of the previous sentence, however, is *say.* The more formal and long-winded alternatives are not sentences that spring to the average person's lips in conversation, but when the average person sits down to write, it is remarkable how often a complicated formulation will come into his or her head in place of a plain statement.

Now, it is difficult to strike the right balance. As has been said, most people's "writing voice" is slightly different from their speaking voice, and it is usually slightly more formal. But it is all a question of degree, and it is easy to go too far. The very act of sitting down in front of a screen, a typewriter, or a piece of blank paper seems sometimes to transform us into stiffer and more pedantic versions of the people we really are. If this happens, we may start, consciously or unconsciously, to divide words and phrases into two classes: those we use on paper, or what we might call "writable words," and those we use when speaking, "speakable words."

Strictly speaking, no such distinction exists; anything that can be written can be spoken and vice versa. In practice, we know that there are some words and phrases that would probably sound out of place if we uttered them in speech and others, for example, very colloquial and slang expressions, that do not look good on paper. Nevertheless, the bulk of what we would normally say can be transferred to paper without alteration. The fact that we are writing rather than speaking should not be the factor that governs our choice of words. Consequently, if "Please give me a list of the things you need" is the wording you would use if you were speaking directly to somebody, there is no need to search around for a more elevated equivalent if you are addressing the same person on paper.

In addition to any self-consciousness they may feel about the act of writing itself, people are also apt to tie themselves into unnecessary knots trying to recall the conventional formulas for the type of writing that they have to do. It is not uncommon, for example, for people who have to write business letters to worry more about producing something that sounds as if it belongs in a commercial environment than about the actual message they have to convey or the person or people they have to convey it to. Here again, it is a question of striking a sensible balance. Tone and register are important, as was said earlier, but clarity and simplicity are more important still.

Consider the following example:

> *With reference to our telephone conversation of yesterday afternoon regarding repairs to my central-heating system, I have since come to the conclusion that the amount that you calculated that the repairs would cost is excessive, and I have decided that I shall make alternative arrangements for carrying out the work.*

Often the way in which you start a sentence or a paragraph sets the tone for the whole piece of writing. A phrase like *with reference to* offers a very tempting solution to the problem of how to begin. It seems to take you to the natural starting point of what you want to say, which is what was said on the same subject on an earlier occasion. It also seems to be the kind of phrase that people write when they are dealing with a business matter. The fact that "With reference to our telephone conversation of yesterday afternoon . . ." is not something most people would naturally say seems irrelevant.

But *with reference to* is precisely the kind of rather formal and conventional phrase that almost inevitably ushers in a vague and wordy sentence. The simpler word it usually replaces is *about*. However, if you begin a sentence of this kind with *about,* it will sound too informal and abrupt. "About those repairs to my central-heating system . . ." is a fine way to start if you happen upon the repairperson in the street, but not when you are writing to him or her. This is one of those phrases that are speakable, but not really writable. To find a beginning that is both speakable and writable—and therefore better written English because it is closer to spoken English—you could forget about trying to damp down the abruptness of *about* and recast the sentence so that it does not start with a preposition or a prepositional phrase:

> *We spoke on the telephone yesterday afternoon about repairs to my central-heating system.*

This is immediately neater and crisper. The words and constructions in the original were not absolutely "unspeakable" and not exactly highfalutin, but they were just far enough away from simplicity and directness to give the sentence a slightly flabby feel. To put it another way, *With reference to our telephone conversation of yesterday afternoon regarding . . .* is business lingo; *We spoke on the telephone yesterday afternoon about . . .* is businesslike.

Having made a crisp beginning—and having decided that what you have to say in this case is too much for a single sentence—you can then set about clearing up all the nervous "that" clauses that follow:

> *I have since decided that the cost you estimated for fixing the system is too high, and I shall ask someone else to do the work.*

Using simpler words generally results in your using fewer words and getting your point across more effectively. Check whether what you have written is what you would normally say. If it is not, consider whether the words you would use for the same purpose if you were speaking to somebody are appropriate to appear on paper. If they are, use them. If they are not, try saying the same thing to yourself another way and use that as the basis for your written sentence.

Let us return briefly to the starting point of this example, the prepositional phrase *with reference to*. It is good discipline to check whether such phrases appear in your writing, especially whether they appear frequently. If they do, think about replacing them with simpler equivalents. Here is a list of some lengthy prepositions and possible alternatives:

as a consequence of	because of
by means of	by, with, using
by virtue of	by
for the purpose of	to (+ infinitive)
for the reason that	because
in accordance with	by, under
in addition to	besides
inasmuch as	since
in association with	with
in case of	if
in excess of	above, more than, over
in favor of	for
in the absence of	without
in the course of	during, in
in the event of	if
in the nature of	like
in the neighborhood of	about, around
in the vicinity of	near
in view of	because of
on the grounds of	because of
on the part of	by, among
prior to	before
subsequent to	after
with a view to	to (+ infinitive)
with the exception of	except

Following is another example that illustrates a slightly different problem for which the best solution would again be to choose words of greater simplicity:

My background in terms of relevant experience has been mainly in inter-facing with the public in retail situations, where I have augmented my intrapersonal skills to the extent that I am now poised to undertake a more demanding position.

It is not clear from this sentence what type of work the writer has been doing, but it would appear that he or she considers it to have been something relatively humble and feels a need to disguise this. Hence the choice of a vague phrase "interfacing with the public in retail situations," instead of something more concrete, such as "serving in a store" or "working as a sales clerk."

Would you say "My background has been mainly in interfacing with the public in retail situations . . ."? You would not, not simply because it sounds highfalutin, but because nine times out of 10 the person you were speaking to would immediately ask what you meant by "interfacing with the public in retail situations." In this case, you should ask yourself not only "Would I say this?" but also "If I said this, what sort of reaction would it provoke?"

It is natural, of course, to want to present yourself in the best possible light when applying for a new job, but it may be counterproductive to try to make what you have done before sound grander than it actually is. A savvy employer's next question might be, "If you're so good with the public, how come you can't communicate more clearly?" An employer is likely to be more impressed by clarity and honesty than by knowledge of a few terms from professional jargon, such as *interface* and *interpersonal skills* (not *intrapersonal skills*).

There are other clumsy expressions in the example: "My background in terms of relevant experience," where just "my background" or "my relevant experience" would have been better; and "I am now poised to undertake a more demanding position," which makes it sound almost as if the writer is practicing yoga exercises rather than applying for a job. Basically, however, the writer would have done better to choose a more direct approach and simpler words:

> *I have relevant experience. I have worked as a sales clerk in a store and feel that I have now become skilled and confident enough in dealing with the public to take on a more responsible job.*

There are other ways in which the original sentence could have been improved. The important thing is to be alert to any tendency you may discover in yourself to use such vague and long-winded phrases as *in retail situations,* or such unnecessarily fancy words as *augment.* Ask yourself whether they would stand up if you were using them in a conversation. Be ruthless about discarding them and seeking simpler alternatives if you come to the conclusion that they would not survive under questioning.

People may be tempted sometimes to resort to longer and more complicated words when writing an ordinary letter, but the temptation is even greater when they are faced with the task of writing something as an academic exercise:

> *In light of this interpretation, "departmentalization" may be seen as a strategy for the involvement of departmental interests in the formulation and implementation of development policies basically following principles of functional representation involving interested parties in the department, through the establishment of forums entitled to the building of a departmental consensus on development objectives and measures.*

Although a high school student is, admittedly, unlikely to produce such a monstrosity, this type of writing is all too common in dissertations and articles in learned journals. It may be the desire to impress that, once again, impels the writer to empty a bucketful of long words into a sentence. On the other hand, it seems equally possible in this case that faced with the problem of defining a concept that is difficult to grasp and has several different aspects, the writer is simply desperate to touch all the bases and get home. It almost reads like a panicky sentence. You can almost imagine the writer thinking, "I know this is terribly complicated, but it's the best I can do. I think it says what I mean. I think it just about hangs together. If it presents problems for the reader, then that's just too bad!"

We have probably all had such thoughts at one time or another. It is much easier to find clear and simple words when the idea you have to put across is relatively straightforward. But the obligation to be clear and simple does not go away if you have something complicated or intricate to write about. You cannot expect your reader to do your thinking for you. Likewise, it is perfectly permissible for a writer to write anything as a first draft, simply in order to get an idea out of the brain and onto the paper or computer screen. It may be very sketchy or very wordy; it may not even be very clearly thought out. What is not permissible is to leave such a first draft unedited, especially in a case like this one where the material is so obviously crying out to be made easier to understand.

Let us see if we can make sense of what this particular writer was trying to say. He or she evidently wanted to do three things: to say what *departmentalization* is, according to "this interpretation"; to state the principles on which it operates; and to show how these principles are put into practice. If we divide up the original material on the basis of this assumption, with very little rewriting we arrive at the following:

> *"Departmentalization" may be seen as a strategy for the involvement of departmental interests in the formulation and implementation of development policies. It basically follows principles of functional representation involving interested parties in the department. It does this through the establishment of forums entitled to the building of a departmental consensus on development objectives and measures.*

That is a little clearer. If we try to simplify and clarify further, we may arrive at the following:

> *In this interpretation, "departmentalization" is a strategy that aims to involve the departments themselves in drawing up and implementing development policies. Interested parties within departments send representatives to forums, which attempt to build a departmental consensus on what the objectives of development should be and what measures should be taken to achieve them.*

The all-important preparation for clear and simple expression is clear and simple thinking. Even if you are writing for your peers, imagine that you are explaining your idea to a nonexpert. If necessary, break down a complex idea into its component parts before attempting to put it down on paper. In the above and previous examples in this chapter, using simpler words has also meant using fewer words. The point has been made before, however, that the interests of clarity and the interests of conciseness are not always the same. If you need to use more words and to repeat key terms in order to express an idea intelligibly, you should never be afraid to do so.

USE FEWER NOUNS

It is often said that one of the distinguishing features of modern writing is a heavy dependence on nouns, and the implication usually is that this is one of the more unfortunate features. Nouns seem to have flourished at the expense of verbs and adjectives, and the result, say critics of the trend, has been to make English prose "flabby" or "flaccid" and to encourage vague and generalized thinking.

The nouns that these critics complain about are not the kind that refer to objects, creatures, or people or to feelings and conditions that have a discernible existence; nobody objects to words such as *cat, dog, home, file, folder, computer, machine, anger, sloth, desire,* or even *defibrillator* and *psoriasis*. The alleged villains are words such as *consideration, experimentation, accountability, sustainability, suspension, furtherance, maintenance,* and *incidence*. None of these words is particularly unusual or difficult to understand, but, in addition to containing many syllables, they all describe activities or states that are abstract or generalized. If students or scientists conduct an experiment, they do so at a particular time and in a particular place using particular instruments and materials; *experimentation* is much less specific and can cover experiments that take place anytime and anywhere. Not even the severest critics suggest that abstract nouns are bad in themselves or that we can manage without them. We need at times to be able to distance ourselves from the particular, and we need words that enable us to discuss things in general terms. It is not their use but their overuse, critics argue, that is detrimental to good style.

The results of using too many abstract nouns are evident in the final example sentence of the preceding subsection. In it we read of "the formulation and implementation of development policies basically following principles of functional representation." Not only is that phrase a terrible mouthful, it never actually seems to touch down on mother earth. It gives no sense of people actually doing things, speaking, or thinking. Instead, it seems to place the activity it is describing in some disembodied realm where formulation and implementation take place almost of their own accord, without any actual person being present to do any formulating or implementing. That may not have been the impression the writer intended to give, but that is how the reader may view the situation. This is why, consciously or unconsciously, people sometimes slip into this kind of writing when they have something to conceal or do not want to take responsibility for something—a fact that political commentators have not been slow to notice.

Where abstract nouns are overused, verbs are almost always underused. It is not difficult to see why. A great many of the nouns that have been cited in the previous paragraphs derive from verbs. *Consideration* means "the act of considering" or "a thing to be considered"; *formulation,* "the act of formulating" or "a particular way of formulating an idea or statement"; and so on. If a sentence contains a noun of this type, it does not need to contain the verb that corresponds to that noun. For this very reason critics complain that nouns are made to do all the work. And, if a sentence is unwieldy or too vague because it contains too many nouns of this type, the best solution, in most cases, is to replace the noun by the verb to which it corresponds.

Let us see how this works in practice:

> *If accreditation and authentication of users are not properly performed, unauthorized people may be able to access the network.*

In the first clause of this sentence, the important conveyors of meaning are the abstract nouns *accreditation* and *authentication.* The verb *perform* is simply there as a prop to the nouns; it has no real meaning of its own in this sentence. *To perform accreditation* means "to accredit"; *to perform authentication* means "to authenticate." Why not, therefore, use those verbs?

> *If users are not properly accredited and authenticated, unauthorized people may be able to access the network.*

It is now the verbs *accredit* and *authenticate* that are doing the work, that is, carrying the meaning, and the result is a better sentence.

Here is another example to analyze:

> *Goods may also suffer deterioration as a result of the improper operation of packaging machines.*

The "overworked" nouns in this sentence are *deterioration* and *operation. Suffer deterioration* is, like *perform accreditation,* another completely unnecessary expansion of a verb. Nothing at all is gained by not saying *Goods may also deteriorate.* The second part of the sentence is a good example of how ambiguous abstract nouns can be. Do these packaging machines have operators who sometimes make mistakes, or do they operate automatically and sometimes go wrong? It is impossible to say for certain without more context, although the choice of the adjective *improper* rather than, say, *defective* suggests human error. In that case, we might improve the sentence like this:

> *Goods may also deteriorate if packaging machines are not operated properly.*

The use of the passive voice in this sentence implies that there is an operator. We do not have to construct a clause in which *operate* is an active verb with, say, *people* or *operators* as its subject. That would actually give too much prominence to those who work the machines. The purpose of the original sentence was to link the deterioration of the goods with the machines, not their operators.

Alternatively, if we assume or learn from the context that the packaging machines do not need human operators, we might say,

> *Goods may also deteriorate if packaging machines fail to operate properly.*

Here is a final example of this particular problem:

> *A loss of clarity may result from the proliferation of abstract nouns in sentences.*

This is indeed true, but there are three abstract nouns in the sentence, *loss, clarity,* and *proliferation.* Two of them derive from verbs, and it would be better to say,

> *When abstract nouns proliferate, sentences may lose clarity.*

That version is considerably crisper than the original, but it has a clipped and rather formal quality that may not fit with everybody's normal style. We could expand and simplify it somewhat to the following:

> *When sentences contain too many abstract nouns, they may become unclear.*

This version is unsatisfactory because it is not immediately clear whether *they,* the subject of the main verb, refers to the sentences or the nouns. With a little further adjustment that ambiguity can be removed:

> *Sentences containing too many abstract nouns may be unclear.*

The simplicity and directness of this version makes the original look positively wordy by comparison.

The tendency to strengthen nouns and weaken verbs is apparent in many short phrases that we tend to use without thinking. In most instances, the meaning expressed by the verb-and-noun combinations given in the left-hand column below would be better expressed by the simple verbs in the right-hand column:

conduct an investigation into	investigate
give consideration to	consider
give thought to	think about
make an assessment of	assess
make preparations for	prepare for
provide justification for	justify

show respect for	respect
subject to scrutiny	scrutinize
take note of	note
undertake a study of	study

Simple verbs seem to be losing ground not only to verb-and-noun phrases but to verb-and-adjective combinations, too. A spokesman during the occupation of Iraq in 2004 remarked that an action "was violative of" the Geneva Convention. Why did he not say that it "violated" the convention? Again, the phrases in the left-hand column below should usually be avoided, and the verbs in the right-hand column preferred:

be deserving of	deserve
be illustrative of	illustrate
be indicative of	indicate
be suggestive of	suggest
be symbolic of	symbolize

Another characteristic of modern English that sometimes causes controversy is its tendency to use nouns in front of other nouns, that is, in the position and with the function traditionally reserved for adjectives. (Nouns used in this position are known, technically, as "attributive nouns" or nouns used as modifiers.) In many ways, this is a very useful and necessary feature. It is usually much neater to say that someone is a *company director* than that he or she is a *director of a company,* and a *help menu* on a computer is very different from a *helpful menu* in a restaurant serving exotic dishes. Some people might complain that the word *development* in *development objectives and measures* is usurping the place of the adjective *developmental,* but others might argue, with good reason, that there are already enough syllables in the phrase without needlessly adding another one.

In itself, this use of nouns as modifiers is not a particularly modern characteristic of English. It is easy to think of compound English words made up of two nouns that are of venerable antiquity: *treasure chest, pocket handkerchief, tennis racket.* Shakespeare has Hamlet refer to himself as a "peasant slave," and Milton writes of the "ocean bed." However, what is new—and often a bone of contention—is the tendency to string more than two words together, as in

transportation facility development personnel

and

accident warning dissemination directive.

It is obviously impossible to replace the nouns that precede the main noun in such compounds with an adjective or even a string of adjectives. The compounds are essentially space-saving devices. Before this kind of multipart noun became fashionable, the only way to express the same idea was to place the modifying nouns after the main noun and link them to it by means of prepositions and other small linking words. Getting rid of the linking words saves space and, perhaps, adds a spurious kind of weight and importance to whatever is being described.

We have become accustomed to this kind of writing by reading newspaper headlines. But newspapers have the excuse that they need to grab their readers' attention and have little space to spare. Ordinary writers are not working under the same constraints. Ordinary readers are unlikely to object if the short linking words, such as *of* and *in,* are put back in. Indeed, they will usually appreciate the greater clarity of

> *personnel involved in the development of transportation facilities*

and

> *a directive on the dissemination of accident warnings.*

The more extended versions have the additional advantage that the key word, the noun that is functioning as a noun and not as a modifier, is placed first, not last. Moreover, there is sometimes a chance of ambiguity when nouns are placed one in front of the other. It is obvious that an *automobile parts salesperson* sells automobile parts, but does an *accident warning* warn you that an accident has taken place or warn you that there is a danger that an accident might take place? Without context, it is impossible to be quite sure.

Where one of the nouns in a string is a word that might, in other circumstances, have a different grammatical function—say, a present participle or an adjective—then the danger is greater. A sign outside an office building in a town in Great Britain reads *Youth Offending Team.* It conjures up a ludicrous image of a youngster making rude gestures at the opposing side in a sports event, or of a group of workers who devote their time to insulting young people. It actually refers to a team of social workers who deal with young people who commit criminal offenses. The person who coined the phrase clearly had no feeling for language and no real sense of the ridiculous.

There is also potential for sometimes comic misunderstanding when an ordinary adjective heads up a string of nouns waiting in line. Is a *large automobile parts salesperson* a seller of large automobile parts or a large person who sells ordinary-sized automobile parts for a living? Is a *green product development engineer* inexperienced, extraterrestrial, or developing environmentally friendly merchandise?

Noun strings present a test of your feeling for language. Remember the point made at the beginning of this book: Written language has to be crystal clear because there is no speaking voice to interpret it. If you link more than two nouns together in a string of this kind, examine the result closely and critically. If you cannot be absolutely sure that the reader will be able to understand what you mean, put the linking words back in.

USE LONGER WORDS CAREFULLY

It sometimes seems as if the writers of books on style are by nature hostile to long, uncommon, or abstract words. If they truly were, then it would probably set them apart from most of the word-loving population. A survey was held in the United Kingdom in the year 2000 to find the nation's favorite word. The winner was *serendipity*. It won thanks as much to its musicality and quaintness as to its cheerful meaning. It is not a particularly short or common word, but then the words that people are especially attached to are not necessarily those that they use every day.

In Shakespeare's play *Henry IV, Part 1*, Hotspur tells his wife to "Swear me, Kate, like a lady as thou art, / A good mouth-filling oath" (3.1.249–250). People like good mouth-filling words: *prestidigitation, deliquescence, fructification, vulturous, discombobulate, infeasibility*. There is pleasure in saying them. There is satisfaction in knowing what they mean. There is even greater satisfaction in being able to use them correctly. Some long words have the romance of exotic place-names; some have the horrible fascination of great carnivorous dinosaurs. They enrich the language and are often a great source of humor—characters in literature are seldom made fun of for habitually speaking in short, simple words. They can sometimes be used to great effect. Turning to Shakespeare again, this time in his play *Macbeth*, "Will all great Neptune's ocean wash this blood / clean from my hand?" asks Macbeth after Duncan's murder. He answers his own question: "No, this my hand will rather / The multitudinous seas incarnadine, / Making the green one red" (2.2.58–61). Those two tremendous polysyllabic words evoke the vast restless ocean, the enormity of the crime, and the troubled state of Macbeth's conscience in a way that the simpler phrase that follows them and ends the speech on its own could not. But few if any of us have Shakespeare's skill in using language.

Long words are usually considered, and treasured, in isolation. *Prestidigitation* is a wonderful word, but when are you likely to use it? Outside the technical contexts to which so many of them rightfully belong, long words exist almost in limbo. It is not easy, for example, to construct a realistic sentence containing the word *serendipity,* or indeed any of the words listed in the preceding paragraph. Technical terms, many of which are very long and very complex—*gyrostabilizer, laparoscopist, metamathematical, ultracentrifuge*—are in some ways easier to put into sentences, perhaps because there are often no simpler one-word alternatives for them. But the nonspecialist is seldom called upon to use such words at all.

Long words, then, have their uses, but their uses are limited. They are not needed, for instance, to produce a grand effect:

[A]sk not what your country can do for you—ask what you can do for your country.

Never in the field of human conflict was so much owed by so many to so few.

[T]hat this nation, under God, shall have a new birth of freedom; and that government of the people, by the people, for the people, shall not perish from the earth.

Great statesmen know rhetoric and are expert users of it, but they do not use long words. They achieve grandeur through the way they arrange simple words and the rhythm they give to their utterances.

Great writers in previous centuries did not use more long words than their modern counterparts do. The standard writing style in earlier times was usually more formal than it is nowadays, but formality is as much a matter of tone as it is of word choice. The famous 18th-century lexicographer Dr. Samuel Johnson is reported by his biographer, James Boswell, to have occasionally expressed an idea in relatively simple language, then decided that a straightforward statement was unworthy of him, and set about reexpressing the same thought more magniloquently. But Johnson was a phenomenon even in his own time, and, in this respect at least, is not a suitable model for a modern stylist.

The disadvantages of longer words have been referred to more than once. They may confuse the reader; they may confuse you; they may make your writing unnecessarily abstract or inflated. Always use long words with care.

ENLARGING YOUR VOCABULARY

Neither the stress on simplicity in most of this book, nor the injunction to use only words that you know well, nor cautionary tone of much of the previous subsection should be interpreted as in any way discouraging the reader from getting to know as many words as possible. Words are the tools of the writer's trade. The more of the language a person recognizes and understands, the easier it is to cope with the everyday business of life, and anyone who aspires to be a writer has a duty not only to maximize his or her passive vocabulary but also to extend his or her active vocabulary as far as possible.

The key to enlarging both vocabularies is to listen carefully, to read carefully, and to consult reference works frequently. Writers should be alive to the language. When you hear or see a word that you are unfamiliar with, check it out.

The first place in which to look is, of course, a dictionary. Even a small dictionary can be helpful, but if you are sufficiently interested in words and writing to read this book, you will probably benefit from owning a dictionary of the size and scope of *Merriam-Webster's Collegiate Dictionary* or *The American Heritage Dictionary of the English Language* or the *Microsoft Encarta College Dictionary.*

If you do not already possess such a work and decide to invest in one, remember at the cash register that you are certainly getting your money's worth. Dictionaries contain a good deal of valuable information in addition to definitions of the senses of words. They will in most cases, for example, tell you how to pronounce the words they list. It may take you a little while to familiarize yourself with the way your dictionary reproduces the various sounds that make up spoken English—there is usually a guide to pronunciation at the front of the book—but the effort is worthwhile. A word only becomes part of your active vocabulary when you know how it is spoken, and English is notorious among foreign learners for the fact that you frequently cannot tell how a word should be pronounced from the way in which it is spelled. This holds good even though you may intend to use a particular word only in writing. If you care about the rhythm of your sentences, if you check the readability of your prose by saying it over inside your head, you need to know how the words you write are supposed to sound and where the stress falls in them. Unless you know that you cannot fully judge the effect they will have on the reader.

Dictionaries also tell you a little about the history of individual words. The etymology of a word, to use the technical term, may seem to be of interest only to the specialist. Sometimes, however, a term's history can open up a new vista on a familiar word. Take the word *helicopter,* for example. Why is an aircraft with a rotating airfoil called a helicopter? The etymology tells us that the word is made up of two elements. These are, though you would not guess it from the way the word is pronounced, *helico-,* meaning "spiral" (as in *helix* and *helical*), and *-pter* meaning "wing" (as in *pterodactyl*). You do not have to be a Greek scholar—both elements come from Greek—to find this interesting. Writers need to cultivate a feeling for words. This is partly inborn, like a sense of musical rhythm, but can also be developed by studying words and thinking about their sound and usage. Knowing where words come from and how they are made helps you to appreciate what they are and what they can do. There is, usually, a logic to the way in which words are constructed, and this is in itself a useful thing to remember.

Because many complex words are logically constructed, you can enlarge your vocabulary and acquire a better grasp of the inner workings of English not only by learning whole words but also by learning to recognize the parts from which complex words such as *helicopter* are made. If you find the four letters *pter,* for example, in any other word, you can deduce that that word must have something to do with wings or flying. Likewise, if you know that the prefixes *hem-, hema-, hemato-,* and *hemo-* all mean "blood" or "having to do with blood," you have a first clue to the meaning of a group of words that take up half a column in an average dictionary. Knowing, as you undoubtedly do already, that the suffix *-logy* means "the study or science of something," you can work out the meaning of the word *hematology,* even if you have never encountered it before and even if there is no dictionary at hand. Modern dictionaries acknowledge the importance of many of these word elements by providing separate entries for them. Their place in the development of the English language has been discussed earlier (*see* THE ORIGINS OF ENGLISH VOCABULARY, page 74). Give them the attention they deserve as part of your effort to get full value from your dictionary.

Most people use dictionaries, thesauri, and similar reference works as aids in cases of particular need. They have one question that needs to be answered; when that question has been settled, the book has fulfilled its purpose. But there is much to be said for browsing in such works, when time allows. This is a good way of learning more words and learning more about words. Follow up on cross-references. If you find an interesting synonym for a particular term in a thesaurus, look up the entry for the synonym as well. Your interest in words will grow as you learn more about them. You may even find that the dictionary and the thesaurus become page-turners as exciting as a thriller or a whodunit.

Words considered in isolation, however, can only really form part of your passive vocabulary. To activate words, you need to consider them in context. Dictionaries can offer only limited help in enlarging your active vocabulary, but what they do offer should not be ignored. Many dictionaries offer quotations from famous and not-so-famous authors to illustrate how words are used in particular senses. They also provide notes that discuss, for example, the distinctions between words that are close synonyms or words whose usage is controversial. Again, read those quotations and those notes, which often contain further quotations, as part of a policy of squeezing the last drop out of your dictionary. But be prepared to look elsewhere as well.

Reading and listening carefully were cited earlier in this subsection as the key to increasing your word power. "Carefully," in this instance, means paying attention not only to the unfamiliar word itself, but to the other words that are used in conjunction with it and to the subject that is being discussed. Let us say, for example, that, along with most Britons, you were attracted by the notion of *serendipity* and the word itself, and that you wanted to be able not merely to explain what it means and where it came from but to drop it into a conversation or use it in a piece of writing.

For all its attractiveness, *serendipity,* as has been remarked before, is not a particularly easy word to put into context. If you are lucky enough to hear someone say it or to read it in a book, it would help enormously if you could remember or note down the whole sentence in which it appeared. You could then begin your own acquisition of the word for your active vocabulary by if not repeating, then at least imitating that sentence. A sentence such as *Can this be serendipity?* is not a great deal of help, since you could replace *serendipity* by a great many other nouns to similar effect, but it is a start. If you heard a person say that such and such a thing or person *was discovered by serendipity in a second-hand bookshop / on a trip to Columbus, Ohio / performing in an amateur production of* West Side Story, you would have more useful context to build on. If you can say (or write) *discovered by serendipity,* then you can also say *found / came upon / happened upon [etc.] by serendipity.* Likewise, if you read that *Without such serendipity, the effectiveness of this remedy might never have been known,* you have another model sentence that you can adapt for your own purposes: *But for serendipity, I might have gone through my whole life without ever knowing the joy of true love.*

Another way of researching the usage of a word is to type it into a search engine and see what results you get from the World Wide Web. You might wonder, for instance, whether it would be appropriate to use the phrase *a piece of serendipity* like a *piece of luck.* One way of finding out whether any other (reputable) writer had ever used it, would be to try to find it on the Web.

Once you have a viable context for your word, you can start to think about using it actively. The advice given in the section USE WORDS YOU KNOW (page 71), still holds good, however. Practice using new words first in communications where it will not matter greatly if you make a mistake. In the days when people frequently exchanged personal letters, these made excellent test beds for writers' new equipment. Modern e-mail is so casual that the sudden appearance of an unusual formal word is perhaps likely to produce the wrong sort of comment. Keep looking out and listening, for once you are alerted to a particular word, it is remarkable how often it seems to present itself to you. Use the new word in practice whenever an opportunity offers, and when you are confident that you have its measure, employ it to the full.

CHOOSING WORDS: AN OVERVIEW

- Always choose the most appropriate word to express your meaning regardless of any other consideration.
- Use words that you are familiar with and know how to handle.
- Where you have a choice, prefer a simple and familiar word to a complex and unfamiliar one.
- Where you have a choice, prefer a concrete word to an abstract one.
- Use no more words than are necessary to express your meaning clearly.
- Avoid making abstract nouns do all the work. Give verbs a chance.
- Avoid long strings of nouns.
- Enlarge your passive vocabulary by using dictionaries and other reference works to the full.
- Enlarge your active vocabulary by listening and reading carefully and collecting context along with the main word.
- Always be aware of the context in which the words you choose will appear.

Constructing Sentences

INTRODUCTION

The basis of a good style is the ability to write clear and effective sentences. This fact has been pointed out by almost everyone who ever attempted to give advice on stylistic matters. However much care you take in choosing your words—and you should take a great deal—all your good work can be undone if you place a well-chosen word in an ill-constructed sentence. If a sentence is incomplete, ungrammatical, or awkward, the effect any of its component words is intended to have on the reader is likely to be severely diminished or entirely lost. Similarly, if you choose the right word, but place it in the wrong position in your sentence, the reader may be confused rather then enlightened. A well-written sentence, however—one that is clear, logical, rhythmical, elegant, and vigorous and in which every word is in its proper place—is a lovely thing in itself and a suitable setting for any of the jewels in the lexicon, from *aardvark* through *serendipity* to *zymosan.*

This chapter, therefore, deals with the art and science of putting words together. It will discuss the finer points of sentence-making under two main headings: the logic of the sentence and the rhythm of the sentence. It begins, however, with a review of the basics: the methods of linking clauses to form sentences, the proper length of sentences, and, first and foremost, the rules of grammar as they apply to sentences. There is probably no other aspect of style in which a solid grammatical foundation is more important. In a book of this nature, however, discussion of grammatical matters must necessarily remain brief, so for a full and systematic account of the grammar of sentences, readers are advised to refer to *The Facts On File Guide to Good Writing.*

SENTENCES—THE BASICS

Grammar

COMPLETENESS

The most important point about a sentence, from the grammatical perspective, is that it should be a unit of language that is complete in itself. Of course, the first word in a sentence should begin with a capital letter, and the punctuation mark that closes a sentence should be a period, a question mark, or an exclamation point, but these are essentially rules of presentation. Their purpose is simply to emphasize that a sentence is a unit of language that can stand alone. The capital letter marks the beginning, just as the period, question mark, or exclamation point marks the end of a complete and independent grammatical unit.

Because completeness is the essential quality that defines a sentence, it is possible for a sentence to consist of no more than a single word. "Yes." is grammatically acceptable as a sentence, therefore, as is "Yes!" or "Yes?" "Go!" "Explain!" or "Really?"

The concept of "completeness" is perhaps not altogether easy to grasp. In what sense, it might be asked, are "Yes!" and "Really?" and "Go!" complete, when some much longer and, on the face of it, more conventionally sentence-like strings of words are not? The answer is that a unit of language is complete when no more needs to be said to make it understandable. Under certain circumstances, particularly when a person has to answer a question or comment on something that somebody else has said, a speaker's attitude or response can be fully conveyed in a single word such as "Yes!" or "Really?" Those words can therefore function as sentences.

> *"Was the victim alive or dead when you found him, lieutenant?"*
> *"Dead."*
> *"Thank you, lieutenant, that is all we need to know."*

Since it is "all we need to know," "Dead." here functions as a sentence.

Completeness and understandability are, admittedly, relative concepts for grammatical purposes. They do not depend on the word or words in the sentence making the situation absolutely clear without reference to anything else. "Yes." and "Really?" fully convey a response or an attitude, but they do not tell us what the speaker is responding to. The same is true of more conventional sentences. "It hurt me" is a sentence. It can stand alone, and it makes sense when it stands alone. But it would only be completely understandable if you knew what "it" was, who was being hurt, and whether "hurt" referred to physical or emotional damage. That kind of explicitness is not required for grammatical completeness, which is necessarily more limited. The best way to describe grammatical completeness is negatively. A sentence is complete when there is nothing missing from it that its words would lead you to expect to be there. This is an issue that will be dealt with in a moment.

VERBS IN SENTENCES

A great deal of what has been said in the preceding paragraphs seems to fly in the face of a rule that most people will remember about sentence construction: To be grammatically correct a sentence must contain a verb, specifically, a finite verb. A finite verb is limited in person, tense, and number. It is, in other words, a verb such as *goes, went, was going, will go, had gone,* or *would have gone,* each of which can be preceded by a personal pronoun of one kind or another, can be defined as either singular or plural, and signifies either past, present, or future time. It is not an infinitive, such *to go,* or a participle, such as *going* or *gone,* on its own.

This is not a universal rule. Not all sentences contain verbs; completeness is not dependent on the presence of a finite verb. Grammarians do, however, put sentences without finite verbs in a special category of their own. They call them "minor sentences." "To return to the matter in hand." and "What an absolutely perfect day!" are, like "Yes!" and "Really?" minor sentences.

MINOR AND MAJOR SENTENCES

Minor sentences are, on the whole, more at home in spoken than in written English. If you are writing dialogue, then you may be called upon to write minor sentences quite frequently. Ordinary continuous prose, especially in a neutral or more formal style, should not contain too many of them. Do not be misled by what has been said in the paragraphs above into thinking that you have grammatical license to write sentences without finite verbs. It is usually advisable to think about making any minor sentences that you write in a first draft into full sentences by combining them with other material.

Let us move the argument forward by turning our attention to sentences that do contain verbs—called "major sentences" by grammarians—and by considering the question of completeness from a different angle.

> *Although that was part of my original plan and was, indeed, the main reason why I had taken the trouble to pay Joan a visit on that gray October day in Columbus, Ohio, when I should have been covering the president's speech in Cleveland, because the election was no more than a few weeks away*

These words do not constitute a sentence of either the major or the minor kind. Despite the fact that there are more than 50 words, including several verbs, despite the fact that they make sense up to a point and do not—at least until such time as a period is placed after *away*—contain any grammatical errors, and despite the fact that they seem to fall away nicely toward a conclusion at the end, they are incomplete. In nongrammatical terms, there is something missing that the words used lead you to be expect to be present. The grammatical reason why these words are incomplete can be stated more succinctly: They contain no main clause.

CLAUSES

A clause is a meaningful group of words that contains a verb. Clauses are of two basic types: main clauses and subordinate, or dependent, clauses. What crucially defines a main clause is what crucially defines a sentence: It must be complete in itself, written in such a way that no more needs to be said to make it understandable. It follows, therefore, that a main clause can function as a sentence by itself, and that if a sentence consists of one clause only, that clause must be a main clause.

It hurt me.

The title character of Moby-Dick *is a great white whale.*

Throughout his period in office as U.S. secretary of state, John Foster Dulles pursued a policy of opposition to the USSR.

These are all sentences that consist of a single main clause. It should also be noted that a main clause in a major sentence must contain a finite verb.

Logically enough, and as their name suggests, subordinate, or dependent, clauses are not complete in themselves. They not only leave unsaid something that needs to be said, they also positively create an expectation that there is more information to come. They depend on the main clause to supply that information. The easiest way to recognize them is that they usually begin with such words as *although, if, because, since, when, where,* or *while.*

Where it hurt me

Because the title character of Moby-Dick *is a great white whale*

Although John Foster Dulles pursued a policy of opposition to the USSR throughout his period in office as U.S. secretary of state

These are not sentences, because the addition of a subordinating word at the beginning has rendered each one incomplete. When someone says or writes *Because the title character of* Moby-Dick *is a great white whale,* we expect a continuation. The word *because* indicates that the following words describe the cause of some particular fact, event, or state of affairs. Until we know the effect or result of that cause, the information the writer is offering us is incomplete. Something is missing that *because* leads us to expect to be there, and so the statement is not a sentence.

If we look again at the lengthy and quite plausible-sounding example given earlier,

Although that was part of my original plan and was, indeed, the main reason why I had taken the trouble to pay Joan a visit on that gray October day in Columbus, Ohio, when I should have been covering the president's speech in Cleveland, because the election was no more than a few weeks away

we shall see that all the verbs it contains are inside clauses governed by sub-ordinating conjunctions: *although, why, when,* and *because.* The example, therefore, consists of a string of subordinate clauses, and the writer never gets to the point. He or she explicitly concedes something by starting the sentence with *although* but does not inform us of what made this concession necessary. To complete the sentence, all that is needed are a few more words:

> *Although that was part of my original plan, . . . the situation had changed dramatically.*

or

> *Although that was part of my original plan, . . . I was no longer convinced of the soundness of the plan.*

Both of these clauses—*the situation had changed dramatically* and *I was no longer convinced of the soundness of the plan*—are grammatically complete in themselves and as such are acceptable as main clauses or as sentences in their own right. As soon as one of them is attached to the original word string, the rules of grammar are satisfied, and the sentence may stand.

It will be noted, however, that neither of the two suggested additions is particularly long in relation to the sentence as a whole. This leads us to an important point. The main clause is the essential part of the sentence for grammatical purposes, but, in terms of size, it does not have to make up the greater part of the sentence, nor does it have to carry all, or even the principal part, of the sentence's information content. The fact that it is the key component, however, means that it always carries weight. When constructing a sentence, you will often have to decide which information you will put in your main clause and which you will convey through subordinate clauses. The balance and the emphasis of the sentence—and some its meaning—will depend on the decision you make.

This topic will be further discussed in the section THE LOGIC OF THE SENTENCE (page 105). For the moment, let us continue to deal with the basics.

Coordination and Subordination

You will often wish to communicate more than one piece of information or combine more than one idea in a single sentence. There are two basic methods of combining ideas in sentences; the grammatical terms used to describe them are "coordination" and "subordination." The basic rule is as follows: Where ideas are of equal importance, they should be coordinated; where one idea is more important than another, the less important idea should be subordinated.

COORDINATION

Coordination is the linking together of clauses, and thus ideas, of equal value through the use of particular words or punctuation marks. The words in question are known as "coordinating conjunctions," "correlative conjunctions," and "conjunctive adverbs," or, more generally, as "coordinators." The relevant punctuation marks are the comma and the semicolon.

The coordinating conjunctions are

and, but, for, nor, or, so, and *yet.*

The correlative conjunctions are

either . . . or, neither . . . nor, whether . . . or, both . . . and, and *not only . . . but also.*

Conjunctive adverbs include

consequently, furthermore, however, meanwhile, moreover, nevertheless, therefore, and *thus.*

Here are some simple sentences in which coordination is used:

Margaret had forgotten, but Carlos most certainly had not.

Either the package has been lost in the mail, or the supplier forgot to send it.

The sergeant had been badly wounded in a previous action; therefore, she was not at her post on the day in question.

Notice that, if you use a conjunctive adverb to join two main clauses, you should separate the clauses by a semicolon and place a comma after the adverb.

All the sentences used as examples above consist of two main clauses. It may seem like a contradiction in terms for a sentence to be able to have more than one main clause, but remember that "main clause" is a technical term. The two statements *the package has been lost in the mail* and *the supplier forgot to send it* are both grammatically complete in themselves, and so both are potential stand-alone sentences, both are main clauses, and the fact that they are conjoined by *either . . . or* does not alter their status. In that particular sentence, we cannot replace the coordinator by a punctuation mark, but in the first sentence we could:

Margaret had forgotten; Carlos most certainly had not.

Main clauses should usually be separated by a semicolon when there is no coordinator in the sentence. When a coordinator is present, commas will usually suffice:

Forget the past, concentrate on the present, and all will be well.

Coordinators can also be used to link two subordinate clauses:

Since we do not have sufficient time to spare, nor can we really afford the expense, it would be better to abandon the project.

Whether because he had mistaken my meaning, or because my meaning was unclear, he continued to behave as if nothing was wrong.

While he was removing the detonator, thus deactivating the bomb, the rest of us watched from a safe distance.

To repeat the basic rule, coordination is the linking together of two or more clauses or phrases of equal value. Subordination, by contrast, is the linking of a comparatively less important idea to a more important one.

SUBORDINATION

Subordinate clauses are introduced by subordinating conjunctions such as

after, although, as, as if, as though, because, before, if, in order that, since, so that, though, unless, until, when, whenever, where, and *while*

or relative pronouns such as

that, which, who, whom, and *whose.*

Here are alternative versions of the examples used earlier. This time they contain subordinating instead of coordinating linkers:

Although Margaret had forgotten, Carlos most certainly had not.

Unless the package has been lost in the mail, the supplier forgot to send it.

Because the sergeant had been badly wounded in a previous action, she was not at her post on the day in question.

As can be seen, the difference between the coordinated and subordinated versions of these particular examples is fairly slight; nevertheless, there is a difference. For a full discussion of that difference, see THE RHYTHM OF THE SENTENCE (page 115).

Length of Sentences

There are no hard-and-fast rules governing the length of sentences. A sentence should be as long as it needs to be to convey all the information the writer wishes to put into it, and no longer. As has already been demonstrated, the minimum length for a sentence is one single word, and there is no maximum length. So long as a sentence obeys the rules of grammar and constitutes a unit that is complete in itself, it can stretch as far as the writer's imagination and vocabulary will take it.

That said, however, there seems to be general agreement among the experts that writers should aim at an average length of between 15 and 20 words. This does not mean that writing sentences above or below that length is in any way to be discouraged, nor that writers should spend much, if any, of their precious time counting the number of words they write and dividing the total by the number of sentences—still less that they should panic if the resultant average is more than 20 or fewer than 15. The figure of 15 to 20 words is intended as a very rough guide.

The length of the sentences you write will partly depend on your personal style. It will also depend on the kind of reader you are targeting.

Sophisticated readers, to put it bluntly, are more able to cope with long sentences than unsophisticated ones. If you are writing for the popular press or for children, it will usually be helpful to make a point of keeping your sentences short. In that case you should aim at an overall average in the region of 10 to 15, rather than 15 to 20 words. If, on the other hand, you are writing for a learned journal, the editor will probably have something to say if you submit an article in which none of the sentences are more than 10 words long.

Guidelines are necessarily given in the form of averages, and averages by their very nature iron out differences. Yet it is the differences between sentences that are important, and this applies as much to length as to any other quality. A paragraph made up of uniform 15- or 20-word sentences is likely a poor paragraph for that reason alone. It is much better, all other things being equal, to provide your reader with a mixture of sentences of different lengths. It will keep your reader alert, vary the pace of the prose and enable you to exploit the different qualities possessed by sentences of different lengths.

SHORT SENTENCES

Short sentences, by and large, generate a fast tempo and can be used effectively to narrate action and create tension.

> *The car was parked right outside the door. Joe revved the engine now and then to remind us to hurry. I stuffed the bills into the bag. Carl kept his gun trained on the cashier. Carl's hand was trembling slightly. The cashier's hand was trembling too as he handed me the bills. I was cool enough till I heard the siren. The cashier stopped. I stopped. Joe didn't stop. He took off with a squeal of tires.*

The excitement and drama of a bank heist is aptly conveyed in a series of short sharp sentences. If you were describing a leisurely picnic by the side of a river, a similar technique might be less appropriate.

> *I sliced the bread. Joe buttered it. Carl was still trying to catch us a fish. He had the line around his big toe. It had worked for Huck Finn. The water flowed. The breeze blew. Nothing happened. The fish in that river just didn't like pastrami.*

A series of short sentences can be even less appropriate outside a narrative context, for example, in a report:

> *The building is in a dilapidated condition. Part of the roof is missing. Water coming through the roof has rotted some of the floor. Paint is coming off the walls. There is no electricity. Squatters have been living in some of the downstairs rooms.*

Short sentences also may be inappropriate in a letter:

I miss you more than I can say. I have been feeling bad. I have been to see the doctor. He never says anything useful. The pills he gave me last time didn't work. I just threw them down the toilet. When are you coming back?

The first passage reads as if a surveyor made notes while going around the building and simply copied out the notes when he or she got back to the office, without attempting to "write them up" at all. If you were the recipient of the second passage, meanwhile, you might be seriously worried that the writer's nerves were about to give way.

Short sentences in large numbers are jerky. Remember that, long or short, a sentence is a complete unit. When you put a lot of short sentences together, it is rather like creating a mosaic from many separate stones except that your reader has to look at them in sequence and cannot stand back to get the overall effect. Remember also that when you put a number of complete units side by side, you leave the reader to work out the relationship between them.

COMBINING SHORT SENTENCES

The following passage illustrates the problem mentioned in the preceding sentence, the missing links that sometimes make a sequence of short sentences less than completely clear:

Ben has resigned from the company. He has had a serious argument with the managing director. The problems have been of long standing. He believes he would have better prospects in another company. He was an extremely popular member of the staff. We are all devastated.

This passage is not exactly unclear, but it could be clearer. We would probably infer that Ben had not been happy in his job, possibly because he was not given a promotion, that these long-standing problems culminated in a serious argument with the managing director, and that this argument finally prompted Ben to resign. But this is, essentially, a story that we make up from the material provided by the writer. It is just as possible that the argument was the result, rather than the cause, of Ben handing in his resignation. Ordinary experience would suggest that this is less likely, but the writer does not rule out the possibility. Nor does the writer tell us precisely what role Ben's ambition played in his decision to leave.

This, then, is a passage where a good deal would be gained by combining one or more of the short sentences into longer ones to make the relationship between the different ideas or actions explicit:

Ben has resigned from the company after a serious argument with the managing director. In fact, his problems here have been of long standing, and he now believes he would have better prospects in another company. He was an extremely popular member of the staff. We are all devastated.

It could also be reworked as follows:

> *Ben has resigned from the company. The problems have been of long standing, and he has always believed he would have better prospects in another company. In the end, he had a serious argument with the managing director and left. He was an extremely popular member of the staff. We are all devastated.*

In both of these versions, combining some of the short sentences and inserting a few linking words or phrases—*in fact* and *now* in the first, and *in the end* in the second—give a much better sense of the sequence of events and of the cause-and-effect relationship between them, albeit the interpretation placed on the original is slightly different in the two cases.

Longer sentences do improve the sense of flow in a piece of writing, as we can demonstrate by giving a similar treatment to the earlier example of the dilapidated building. In the passage, the second, third, and fourth sentences are all of equal value, in that each one illustrates a particular aspect of the dilapidated state of the building. Simply linking them to the first sentence by means of a colon and listing them in order would make this plain and, at the same time, give a better flow. It would also indicate that some thought had been given to presenting the information in a sophisticated way.

> *The building is in a dilapidated condition: Part of the roof is missing, water coming through the roof has rotted some of the floor, and paint is coming off the walls. There is also no electricity, and squatters have been living in some of the downstairs rooms.*

If you feel that you have produced a passage in which there are too many short sentences, then combine them. Decide which sentences contain major ideas and which contain minor ones, coordinate ideas of equal value, and rework minor points as subordinate clauses or phrases in sentences that center on a major point. (*See* ORGANIZING AND COMBINING IDEAS IN SENTENCES, page 106, for techniques that can be used to construct sentences from separate pieces of information.)

LONG SENTENCES

Although problems can arise when writers string several short sentences together, sentences that are short or of medium length have the advantage that they are, on the whole, easy to keep under control. As the length of a sentence starts to grow, inexperienced writers or writers whose attention slips may find that the sentence loses shape or focus.

Let us refer again to an example used earlier:

> *Although that was part of my original plan and was, indeed, the main reason why I had taken the trouble to pay Joan a visit on that gray October day in Columbus, Ohio, when I should have been covering the president's speech in Cleveland, because the election was no more than a few weeks away.*

By the time he or she reaches the "end," the writer seems simply to have forgotten how the sentence started and so fails to provide the crucial main clause. This can and does happen quite frequently:

> *Busy with the tasks of everyday, the cleaning, the cooking, the washing, the sewing, the hundred and one tasks that wearied my body, filled my mind with trivial thoughts on which I would have spent no time at all— or so at least it seemed to me then—in the happy days when I was a blessedly unmarried, childless Virginia spinster, my soul shrank and became a small, flaccid, defeated thing.*

Busy with the task of evoking her mood, the writer loses track of her starting point and forgets that it is she herself, not her *soul* (the subject of the main clause, to which, grammatically, all the introductory material relates), that is cleaning the house and washing diapers. She has built a progression into the sentence—*wearied my body, filled my mind*—that leaves us perhaps waiting to hear what effect all these domestic duties had on her soul. But her soul should take its rightful place in the series, and the subject of the main clause should be the woman herself, since it is she who is *busy with the tasks of everyday.*

The writer is perhaps justified in trying to convey a wearisome, repetitive routine in one long, drawn-out sentence rather than a series of short, sharp, crisp ones. Nevertheless, there is nothing to be gained from boring and mystifying the reader. A more satisfactory version of the sentence might look like this:

> *Busy with the tasks of everyday—the cleaning, the cooking, the washing, the sewing—that wearied my body, filled my mind with trivial thoughts, and made my soul shrink until it became a small, flaccid, defeated thing, I had scarcely time to stop and wonder how all these things, on which I would have spent no time at all in the happy days when I was a blessedly husbandless, childless, and possibly feckless Virginia spinster, had come to make up the totality of what I called my life.*

You cannot always repair a long sentence by cutting it into shorter ones. In cases like the two dealt with above, the sentences actually need to be made longer to work properly. The critical point is not to lose your grip on the logic of the sentence, not to become so involved in the development of your ideas or the evocation of a scene or mood that you forget about the basic structure you are working with.

DIVIDING UP LONG SENTENCES

Despite what was said in the previous paragraph, many longer sentences would benefit from being broken up. Dividing up excessively long sentences not only makes the text more readable; it also allows ideas that have been sharing space and possibly competing for the reader's attention to have both room to breathe and the prominence that comes from being encapsulated in an independent unit. Consider this example:

> *Too many of us forget that wonderful instruction of the Psalmist "Be still and know," and we seek knowledge instead in the rush and tumble of experience, where impressions fall upon us continually from every side, where, indeed, we are threatened with "information overload," for only knowledge that is reflected upon and assimilated can become usable knowledge and not a burdensome excess, but reflection and assimilation can take place only in stillness.*

Coordination is a very simple and useful way of linking ideas, but it should not be used to excess. If you try to string too many clauses together using *and, but,* and so forth, the end result is likely to seem as breathless as a child's list: *We went to the zoo, and we went to the diner, and we went to the movies, but I didn't like the movie so much, and we went to . . .* A sentence that contains a great many coordinators, therefore, is often a sentence that would benefit from being divided up. The task is usually fairly simple, because the coordinators generally mark the natural breaks. So we could recast the previous example in sentences of more manageable length like this:

> *Too many of us forget that wonderful instruction of the Psalmist "Be still and know." We seek knowledge instead in the rush and tumble of experience, where impressions fall upon us continually from every side and where we are, indeed, threatened with information overload. Only knowledge that is reflected upon and assimilated can become usable knowledge. Knowledge that we cannot use is a burdensome excess. Reflection and assimilation, however, can take place only in stillness.*

If the passage is split up into smaller units, readers are better able to follow the writer's arguments; indeed, we are more likely to be able to reflect upon and assimilate thoughts that are not poured over us in a flood.

Sentences do not even have to be excessively long to benefit from being divided up.

> *A no-fly zone is an area over which aircraft, especially those of another country, are forbidden to fly and in which they are liable to be shot down if they enter it.*

The latter part of that sentence is extremely clumsy. The definition would surely be clearer and crisper if the two parallel clauses, *over which . . .* and *in which . . .* , became two separate sentences.

> *A no-fly zone is an area over which aircraft, especially those of another country, are forbidden to fly. Any aircraft that enter it are liable to be shot down.*

Finally, consider this example:

> *Within this general context, this article aims to present and discuss changes that are emerging in the framework of Italian local government*

policies; and discussing critically, with reference to the Italian case, the relationship between change in the idea of local territories and change in urban and territorial policies.

The semicolon here seems to represent a frantic and ultimately forlorn attempt by the writer to stitch together two elements that are grammatically incompatible: The first clause centers on a finite verb—*aims*—the second, on a participle—*discussing*. (The writer should also, incidentally, make it clear whether the "framework" itself is changing or whether more general changes are emerging *within* that framework.)

Within this general context, this article aims to present and discuss changes that are emerging in Italian local government policies. It also discusses critically, with reference to the Italian case, the relationship between change in the idea of local territories and change in urban and territorial policies.

SUMMING UP

To sum up, both long and short sentences have their uses, their special qualities, and their disadvantages. You may weary your readers by bombarding them with staccato statements, but you may just as easily weary them by stretching their attention span beyond a reasonable length, and you run the risk of confusing yourself in the process. Never hesitate, therefore, to divide sentences that seem too long or to integrate sentences that seem too short. Finally, you should be alert to the length of your sentences not to keep to a mathematical average but to ensure that your prose is appropriate to your subject matter and your readership and that it has sufficient variety to retain your reader's interest.

THE LOGIC OF THE SENTENCE
Language and Basic Logic

A great deal of what we say or write consists of straightforward statements or questions: "I got a letter from the bank this morning." "Did you remember to put gas in the car?" Simple as they are, such statements and questions have an underlying structure, based on grammar and usage, and in order to communicate successfully we have to get that structure right. Words do not always communicate meaning on their own. Meaning relies on the way the words are ordered, as we can easily see if we jumble up the words in the sentences above: "This morning a letter got I from the bank," which sounds like a foreigner attempting, unsuccessfully, to render his or her own language word for word into English, or "This I letter bank got from a morning the," a sentence that is intelligible only to speakers of double Dutch.

If sets of very simple words need to be logically ordered before they can form straightforward statements, it stands to reason that the elements of more complex structures require logical organization as well. To talk about "putting" or "stringing" words, phrases, and clauses together may give the impression that the elements of language are like building blocks or beads on a string, which can be juxtaposed in any way the writer likes. But just as writers cannot abandon the normal word order of English and still expect to be understood, so they cannot afford to overlook the demands of logic and grammar in arranging their material in sentences. Only a logically structured sentence will convey precisely the meaning that the writer intends. Consequently, a good deal of thought needs to go into sentence organization.

Now, this does not mean that you, as a writer, necessarily have to sit down and construct every sentence from its constituent parts in a conscious and deliberate way. As has been said before, when you are writing, especially when the work is flowing along, you will often achieve a good result spontaneously. You will automatically make the sort of decisions that are going to be analyzed at length in the rest of this chapter. Too much thinking, as everyone knows, can often stifle creativity.

It does mean, however, that you should have the basic knowledge to be able to construct a sentence consciously, on sound grammatical principles, if the words and ideas do not fall naturally into place. It also means that you must be prepared, especially during the revision stage, to look at your sentences critically, analyze them, take them apart, and reorganize them, if for any reason you feel that they do not work. Too little thinking, as everyone also knows, produces poor results.

Organizing and Combining Ideas in Sentences
COORDINATING AND SUBORDINATING IDEAS
So, how do we go about making ideas into good sentences? We have already established that coordination and subordination are the two basic methods of combining ideas. Coordination, let us remind ourselves, is a method of linking two or more ideas or clauses of equal value; subordination is a method of linking a less important idea to a more important one.

If you are consciously constructing a sentence, therefore, your first task to sort out your ideas and assess their relative importance.

Johnny threw his ball—the ball broke a window—the window was in the kitchen.

Here are three very simple ideas. The first two would be of equal importance in most sentences. There would be nothing to report if the ball that Johnny threw had not broken a window, and the breaking of the window would be something of a mystery if we did not know that Johnny had thrown the ball. The fact that the broken window was in the kitchen would, in most cases, be a detail. On the principles set out in the preceding paragraph, then, the first two ideas should be coordinated and the third subordinated, probably to a mere phrase or even to a noun modifier. The result of what may sound like a complicated grammatical operation would therefore be

Johnny threw his ball and broke a window in the kitchen.

or

Johnny threw his ball and broke a kitchen window.

Let us look at a set of slightly less simple ideas:

Chop the meat into cubes—the cubes should measure about two inches—heat the oil in a frying pan—wait until the oil is ready—the oil is ready when it starts to smoke—brown the meat lightly on all sides.

The most important component of the recipe, and therefore of the sentence, is the meat. Consequently the two actions that involve the meat—chopping it and browning it—would seem to be of equal importance. The size of the cubes is a detail. Heating the oil—precisely how hot the oil has to be is an important detail, but nevertheless a detail—could be considered an action of equal importance to the handling of the meat or it might be considered slightly less important. In other words, the information about the oil could either be coordinated with or subordinated to the information about the meat.

The results would be

Chop the meat into two-inch cubes, heat the oil until it starts to smoke, then brown the meat lightly on all sides.

or

Chop the meat into two-inch cubes, meanwhile heating the oil until it starts to smoke, then brown the meat lightly on all sides.

Notice how the commas perform slightly different functions in the two sentences. In the first sentence the two commas work individually, so to speak, each marking the end of the clause. In the second sentence, they work together, enclosing the central section and emphasizing the fact that it is to some extent incidental to the main thrust of the sentence.

Here is a final example:

People had more money to spend in the 1950s—they wanted to show it—they no longer wanted to drive the same car until it wore out— automobile manufacturers realized this—they also realized sales would increase if people could be persuaded to change their cars more often—they wanted them to change cars every two or three years— they began to change the design of cars regularly to make older cars seem out of date.

There is much more information here than in either of the two previous examples. The ideas are obviously related and belong together, but it is by no means certain that they can all be accommodated within a single sentence. Let us consider them and try to work out the best solution.

There are two active agents in this situation: "people" on the one hand and "the automobile manufacturers" on the other. The things that connect the people to the manufacturers, obviously, are cars. The crucial pieces of information seem to be, first, that the people no longer wanted to keep the same car until it fell apart and, second, that the manufacturers realized that sales would increase if people could be persuaded to change their cars more often. Given that basic connection, the rest of the material is of relatively secondary importance and probably needs to be subordinated in some way.

Whatever decision we take as regards organizing all these ideas will depend on whether we intend to focus mainly on the people or the manufacturers, or on both equally. If we decide that both merit equal attention, we might think about coordinating the two main ideas:

> *People no longer wanted to drive the same car until it wore out, and automobile manufacturers realized that sales would increase if people could be persuaded to change their cars more often.*

These two main clauses would then form the heart of the sentence, and the rest of the information would need to be arranged around them:

> *People, having more money to spend in the 1950s and wanting to show it, were no longer content to drive the same car until it wore out, and automobile manufacturers realized that sales would increase if people could be persuaded to change their cars more often, say every two or three years, and began to modify the design of cars regularly to make older models seem out of date.*

The result we have arrived at, however, is far from satisfactory. The sentence is overly long and shapeless. Anyone who drafted a sentence in this form and went back to look at it again later, would want to divide it up into two or three separate units:

> *People had more money to spend in the 1950s and wanted to show it, so they were no longer content to drive the same car until it wore out. Automobile manufacturers, realizing this, also realized that sales would increase if their customers could be persuaded to trade in their cars more often, preferably every two or three years. As a result, they began to modify the design of their cars regularly to make older models seem out of date.*

This is a far more satisfactory solution. When you have complicated ideas to organize, even if they are interrelated, always keep an open mind about how many sentences you should make with them, until you have conducted a few experiments.

This particular solution, you may recall, is based on a decision to give the people and the automobile manufacturers equal status. But suppose you had chosen instead to focus on one of them rather than the other, how would that

affect the way you organized the material? The answer is that you would subordinate the material relating to the agent whom you were less interested in.

> *Because people had more money to spend in the 1950s, wanted to show
> it, and were no longer content to drive the same car until it wore out,
> automobile manufacturers realized that they could increase their sales
> by persuading their customers to change their cars more often, prefer-
> ably every two or three years, and so began to modify the design of cars
> regularly to make older models seem out of date.*

This version puts the people firmly into a subordinate clause, but once again
the keen-eyed reviser would be likely to regard this sentence as an obvious
candidate for remodeling.

Hitherto, we have tended to discuss subordination as if it meant only the
incorporation of material into subordinate clauses. But there are many other
ways of subordinating ideas: by reducing them to phrases instead of clauses,
for instance, or by expressing them in the form of a single word, an adjective,
say, or an adverb or a noun modifier, as with the idea "the window was in
the kitchen" in the first example of the present series.

Suppose you were working on the ideas

> *I met a bear in the forest—the bear was hungry—I ran for my life,*

You might very well boil it down to

> *I met a hungry bear in the woods and ran for my life.*

Likewise, if the ideas were

> *The tree is very tall—it is a sequoia—it is taller even than most sequoias,*

you would probably render them as

> *The tree is unusually tall even for a sequoia.*

In the first instance, one idea has been accommodated in an adjective; in the
second, an adverb performs the same role.

What can be done when the ideas are simple can also be done when the
ideas are more complex. Returning to the automobile example, if we are to
give prominence to the manufacturers, we will probably need to subject the
material relating to the people to more drastic subordination:

> *In the 1950s, automobile manufacturers realized that they could increase
> their sales by persuading their increasingly wealthy and status-conscious
> customers, who were no longer content to drive the same car until it wore
> out, to trade in their cars every two or three years. Accordingly, they
> began to modify the design of cars regularly to make the older models
> seem out of date.*

The purpose of this lengthy analysis of material relating to automobile manufacturers in the 1950s has been twofold. It was partly intended to show that if you worry away at your material and, if necessary, experiment with different ways of organizing it, you can usually come up with a sentence that fulfills your requirements. It was also intended to show that it is possible to structure material in different ways to suit different purposes.

DISTINGUISHING THE RELATIVE IMPORTANCE OF IDEAS

You need to know what your purpose is so that you can assess the relative value of ideas and assign them to their proper places in the sentence. Likewise, when you are revising your work, you need to have your essential purpose in mind so that you can check that you have not coordinated an idea that deserves to be subordinated or subordinated an idea that really belongs in a main clause.

Let us think a little more about distinguishing between more and less important ideas:

> *Professor Paul Dyson is a scientist of international renown and a Nobel Prize laureate, and he lives in Tulsa, Oklahoma.*

This sentence is fine as it stands if your purpose is to praise Tulsa, Oklahoma, at least as much as the distinguished Professor Dyson. That is the effect of coordinating the piece of information about his place of residence with the rest of the sentence. But normally, where a person happens to live would be considered of less interest than his or her personal achievements, especially when these are considerable. A more logical course, therefore, would be to subordinate the reference to Tulsa:

> *Professor Paul Dyson, who lives in Tulsa, Oklahoma, is a scientist of international renown and a Nobel Prize laureate.*

or

> *Professor Paul Dyson of Tulsa, Oklahoma, is a scientist of international renown and a Noble Prize laureate.*

Consider this further example:

> *There were flames leaping from the windows of the second story and people were gathering on the roof of the building, but the sun still shone brightly through the pall of smoke.*

What are we to make of this sentence in which the weather conditions are given equal importance—as the use of the coordinator *but* implies—as the plight of the people escaping from a blazing building? Does the writer intend to suggest the indifference of the universe to human suffering, or was he or she rather careless in attaching a note about a phenomenon observed at the scene to a sentence mainly concerned with conveying the drama of the situation? The second is the more likely alternative. In this instance, there is no easy way of simply subordinating that piece of information, so the best solution would be to reorganize it and reposition it so that it accords with the logic of the sentence as a whole:

> *A pall of smoke partially obscured the sun, flames were leaping from the windows of the second story, and people were gathering on the roof of the building.*

There are also occasions in which material of primary importance is inappropriately subordinated:

> *Although he built his own house, he had no skills as a builder when he started.*

It seems excessively grudging to concentrate on the man's initial lack of skill and subordinate his achievement. This is an obvious case of "putting the cart before the horse" and should be changed to:

> *Although he had no skills as a builder when he started, he nevertheless succeeded in building his own house.*

Consider another example:

> *The city of Salzburg, which was the birthplace of Mozart and home to several other composers who were in many cases notable precursors of the city's most eminent son, lies between a low rocky ridge and a river dominated by a great castle and has many fine palaces and churches, in which concerts are given during the annual festival of music hosted by the city.*

The fault with this sentence is not so much incorrect subordination as excessive subordination and, indeed, an excess of ideas. It is often tempting to try to pack a lot of information into a single sentence by using subordinate clauses, but that temptation ought to be resisted. If you wish to talk about the city's topography and its musical history, by all means do so, but it would better to do so in two or more separate sentences:

> *The city of Salzburg lies between a low rocky ridge and a river, is dominated by a great castle, and has many fine palaces and churches. Its chief claim to fame, however, is its musical heritage. It was the birthplace of Mozart, as well as being home to several composers who were precursors of its most eminent son. It also hosts an annual music festival, and many of the concerts take place in the city's great buildings.*

This is a more logical arrangement of the material, which gives the important ideas due prominence, in particular, not confining Mozart in a subordinate clause. It also, incidentally sorts out one ambiguity in the original, with regard to the exact positioning of the castle in relation to the rest of the topography. For more on the subject of positioning within a sentence, see the section POSITIONING, which immediately follows.

To round off this discussion, here is an interesting example from literature of a sentence in which the usual expectations as to how information might be evaluated are perhaps upset. The sentence in question is the second of the three quoted below.

> *At the sight of this, the man with the blue and white plumes fainted away. But Kohlhaas, while the man's dismayed attendants bent over him and lifted him up off the ground, turned to the scaffold, where his head fell to the executioner's ax. Here ends the story of Kohlhaas.*

This passage is taken from the final paragraph of a novella entitled *Michael Kohlhaas* by the early-19th-century German writer Heinrich von Kleist. It is an intricately written, philosophical story, but one of its chief claims to fame is that its hero dies in a subordinate clause. Kleist tells us in the main clause that "Kohlhaas . . . turned to the scaffold," and in the following clause informs us of the striking of the fatal blow, almost as an afterthought. Was this carelessness on his part, or is Kohlhaas's turning toward the scaffold the more significant of the two actions and, if so, why? To decide, you will have to read the whole story. But if you do not wish to cause scholarly controversy, it is undoubtedly safer to put what most people would consider the main event into the main clause.

Positioning
THE IMPORTANCE OF POSITIONING

Logical ordering is required not only for clauses and the larger elements of a sentence but for the smaller elements, too. Words and phrases should be positioned in a sentence in such a way as to make their relationship to one another perfectly plain. This usually means that if word or phrase A modifies or otherwise relates to word or phrase B, then A and B should be placed quite close together in the sentence. Confusion or unintentional humor usually results when items that belong together drift apart:

> *The professor told me that he had lost his way while waiting for the bus.*

> *The machine had several vital parts missing that you lent me.*

Put the wandering elements back in their proper places, and, magically, sense is restored:

> *The professor, while waiting for the bus, told me that he had lost his way.*

> *The machine that you lent me had several vital parts missing.*

In unguarded moments, we can all be guilty of such howlers. But similar and less amusing mistakes can occur in everyday prose and cause a lot of unnecessary confusion:

In many ways the book is great for researchers who are tackling images for the first time, because it is sure footed regarding the way it deals with methods arising from different theoretical concerns, working around a clear framework.

This is not an inordinately long sentence, but neither is it a very clear one. It reads like a piece of academic waffle, yet there is nothing in the writer's choice of words that makes the meaning unclear. It is actually the organization of the material that is mainly at fault, as we can see if we simply cut off the final phrase:

In many ways the book is great for researchers who are tackling images for the first time, because it is sure footed regarding the way it deals with methods arising from different theoretical concerns.

In that form, though still hardly elegant, the sentence seems much clearer. It has a basic logical structure: "The book is great . . . because it is sure footed." The writer did not help matters by spelling *surefooted* as two words, but that is a minor quibble. The real problem arose when the writer felt it necessary to add the additional phrase "working around a clear framework." Ironically, the intention was to clarify matters, but the writer failed to make it clear how that phrase relates to the ideas in the rest of the sentence.

It is probable in this instance that the writer wanted to explain how the book comes to be surefooted. The book deals "surefootedly," that is, competently and confidently, with different methods because it is based on a clear framework. That makes sense. In the sentence as originally framed, however, the reader's first instinct is to associate the phrase with the material immediately adjacent to it "methods arising from different theoretical concerns," but the phrase *methods arising from different theoretical concerns, working around a clear framework* is gobbledygook.

If we reposition the offending phrase, we have a sentence that is on its way to being satisfactory:

In many ways the book is great for researchers who are tackling images for the first time, because, working around a clear framework, it is sure footed regarding the way it deals with methods arising from different theoretical concerns.

There is a more work to be done on this sentence before it is really fit to appear in a handbook on style, but that work is not relevant to our immediate concerns.

AMBIGUOUS POSITIONING

Words and phrases sometimes appear in a position where their meaning is ambiguous:

> *Rereading a favorite novel occasionally may be a disappointing experience.*

Is the disappointment caused by occasional reading, or is rereading an occasional disappointment?

> *His confession that his inspiration had dried up completely stunned me.*

Has the inspiration dried up completely, or is the speaker completely stunned?

If you accidentally produce such a sentence, think about what precisely you want to say and then reposition the ambiguous word or rewrite the sentence so that the meaning becomes crystal clear:

> *Rereading a favorite novel may occasionally be a disappointing experience.*

> *When he confessed that his inspiration had dried up, I was completely stunned.*

or

> *His inspiration, he confessed, had dried up completely. I was stunned.*

DANGLING MODIFIERS

There is a particular form of the displacement problem that grammarians call the "dangling modifier," or sometimes the "dangling participle" or "hanging participle." Here a phrase or clause, usually without a finite verb, positioned at the beginning of the sentence, has nothing to connect to in the main part of the sentence. Again, confusion or hilarity generally result:

> *Prizing open the lid, the box was completely empty.*

> *Lazing on a lounger in the hot sun, the swimming pool looked more and more inviting.*

Positioning is vital, remember, so the reader naturally connects the opening phrase to the noun that comes next, but boxes do not prize open their own lids and swimming pools do not laze on loungers. Repositioning the phrase does not suffice in such cases. The best solution is one of two. You can upgrade the phrase to a full clause with a finite verb and the correct subject:

> *When I prized open the lid, the box was completely empty.*

As she lazed on a lounger in the hot sun, the swimming pool looked more and more inviting.

You can also recast the main clause so that it has a subject to which the opening phrase can appropriately connect:

Prizing open the lid, I found the box to be completely empty.

Lazing on a lounger in the hot sun, she thought the swimming pool looked more and more inviting.

ONLY GET THE POSITION RIGHT
If there is one single word that illustrates the necessity of precise positioning, then that word is *only*.

Only I met him at the airport. [Nobody else did]

I only met him at the airport. [I had nothing else to do with him]

I met only him at the airport. [And no one else]

I met him only at the airport. [And nowhere else]

I met him at the only airport. [It was a small city]

These are five arrangements of the same words, with five slightly differing senses depending on the positioning of *only*. Remember *only* and you will never be in any doubt as to the importance of the placement of words for the meaning of sentences.

THE RHYTHM OF THE SENTENCE

In this section we will be dealing with issues that go beyond logic and grammar and call into play our feeling for words, our aesthetic sense, and our sense of emotional logic, for they too have a part to play in assessing how words can best be organized to convey meaning.

Prose Rhythm
The rhythm of prose is somewhat different from the rhythm of poetry. The regular ti-tum-ti-tum-ti-tum beat of iambic pentameter—or the beat of any other kind of poetic meter—is generally out of place in prose:

I saw at once how it would be, that nothing else would ever have the wonder of that first caress.

Going homeward from the drug store, I met up with Bob Kowalski, who was walking his pet poodle.

If you find yourself writing sentences like these, either go ahead and cut them up into verse lines or change them!

> *I realized it at once: Nothing else would have the wonder of that first caress.*

The sentiment may be no less corny in this version, but this sentence is genuine prose and has a genuine prose rhythm. Rhythmically everything hinges here on the dramatic pause produced by the colon. It suggests the heart-stopping moment of awareness, when you realize that something important has happened but are as yet unable to put into words what it is or why it is important. The second part of the sentence gives us the verbalization of that insight, the rush or patter of words as they come into the speaker's mind. That is the emotional situation that the writer intends to convey. The rhythm of the sentence helps to convey the situation; indeed, we might almost say that the rhythm of this particular sentence "enacts" what is taking place.

This idea is quite familiar in poetry. Here is Alexander Pope discussing and illustrating the idea in his *Essay on Criticism,* written at the beginning of the 18th century:

> When Ajax strives some rock's vast weight to throw,
> The line too labors and the words move slow;
> Not so when swift Camilla scours the plain,
> Flies o'er the unbending corn, and skims along the main.

This is something in which prose can emulate poetry, though in different rhythms:

> *Stooping, Bartholomew felt for a hold under the chassis, then suddenly jerked the front end of the vehicle high up off the ground.*

> *She was off in an instant, flying down the corridor with her little legs twinkling under her skirt.*

> *Slowly at first, one step taken with infinite caution, then a second step, then a third—she was gaining in confidence now—a fourth, a fifth, and she knew she was free and broke into a run.*

The rhythmic effect is produced, first, by choosing words on the basis of their sound and stress pattern, as well as their meaning. You would not, for instance, include words such as *lugubrious, onerous,* or *ponderous* in a sentence where you wanted to give the impression of speed and lightness, any more than you would put *quick, bright, shimmer,* or *scintillate* into a sentence that was intended to convey heaviness or dismalness. And that choice of words is complemented by what we might call the general distribution of pace, weight, and energy throughout the sentence. To illustrate what this last phrase means, let us look again at an example used earlier:

I realized it at once: Nothing else would have the wonder of that first caress.

There is a slight buildup of energy before the colon and a release of it after the colon. The first part of the sentence is relatively weightier and slower; the second, lighter and quicker.

All the examples used so far in this section illustrate, to a greater or lesser extent, what we might call rhythmic special effects. There is limited scope for the writer to use rhythm to "enact" something other than when he or she is describing an action of some kind, and even then the scope is somewhat limited. A student once enthused about a particular sentence in James Joyce's *Ulysses:* "It's written in the rhythm of the peristaltic action of his bowels!" But that is a feat that few of us, probably, would feel inclined to emulate.

Where to Find Rhythm

Where else, then, does rhythm play a part? There are rhythms in everyday speech that we cannot exactly reproduce on paper but that we can try at least to remind the reader of, where appropriate:

Never, ever, ever do that again!

You angel, you absolute angel!

I'm coming, I'm coming, wait for me!

There are rhythms in rhetoric, which more often than not rely on repetition:

Do we want freedom? Yes! Do we want unlimited freedom? No!

"A man who is good enough to shed his blood for the country is good enough to be given a square deal afterwards. More than that no man is entitled to, and less than that no man shall have."

Notice how the second half of Theodore Roosevelt's last sentence exactly balances the first half not only in sense but also in rhythm.

There are rhythms, too, in wit and comedy, and a writer should in particular pay attention to these:

"To cease smoking is the easiest thing I ever did. I ought to know because I've done it a thousand times."

"Twenty years of romance make a woman look like a ruin; but twenty years of marriage make her something like a public building."

The first quotation is attributed to Mark Twain; the second comes from Oscar Wilde's play *A Woman of No Importance.* We know from the testimony of many great comedians that timing is of the essence in comedy. The joke falls flat if you do not deliver the punch line at the right moment and in the right way. This is true of written comedy as well. The sting in an epigram, the kernel of the joke, comes at the end. Rhythm has to be imparted to the sentence in such a way that the energy flows through it toward the end and emerges there with greatest impact.

Rhythm and Positioning

Whether you intend to write in a comic style, there is a lesson to be learned here. The position of a word, phrase, clause, or idea within the overall layout of a sentence is very important, as has been said before, because positioning plays a major part in establishing the relationship between the various elements and thus conveys meaning. Above and beyond this, however, there are certain positions within a sentence that give a word or group of words greater impact. The position of greatest prominence is usually the end. The reason is partly the direction of the usual rhythmic flow, partly the fact that the end of one sentence is, generally speaking, the springing-off point for the next sentence. The word or words just preceding the period are naturally well placed to lead into the continuing narrative. The position of next greatest prominence is, as you would expect, the beginning. The first word, or the first significant word, in a sentence is generally stressed in speech. Something of that stressed quality carries over into writing.

These are statements of fact that the writer should bear in mind, rather than hard-and-fast rules that should govern all of his or her thinking on sentence construction. They are quite important facts, nonetheless.

Rhythm and Sentence Construction

It is now time to try to apply some of what has just been said about rhythm in sentences and positions of prominence to more ordinary material, and also to link this aspect of sentence-making to aspects discussed earlier. For this purpose, we shall use examples from an earlier subsection discussing the basic principles of coordination and subordination. There, various sentences were shown in subordinated and coordinated form, and it was remarked that the difference between the two forms was slight but significant. The subsequent discussions will enable to see more clearly what that significance is.

Two of the sentences in question were these:

Margaret had forgotten, but Carlos most certainly had not.

and

Although Margaret had forgotten, Carlos most certainly had not.

The first is the coordinated version. As befits a sentence in which two clauses of equal value are joined, the first version is the more equally balanced of the two. The word *Margaret* is the first word in the sentence. It thus has considerable prominence and is stressed. The next word that would naturally be stressed is *Carlos*. This puts the two "actors" in the sentence on an equal footing. You feel, as a result, that the next sentence could say something more about Margaret, something more about Carlos, or continue to compare or contrast their reactions:

> *Margaret had forgotten, but Carlos most certainly had not. She was sufficiently wealthy to be fairly unconcerned about the small sums that people owed her. . . .*

> *Margaret had forgotten, but Carlos most certainly had not. He was not one to forgive small debts or small slights. . . .*

> *Margaret had forgotten, but Carlos most certainly had not. She was much more inclined to forgive small slights than was her prickly brother. . . .*

Any one of those three continuations seems acceptable.

But this is not the case when the second version is used. The first word in that sentence, the stressed word, is *Although.* The emphasis is on the subordinating conjunction, and *Margaret* is deemphasized, whereas *Carlos* is in the same position as before. The effect of this is to place the focus on Carlos and his reaction to the extent that you would feel it was almost inappropriate to continue talking about Margaret. For example, if you add the following continuation,

> *Although Margaret had forgotten, Carlos most certainly had not. She was sufficiently wealthy . . .*

the feminine personal pronoun startles the reader. *She?* But we were talking about Carlos! A continuation that said more about Carlos's attitude would follow much more naturally:

> *Although Margaret had forgotten, Carlos most certainly had not. He was not one to forgive small debts or small slights. . . .*

Changing the structure of the sentence has changed the stress pattern and the rhythm and consequently shifted its focus. By putting the words that refer to Margaret into a subordinate clause, we have implicitly suggested that she is less important than Carlos at this particular point in the narrative, and the rhythm of the sentence bears this out. The expectation is thus raised that Carlos will be the subject when the narrative continues. The weight carried by a main clause has been referred to before; this example further illustrates the point.

But let us suppose that Margaret is the main character. How should we alter the sentence to shift the focus firmly onto her? Following from what was said in the previous paragraph, the obvious solution would seem to be to allow Margaret to figure in the main clause and to subordinate Carlos:

> *Margaret had forgotten, although Carlos most certainly had not. She*
> *was sufficiently wealthy . . .*

or

> *Although Carlos had most certainly not forgotten, Margaret had. She*
> *was sufficiently wealthy . . .*

Of these two versions, the first is probably the more satisfactory, but it only really takes us back to where we were when we used the coordinated sentence as our base. *Margaret* is stressed, but because it falls in the middle of the sentence and not at the beginning, *although* is not stressed, so *Carlos* continues to be the second emphasized word. The second version seems unbalanced, rhythmically or proportionally. The last two words seem out of proportion to the first seven, despite the fact that the end is usually the position of prominence and that the word *Margaret* is stressed. This is because in the subordinate clause the initial stress has shifted away from *Although* and onto *Carlos*. It must, in a natural reading of the sentence, to cope with the emphatic negative—*most certainly not*—that follows.

Because they demand to receive some measure of stress, these emphatic words largely counteract the effect of putting Carlos into a subordinate clause. We have to think again to find a method of putting the spotlight on Margaret. Two solutions suggest themselves.

The first solution is simply to transfer the emphatic words to Margaret's clause:

> *Although Carlos had not forgotten, Margaret most certainly had. She*
> *was sufficiently wealthy to be fairly unconcerned about the small sums*
> *that people owed her. . . .*

Again, however, the result is far from perfect. It is not that the words *most certainly* belong by nature with a negative. It is easy enough to think of sentences in which they reinforce a positive statement—*I most certainly do; there is most certainly a case to answer.* It is rather that with this particular continuation, in which Margaret is said to be "fairly unconcerned" about small debts, seems to go against the grain to emphasize Margaret's nonchalance. It runs counter to what we might call the emotional logic of what is being said. It is more logical to link emphasizing words or phrases with the stronger emotion, where two states of feeling are being compared:

> *Although Carlos did not bear a grudge, Margaret most certainly did.*
>
> *If Carlos was relatively calm about the whole affair, Margaret most cer-*
> *tainly was not.*

The effect would be actually comic if we said:

> *Carlos was screaming his head off, but Margaret most certainly was not.*

The alternative solution, since transferring the emphatic phrase will not do the trick, is, somewhat paradoxically, to say more about Carlos:

> *Although Carlos was of an unforgiving nature and most certainly had not forgotten, Margaret had.*

or

> *Although Carlos most certainly had not forgotten, because he never forgave the slightest offense or failed to collect the smallest debt, Margaret had.*

What we have done here is to break up the emphatic rhythm of the shorter subordinate clause by adding extra syllables. As a result, the two final words appear as a succinct, even pithy riposte to the more elaborate statement of Carlos's attitude, and Margaret gets her position of prominence.

Summing Up

Rhythm can be a significant factor even in fairly everyday sentences and thus earns its place alongside logic. To hear rhythm we must listen carefully to the way our prose sounds to the ear or "the mind's voice." That is a discipline every writer must become used to, not simply for the relatively short span of a sentence, but over the course of longer units such as paragraphs.

CONSTRUCTING SENTENCES: AN OVERVIEW

- A sentence, in grammatical terms, is a unit of language that is complete in itself.
- Most sentences contain a finite verb and consist of one or more clauses.
- There are two types of clause: main clauses and subordinate clauses.
- There are two methods of linking ideas in a sentence: coordination and subordination.
- Ideas of equal value should be coordinated. An idea of lesser importance should be subordinated to one of greater importance.
- Sentences can be of any length as long as they are grammatically and logically viable and suit the writer's purpose. The best policy is to vary the length of your sentences.
- Evaluate the ideas that are going to make up your sentence and link them using coordination or subordination.
- Make sure your sentences obey natural logic.
- Check the position of the various elements in your sentence to ensure that their relationship to one another is clear.
- Use your ear and "the mind's voice" to appreciate the rhythm of sentences.
- Put your sentences together to form a paragraph.

Constructing Paragraphs

INTRODUCTION

The same craftsmanship that produces a well-constructed sentence should also go into the making of all the larger units of which a piece of writing is composed. The careful writer will take the same pains to ensure that a paragraph is more than a string of sentences as he or she does to ensure that a sentence is more than a string of words—if by "a string" we mean a sequence of items that has no organizing principle behind it and is not consciously shaped. In fact, he or she will go further and make certain that each chapter or section is likewise more than a simple string of paragraphs. If a piece of writing is to be truly stylish and effective, all its larger units, like all its sentences, should be well-made artifacts distinguished by good planning, careful design, and skillful execution.

The principal concern of this chapter, therefore, will be with the techniques that writers can use to organize their ideas into larger units. It will concentrate on the paragraph but will occasionally look beyond the paragraph to bigger structures. It will also sometimes refer to methods of sentence construction, for the same skills that enable a writer to construct a good sentence—the ability to create a logical structure and a feeling for the rhythm of words and of larger units of language in combination—are used in the task of putting those sentences together in a clear, effective, and imaginative way. The art of constructing paragraphs is essentially the art of deploying those skills on a larger scale, while still retaining the qualities of logicality and shapeliness that we expect in smaller units.

The keyword in this process is *coherence*. We have been speaking of units. Units ought, by definition, to be unified. The techniques in question are, therefore, those that link smaller units together so that they form coherent larger ones, principally those that make sentences into coherent paragraphs. These techniques will be dealt with in subsections entitled "Making Paragraphs" and "Unifying Paragraphs." When we look beyond the individual paragraph, the concept of continuity becomes equally important. That will be the main theme of the final subsection, "Connecting Paragraphs." As in the preceding chapter, however, let us begin with a brief review of the basics.

PARAGRAPHS—THE BASICS

A paragraph, according to Sir Ernest Gowers, the British advocate of a plain style in official documents and letters, "is a unit of thought, not a unit of length" (*The Complete Plain Words,* edited by Greenbaum and Whitcut [London: Her Majesty's Stationery Office, 1986], page 170).

Gowers puts the essential about paragraphs in a nutshell. Yes, a paragraph is a subdivision of text, consisting of a number of sentences, marked off from the rest by beginning on a new line. Yes, the first line of a new paragraph is usually indented, or a blankline space is left between the end of one paragraph and the beginning of the next. But, crucially, a paragraph is a container for thought.

The golden rule for dividing text into paragraphs is, One idea or topic, one paragraph. A paragraph should consist of a particular thought and the explanatory or illustrative material required for its presentation. The indentation at the beginning of a paragraph and the line break at its end have the same role as the capital letter and the period that define the beginning and the end of a sentence. They indicate to the reader that this portion of text forms a unit. It is about something particular. It is substantially complete in itself. It presents one thought. When you have dealt with that thought and wish to describe or discuss something else, you should begin a new paragraph.

The Function of the Paragraph

The primary function of the paragraph, therefore, is to present, in a relatively compact and self-contained form, a particular idea that contributes to your argument or a particular aspect of something that you wish to describe. When the reader has read through the set of sentences that make up the paragraph, he or she should have become acquainted with one significant element in an ongoing narrative or discussion, together with its attendant details or supporting evidence. At that point, he or she might like to pause momentarily and think about what has been said.

To understand the function and the value of paragraphs, it is only necessary to consider what text is like when it is not divided up into smaller units. A writer who does not use paragraphs delivers ideas and information in a continuous stream, providing no places where the reader can pause, no obvious opportunity for the reader to go back a manageable distance and reconsider what he or she has just read. The text proceeds in a relentless onward march. Ideas or pieces of description follow one after the other, and there is nothing to indicate where one ends and the next begins. Amid the flow of undifferentiated text, it may become difficult for the reader to distinguish matters that are particularly important or to see at a glance that certain ideas belong together. In short, by not using paragraphs, the writer foists a great deal of organizational labor onto the reader, who may be unwilling to accept the burden.

Whether they are motivated by a concern not to overburden their readers, most writers will want to keep their hands on the levers of communication: They will want to control the rate and the manner in which the information they are providing is fed to their readers. Most writers, therefore, need paragraphs as much as their readers do, because paragraphs are their principal means of exercising that control. They would prefer a reader to pause in order to make sure that he or she has fully grasped a particular idea—and perhaps to appreciate the skill with which the idea has been presented—rather than to go rushing on receiving perhaps only a general and rather inaccurate impression of what was said. They welcome (or ought to welcome) the opportunity that the paragraph offers to deliver information in portions of manageable size, which are precisely organized so as to produce just the right response from the reader.

There are cases where a writer deliberately chooses to forgo the advantages of paragraphing and puts down a length of unbroken text in order to achieve a special effect. Stream-of-consciousness writing is the obvious example. Outside specialized literary writing, however, undivided text is rarely if ever needed. Generally speaking, writers produce it not so much as a deliberate policy, but because they are in a hurry or on a roll, drafting furiously to catch the ideas as they unfold.

As has been said before, anything goes when you are writing a draft. You may choose to dispense with punctuation altogether, let alone such sophisticated mechanisms as paragraph breaks. This is fine as long as you realize that you will have to go back at the revision stage and put your material into proper form. Do not be tempted to omit paragraph breaks because you believe that the reader might enjoy sharing the excitement that you felt when you were in the flow. In 999 cases out of 1,000, to do so is a mistake. Even a fast-paced narrative is usually divided into paragraphs. Dialogue is always presented in separate paragraphs, as we shall see later in this chapter (page 131). The fact that each speaker's contribution is presented in a separate paragraph does not diminish the impression that a conversation is in progress or suggest that there is always a pregnant pause before the next utterance. The skilled writer is able to maintain a sense of flow across paragraphs, while still dividing up the text into units of manageable size. And the reader, after all, is in all likelihood approaching the text in a much more sober frame of mind than the writer who excitedly penned it.

To sum up then, the function of the paragraph is, first, to provide a container for thought and, second, to provide readers and writers alike with a measure of control over the flow of the text. It also has one further practical function. Text looks better and reads more easily when it is broken up into paragraphs. To have to work through a long stretch of unbroken text tires the reader's eyes, as well as his or her mind; indeed, a page that presents a solid block of words wedged in between the margins may actually deter the reader from reading it. The look of text on the page is not the first priority of a writer, but it is nonetheless important. The combination of words and clear space that results when there are a number of paragraphs aligned down a page usually produces the best effect.

The Length of Paragraphs

There is no set length for a paragraph any more than there is for a sentence. A paragraph may consist only of a single sentence—and, since a sentence may contain only a single word, one-word paragraphs are neither unknown nor inherently incorrect, though they are relatively rare. As a general rule, a paragraph should contain at least two or three sentences. A paragraph that contains more than six or seven sentences—that is, given an average sentence length of around 15 words, more than 100 words or so—is starting to grow into a long paragraph.

The length of your paragraphs will be determined, like the length of your sentences, partly by the kind of readership you have in mind. If your readers can cope better with short sentences, then they will also prefer short paragraphs. The function of a particular paragraph within a longer section of text may also have a bearing on its length. Introductory and concluding paragraphs tend to be shorter than "body" paragraphs, as do so-called transition paragraphs. (For more information on the different types of paragraph, see the subsection immediately following.)

As always, variety is important. Vary the length of your paragraphs both to suit the demands of your material and to keep your reader's attention. As always too, brevity is what usually grabs attention. A very long paragraph amid a set of short ones will obviously stand out, but it is not in the nature of long paragraphs to deliver a telling punch. A short paragraph in the midst of several long ones, however, can often be used as a point of focus, especially if it encapsulates a particularly significant piece of information.

Types of Paragraph

Most pieces of writing conform to a standard pattern. They begin with an introduction, move into the body of the text in which the main ideas are presented and discussed, and end with a conclusion. This basic pattern—introduction, body, conclusion—recurs at many levels in writing and can be used, as we shall see, as a guide to the construction of paragraphs as well as of longer units.

Paragraphs are sometimes labeled in accordance with their place within this scheme. There are four different types: introductory paragraphs, concluding paragraphs, body paragraphs, and transition paragraphs.

The function of introductory and concluding paragraphs is obvious from their names. Body paragraphs, as their name suggests, make up the bulk of any text. They convey information, continue a narrative, or develop an argument. Transition paragraphs are paragraphs that writers sometimes insert when they have to change from one topic to another and wish to announce the fact to the reader. They frequently contain a brief conclusion or farewell to the earlier topic and an equally brief introduction to the topic that is to be dealt with next.

Most of the discussion in this chapter centers on body paragraphs, so they need no further treatment here. The other three, more specialized types of paragraph are dealt with briefly below.

INTRODUCTORY PARAGRAPHS

An introductory paragraph briefly sets out what you intend to show within a particular section of the work. It is usually a mistake to allow an introductory paragraph (or an introduction of any kind) to become too lengthy for the simple reason that the same material is going to be covered in full in the body paragraphs that follow. An introductory paragraph has the additional task of awakening the reader's interest, so it pays to make it lively.

A paragraph such as the following, for example, does not make a particularly effective introduction to a text:

> *This article is the fruit of a lengthy period of research into the historical reasons for the particular hostility shown by the Bush administration toward France in general, and the French government in particular, as a result of France's failure to participate in and support the military action against Iraq undertaken by the United States and its allies in 2003. We shall endeavor to show that the roots of the grievance go back in part to the period of World War II and its immediate aftermath. Not only did U.S. military personnel make extraordinary sacrifices during the Normandy landings of 1944 and the subsequent battles to liberate France, but the U.S. government of the time committed itself to a lengthy diplomatic effort to ensure the establishment of a free and democratic government in France at a time when the Communist Party was particularly strong and enjoyed immense prestige through having taken a leading role in the resistance to German occupation. Furthermore, the United States provided massive financial and material assistance to the country at the end of the 1940s through the Marshall Plan. We shall show by quotations from speeches and from published sources, that the events of the immediate postwar period were very much in the minds of leading members of the Bush administration and helped to shape their attitude toward French nonparticipation in efforts to topple the regime of Saddam Hussein. It should also be remembered that the approaching 60th anniversary of the Liberation—felt by many to be the last occasion in which surviving veterans of World War II would be able to participate in acts of commemoration in large numbers—gave particular prominence to this period of history in 2002–03. We shall therefore begin by outlining the role played by the United States in the restoration of France after one of the darkest periods in its history.*

The writers of this passage, we might say, show too much of their hand too early. The third and fourth sentences (*Not only did U.S. military personnel . . . Furthermore, the United States . . .*) and the sixth sentence (*It should also be remembered . . .*) in particular start to go into too much detail. Simply excluding them produces a better result:

> *This article is the fruit of a lengthy period of research into the historical reasons for the particular hostility shown by the Bush administration toward France in general, and the French government in particular, as a result of France's failure to participate in and support the military action against Iraq undertaken by the United States and its allies in 2003. We shall endeavor to show that the roots of the grievance go back in part to*

the period of World War II and its immediate aftermath. We shall show by quotations from speeches and from published sources, that the events of the immediate postwar period were very much in the minds of leading members of the Bush administration and helped to shape their attitude toward French nonparticipation in efforts to topple the regime of Saddam Hussein. We shall therefore begin by outlining the role played by the United States in the restoration of France after one of the darkest periods in its history.

Now, the three sentences in question have been omitted not because they contain information that is irrelevant to the subject as a whole but simply because that information is irrelevant in the context of an introductory paragraph. In this instance, it is enough to state the general thesis—the attitude of the administration in 2003 was partly shaped by historical events—to indicate the period of history during which those events occurred, and to provide a lead-in to the discussion proper in its final sentence. The omitted sentences went some way toward "outlining the role played by the United States" and consequently stole the thunder of the paragraphs that follow.

We will have a good deal to say about relevance as a criterion for the organization of material in paragraphs in the rest of this section. There, it will be mainly a question of the relevance of subsidiary matters to the central idea. But the function of a particular paragraph also has a bearing on what belongs inside it. If the function of a paragraph is to introduce something, then it should do that and no more.

Deleting the unnecessary sentences has considerably improved the above example. Nonetheless, it could benefit from some further work to tighten and liven it up. It contains, for instance, three sentences beginning with the same two words—*We shall*—and the repetition serves no pressing rhetorical purpose.

Posing a question is often an effective way of catching the reader's attention from the outset. In this instance, if we pose a question in the first sentence, answering the question in the second will also enable us to get rid of one *We shall*:

> *. . . Why did the Bush administration feel so aggrieved at the failure of France to undertake or support military action against Iraq in 2003? The answer, we believe, lies in part in "the period of World War II and its aftermath . . ."*

However, a simple statement that centers on the matter in hand—and not on the person or persons who are writing about it or on the effort that they have expended to compile their material—can be equally effective:

> *The Bush administration showed particular hostility toward France in general, and the French government in particular, as a result of France's failure to participate in and support military action against Iraq in 2003. The reasons for the sense of grievance felt by the administration and*

expressed in the speeches and publications of some of its leading members are in part historical. They go back to World War II and its immediate aftermath, for the debt of gratitude that the French owed to the United States and was, in the administration's view, refusing to honor, dates from that period. We shall therefore begin by outlining the role played by the United States in the restoration of France after one of the darkest periods in its history.

These four sentences adequately state the subject matter of the article as a whole and lead into the exposition of the first piece of evidence that the writers offer in support of their thesis. That is all that they are required to do.

CONCLUDING PARAGRAPHS

Endings are often even more difficult to write than beginnings. A concluding paragraph should sum up the argument that has gone before and present the writer's verdict on it. The verdict is the important part. The reader may need reminding of the means by which the writer arrived at the verdict—especially if the preceding argument has been long and complex—but does not need to be taken through the whole process again. A concluding paragraph should not, as a rule, contain new material other than the verdict, if that has not been given before, because the reader would expect all the relevant aspects of the subject to have been fully discussed in the body of the piece of writing. So, like an introductory paragraph, a concluding paragraph should usually be kept short.

Consider the following example:

Let me then give you my considered opinion on the matter. Because undertaking the project would require us to take on specially trained staff, because we know that there is a general shortage of staff with such training, and because we have neither the facilities nor the personnel to train new recruits ourselves, I believe that the project is not a practical proposition for this company at this time. I should be grateful if you would communicate my opinion to the other members of the board.

Sincerely yours,

The writer neatly and forcefully sums up the situation, as he or she sees it, and leaves the impression that there is no more to be said at this stage. Notice how the points that lead up to the verdict, which would have been fully argued in earlier paragraphs, are presented in subordinate clauses—in this case a series of *because* clauses (*see* COORDINATION AND SUBORDINATION, page 97). If you wish to remind the reader of information or arguments that you have made before without seeming repetitious or giving them undue prominence, then remember the usefulness of subordinate clauses. The reminders can be put into subordinate clauses, and the verdict, delivered in the main clause. That, if your material will allow it, is the best principle to adopt in a concluding paragraph.

TRANSITION PARAGRAPHS

A transition paragraph is a short paragraph inserted between two longer ones to act as a bridge when you are moving from one major topic to the next. The following example consists of a transition paragraph placed between the last and first sentences of longer paragraphs:

> . . . *As a result, the committee decided to reject the proposal to open the competition to nonmembers and, as in previous years, restricted entry to registered members of the club.*
>
> *When they came to this decision, the members of the committee seem to have been completely unaware that they were acting in a way that might leave them open to a legal challenge. Few if any of them, apparently, were familiar with the details of their own constitution. They were in for a considerable surprise.*
>
> *A legal action was brought by Mr. Cuthbert Johanssen of Taos, New Mexico, who claimed that . . .*

The paragraph preceding the transition paragraph deals with the reasons why the committee rejected the proposal; the paragraph after the transition paragraph sets out the grounds for Mr. Johanssen's action. The three sentences in the transition paragraph bridge the gap in the story and prepare the way for the new topic. The first sentence actually does most of the work. It refers to the end of the preceding paragraph—the noun *decision* echoes the verb *decided*—and also contains a pointer to what is to follow inasmuch as it mentions a "legal challenge."

A transition paragraph is perhaps better compared to a hinge than a bridge. It turns the argument in a new direction. But transition paragraphs are only needed occasionally, usually between two long paragraphs or two series of shorter paragraphs, and only when there is good reason to emphasize a change of topic.

When to Insert a Paragraph Break

The basic rule that determines when a paragraph should end has already been given. When you have dealt fully with one particular idea—or with one particular aspect of a complex idea that it takes you several paragraphs to cover appropriately—you should finish a paragraph and begin another. How this works in practice will be shown in MAKING PARAGRAPHS (page 133).

CHANGING THE POINT OF VIEW

It is also usual to begin a new paragraph when you change the point of view from which you are writing. This can occur quite frequently in narrative, when the writer presents a scene or an incident from the point of view of one character and then switches to another character to present his or her possibly very different perception of the same scene or incident. Such is the case in the following example:

> *Mary suddenly became conscious that she was saying things that she did not necessarily want the rest of the company to overhear. She huddled*

down in her chair and leaned closer to the wall, at the same time picking up the handkerchief that lay in her lap and placing it over the mouthpiece of the telephone. Not satisfied that these measures alone sufficed to ensure her privacy, she also dropped her voice to a very low whisper.

Her mother, at the other end of the line, was completely nonplussed when Mary's speech suddenly degenerated into a series of barely audible sounds in the middle of what had appeared to be a perfectly normal conversation. Her first thought was that there was something wrong with her phone. . . .

There is an obvious shift in perspective here. We are presented first with a description of Mary's actions, then with a description of her mother's reactions. The point of view changes, and to mark that change the writer begins a new paragraph.

Shifts in point of view are not restricted to narrative, however:

There are cases where a writer deliberately chooses to forgo the advantages of paragraphing and puts down a length of unbroken text in order to achieve a special effect. Stream-of-consciousness writing is the obvious example. Outside specialized literary writing, however, undivided text is rarely if ever needed. Generally speaking, writers produce it not so much as a deliberate policy, but because they are in a hurry or on a roll, drafting furiously to catch the ideas as they unfold.

As has been said before, anything goes when you are writing a draft. You may choose to dispense with punctuation altogether, let alone such sophisticated mechanisms as paragraph breaks. This is fine as long as you realize that you will have to go back at the revision stage and put your material into proper form. Do not be tempted to omit paragraph breaks because you believe that the reader might enjoy sharing the excitement that you felt when you were in the flow. . . .

This passage occurs a little earlier in this chapter. The first three sentences speak of writers generally and impersonally. The remainder of the passage addresses the reader (as writer) directly. The shift from general description to direct address constitutes a change in angle of attack, so to speak, which is tantamount to a change in point of view. At the point of change, therefore, a new paragraph begins.

DIALOGUE

It is usual practice to present the words of each speaker in a dialogue or conversation as a separate paragraph. The "attribution" of the words used—that is, a phrase that tells the reader who is speaking, such as *he said, Mrs. Hollinger remarked,* or *they chanted in unison*—should be included in the same paragraph, as should any material that describes the way in which the words are uttered or what the speaker is doing when he or she utters them.

Grant leaned across the table and said softly, "Don't turn your head, but that woman's just come into the restaurant."

> *"Which woman?" Despite Grant's warning, Josie swiveled around in her seat to see.*
>
> *A tall, thin woman in a long black evening gown was already making her way toward their table. She walked with unsteady steps and was holding a glass in her hand.*
>
> *"Oh my God!" exclaimed Josie and immediately looked away again.*
>
> *"Who is it? What's the matter?"*
>
> *"It's my mother!"*

There are several points to note in this short passage. First, as at the end of the passage, it is not necessary to attribute spoken words to a particular person explicitly if it is obvious from the context who says them. But note that this can be done with safety only when there are no more than two, or perhaps at most three, people involved in the exchange. Second, it is not necessary to use a reporting verb—that is, a verb such as *said, exclaimed, muttered,* or *whispered* that explicitly describes a speech act—to attribute words to a particular person. The writer makes it quite clear that Josie speaks the words "Which woman?" by simply going on, in the same paragraph, to describe the action that accompanies those words. Third, material that is not directly connected with any spoken words—in this instance, the sentences that describe Josie's mother—is placed in a separate paragraph.

The reason this particular piece of description is placed in a separate paragraph—indeed, why most pieces of contextual information that fall within passages of dialogue are similarly separated out—relates back to the rule set out in the previous subsection: There is a change in the point of view. If this scene were in a movie, the director would probably show Grant and Josie exchanging their opening remarks in close-up, then change to a different camera to give a broader view of the whole room and show the woman in black moving toward their table. The writer has chosen to present the scene in the same way, moving from a narrow focus on the couple to a broader and more general perspective, thus requiring a new paragraph.

It would, however, be possible to introduce the woman in black, not from the angle of an independent observer somewhere in the room, but from the angle of Josie herself, as he swivels around and spots her. In that case, the paragraphing would be done rather differently:

> *Grant leaned across the table and said softly, "Don't turn your head, but that woman's just come into the restaurant."*
>
> *"Which woman?" Despite Grant's warning, Josie swiveled around in her seat and saw a tall, thin woman in a long black evening gown making her way toward their table, walking with unsteady steps and holding a glass in her hand.*
>
> *"Oh my God!" exclaimed Josie, and immediately looked away again. . . .*

Once the woman in black becomes something that Josie perceives as she swivels in her seat, she can be appropriately accommodated in the same paragraph as Josie's spoken words.

MAKING PARAGRAPHS

Composing and Revising

Writers make paragraphs under two slightly different sets of circumstances: when they are composing and when they are revising. When writers are composing, they organize the ideas that come into their head or the material that they have gathered from research into paragraphs as they go along, though many writers, in fact, plan their work in such a way that their material is organized into potential paragraphs, or sections of paragraph length, before they even begin to draft the text. When writers are revising, they reshape existing paragraphs or, if they are in the habit of drafting text in lengthy sections, they divide up what they have written into proper paragraphs. In general, therefore, writers usually find themselves making paragraphs either from notes or from existing text.

Both of these procedures will be dealt with here. First, however, let us recall the concept that is key to successful paragraphing, under whatever circumstances paragraphs happen to be made: coherence. According to most experts, coherence can be most easily achieved when a paragraph contains what is known as a "topic sentence." The next subsection briefly outlines the nature and function of this vital element.

The Topic Sentence

A topic sentence, also sometimes referred to as a "thesis sentence," is a sentence that encapsulates the subject matter of the paragraph. The golden rule, remember, is One idea, one paragraph. The topic sentence is the sentence in which that one basic idea is set forth most explicitly. It thus forms the nucleus of the paragraph. The material contained in all the other sentences in the paragraph should in some way relate to the idea encapsulated in the topic sentence, elaborating on it, illustrating or exemplifying it, commenting on it or arguing with it. Material that does not relate to the topic sentence in some way is irrelevant and should be cut or transferred to another paragraph.

The topic sentence in the previous paragraph is the first sentence. It contains a definition of the term *topic sentence*. The remaining sentences expand on that basic definition. The topic sentence of the first paragraph of "Composing and Revising" is likewise the first sentence—"Writers make paragraphs under two slightly different sets of circumstances: when they are composing and when they are revising"—the rest of the paragraph builds on that statement and explains in more detail when and how writers make paragraphs.

Consider this paragraph, however:

> *The days dragged on wearily toward Christmas. Despite having been brought up in a Christian household, Daniel did not know of any rea-*

son why he should celebrate December 25 more than any other day of the year. Its main advantage was that he did not have to go work on that day; its main disadvantage was that he had to spend it with his family going through a series of meaningless rituals and pretending to enjoy them. He did not enjoy giving gifts, nor did he particularly enjoy receiving them. Even if he made a list of what he wanted, his friends and family would invariably choose an article that was the wrong brand or the wrong color. No one had ever seemed able to match a gift precisely to his needs or desires, and, as far as Daniel was concerned, God was as much at fault in this as any of His creatures.

Here, the topic sentence is the second sentence. The paragraph is about Daniel's attitude toward Christmas and gift giving. The first sentence establishes the time of year and hints at Daniel's feelings in the verb phrase "dragged on wearily," but its function is merely introductory. It is only in the second sentence that the writer presents us with the idea that is to be developed further in the remainder of the paragraph.

A topic sentence can, in theory, be placed anywhere in the paragraph. There are obvious advantages, however, to letting the reader know early on what the substance of the paragraph is. Consequently, the topic sentence is often the first sentence and is usually positioned close to the beginning.

A topic sentence has a good deal in common with a main clause, leaving aside the latter's grammatical function. (There are no grammatical rules, incidentally, that apply specifically to paragraphs.) The main clause is usually the heart of the sentence, and the subordinate clauses are grouped around it. The relationship of the topic sentence to the subsidiary sentences is similar. Likewise, just as it is possible to construct a sentence that does not have a main clause, so it is also possible to construct a paragraph that does not have a topic sentence. Transition paragraphs, for example, do not require a topic sentence, because their main function is to be the hinge between different topics. It is also possible to construct perfectly acceptable body paragraphs that do not have topic sentences. This is especially so in narrative, where you might, for instance, write a paragraph describing a sequence of events or a set of character traits, none of which is necessarily more important than the others. In these circumstances, it would be inappropriate to try to encapsulate the substance of the paragraph in a single sentence. Such is the case in the example that follows:

Taggart felt in his jacket pocket for a pack of cigarettes. He kept the gun pointing in my direction. He felt again for his lighter. The gun wavered slightly. I could see he was trying to figure out how to extract his cigarette and light it while still keeping his pistol trained on me. The cops would be here in minutes. As he tapped the top of the pack on the edge of the table, his eyes went down, and the muzzle of his pistol went sideways. In that fraction of a second, I leaped forward, grabbed his arm, and wrenched it upward. The bullet went into the ceiling. The cigarette dropped to the floor.

The above example is a genuine paragraph. It has unity, not simply because it deals a single moment in an ongoing story, but because it concentrates on the gun and the cigarette and the relationship between the two, and uses them to provide focus and, in a way, to tell the story. But there is no topic sentence. It is possible to imagine how this same event might have been recounted in a paragraph with a topic sentence. The writer might have begun with a sentence such as this:

> *I guess I would never have gotten out of there before the cops arrived if Taggart hadn't been such a heavy smoker. I could see that he was dying for a cigarette. He felt inside his jacket pocket for a pack. . . .*

That first sentence sums up the action that the rest of the paragraph describes in more detail. This approach has one disadvantage, however: It removes the element of suspense.

Although there is no rule that each paragraph must contain a topic sentence, most paragraphs, especially in work that is primarily concerned with discussing ideas or providing information rather than telling a story, do contain them and benefit from containing them. It is often helpful to write a topic sentence first and then construct the rest of your paragraph around it. If you start writing a paragraph, and no sentence emerges that could function as its nucleus, then you probably need to clarify what precisely it is that you are trying to say. Similarly, if you look back at a paragraph that you have written and cannot identify a topic sentence, then the chances are that you need to rewrite the paragraph so that a central idea emerges more clearly. (For further discussion on topic sentences in writing essays, *see* THE THESIS STATEMENT, page 257).

Constructing Paragraphs from Notes

The procedure for constructing a paragraph from notes is very similar to the procedure for constructing a sentence from ideas, which was discussed and exemplified in the preceding chapter. First, group together the notes that belong together; second, identify the core idea that will be expressed in the topic sentence; third, arrange the remaining material in an appropriate order around the topic sentence.

Let us assume that you are writing a review of an amateur performance of Arthur Miller's famous play *The Crucible*. You scribbled down as many notes as you could in the theater and added to them after you returned home, while the performance was still fresh in your memory. You clearly want to devote at least one paragraph in your review to the performance of the actor playing the leading role of John Proctor. Your notes read as follows:

> *John Proctor (Peter O'Brien) doesn't look the part—too thin? too slight?—looks more like an intellectual than a Massachusetts farmer— costume too neat?—has good voice—delivers lines well—understands what he is saying, unlike, e.g., Giles Corey—terrible—hasn't a clue—JP badly positioned behind table in scene with Abigail—good chemistry*

with Abigail—less good with Elizabeth—plenty of passion—positioning poor in examination scene with Elizabeth—JP too far downstage—very good at end—very moving—very dignified.

The rule is One idea, one paragraph. The first task, therefore, is to remove any material that does not relate to the actor's performance as John Proctor and to reassign it to another paragraph. From the above, you might omit, for example, the note you made on the bad performance of Giles Corey, unless you particularly wanted to compare Proctor favorably with Corey. You would probably also not need to mention the fact that Proctor was badly positioned in certain scenes. The positioning of the actors on stage is essentially the business of the director, and your assessment of the director's skills—or lack of them—would normally belong in another paragraph.

The next task is decide your overall impression of the performance. This, obviously, will inform what you say in the paragraph as a whole and, in particular, determine what you say in your topic sentence.

Whether or not the topic sentence will be the first sentence in the paragraph, it is, as has been said, usually a good idea to construct it first—in your head, if not on the page—since it gives the keynote to the paragraph. In framing the topic sentence you make a decision as to what the paragraph is actually about. On that basis, you can then sift your material further, perhaps again rejecting some of it as irrelevant or reshaping it to fit in with the main theme.

In this instance, you would probably decide that on balance Peter O'Brien has given a good performance as John Proctor. There were certain matters that you were not entirely happy with—for example, his appearance—but he got many important matters right. You might, therefore, decide to frame your topic sentence like this:

Despite certain physical disadvantages, Peter O'Brien gave a very powerful performance as John Proctor.

or like this:

Peter O'Brien's fine speaking voice and intelligent delivery of the lines made him a very powerful John Proctor, despite his physical disadvantages.

or even like this:

In Peter O'Brien, this production had a John Proctor who was fully equal to the part in passion, in dignity, and in his intelligent delivery of the lines throughout.

Each of these three keynote sentences encapsulates a slightly different attitude toward the performance. The importance of the way you construct your topic sentence becomes obvious when we consider the sort of paragraphs that you might build upon them. There is no doubt which of them Mr. O'Brien would prefer to read in the local newspaper on the day after his first night, but your choice would obviously depend on your particular assessment of his performance and on the tone of your review as a whole.

Because the topic sentence is the nucleus of the paragraph, its logic determines the logic of the paragraph as a whole. Its emphases and its attitude, we might say, demand to be carried over into the rest of the paragraph. If, therefore, you chose to write the first of these sentences, which highlights the fact that O'Brien did not look the part by referring to it first, even if only in a subordinated phrase, you would be committing yourself to a full description of his physical inadequacies. Any praise you went on to award him would nevertheless be seen against the background of this basic failing:

> *Despite certain physical disadvantages, Peter O'Brien gave a very powerful performance as John Proctor. With his slight build, his intellectual air, and his overly neat costuming, Mr. O'Brien looked anything but the very model of a 17th-century Massachusetts farmer, but his vocal talents and his intelligent delivery of the lines enabled him to overcome this handicap. He was particularly convincing in his scene with Abigail and in the final scene, where he achieved real dignity and was very moving. He was less convincing in his scenes with Elizabeth, where he was sometimes not helped by bad positioning. All in all, it was a very commendable effort at a very difficult part.*

But what if you selected the second example sentence? This sentence strikes a rather more positive note insofar as it relegates the chief criticism to a closing phrase. Nonetheless, that criticism still features in the topic sentence. Logically, therefore, it has to be given due weight in the paragraph as a whole. Let us this time place the topic sentence second:

> *Any production of* The Crucible *is likely to stand or fall by its John Proctor. Peter O'Brien's fine speaking voice and intelligent delivery of the lines made him a very powerful performer in this part, despite his physical disadvantages. He conveyed all the passion and the torment of the man in the scene with Abigail and was particularly dignified and moving in his final scene. His achievement was all the greater, because he did not really look the part, being slighter and more intellectual in appearance than one would normally expect John Proctor to be. His vocal talents more than made up for any physical deficiencies, however, and this was the rocklike central performance that the play needed.*

Choosing the second of the proposed topic sentences gives you the cue perhaps to add "spin" or "finesse" to the actor's physical disadvantages. They still must be mentioned, but they can be presented in the most positive possible light: "His achievement was all the greater because . . ." Choosing the third topic sentence, meanwhile, would enable you to avoid mentioning them altogether or to give them very little prominence:

Any production of The Crucible *is likely to stand or fall by its John Proctor. In Peter O'Brien, this production had a John Proctor who was fully equal to the part in passion, in dignity, and in his intelligent delivery of the lines throughout. The audience was immediately gripped by the tormented power of his first scene with Abigail. In his scenes with Elizabeth, despite sometimes being poorly served by the director, he was scarcely less convincing, and his final moments were intensely moving. This was indeed the rocklike central performance that the play requires.*

Mr. O'Brien could scarcely ask for anything more.

The need for a logical relationship between the topic sentence and the rest of the paragraph can perhaps also be demonstrated if we take the first of the keynote sentences and attach it to the body of the third paragraph.

Despite certain physical disadvantages, Peter O'Brien gave a very powerful performance as John Proctor. The audience was immediately gripped by the tormented power of his first scene with Abigail. In his scenes with Elizabeth, despite sometimes being poorly served by the director, he was scarcely less convincing, and his final moments were intensely moving. This was indeed the rocklike central performance that the play requires.

Here, an important part of the first sentence has no follow-up at all in the remainder of the paragraph. The reader wonders why the writer bothered to mention the actor's "physical disadvantages," the first sentence effectively loses its status as a topic sentence, and the paragraph as a whole loses the logicality and shape that the previous three examples possessed.

The same set of notes can be made into several different paragraphs, as this exercise has shown. The crucial point, as always, is to decide precisely what you want to say. On that basis you construct your topic sentence, and from that the rest of the paragraph should logically flow.

Constructing Paragraphs from Text

Let us suppose that you have drafted a piece of work on the pleasures and problems of retirement and that you are now setting out to revise it. Part of it reads as follows:

At last the day you have been waiting for arrives. You've cleared your desk, you've been to all the parties, you're richer by several fishing poles or clocks or loungers, you've said a fond farewell to all your colleagues and accepted all their good wishes, and you've finally walked out of the old place, probably with a good deal of sadness. All that was yesterday. Today is the first day of the rest of your life. So what are you going to do? There is so much you want to do, so much you could do, so much you never had time to do while you were a working man or woman. At the same time, there's nothing to do. At least there's nothing that you have to do. And maybe that's the greatest thing of all. You're free and you're going to enjoy your freedom more than anything else. And maybe the best way to enjoy your freedom is just to sit comfortably and think about all the wonderful things you're going to do with the time you have left. You'll go on vacation more often, take that trip to Europe or Peru or China you always promised yourself, and see more of the kids and the grandchildren. Great! Except it doesn't take very long to think this and suddenly you realize you're bored. Suddenly you're walking up and down looking for jobs to do. Suddenly you miss the old place like hell, and this whole retirement thing feels like a big mistake. So, what are you going to do now?

You cannot fault what you have written as far as liveliness goes, and you have deliberately chosen to write in an informal style. But there is informal and there is formless, and this, as it stands, falls into the latter category. It needs breaking into paragraphs.

Breaking text into paragraphs—that is, into text without a lot of crossing out and overwriting—should be a fairly simple task. Even when you are in the flow and drafting speed, you will naturally tend to arrange your ideas in a reasonably logical sequence. It is essentially a question of finding the best places to break the sequence, and then doing a little shaping to make the resultant sections into satisfactory paragraphs.

In order to find the best points at which to begin new paragraphs, you will first need to isolate the different ideas that are contained in the passage. If you are lucky, you may find that you have already written sentences that will serve as topic sentences on which to base the new paragraphs.

The example passage above seems to fall into three basic sections: first, a retrospective look at the day before the first day of actual retirement; second, the retiree's thoughts; third, the retiree's second thoughts, as it were, when he or she finds that thinking of things to do is no substitute for actually doing something. So, we might roughly chop the passage up like this:

At last the day you have been waiting for arrives. You've cleared your desk, you've been to all the parties, you're richer by several fishing poles or clocks or loungers, you've said a fond farewell to all your colleagues and accepted all their good wishes, and you've finally walked out of the old place, probably with a good deal of sadness. All that was yesterday. Today is the first day of the rest of your life. So what are you going to do?

There is so much you want to do, so much you could do, so much you never had time to do while you were a working man or woman. At the same time, there's nothing to do. At least there's nothing that you have to do. And maybe that's the greatest thing of all. You're free and you're going to enjoy your freedom more than anything else. And maybe the best way to enjoy your freedom is just to sit comfortably and think about all the wonderful things you're going to do with the time you have left. You'll go on vacation more often, take that trip to Europe or Peru or China you always promised yourself, and see more of the kids and the grandchildren.

> Great! Except it doesn't take very long to think this and suddenly you realize you're bored. Suddenly you're walking up and down looking for jobs to do. Suddenly you miss the old place like hell, and this whole retirement thing feels like a big mistake. So, what are you going to do now?

This is a start, but it looks like one of those starts where the partially improved passage looks, if anything, slightly worse than the unimproved passage. Making rough divisions can leave rather rough edges. That, however, is something you can work on.

Since this is a passage in an informal style, it may be a good idea to think in terms of short paragraphs, even really short paragraphs. For example, the middle paragraph might benefit from being split again. The first sentence ("There is so much you want to do . . .") could be a topic sentence for a short paragraph of five sentences. The present sixth sentence ("And maybe the best way to enjoy your freedom . . .") perhaps introduces a different thought. It is also, incidentally, constructed on a very similar pattern to the next-to-last sentence and others preceding it. There are instances where, as we shall see in the next subsection, parallel construction is an asset. But there is parallelism by design and parallelism by accident, and this looks like the latter.

Furthermore, there is the question that hangs onto the end of the first paragraph. The previous sentence ("Today is the first day of the rest of your life.") makes a rather nice conclusion and has the additional advantage that it harks back to the opening sentence. You could detach the question and reattach it to the front of the following paragraph, but it does not altogether fit there either. Perhaps you could take advantage of the freedom offered by the comparative informality of tone and structure and leave it isolated as a separate one-sentence paragraph. And if you can be so bold with the question at the end of the first paragraph, might it not be a good idea to be equally bold with the question at the end of the present third paragraph and, possibly, with the "Great!" that introduces it?

A final version of the original text, reparagraphed along the lines herein suggested and otherwise generally tidied up, might look something like this:

> *At last the day you've been waiting for arrives. You've cleared your desk, you've been to all the parties, you're richer by several fishing poles or clocks or loungers, you've said a fond farewell to all your colleagues and accepted all their good wishes, and you've finally walked out of the old place, probably feeling pretty sad. But all that was yesterday. Today is the first day of the rest of your life.*
>
> *So what are you going to do?*
>
> *There is so much you want to do, so much you could do, so much you never had time to do while you were working. At the same time, there's nothing to do. At least, there's nothing that you have to do. And maybe that's the greatest thing of all. You're free, and you're going to enjoy your freedom more than anything else.*
>
> *The best way to enjoy your freedom may be just to sit comfortably and think about all the wonderful things you're going to do with the*

time you have left. You'll go on vacation more often, take that trip to Europe or Peru or China you always promised yourself, and see more of the kids and the grandchildren.

Great!

Except that it doesn't take very long to have these thoughts, and suddenly you realize you're bored. Suddenly you're walking up and down looking for jobs to do. Suddenly you miss the old place like hell. Suddenly this whole retirement thing feels like a really big mistake.

So, what are you going to do now?

The original text was lively; the revised text is even livelier. There is a real sense that the writer is speaking directly to the reader and, indeed, having fun with the reader. The questions have an almost teasing quality, now that they are separated out from the rest of the text.

This example in particular is intended to show that making paragraphs need not be—ought not to be—a humdrum task undertaken simply for reasons of literary or academic propriety. When you divide your work up into well-constructed paragraphs, you add value to it. You not only clarify it, you often enliven it; you not only make it easier for the reader to read, you usually make it look better on the page; you not only give your thoughts distinctness, you put them in a context designed to show them to best advantage. A writer's stylistic skills are shown as much in the way he or she makes paragraphs as they are in the way he or she chooses words or constructs sentences.

UNIFYING PARAGRAPHS
Coherence

Why is coherence in paragraphs a feature of good style? The answer, first and foremost, is that coherence is a valuable quality in itself. Certainly, no writer worth his or her salt would want to produce paragraphs that could be described as incoherent. Coherence is a quality of art. It is to writing roughly what shape is to a physical object. There is usually little point in trying to give text a pleasing shape on the page. Neatness of presentation is all that is required of the writer; the design editor and the typesetter will do the rest. But the mind is nevertheless able to apprehend and appreciate formal qualities in written work even when the eye cannot see them. A coherent, well-rounded paragraph will satisfy the aesthetic sense of more sensitive readers, and even readers who do not respond to aesthetic qualities will value the fact that a paragraph delivers its message clearly and does not distract them with irrelevant material.

That is the practical value of coherence above and beyond its aesthetic virtue. If the reader is uninterested in aesthetic satisfaction, he or she will definitely want the satisfaction of having information delivered efficiently. If the thought being offered is an interesting one, then the reader will be eager to receive it and will be dissatisfied if anything interferes with the reception. He or she will not want the thought process that is being presented in the paragraph to be disrupted. The topic sentence might even be seen as a kind of writer's contract with the reader. This, the writer seems to say, is what I intend to write about; you can judge my performance on whether I deliver. If the ensuing paragraph fails to fulfill that contract or fulfillment is unnecessarily delayed, then the reader has the right to feel dissatisfied.

So if, to refer to an example used in a previous subsection, the writer contracts in the topic sentence to write about the performance of an actor playing John Proctor, but then uses a good deal of the space in the paragraph to talk about the 17th-century context of *The Crucible* or its other historical roots in the McCarthy era, the reader may feel that the contract has been broken. Coherence is the quality that ensures that the writer fulfills the contract.

There are two basic methods of achieving coherence and unifying paragraphs: through structural organization and through the use of linkers. These two are not mutually exclusive. A well-knit paragraph will probably contain elements of structural organization as well as judiciously placed linkers. Let us deal first with structural organization.

Structural Organization

RECURRENCE

The key to achieving coherence through structural organization is repetition or, to use a word with fewer negative overtones, recurrence. What gives coherence to a piece of music—over and above the fact, which may not be obvious to nonmusicians, that it is written in a particular key—is a recurring tune or motif. What gives coherence to poetry—the kind of writing in which formal qualities are most evident—are recurring rhythms, rhymes, and lengths of line. What gives coherence to a paragraph of prose are likewise recurring elements: recurring words or phrases and recurring constructions, together with a general roundedness that links the beginning to the end and a strict concern for the relevance of the contents of the paragraph to its central idea.

Recurrence is deliberate repetition that creates a framework. It signals to the reader that a conscious shaping process is at work. As in music, however, when a motif recurs, it may be varied. Instead of repeating a key word in exactly the form in which it occurs in the topic sentence, you may, for instance, use a derivate or a related word. Let us see how this works in practice.

KEY WORDS

One relatively simple way of unifying a paragraph is to repeat or allude to key terms in it, usually words that feature prominently in the topic sentence. Here, from the previous subsection, is an obvious example of this technique:

> *So, what are you going to do?*
> *There is so much you want to do, so much you could do, so much you never had time to do while you were working. At the same time, there's nothing to do. At least there's nothing that you have to do. And maybe that's the greatest thing of all. You're free, and you're going to enjoy your freedom more than anything else.*

The key word is *(to) do*. Picked up from the question, it is repeated almost to excess in the following paragraph. But there is no mistaking the paragraph's dominant theme.

Following is a somewhat subtler use of the same technique in an earlier paragraph from this book. The topic sentence is the second sentence; the key words and other words that relate to them are underlined:

> *Why is coherence in paragraphs a feature of good style? The answer, first and foremost, is that <u>coherence</u> is a <u>valuable quality</u> in itself. Certainly, no writer worth his or her salt would want to produce paragraphs that could be described as <u>incoherent</u>. <u>Coherence</u> is a <u>quality</u> of art. It is to writing roughly what shape is to a physical object. There is usually little point in trying to give text a pleasing shape on the page. Neatness of presentation is all that is required; the design editor and the typesetter will do the rest. But the mind is nevertheless able to apprehend and appreciate formal <u>qualities</u> in written work even when the eye cannot see them. A <u>coherent</u>, well-rounded paragraph will satisfy the aesthetic sense of more sensitive readers, and even readers who do not respond to aesthetic <u>qualities</u> will <u>value</u> the fact that a paragraph delivers its message clearly and does not distract them with irrelevant material.*

The repetition is not intended to hit the reader in the eye, in this instance. It keeps the paragraph on track. It gently reminds the reader of the principal theme. If the word *valuable* perhaps does not seem to get its fair share of recurrence, nevertheless the paragraph is full of words that express value or the act of valuation, such as *pleasing, neatness, appreciate,* and so on.

PARALLEL STRUCTURE

Another means of achieving unity in a paragraph is to use the same, or a similar, structure in several of the sentences that it contains. Consider the following paragraph:

> *With my 60th birthday only a few months away, I resolved, knowing that my remaining period of active life must necessarily be limited, to use what time I had more productively. Where I had wasted time before, I would now use every minute to the full. Where I had previously given up when faced with difficulties, I would henceforth persevere to the end. Where in my earlier life I had entered into projects half-heartedly, with only faint expectations of enjoyment or success, from this moment I would devote myself to them body and heart and soul, with confidence that the more commitment I put into them, the more pleasure and benefit I would derive. In short, I resolved to wring every last drop of goodness out of myself before night fell and I went home to my final resting place. But 60 years is a long time to live on this earth, productively or unproductively, and not realize that resolutions are easy to make and hard to sustain.*

Much of the strength of this paragraph lies in the three sentences, each beginning with *Where,* that the writer uses to elaborate the idea, put forward in the topic sentence, of resolving to use time more productively. Without this parallel structure, the paragraph would be much less effective, as in the following version:

With my 60th birthday only a few months away, I resolved, knowing that my remaining period of active life must necessarily be limited, to use what time I had more productively. I would use every minute to the full and not waste time. Difficulties tended to make me lose heart, but I would henceforth persevere to the end. I had often entered into projects half-heartedly, with only faint expectations of enjoyment or success, but that was going to change, and I would, instead, devote myself to them body and heart and soul. . . .

In the original, the parallel structure—which involves not merely the use of a *where* clause followed by an *I would* clause, but repeated contrasts between time before and time after, as in *before . . . now, previously . . . henceforth,* and *in my earlier life . . . as from this moment*—is far more emphatic and particularly befits the usual mode of thought or utterance of someone who is making resolutions.

ROUNDING OFF A PARAGRAPH

The sense of unity in a paragraph is usually considerably enhanced if it can be brought to an effective close. A paragraph is most effectively closed by the kind of sentence familiarly known as a "clincher." A clinching sentence recalls the main theme of the paragraph and/or its opening sentence, sums up the discussion, or offers a comment by the writer on what has just been said. Ideally, a clincher should also provide a lead-in for the next paragraph.

Consider again the passage used to exemplify parallel structure. It ends with quite an effective clincher:

. . . But 60 years is a long time to live on this earth, productively or unproductively, and not realize that resolutions are easy to make and hard to sustain.

It recalls the opening sentence:

With my 60th birthday only a few months away, I resolved, knowing that my remaining period of active life must necessarily be limited, to use what time I had more productively.

It also reuses the key words *resolution* and *productively* from the topic sentence, offers the writer's ironic comment on his own earnestness, emphatically expressed in the repeated sentence pattern of the central section, and, finally, opens the way for the next paragraph, which deals with his failure to put those resolutions into practice.

The "clincher" is to a paragraph roughly what a conclusion is to a larger section of a work. And if a paragraph has a conclusion, it ought in most cases to have an introduction as well. The familiar template of introduction, discussion, conclusion can be a useful guide in constructing paragraphs. Consider again this example paragraph from an earlier subsection:

> *Any production of* The Crucible *is likely to stand or fall by its John Proctor. Peter O'Brien's fine speaking voice and intelligent delivery of the lines made him a very powerful performer in this part, despite his physical disadvantages. He conveyed all the passion and the torment of the man in the scene with Abigail and was particularly dignified and moving in his final scene. His achievement was all the greater, because he did not really look the part, being slighter and more intellectual in appearance than one would normally expect John Proctor to be. His vocal talents more than made up for any physical deficiencies, however, and this was the rocklike central performance that the play needed.*

The first sentence is an introduction, emphasizing the importance of the role, but not discussing the actual performance. The second, third, and fourth sentences convey the reviewer's essential message. The fifth sentence, or, rather, the second half of the fifth sentence, sums up the reviewer's assessment of the performance in words that continue the main theme—the actor gave a powerful performance—and at the same time alludes again to the introductory comment on how essential this particular role is to the play. The paragraph, as a result, not only comes to a satisfactory close but has an equally satisfactory overall roundedness.

LINKERS

Linkers, as their name suggests, are continuity words. Their task is to ensure that sentences, though units, are not isolated units but relate to one another and form part of a greater whole. It is possible to write paragraphs in which the sentences seem to stand back to back ignoring one another, like embarrassed guests at a party. Linkers—words and phrases such as *but, however, still, next, also, in addition, in contrast*—are, like small talk, a great aid to intercommunication. They indicate that the writer is aware of what he or she has said in the previous sentence and is responding to it in some way in the sentence that follows. In short, they enable a paragraph to flow.

Here is a paragraph with no linkers:

> *My brother and his family live in Australia. Opportunities for us to see one another are rare. We do occasionally keep in contact by e-mail; we send gifts at Christmas and on birthdays. While my parents were alive, they acted as a communications center for the whole family. They would pass on news and good wishes and ensure that each of us kept up to date with the doings of the other. Since they died, contact between us has dwindled. This happens in a lot of families. Imagine my surprise when one day I heard a ring at the door and found a young man standing on my doorstep who announced that he was my nephew.*

Here is the same paragraph with linkers, which are underlined:

> *My brother and his family live in Australia. Opportunities for us to see*
> *one another are, <u>consequently,</u> rare. We do, <u>however,</u> occasionally keep*
> *in contact by e-mail; we <u>also</u> send gifts at Christmas and on birthdays.*
> *While my parents were alive, they acted as a communications center for*
> *the whole family. They would pass on news and good wishes and ensure*
> *that each of us kept up to date with the doings of the other. <u>But</u> since*
> *they died, contact between us has dwindled. <u>No doubt</u> this happens in a*
> *lot of families. Imagine my surprise, <u>therefore,</u> when one day I heard a*
> *ring at the door and found a young man standing on <u>my</u> doorstep who*
> *announced that he was my nephew.*

The difference between the two versions is, on the face of it, slight. The first version is not incorrect; it simply seems, rather abrupt or staccato. There are occasions when, as a writer, you may want to produce a rough-hewn or unpolished effect, but most writers on most occasions aim at smoothness. Inserting linkers helps to achieve that effect.

You might argue that if the writer's brother lives in Australia and the writer lives in the United States, it is obvious that opportunities for contact between them will be rare and that, therefore, to put *consequently* into the second sentence to point out the fact that the latter situation is the result of the former, is superfluous. Strictly speaking, this is true, and if you were rationed as to the number of words you were allowed to use in a passage, you might have to delete some of the linkers. Under normal circumstances, however, when you are more concerned with the overall effect of a paragraph and its coherence and flow than with an exact word count, the linkers should be left in. Even under circumstances where words are rationed, it would be difficult to pretend that the bald and disjointed third sentence of the first version does not benefit from the insertion of *however* to indicate the contrast with sentences one and two and of *also* to connect the second part of the sentence to the first. That sentence in particular needs to be integrated with the rest of the paragraph, and, in this instance, that can best be done by the use of linkers.

COMMONLY USED LINKERS

Listed below are some of the most frequently used linking words and phrases, organized by category.

When dealing with a new aspect of the subject:
And so
Another example/factor/possibility
As will now be proved/shown
First, . . . second, . . . third, . . . etc.
Following this
Next
Then
Turning now to

When reinforcing a point already made:
 Again
 Besides
 For example
 For instance
 Furthermore
 In addition
 It should also be borne in mind that
 Moreover

When introducing a difference or contrast:
 Alternatively
 Although
 Conversely
 Despite this
 However
 I/we will now turn to
 In comparison
 In contrast
 In spite of this
 Meanwhile
 Nevertheless
 Nonetheless
 On the other hand
 Still
 Yet

When indicating similarity:
 By the same token
 Furthermore
 Likewise
 Moreover
 Similarly

When indicating a result:
 Accordingly
 And so
 As a result
 Consequently
 Then
 Therefore
 Thus

To indicate a summary or restatement:
 All things considered
 In other words

In short
On the whole
To put it differently/another way

When concluding:
All in all
Finally
In conclusion
Lastly
On balance
To sum up

Small words and phrases such as these are useful signposts for the reader. They show him or her what you are doing; they also show him or her that you know what you are doing. They help to create structure in paragraphs; at the same time they give the paragraph coherence by relating sentences to one another. They are extremely useful as writing tools and should not be forgotten or neglected.

LINKING IN TIME AND SPACE

There is another class of linkers that perform a similar function. These are words that express relationship in time and space. Consider the following paragraph, from which the linking words have been removed:

> *Jessica and Raul had moved to San Francisco in the fall of 1992. It was what they both had wanted, and they were very happy there. They both found jobs and began to make new friends. The West Coast seemed their natural home. However, developments were taking place back in New Jersey that would change everything for them. Jessica always dated the turning point to July 16, 1994. She received a telephone call from her father, and nothing was ever the same again.*

Now look at the same paragraph with the linking words and phrases restored (and underlined):

> *Jessica and Raul had moved to San Francisco in the fall of 1992. It was what they both had wanted, and <u>at first</u> they were very happy there. They both found jobs and <u>soon</u> began to make new friends. <u>It was not long before</u> the West Coast seemed their natural home. <u>In the meantime,</u> however, developments were taking place back in New Jersey that would change everything for them. Jessica always dated the turning point to July 16, 1994. <u>On that day</u> she received a telephone call from her father, and <u>afterward</u> nothing was ever the same again.*

The differences between the two versions are again slight, but, as in the previous example, significant. There is a considerable gain in clarity for the reader from the inclusion of small signposts indicating the relationship in time of the various events referred to. There is also a considerable gain in coherence and continuity.

Where there is an opportunity to organize the ideas contained in a paragraph in terms of relationship in time and space, that opportunity should be taken. The sort of words and phrases that can enable you to do this are again listed below.

To indicate a relationship in time:
>   afterward
>   at the same time
>   earlier
>   formerly
>   later
>   meanwhile
>   next
>   simultaneously
>   soon
>   then
>   while

To indicate a relationship in space:
>   beyond
>   here
>   in the distance
>   nearby
>   on/to the left
>   on/to the right
>   opposite
>   over there
>   there

These are all small, simple words and phrases. It will probably come quite naturally to most writers to include them in their texts. They deserve highlighting, however, because their value in giving coherence to paragraphs that describe processes or scenes is out of proportion to their ordinariness.

CONNECTING PARAGRAPHS

Just as sentences need to be skillfully linked together to form coherent paragraphs, so paragraphs need to be linked with equal skill to form coherent larger units. Many of the techniques outlined in the previous subsection can also be used to ensure that the message or argument in a piece of writing flows on from one paragraph to the next.

Linkers

The same linking words that indicate that one sentence has a logical, temporal, or spatial connection with the next can also be used to express similar relationships between paragraphs, as the following examples (with under-lined linkers) demonstrate:

> *. . . In short, everything was prepared, and the organizers were satisfied that they had made plans to deal with any contingency.*
> *<u>But</u> the one thing they apparently had not foreseen was that members of the public would object to paying $30 for admission. . . .*

> *. . . The rescue services, accordingly, called off their search of the area immediately around the crash site and concentrated their efforts on the river valley below.*
> *<u>Meanwhile,</u> in the cave where they had taken shelter from the blizzard, the small band of survivors was gradually growing weaker. . . .*

> *. . . and in the very center of the village stood the church, an imposing Gothic edifice with a tall tower and a pair of wooden doors, carved with the figures of St. Peter and St. Paul, that faced out across the main square.*
> *<u>Directly opposite</u> the church, on the other side of the square, the café Georges Dandin sprawled along the sidewalk. . . .*

It is also possible to build into your text introductory or linking phrases designed to create a framework into which subsequent paragraphs will fit. For example:

> *I will describe the process in four steps. First . . . Second . . . Third . . . Fourth . . .*

> *There are four different aspects of this problem . . . First . . . Second . . . Third . . . Fourth . . .*

> *To begin with . . . I will then . . .*

There are also phrases that usefully indicate the way your argument proceeds from one paragraph to the next. For example:

> *Another factor to be taken into account is . . .*
> *As I/we have already stated/mentioned/shown . . .*
> *As I/we have shown in the previous paragraph . . .*
> *As I/we shall now show/demonstrate/prove . . .*
> *I/we can best illustrate this point by means of an example . . .*
> *I/we shall now move on to discuss . . .*
> *I/we shall now turn my/our attention to . . .*
> *Let us now consider . . .*
> *On the basis of what has been said before . . .*
> *The next step/stage is to . . .*
> *Turning now to . . .*

Such phrases indicate to the reader that you are following a planned route and are fully in control of your material.

Perhaps the most important means of linking paragraphs together, however, is a rather more subtle one.

Cues

The best way of ensuring continuity between paragraphs is to write so that the following paragraph picks up a cue from the preceding one and carries it forward. The cue usually takes the form of a word or phrase that occurs toward the end of the earlier paragraph and is either used in the introduction to the following paragraph or, indeed, plays a key role throughout that paragraph.

Here are some examples. The words that serve as cues to the succeeding paragraph are underlined:

> . . . *In their final report, the investigators restated their initial finding that the crash was caused by <u>pilot error,</u> and the case was officially <u>closed.</u>*
>
> *Colleagues of the <u>pilot,</u> Captain Higgins, were far from convinced by this verdict, however. They pointed to his unblemished 20-year record of service and immediately began to press for the case to be <u>reopened</u>. . . .*

> . . . *Economic factors aside, agriculture in South Africa is mainly determined, as one would expect, by the country's <u>climate,</u> and, in particular, by the time of year during which <u>rain</u> can be most confidently expected. On <u>climatic</u> grounds, therefore, the country is divided into two distinct regions.*
>
> *The southern part of the country has a Mediterranean <u>climate,</u> with hot, dry summers and cold, wet winters. It is known as the winter <u>rainfall</u> area and produces soft fruits of European origin, particularly apples and grapes. . . .*

It was suggested in an earlier subsection that the reuse of key words was a useful way of giving internal coherence to a paragraph. The technique recommended here for linking paragraphs is essentially an extension of that technique. It depends again on the writer being alert to the words that he or she is using and either seizing opportunities that occur in the natural course of composition to link one paragraph to another or reworking the beginning and end of existing paragraphs during revision to ensure that language and, consequently, thought appear to flow across the gap that is left on the page. It would not be wrong to start the second paragraph of the first of the examples given above like this, for instance:

> . . . *In their final report, the investigators restated their initial finding that the crash was caused by pilot error, and the case was officially closed.*
>
> *Colleagues of Captain Higgins were far from convinced by this verdict,*

however. They pointed to his unblemished 20-year record of service and immediately began to press for the case to be further investigated. . . .

It would not be wrong, but it would be a missed opportunity.

Always try to think across the paragraph gap. Always be aware as you bring one paragraph to an end that another paragraph is about to begin, and try to cue in the new paragraph from the old. Always be sensitive to the words you are using, for you will often find when you are looking for a way to start a new paragraph that the inspiration will lie in something you have just written. If you can link sentence to sentence and paragraph to paragraph effectively, you will be well on the way to becoming a good writer.

CONSTRUCTING PARAGRAPHS: AN OVERVIEW

- The basic rule: One idea, one paragraph.
- A paragraph should consist of one basic idea and the material needed to support or illustrate that idea.
- The paragraph's main idea should normally be expressed in a topic sentence.
- The topic sentence is a nucleus to which all the other sentences in the paragraph should relate.
- Coherence is the basic virtue required of a good paragraph.
- Coherence can be achieved through structural organization and the use of linkers.
- Wherever possible, a paragraph should be linked to the paragraphs that precede and follow it.
- Use linkers and cues to connect paragraphs.
- Always think across the gap—the gap between sentences and the gap between paragraphs—to make your writing flow.

Using Figurative Language

INTRODUCTION

Most of us are as familiar with the nonliteral senses of words as we are with the literal ones, and we use them continually. We are as likely to say that something is *in short supply* as to describe a person, piece of apparel, or length of time as *short*. These days we are perhaps more likely to say that someone *weaves* his or her way through the traffic or *weaves* something into a discussion than that someone *is weaving* a piece of cloth. Figurative expressions and meanings are part of our linguistic heritage. Almost all English idioms are figurative—*hold a candle to, hold your horses, hold your tongue, hold the line*—and we use them continually. In short, most of us are completely at ease with figurative language and take it more or less for granted as part and parcel of our everyday vocabulary.

Yet when the topic of figurative language arises, the discussion frequently takes the form of a long series of illustrations of what to avoid. However familiar we may be with figurative terms, using them, it seems, is rather dangerous.

There is, unfortunately, good reason for the negative approach adopted by many writers on this subject. Familiarity, in this particular area, seems to breed not so much contempt as insensitivity. We tend to overlook the fact that some of the words and expressions we are accustomed to using in their modern, usually abstract, senses still retain traces of their original meanings that applied, as often as not, to concrete objects and events in everyday life. We do not realize that these old concrete senses sometimes clash with the newer abstract ones. Alternatively, we may grasp at an idiomatic expression, because it seems lively or picturesque, or simply because it is very familiar, without stopping to think whether it expresses an idea exactly or expresses it in a fresh and individual way.

An ability to use figurative language effectively is one of the qualities that distinguishes good writers from bad, precisely because it involves sensitivity not only to the dictionary meanings of words but to what we might call their background and their aura. It involves being aware of the mental images that words are likely to conjure up in the minds of readers. It involves accurate knowledge of the real world, too, and some knowledge of history. Last but not least, it involves awareness of what other people say and write, because if most idioms are figurative, so too are most clichés, and how are we to avoid clichés if we do not know what expressions are common currency among our fellow speakers and writers? There may be dangers in using figurative language, but those dangers should not deter us from deploying the kinds of knowledge and skill mentioned above to good effect. This chapter will endeavor to show how this can be done, in addition to pointing out the perils along the way. First, however, we will examine the nature of figurative language.

THE NATURE OF FIGURATIVE LANGUAGE

The adjective figurative, as most, if not all, readers of this book will already know, is used to describe any use of language that is not literal. A *spade* is an implement used for digging. When we use the word *spade*, we will, in the vast majority of cases, be using it literally. We will be referring to an actual physical object that the person we are speaking to can see at the time or that he or she can easily visualize. When we use the word *spadework*, however, we are more likely to be using it figuratively. We will, again in the vast majority of cases, be referring not to the work of turning over the ground with an actual spade but to the hard or routine preparatory work required for any undertaking, work that may be mental rather than physical, work that may have nothing in common with the act of digging except that it is necessary, demanding, and fairly humdrum.

When we use the word *spadework*, therefore, we are implicitly comparing one kind of labor with another. If we say, for example, *Jim did all the spadework,* we are implicitly saying that the work that Jim did was comparable to that of a gardener who prepares an area of ground so that seed can be sown or plants set. It is important to recognize this fact because comparisons, either implicit or explicit, are the basis of almost all figurative use of language. We are also, at least in theory, asking our listeners or readers to make the same comparison.

In practice, most people know what is generally meant by *spadework*. If by any chance they do not, they can look the word up in a dictionary, which will give the figurative senses of most words alongside their literal ones. There is certainly no need for them to visualize someone working with a spade in order to understand what kind of work is involved. In fact, any attempt to visualize spadework as such is likely to lead to confusion rather than enlightenment.

If you were trying to describe an object that was unfamiliar to someone, it might be useful to say that it was "shaped like a spade" or "about the same size as a spade" or that "you use it like a spade." When you say something of that kind, you invite your listener or reader to visualize a spade, an object that they are likely to be familiar with, in order to understand what the less familiar object is like. But it would make little sense to tell someone who was unfamiliar with a particular kind of work that it was "like spadework." That would, in the first place, involve comparing it with something that derived its meaning only from being compared to something else. In the second place, *spadework* as generally understood—that is, in its more common figurative sense—is too abstract and general a term to be much help in explaining a particular, concrete task.

This simple example enables us to take our definition of figurative language a little further. Figurative language is based on comparison. The comparisons on which it is based usually refer to things that are, or used to be, concrete, familiar, and easy to visualize. This is how the many familiar words that now have dictionary-attested figurative senses originally acquired them. The adjective *cold,* for example, is used in meanings that extend into realms far from that of temperature, where the word literally belongs. For warm-blooded beings, the imaginative leap that had to be made from *a cold day, cold water,* or *cold hands* to *a cold heart, cold comfort,* or *cold eyes* was not a very great one, and the association between low temperature and lack of humanity or emotion is one that still comes naturally to almost every person. It must have come equally naturally to the people who developed the usual modern sense of *spadework* to equate basic humdrum work of any kind with the everyday labor of turning the soil. It might not come so easily to us today when gardening is thought of mainly as a leisure activity, and many city dwellers may not lay hands on a spade from one year's end to the next. This simply goes to show that an awareness of history, the history of everyday life rather than that of great events, is a great asset to anyone who wishes to understand figurative language and use it correctly.

Figurative language as we know it today, then, derives mainly from an effort on the part of our ancestors to explain more abstract or complex concepts by relating them to simpler and everyday ones. There is a process of comparison implicit in the figurative use of words. Because we are now so familiar with the figurative senses of words such as *cold* or *spadework,* we tend to skip over the process of comparison and may even be unaware that a process of comparison is involved. That is where danger sometimes lies.

THE FUNCTION OF FIGURATIVE LANGUAGE

The basic function of figurative language derives from its essential nature. Figurative language is used to present something more vividly to the reader's imagination, and his or her understanding, than would be possible through the use of literal language alone. Its purpose is to bring an idea home to the reader or listener and make it stick in his or her mind. In particular, figurative language aims to bring home something abstract, complex, or unfamiliar by comparing it to something concrete, simple, or familiar to the reader's or listener's experience.

In act 1, scene 5 of *Macbeth,* for instance, when Macbeth returns home for the first time after encountering the witches, Shakespeare could have made Lady Macbeth say to him something to the effect of: "It would be quite obvious to anyone who looked at your face, my thane, that you were preoccupied with thinking about things that you find strange and worrying." That statement is perfectly clear. It is easy to understand, because the language is simple and straightforward, but there is nothing in those plain and, in fact, fairly abstract words that activates the inner eye of the imagination. You can read those words and by an intellectual process note what is being said, but there is nothing in them that, to change the metaphor, reaches out to you in such a way that you can grasp it with more than the neutral intellect. The fact that the statement is neither poetic nor dramatic and makes Lady Macbeth sound like a disinterested observer, which she emphatically is not, is, for our purposes, incidental.

Shakespeare was acutely aware that he was presenting a dramatic moment and equally aware that if his words did not hit home immediately the moment would be gone. So he has Lady Macbeth express herself far more pithily and memorably: "Your face, my thane, is as a book where men / May read strange matters" (1.5.61–62). Instead of presenting us with such abstract words as "obvious," "preoccupied," "thinking," he gives us a word for a concrete and familiar object, a book. Although a person's face does not greatly resemble an open book, the idea that a people's emotional or mental states can be as easily perceived from their facial expressions as information can be derived from the page is one that almost anyone can respond to immediately. The comparison seems apt, just as it seems apt to equate lack of a normal human response with low temperatures. The image has certainly stuck in the minds of English-speaking people, for we still say that "someone's face is like a book," just as we say that guilt or some other feeling is "written all over someone's face."

Shakespeare, then, is using figurative language precisely as it ought to be used—to imprint something in the mind by using the concrete and familiar to represent the abstract and unfamiliar and make the latter easier to visualize and understand. But it is comparatively easy to appreciate figurative use in a great writer, especially a great poet. It is not always so easy to use it in your own writing.

USING FIGURATIVE LANGUAGE

We need to draw a distinction here between what we might call the everyday use of figurative language and its use for special effect. As was said in the introduction to this chapter, we use figurative language all the time. It is actually quite difficult to write more than a few sentences without using some word or phrase that is not intended to be understood in its literal sense. If an expression like *a cold heart* or a word such as *spadework* best expresses your idea in a particular context, then you should go ahead and use it, bearing in mind the warnings about dead metaphors and clichés (*see* THE PERILS OF FIGURATIVE LANGUAGE, page 161).

Using figurative language for special effect is a rather different matter. The opportunities for writers of ordinary prose to use the kind of imagery that occurs on every page in Shakespeare's works is limited. If you are not writing to entertain your readers but principally to inform them, figurative devices are probably best reserved for occasions when you want to make a point particularly strongly—and when your inspiration is operating at a particularly high level. A powerful image will stand out in a passage of ordinary literal prose, and if the image is not powerful, then there is probably no point in using it at all. Above all, you should resist the temptation to use figurative language as a kind of decoration. Even in literary contexts, readers will soon weary of prose poetry, unless it is very well done:

The Moon rose like a golden penny in a night as black as a magician's cape.

The above sentence tells you very little about the Moon or the night or what is going on, but it tells you a lot about the writer's attitude and skill. Figurative devices should always serve a purpose, and their original purpose, it should be remembered, is to make unfamiliar things more intelligible. That original purpose may sometimes be modified. It is perfectly acceptable to use a telling image to make the reader look at a familiar object in a new way or to give what is being said greater emphasis. But merely prettifying your prose is not a serious or worthwhile purpose.

Before we proceed with this discussion, however, let us briefly review the range of figurative devices available to the writer.

FIGURATIVE DEVICES

Figures of speech come in many varieties, but the two most common, and the two that most concern us here, are metaphors and similes. Both involve comparison. In a simile, the comparison is made explicit by the use of a word such as *as* or *like*. In a metaphor, there is no explicit pointer to the fact that a comparison is being made.

Consequently,

His hair was as white as snow.

My love is like a red, red rose.

She dances like a pregnant camel.

and

Your face, my thane, is as a book where men / May read strange matters.

are sentences that contain similes. Conversely,

All flesh is grass.

Love is a butterfly with gilded wings.

My heart was dancing for joy.

and

I am in blood / Stepped in so far that, should I wade no more, / Returning were as tedious as go o'er.

are sentences that contain metaphors. (The latter, by the way, is also from *Macbeth* [3.4.135–137].)

Two other devices deserve a very brief mention. Personification is a metaphorical use of language in which inanimate objects or animals are described as if they were human, as in:

The Sun peeped over the edge of the world and looked around.

Hyperbole is deliberate exaggeration:

If she was holding forth in New York, her voice would be heard in New Jersey, and probably in New Hampshire as well.

Personification is unlikely to be used very frequently by the writer of ordinary, informative prose. Hyperbole is frequent in informal language (*I had to wait ages; There's a mountain of work waiting for me in the office*) but rare in serious writing. Both devices may have a place in what is nowadays probably one of the main repositories of figurative writing for effect: comedy.

THE PLACE FOR FIGURATIVE LANGUAGE

Let us resume our discussion of where figurative devices, as opposed to everyday figurative senses, can best be used.

The basic purpose of similes, metaphors, and other figurative devices is to bring something home to the reader vividly and immediately. Hence, instead of writing

Trying to stop money being wasted in this organization is a frustrating and ultimately futile task.

we might write,

Trying to stop money being wasted in this organization is like trying to hold water in a sieve.

Instead of

It was not a constructive criticism; it was a direct personal insult.

we might choose to say,

It was not a constructive criticism; it was a slap in the face.

In both instances, the images used are appropriate to the idea that is being expressed and are more graphic and forceful than the literal statements. Neither image is particularly original, but neither is among the most overused clichés. On the whole, this is the safest kind of image to use. If you choose more original or out-of-the-way images, you run two risks. The first is that the reader may not know what you are talking about. If you wrote, for example,

> *Trying to stop money being wasted in this organization is like trying to repair a leaking faucet with a paper washer.*

you would undoubtedly have produced a more original simile, but it might take those of your readers who were not plumbers or do-it-yourselfers a while to understand what you were implying. The second is that the image may claim more than its fair share of the reader's attention. If you wrote,

> *It was not a constructive criticism; it was a bucket of spit poured over the man's best suit.*

you would have produced a more arresting metaphor than the customary *slap in the face,* but you might find the reader savoring the details of the image rather than attending to the essential point. You need to bear these considerations in mind when choosing or coining a figurative expression. You may also need to think carefully about how you will follow up on your image.

Figurative expressions tend to be showstoppers. They are by nature more vivid and arresting than factual statements, and they tend also to be complete in themselves, inasmuch as they are easy to grasp and, thus, self-explanatory or else they have failed in their basic purposes. If you say,

> *It was not a constructive criticism; it was a bucket of spit poured over the man's best suit.*

you cannot really go on to develop the idea and explain what you mean by it, because that would defeat the basic purpose of using an image and be tantamount to confessing that the image was there primarily for effect and not to aid the reader's understanding.

If you say,

> *Trying to stop money being wasted in this organization is a frustrating and ultimately futile task.*

you can cue in your next sentence from any of the words or phrases contained in it:

> *Trying to stop money being wasted in this organization is a frustrating and ultimately futile task. None of its members seems to realize that a dollar saved is a dollar earned. . . .*

> *Trying to stop money being wasted in this organization is a frustrating and ultimately futile task. I have striven in vain to inculcate habits of economy in the staff, but . . .*

> *Trying to stop money being wasted in this organization is a frustrating and ultimately futile task. It is frustrating because it is so obvious where savings could be made, and it is futile because . . .*

However if you say,

> *Trying to stop money being wasted in this organization is like trying to hold water in a sieve.*

perhaps only the second of the three options suggested above makes a satisfactory continuation. You would probably not wish to follow a homely image with a homely saying in the next sentence, as in option one, and option three is individually tailored to the factual sentence. You might be tempted to try and continue the simile, but it is usually difficult to stretch an image without its starting to seem contrived:

> *Trying to stop money being wasted in this organization is like trying to hold water in a sieve. The whole setup is full of holes through which cash is continually leaking. . . .*

On the whole, it is usually best to reserve an image for a point in your argument or story where it can act as a kind of clincher, expressing something or summing up something decisively. Treat it as something that temporarily stops the show. Be prepared to make a fresh start in the next sentence.

COMIC IMAGERY

We live in a rather prosaic age in which the predominant style in most kinds of writing is sober and factual and we are usually ill at ease with the high-flown and poetic. If writers attempt anything very original or imaginative in serious contexts, they are likely to feel that they are sticking their necks out. We are continually reminded that "less is more," and understatement is, quite rightly, held to be more effective in most situations than overstatement.

The one area where a writer can allow the imagination free rein is in comedy. There the usual criteria of appropriateness, good taste, and accuracy do not apply so strictly, and overstatement need not be out of place. If amusing your readers is your primary aim, or if you wish to provide your readers with a little light relief, then you may well find a space for the extravagant metaphor or simile that would be difficult to accommodate elsewhere:

> *Freud explaining humor is like a boa constrictor squeezing the life out of some rather charming little animal.*

> *Margaret swanned into the room, but ducked out again as soon as she caught sight of Father O'Reilly.*

> *Henry shot out of his seat like a cork from a champagne bottle.*

A degree of correspondence between the event described and the image used to describe it is as necessary in a humorous image as in any other kind, but otherwise the more inventive and exuberant you can be, the better. But where a sense of humor is a useful asset to anyone who wants to use figurative language, a sense of the ridiculous is vital to anyone who wants to avoid using it incorrectly.

THE PERILS OF FIGURATIVE LANGUAGE

There are three things to be especially wary of when using figurative language: choosing the wrong image through ignorance of the meaning of an established phrase or a faulty knowledge of the real world or history, mixing metaphors, and inadvertently bringing dead metaphors back to life.

Ignorance of Meaning

Consider the following example:

> *Besides, a well-chosen image can pull an unexpected punch. As the old saying goes, "One image is worth a thousand words. . . ."*

What the writer meant to say, evidently, was that a well-chosen image can *pack* an unexpected punch. To *pull* a punch, as anyone with an elementary knowledge of boxing knows, or as anyone can find out from the dictionary, is to refrain from putting the usual amount of force into it or to stop your fist before it makes contact with the other person.

Now take a look at this example:

> *It was a missed opportunity—that much was certain—but she was not greatly concerned. Like the proverbial musician, she had more than one string to her bow.*

A careful look at a violin bow would soon put this writer back on track. It was medieval archers who carried a spare bowstring and whose habits gave rise to this saying. You should always check in a dictionary or other reference work if you are uncertain about the usual wording of a familiar phrase or do not know its exact meaning or provenance.

Mixed Metaphors

A mixed metaphor is one in which two different images or figurative expressions are used together inappropriately. For instance, when a new opera house was opened in Cardiff, the capital of Wales, a prominent politician announced:

> *Wales has taken the stage on the map of the world.*

He was obviously trying to express his sense that the country had gained a new international prominence. He could hardly have chosen a more ham-handed way of doing so, mixing the idea of *taking the stage* with the idea of being *put on the map.*

Here is another example:

> *I warn you that, if we go down that road, we shall be entering a mine-*
> *field, and I, for one, will be walking on eggshells until we are clear on*
> *the other side.*

It is clear how the first image, *go down that road,* (though a terrible cliché) suggests the others. If the writer had stopped after *minefield,* the result would have been an acceptable sentence. To add the idea of *walking on eggshells* to the idea of entering a minefield reduces the whole sentence to absurdity.

The way to avoid such disasters is to put back the element that we so often leave out—visualization. If you try to visualize the literal sense of what you are saying—visualize someone entering a literal minefield, then visualize someone walking on literal eggshells; or, visualize an actor taking the stage, and then visualize a map of the world—you are far less likely to commit this kind of offense against common sense.

Dead Metaphors

Dead metaphors are words and phrase that have become so familiar that readers and writers usually use them without any sense at all of their metaphorical origins. We would never think of choosing them in order to make the unfamiliar more familiar or to bring something home to a reader's imagination. If you call someone or something a *lame duck,* you do not expect the reader's mind to flash up an image of an unfortunate bird that needs help in walking. *Spadework,* referred to at the beginning of the chapter, is a similar case.

There is nothing wrong with dead metaphors and no need to avoid them. They are the staple material for the everyday use of figurative terms. But there are situations where a mischievous person or an inappropriate context can suddenly bring the long-gone original senses of these words back to life, usually with unintended comic effect:

> *They were left with 500 pairs of men's fashion boots on their hands.*

> *Many women still find they are left dangling under the glass ceiling.*

Tired and unresponsive readers may take these sentences at their face value and not notice the howlers. Writers should always be on the lookout for them. The fact you intended a word to be understood in one sense does not mean a reader may not decide to take it in another. Many words carry, as it were, unexploded alternative meanings. Here, to take a less obviously ludicrous example, is the first draft of two sentences from earlier in this chapter:

> *When we use the word* spadework, *however, we are more likely to be*
> *using it figuratively. We will, again in the vast majority of cases, be refer-*

*ring not to the work of turning over the ground with an actual spade,
but to hard or routine preparatory work in any field.*

In most contexts, it would be perfectly acceptable to use the word *field* to
mean "area of activity." In this instance, the proximity of the words *ground*
and *spade* brings the original agricultural sense of *field* back to life. Fortunately, we realized at once that this was a mistake and recast the sentence.

When you choose a word, always bear in mind the context in which it
will appear and make sure it is right for that context. Again, visualize the literal sense, and, if in doubt, stick to the plain and literal:

They were left with 500 pairs of men's fashion boots to dispose of.

*Many women still find that there are limits to how far they can advance
in their profession.*

USING FIGURATIVE LANGUAGE: AN OVERVIEW

- Figurative language is based on comparison, particularly comparison of
  the abstract and unfamiliar with the concrete and familiar.
- Figurative language is particularly vivid, and its main purpose is to bring
  something home forcefully to the reader.
- Use figurative devices such as metaphors and similes sparingly in ordinary prose.
- Be wary of extended metaphors or similes, mixed metaphors, and dead
  metaphors.
- Be aware of the context in which a figurative word or expression
  appears.
- If in doubt, stick to the plain and literal.

Choosing a Style

INTRODUCTION

A good deal of the discussion so far has had to do with making choices. Do we accept, reject, or modify the words in which an idea first presents itself to us? How do we choose, from among all the options that the English language offers us, the word or phrase that most effectively expresses our meaning?

In endeavoring to decide how to make these choices, we have been guided by a concept of style in the abstract. We have had our attention fixed on those qualities that characterize good writing under any circumstances, as well as on the techniques that should enable us to produce it. Every piece of writing should aim to be clear, elegant, and vigorous; every sentence and paragraph should be grammatically sound and constructed in such a way as to present the thought it contains most advantageously to the reader.

But although there are choices to be made at every stage in the process, if we want to achieve good style, we really have no choice at all. We cannot deliberately choose not to try to be stylish—or, at least, we can only do so on the same terms that a worker in any other sphere might choose to be incompetent, choose to do a bad job, or choose to lose money for the business he or she works for.

There is no choice as regards the basics of style. So, when we talk about choosing a style, we are moving on to deal with particular styles, as discussed at the beginning of this book (*see* DEFINING THE TERM, page 5). We have to choose among different styles for different circumstances and readers.

Even so, it may seem peculiar to some readers that a writer might want to adopt a particular style in order to carry out a particular writing task. Can you really change the whole way in which you write? Could it really ever happen, for instance, that a novelist would wake up in the morning and say, "Yesterday I wrote like Donna Tartt, but today I'm going to write like John Grisham." In fact, it may seem not only peculiar but also dishonest. What happened to spontaneity? What happened to sincerity? Is it not every writer's aim to express himself or herself? Does every writer not owe it to his or her readers to tell them the truth as he or she sees it? If the best style is clear, transparent, and more like see-through clothing than a fancy getup, as was suggested earlier in this book (*see* HOW DOES STYLE RELATE TO CONTENT? page

12), how does this square with the idea of choosing a style, which sounds more like searching through your closet for a suitable outfit than stepping out proudly naked into the world?

Well, most of us do go out clothed rather than naked, yet we remain the same people underneath. It is seldom possible to change the whole way in which we write, but then there is seldom any need to do so. Whatever the circumstances, our writing will—and ought to—retain its personal stamp. Whatever the circumstances, our writing should conform to the basic requirements of good style. At the same time, however, it makes sense to adjust our writing, when necessary, to meet the demands of a particular situation. This means imposing an additional set of stylistic criteria on our work either as we produce it or when we go back and revise it. There is nothing dishonest in this. It is, after all, what people in all walks of life have to do every day.

People Who Adjust

Businesspeople are sensitive to the needs and demands of their customers. They will try to ensure that there is a market for a new product before they begin to produce it. If a particular product is not selling well, they will adapt it to make it more attractive to potential buyers. They may, as many successful entrepreneurs have done, set out to create a market where none existed before, but even in these cases they will realize that they cannot simply command their customers to desire and buy their goods. They have to take their customers into account, persuade them, and negotiate with them until they win their acceptance of the new line.

In the same way, writers have to consult the needs of their "customers," that is, their readers. It makes obvious sense to write in a way that will suit your readers. If you wish to get your ideas across to them, you will need to write in a way that speaks to them and their concerns. You will need to make your writing understandable to them, and you will need to keep their interest. There are circumstances when writing in accordance with your own personal tastes and even writing in accordance with the dictates of good style will not be enough. If you are writing for a readership that is in any way specialized, you may well need to adapt your writing to suit that specialization.

A writer may sometimes be in the position of the cutting-edge entrepreneur whose idea is ahead of its market. Original writers and original artists in any field sometimes create work for which there is as yet no audience. If what they have to offer is genuinely valuable, then, in time, it will create a new audience or win over an old one. When you are not operating at the cutting edge, however, then the normal principles of good business apply: You need to be attentive to the requirements and tastes of your readers and to "customize" your writing, as far as possible, for their benefit.

If you are, or wish to become, a professional writer, you will most definitely have to apply business principles to your work. You will need to know what publishers and readers want and try to cater to their wishes. You will need to conduct basic market research to find out, for example, what kind of material is usually published in the magazine you would like to write for or in what form scripts should be presented to the TV show you hope to write for. But perhaps you do not have professional ambitions. In that case, the comparison with business practices elaborated in the preceding paragraphs may seem irrelevant or inappropriate. Let us consider another type of person who at all times has to take his or her audience into account.

Imagine an actor in a large theater playing, let's say, Shakespeare's Hamlet and delivering a speech to an audience of 2,000 people or more. However private the sentiments contained in the speech and however intimate the setting—for Hamlet is a character with a personal mission and he has been entrusted by his father's ghost with a highly dangerous secret—every syllable the actor utters must be clearly audible and every gesture he makes must be clearly visible to everyone in the theater, including the people seated in the very back row of the gallery. Consequently, the actor must speak louder than he would in real life and project his voice outward toward the far end of the theater. He must also ensure that his hand and facial movements are very clearly defined.

Now imagine that actor delivering the same intimate soliloquy in close-up to a movie or TV camera, with a microphone a few feet away from his mouth. In that situation, he has no need to throw his voice. He can speak in a real-life whisper if he so chooses and still be heard. He knows that, with his face projected giant-size on a movie screen, the blink of his eye or the twitch of his cheek muscle can convey as much as the most elaborate hand gesture would in live theater. In fact, he will know that the larger-than-life body language that is acceptable and often necessary on stage can look exaggerated and out of place on screen. The different media—the different situations—demand different acting styles.

Different media and different situations likewise demand different writing styles. And when we are discussing style in this sense, we cannot really say that one style is necessarily better than another any more than we can say that screen acting is necessarily better than stage acting. An actor who tried to reproduce his or her style of stage performance on screen might well fail, as might a screen actor who performed on stage as he or she would on set. If you tried to write a speech in exactly the same style in which you would normally write a letter, you could be equally unsuccessful. There are conventions that govern different types of acting and different types of writing. You need to know these conventions, and you need to observe them. There are certain actors who, as the saying is, can "only ever play themselves." You should not set out to become in any way typecast as a writer—at least not until you become a best-selling author, by which time you will probably have ceased to have any need for this book!

Let us, however, return to the question of adjustment of style, and consider the process from one final angle that should bring it even closer to home.

Joining the Party

Imagine that you are about to join a gathering. You are among the last to arrive, and by the time you arrive, an atmosphere has already established itself among the people there. What kind of atmosphere it is will depend on who those people are, how well they know one another, and what sort of occasion it is. It might, for argument's sake, be a wedding, a funeral, or a board meeting. Each of those situations is likely to impose slightly different "conventions" on the people who attend it.

Something has happened to you on the way to this gathering, and you are very eager to tell the people who are already there chatting among themselves all about it. How do you go about announcing or spreading your news?

That will depend to a large extent, of course, on the sort of person you are and the sort of news you have to give. If what you had to say was "I came up the driveway just ahead of the President and the First Lady" or "The house across the street is on fire," you would probably be justified in announcing it at the top of your voice no matter what anyone else was saying or doing. If your news was less urgent, however, you might well stop and think for a moment.

You would have a choice. You could assert your presence immediately and make your announcement to all and sundry or to anyone who happened to be listening, in which case you might perhaps change the whole mood of the gathering. Alternatively, you could hold back your announcement for a while, mingle with the other guests or attendees, gauge the atmosphere, find out who was there, and wait for a suitable opportunity to deliver your news. You might also adjust the volume and tone of your voice to suit the occasion. Indeed, since there is probably more than one way of wording the announcement you have to make, you might adjust your vocabulary to the circumstances as well. If you were telling your bowling buddies that a driver had just dented your fender in the parking lot, you would probably do it one way; if you were presenting the same story to the judge as a reason for being a few moments late coming to court, you would probably do it in another way.

The writer is in a similar position to the latecomer at a gathering. He or she has a story to tell or information to impart and is often faced with the same choice: to be assertive or to blend in. On many occasions he or she will want to blend in as a matter of courtesy on the one hand and as a matter of self-interest on the other, for it is in the writer's own interest to obtain a proper hearing for what he or she has to say. To "blend in," the writer must adopt the appropriate tone, vocabulary, and conventions to suit the circumstances; in other words, he or she must choose the appropriate style.

We have all probably been present on some occasion when somebody has misjudged the tone completely, made a joke that has fallen completely flat because the audience was not attuned to it or, worse, made a joke or remark that offended people. The embarrassment under these circumstances extends far beyond the maker of the gaffe, assuming he or she is even aware of what has happened. Writers are often not present to witness what happens when they get it wrong, but they should remember the equivalent social situation and, if in doubt, take the temperature of the situation before plunging into it.

Even if your temperament inclines you to assert yourself, it is worth examining the techniques that writers can use to adapt to circumstances. Once you have internalized them, they become as much part of your writing equipment as any other of your more innate qualities, and any writer should try to extend his or her range as far as possible.

This, then, is the concern of this chapter of this book. It will examine the nature of the relationship between writer and reader. It will suggest ways in which you can adjust your natural style, or the neutral style, to fit a variety of readers and circumstances. It will deal in some detail with the question of tone. Tone is, in fact, the keyword in this chapter, so let us begin by defining and discussing it.

FINDING THE APPROPRIATE TONE
What Is Tone?

Tone in writing is similar to, but not exactly the same as, tone of voice in speaking. The tone of a speaker's voice, as everyone knows, can convey a meaning—often an emotional meaning—that is additional to the plain meaning of the words spoken. It is possible, indeed, to take a particular set of words and imagine them being uttered in any number of different ways. Take the simple question "How many are there?" The meaning of these words will, in the first place, differ slightly depending on whether the speaker puts the stress on the word *are* or the word *there*, or, indeed, decides to stress the first word *How*. Moreover, you can easily imagine these words being spoken in a loud and bullying way by somebody who is trying to force information out of somebody else; in a timid and fearful way by somebody who is afraid that if there are a great many, he or she might be unable to cope; or in a tone of righteous indignation or shocked surprise by somebody who was expecting only a few and finds that there are in fact many.

In each of these cases, the speaker will vary the stress pattern and, more important, impart an appropriate quality to his or her voice. Quite possibly he or she will accompany the question with a gesture or with some kind of body language in order to reinforce that voice quality. If accompanied by a reassuring arm around the shoulders, the question could be made to sound encouraging and be made to carry the implication "Don't worry. However many there are, we'll cope." If accompanied by a wide-eyed look of wonder, it could convey the notion "You must be a very extraordinary person to have so many."

Unfortunately, as far as the writer is concerned, all of this is neither here nor there.

How many are there?

That is how the words look on the page or on the screen. You can put them into upper case, italic, or bold, you can write them in any color you like, but there is nothing you can really do with them, as they stand, to convey any of the richness of meaning that a speaker could communicate by flexing his or her vocal cords in a particular way, stretching out an arm, angling the body, or fluttering an eyelash.

How many are there?

There is nothing that the reader can do with these words, either. This is something that is very important for writers to understand. Until informed or persuaded otherwise, readers will assume that what they are reading is neutral.

If they associate the words on the page with any tone of voice at all, they will take it for granted that they are being delivered in an even voice, one that is not necessarily expressionless but carries no particular expression. Most words do not leap off the page. They sit firmly on the page. The reader looks at them, and they, so to speak, look right back at the reader, evenly and dispassionately. It is only when the reader's imagination begins to work on them that they acquire any distinctive tone. And it is you, the writer, who has to set the reader's imagination to work.

In the majority of cases, you would not, of course, be limited simply to the four words we have been using as an example. As a writer, you may not be able to utilize tone of voice, body language, or action, but you can at least describe it:

"How many are there?" he thundered/whispered/quavered/cooed.

"How many are there?" she asked impatiently/impulsively/ingratiatingly.

"How many are there?" they chorused, rushing to the window to see for themselves.

Nevertheless, there are occasions when you want the reader to understand the feeling that underlies the words without having to be explicitly told what that feeling is. In order to do this, you have to impart a certain emotional coloring to what you write. You have to choose your words and structure your sentences in such a way that the reader knows immediately what feeling you intend to convey. This coloring is what is meant by "tone." Tone is feeling or attitude embedded in text.

If we experiment a little, we will probably find that even a question as simple as the one we have been using as an example can be adjusted so as to convey a certain amount of tone. To put it another way, that we can usually embed a small amount of feeling or attitude in it:

"How many would you say there are?"

"How many are there, then, at a rough estimate?"

"I don't want to know roughly, approximately, or a ballpark figure. I want to know precisely. How many there are?"

As soon as we start to expand the question—in fact, as soon as we add quotation marks to indicate that the question is asked by somebody in the course of a conversational exchange—we begin to offer clues to the reader as to the tone of voice in which the words were spoken, and we prompt the reader to imagine the words being spoken in a particular way. A sensitive reader will register the fact that the way the first of the three examples above is phrased implies a relationship of some sort between the asker and the person to whom he or she poses the question. Most readers will easily perceive that the speaker in the third example asked the question in an irritated or peremptory tone and put the chief stress on the word *precisely*.

But, as was said at the beginning of this section, tone in writing is not exactly the same as tone of voice. It is useful to be able to reproduce tone of voice if you are engaged in the kind of writing in which you put words into the mouths of characters. You should, as has been said several times before, always be aware of how the words you write would sound if they were read aloud. You should read passages over to yourself in "your mind's voice," and, consequently, the tone of your inner voice is likely to be reproduced to some extent on paper. Nevertheless, when we are making specific comparisons between tone in writing and tone of voice, we find ourselves concentrating on relatively short passages of text. When people speak, they do not usually go on for page after page after page. Somebody says something, somebody else replies or something happens, the person who spoke first then speaks again, and his or her tone may change from remark to remark. Writing often involves a much more extended effort. Tone in writing frequently does have to be sustained for page after page after page. As a result, tone in writing is generally something less variable, less nuanced, and less pronounced than tone of voice.

If we were making a comparison with color, we would probably say that tone in writing often has to be fairly neutral. Precisely because writers and readers often have to "live with" pieces of writing for some considerable length of time, when we are discussing tone, we are more likely to be talking about shades of gray or pastel shades than about stark black and white or vivid red.

Strong and Neutral Tones

Tone, it was suggested earlier, is "feeling or attitude embedded in text." It is, naturally, easiest to write in a particular tone if you happen to have the feeling that you wish to communicate at the time of writing. If you are angry or hurt and write from inside that feeling and simply allow that feeling to spill over onto the page, then you will obviously tend to write in an angry or injured tone:

> *You are the most loathsome, disgusting reptile it has ever been my misfortune to meet. I would rather have dinner with an alligator in a swamp than accept any kind of invitation from you ever again.*

The reader or recipient is unlikely to mistake the way you are feeling if you write like that. Likewise, you might write,

> *This has to be the most gripping thriller I have read this year. It was taut; it was electrifying. It kept me guessing till the very last moment. I literally could not put it down. Every time I tried to put it aside, I felt I was deserting the characters and leaving them to their fate. I just had to know whether they made it safely onto the next page. How does Julie manage to get under her readers' skin like that?*

Prose of this type is exciting to read and also exciting to write. But feelings tend to wax and wane. Like any other special effect in writing, a tone of venomous hatred or breathless enthusiasm may be difficult to sustain extensively. It is easy to imagine a person writing a blazingly angry letter, but less easy to imagine somebody writing a blazingly angry report. Rave reviews for books or plays appear quite often; a dissertation that maintains its enthusiasm at the level shown in the example above must be a rarity, and such a production would not necessarily be appreciated by its academic assessors.

There are occasions when a writer feels the need to write with strong feeling and in a tone that adequately matches that feeling. He or she may even deliberately attempt to re-create such a feeling inside himself or herself, if it is not present at the time of writing, in order, for instance, to give authenticity to the words that a character says or to a description of that character's feelings. But more often than not, what is required is prose that does not wear its heart on its sleeve, prose that is fairly reticent and, as has been suggested before, does not call attention to itself but rather to the author's ideas or the information he or she wishes to communicate. Reasonably sober and reticent writing is not, therefore, necessarily toneless. It has tone of a different kind.

Writers do not usually need to ask themselves, "How angry or how enthusiastic should I be about this?" More often, writers are likely to find themselves pondering questions such as "Should I adopt a formal or an informal style in writing to this person or on this subject?" or "Should I treat this subject seriously, or should I treat it lightly?" or "How can I appear to be moderate, sober, and responsible and still be lively enough to hold my readers' interest?" Such questions relate to attitude as much as to feeling, to the writer's attitude both toward the subject and toward the reader. They dictate the tone that the writer will try to maintain. They are not, however, irrelevant, even when there is a strong emotion underlying the writing. After all, instead of

This has to be the most gripping thriller I have read this year.

you could write,

No other thriller that I have read this year has exerted such a powerful and tenacious hold on my imagination.

or

Wow! Gripping? You bet! Thriller of the year? It gets my vote!

The emotion and, therefore, the emotional tone remain the same in all three versions, but the level of formality and, therefore, the overall tone differ in each case.

The question of what precisely is meant by terms such as *formality* and *informality,* together with the larger question of how you impart tone to your writing, will be dealt with in chapter 9 (*see* EXPRESSING TONE THROUGH

WORDS, page 185). For the moment, having established what tone is and that it is often a quiet or subtle factor, let us concentrate on the factors that decide which tone you ought to adopt.

These are simple: the circumstances and your readers. The force of circumstances barely requires discussing. You would not write the same kind of speech for a wedding as for a funeral; you would not write a letter of appreciation in the same tone as a letter of complaint. Specific kinds of writing are discussed in part II. So let us turn our attention to the reader, because the relationship between writer and reader is not always entirely straightforward.

Writers and Readers

One of the most often quoted maxims with regard to writing is "Know your reader." Now, in any particular instance, the relationship between writer and reader may be based on knowledge, but it may equally well, at least at the outset, be a relationship of mutual ignorance. You may be writing to a friend; you may be writing to somebody who is just a name on an advertisement or in the phone directory. You may be presenting your work to a group of colleagues; you may be writing for the vast, anonymous public at large. If you know who is going to read your work, your task is much simpler. On the basis of your social or professional acquaintance with the person or people involved, you should know roughly what tone to adopt with them, how polite or formal you need to be, whether you can afford to make attempts at humor, and so on.

It is important to know your readers not only because you want to communicate with them appropriately and effectively—you do not want to offend them; you do not want to seem to be overestimating or underestimating their intelligence; you do perhaps want them to like what you have written and find it suitable, of appropriate, acceptable, or correct—but also because knowing them, to some degree, personalizes and thus facilitates the task of writing.

THE LONELY WRITER

Writers' magazines frequently print letters from their subscribers complaining about the loneliness of being a writer. There is the writer, shut away in a room, working at the computer or typewriter alone, often having no interaction with or feedback from the people he or she lives among, let alone the people he or she is writing for. Somewhere out there is the reader, perhaps shut away in another little room or going about his or her daily business, in any case, utterly oblivious of the writer's existence. The gulf between the two can seem enormous. A writer may feel that he or she is like a person sitting in front of a microphone in a radio studio sending messages out to receivers dotted at random across the city or countryside—except that the writer is never sure whether the microphone or the receivers are actually turned on.

Under such circumstances, it is easy for writers to become discouraged. Most types of communication are two-way processes. Writing often seems as if it is all one way.

But the writer who knows his or her reader does have a communications partner. He or she is not sending out messages into a void and so is probably less likely to feel alone and unloved and less likely to become disenchanted with the business of writing as a whole. It therefore makes sense to find out as much as you can about your potential readers, to ascertain their tastes, interests, and abilities, so that you can make them into full-fledged partners in communication and pitch your writing directly to them.

Promotional writing, for instance, usually seems to start out from the assumption that readers respond more favorably to communications that are addressed to them as individuals and that take their personal preferences into account. There is an information-gathering industry at work collecting, or deducing, as many facts as it can about the habits, opinions, and lifestyles of sectors of the public so that organizations such as commercial companies and political parties can more effectively target potential buyers, voters, and so on. Much of the information acquired in this way is probably far less accurate and certainly less personal than it is sometimes made to appear. Some recipients may even be put off by the familiar tone adopted in some promotional literature and by its assumption that it knows even better than they do what they need or think. But the ordinary writer is not being asked here to buy into the ethos of promotional writing, simply to take note of the importance it attaches to collecting every scrap of information it can about the people on the other side of the gulf.

Most ordinary writers will not have access to professionally gathered market research. Most ordinary writers can, however, conduct a certain amount of research into their readers' status and preferences and should seriously consider the merits of doing so. Let us repeat the points made before. To know your reader usually ensures that your writing will get a better reception; it also makes the task of writing easier.

THE INVISIBLE READER

If, for whatever reason, it is impossible for you to find out anything about the actual reader who is most likely to peruse your work, then try to imagine an invisible reader—either the average or the ideal reader for your work, whichever suits your temperament better—and dedicate your writing to that person. An effort of the imagination is required, even when you do know your reader, because that real reader is not sitting in the room with you. If you can listen, as this book has often advocated, to your inner voice, it is perhaps not so difficult to conjure up an "inner reader" who responds to and comments on what you are writing.

When, for example, you are putting the case for something, you will obviously wish to consider and deal with views that oppose your own. It is a relatively simple step to imagine a person who holds those opposing views with whom you are conducting a vigorous debate about the issue in question. You put forward an argument, the invisible reader or invisible debater—who is a skeptic if you are a believer, and a critic if you are an advocate—counters with an objection, which you should make as convincing as possible. This objection sparks off a further point on your side, and so the argument proceeds, and so, with luck, the piece starts to write itself.

This kind of imaginary conversation need not be limited to writing with an adversarial element in it. It can be applied to most kinds of writing. You can imagine, for instance, that you are reading your poem or story aloud to an audience of the people you would most like to impress or appeal to.

This technique does help. Engaging with an imaginary conversation or communications partner is often recommended as a method of getting your writing going and of keeping it going when you have problems putting down words on the page. For our immediate purposes, however, the main function of the invisible reader, like that of a real reader, is to guide you in your choice of tone and style and to help you stick consistently with that tone and style once you have chosen it.

RELATIONSHIP

Let us try to focus on the qualities in a real or an imagined reader that are going to affect your choice of tone and style. The first among these will be your relationship with the person you are writing to or for. Is he or she known to you? Is he or she a friend or colleague of yours?

The closer the relationship between you and the reader, the easier it is to assess the kind of reception that your writing will meet with, and the fewer constraints there are on the way in which you write. You may write informally; you may use any kind of specialized or even private language as long as you are sure that it can be understood equally well by both of you; you will probably possess roughly the same range of reference on the basis of experiences you have shared in the past (*see* RANGE OF REFERENCE, page 179). Indeed, you probably will not have to worry much about choosing a tone, since a friendly or collegial tone will emerge naturally from the writing situation.

But we need to generalize this discussion somewhat, for most people who are interested in style will be aiming at an audience beyond their immediate circle of acquaintances, and in any event, it is usually fairly obvious how you should go about addressing somebody you know. Let us assume that, as far as you are concerned, the wider world is composed of two types of people: peers and nonpeers. A peer is somebody who has the same status as you, somebody who is like you in most respects; a nonpeer is somebody who differs from you.

WRITING FOR PEERS AND NONPEERS

Peer-to-peer writing is probably the easiest kind of writing to accomplish apart from writing to somebody who is a personal acquaintance. When you write peer to peer, you can assume more or less that you are talking to yourself and do as you would be done by, adopting the kind of tone for your work that you would be happy to find in a similar work directed to you.

It is when you are writing for a nonpeer that the choices become more difficult. When you are writing to a nonpeer, you are most likely to have to consider adjusting the way you write.

First, however, you have to decide whether the reader you have in mind is a peer or a nonpeer. If you are an adult writing for other adults, you would assume you should write on a peer-to-peer basis. But suppose you were an adult female writing for a readership that consists mainly of adult males, or vice versa. Should you assume that difference in gender makes your likely readers nonpeers and adjust your style accordingly?

That is quite a tricky question and possibly a contentious one, too. There are circumstances where a readership of one gender would appreciate being addressed by a person who comes across strongly as a member of the other. There are, equally, circumstances in which any consideration of gender differences would be considered inappropriate. It is this sort of factor that a writer may have to weigh. The sensible course in this particular case would usually be to start out on the assumption that you are writing peer to peer and adopt a determinedly neutral approach and style, while making sure, as always, that your range of references is suited to your readers. Do not, for instance, if you are a man, attempt to explain something to a general female readership using obscure sporting metaphors.

Let us move on to less disputed ground. How should you proceed if you are a student writing for an instructor or an employee writing for your boss? Different people use different teaching and managerial styles, and consequently, there are different degrees of aloofness in relationships between teachers and their students and between managers and their staff. In many cases there will be no aloofness at all, and the relationship will be one of peer to peer. But if you regard the person you are writing for as senior to you, and that person tends to assume seniority, what course should you take?

There is a perhaps natural tendency in most of us to express respect through greater carefulness in what we say. We do not wish to offend a person whom we do not know, particularly a person who is senior to us. We tend to think twice before inserting slang or colloquial expressions or jokes, whereas we would not hesitate to use them when writing to a friend. In short, we formalize our style and language. Formality is a gesture of respect.

Informal or colloquial language, in fact, is often defined as the kind of language people use when communicating on easy terms with their friends and peers. When you start a letter with *Dear George* or *Dear Friends* or *Hi,* you will probably continue in something approximating the style of ordinary casual conversation. If you are communicating with people whom you do not know or who are senior to you in age or position, just as when you begin a letter *Dear Ms. Wanamaker* or *Dear Sir or Madam,* you expect to continue in "written" English and a more formal style.

This instinctive tendency to heighten style when addressing a senior nonpeer is essentially a sound one. Nevertheless, the modern age is in most respects far less formal than its predecessors. People are less deferential than they used to be and also perhaps less conscious of their own dignity. The days when ladies and gentlemen seemed to owe it to themselves and to their readers and listeners to raise themselves on lofty stilts when holding forth on a subject are over. Language itself seems less deferential, and campaigns for simple English and for making official documents more accessible have tended to reduce people's acquaintance with the higher levels of vocabulary and style. Regular readers of academic journals still sometimes have to wrestle with obscure concepts and stylized prose, but the majority of us do not.

This is essentially a good thing. But it has had the effect of making writers less familiar with formal language and style and so less able to use it confidently. Nevertheless, if people do not stand so much on their dignity, they still have it. They want to be respected and consequently want to be written to with respect, which is different from deference. It is of the utmost importance that writers should master a tone and style that is adequate for this purpose. In keeping with the spirit of the present age, however, this tone and style is better described as "neutral" than as formal. It is, in other words, a style that is not informal—it preserves a certain respectful distance between the writer and the reader—but at the same time it is not formal—it does not consciously strive to elevate itself and create greater distance either between writer and reader or between itself and the spoken language. This book, for instance, is written in a neutral style.

The subject of the "neutral style," which, it should be noted, does not have to be defined solely by negatives, is further discussed in chapter 9 (*see* EXPRESSING TONE THROUGH WORDS, page 185). Let us now return to the subject of the writer-reader relationship.

AS SMART AS YOU ARE?

We have been discussing the respect that a writer owes to certain categories of readers. There is one kind of respect, however, that the writer owes to all readers, which is best summed up as follows: Remember that your reader is as smart as you are.

Most readers do not want to be deferred to; no reader wants to be condescended to. This is another tricky point. It is a common enough situation for a writer to possess information that he or she assumes the reader does not possess. The principal exception to this is a student writing an essay for a teacher. At whatever level the student ought usually to take for granted that the teacher is better informed on most subjects than he or she is. The main purpose of student writing is to demonstrate the student's ability to understand a subject; form personal, and hopefully interesting, opinions about it; and present those opinions in lively and literate prose. Outside the academic context, however, the purpose of writing is generally to inform and/or entertain. The writer has information to give and should assume at the outset that he or she understands the subject in question better than the reader does. Otherwise, what is the purpose of making demands on the reader's time and attention?

This knowledge does not make the writer more intelligent than the reader, but it does mean that the writer is not always addressing the reader exactly as peer to peer. The writer, therefore, has to make allowances for the reader's lesser degree of understanding without seeming to imply that the reader is less intelligent than he or she is.

It might appear that this has a great deal to do with the writer's attitude, and that the number of writers who actually start out with an attitude of arrogant superiority toward their readers is probably, and thankfully, small. But it also has something to do with the writer's choice and use of language. As long as a writer cultivates the qualities of style as defined in chapter 3 of this book—particularly clarity and simplicity—all should be well. If your writing is clear and simple, it stands to reason that it should be understandable to almost everybody. But, like all such qualities, clarity and simplicity can be to some degree relative and subjective. In particular, if you happen to be well versed in a subject because it is how you make your living or because you have researched it long and thoroughly, you may, almost unawares, have reached such a level of familiarity with it that what seems clear and straightforward to you is nevertheless Greek to the ordinary layperson.

Here is a case in point. A student once took a vacation job in a small nursery where tomatoes and cucumbers were grown in greenhouses for the local market. One of the tasks he was asked to perform by the owner was to sort recently picked tomatoes. His instructions were to separate the tomatoes into pinks, pink and whites, and whites and to put the different kinds into separate boxes ready for delivery.

The instructions seemed perfectly clear and simple to the student, and the owner must have assumed they were perfectly clear and simple as well, for he immediately left to attend to some other matter. When the student set about the task, he found that the task was not quite as straightforward as he had at first imagined. The vast majority of the tomatoes looked red or near-red, naturally enough, since they were about to be sent off for sale, and there were very few that looked pink and white, let alone white.

Not wishing to appear stupid, because the instructions were, after all, very simple, and he was, after all, a college student and a pretty intelligent fellow, he did not set out to find the owner and ask for clarification but instead interpreted the instructions as meaning that he should sort the tomatoes into those that seemed ripe, those that seemed fairly ripe, and those that seemed fairly unripe. Since he was dealing with a fruit that began pale and got redder as it ripened, this seemed to be a not unreasonable way to proceed.

Reasonable-seeming or not, it was totally wrong, as the student found out when the owner returned and immediately lambasted him for mixing up the pinks, pink and whites, and whites. The owner then demonstrated, as if for the benefit of a very slow-witted individual, the correct method of sorting tomatoes, which was by size. "These are your pinks," he said assembling a group of large tomatoes, "These are your pink and whites," assembling a group of medium-sized ones, and so on.

As the somewhat mortified student began the task of resorting the whole delivery, he was left to reflect on the pitfalls that can be hidden in even the most apparently simple language. It was only later, and from somebody else, that he discovered that traditionally, large tomatoes had been wrapped in pink paper, medium-sized tomatoes in pink and white paper, and small tomatoes in white. Despite the fact that tomatoes were no longer individually wrapped, the color coding had stuck—at least in that nursery.

There are, no doubt, lessons in life to be learned from that anecdote; there are certainly lessons to be learned about the use of language. The terminology that you use in your trade or profession may not be comprehensible to other people. And a technical term does not have to be a multisyllabic jawbreaker or borrowed from a foreign language to be incomprehensible. A simple everyday word can cause confusion if it is used in a specialized meaning with which the listener or reader is not familiar. Use your imagination. Writers usually expect to be told to use their imaginations to conjure up new and exciting ideas or visions, but it is equally important that they should use their imaginations to place themselves in their readers' shoes and avoid misunderstandings.

RANGE OF REFERENCE

When we are writing on a subject, we naturally tend to draw on our experience of life and the world to illustrate and explain our arguments. We may need a concrete example to support a general point we are making. If we do, we automatically delve into our memory to find an incident or an experience that fits the bill. Our experience also weaves itself into the way we use language in more subtle ways. If somebody took the trouble to analyze the metaphors and similes that we habitually use, that person might well be able to discover a great deal about who and what we are. You are less likely to say that you will leave somebody or something to "simmer slowly" if you know absolutely nothing about cooking; you are not likely to find British people saying that someone has to "step up to the plate," because most British people have never played or watched baseball.

Our "range of reference," therefore, comprises those things from within our experience and knowledge that we draw on in our writing for purposes of illustration, explanation, and comparison. There is a common stock of experiences and knowledge that almost any person can reasonably be assumed to share. When we are writing for friends and peers, we can also assume a good deal of correspondence between their experience and our own. When we are writing for nonpeers, however, the situation may be different. Again, we should at one and the same time be cautious and imaginative—cautious in not making too many assumptions, imaginative in trying to empathize with the potential reader and in finding alternative and more generally understandable replacements for expressions that may not fall within his or her range of reference.

WRITING FOR CHILDREN

We can perhaps best sum up the points made in this section on the writer-reader relationship by considering a case study: the art or business of writing for children. Writing for children is a specialty. There are authors who have made their names by writing children's books, and all other authors owe them a special debt for fostering the reading habit among the young and preparing the next generation of adult readers. At the same time, many ordinary writers will on occasion have to produce text that is suitable for young readers. To attempt to do so is a good test of an (adult) writer's ability to empathize with a nonpeer reader and, in particular, to write for people who may be essentially as smart as he or she is, but who do not have the same vocabulary at their disposal or anything like the same knowledge of the world and range of reference.

You could, if you were so minded, practice making a text child-friendly by, for instance, taking definitions from a standard dictionary and reworking them. Here is the definition of the main sense of the word *otter* from the 10th edition of *Merriam-Webster's Collegiate Dictionary*:

> any of various largely aquatic carnivorous mammals (as genus *Lutra* or *Enhydra*) that are related to the weasels and minks and usu. have webbed and clawed feet and dark brown fur.

The editors have thoughtfully provided a picture of an otter beside the definition.

Now, there is nothing wrong with this definition as far as it goes. It is perfectly accurate and reasonably comprehensible to an adult, at least to an adult who is familiar with the ways of dictionaries. Dictionaries have to provide a great deal of information in a small space. They also have to try to be exhaustive. There are many kinds of otter, and they spend most but not all of their time in water. The desire for strict accuracy and considerations of space are like two opposing forces pulling in opposite directions. The solution to the problem is a use of language that employs few words but suggests manifold possibilities: "any of various largely aquatic carnivorous mammals . . ."

But where else, outside a dictionary, would you find such a phrase? In order to solve their own problems, lexicographers have invented a style of their own, sometimes referred to as "dictionaryese," that the reader has to become familiar with if he or she is to get full value out of an indispensable work of reference. Those of us who use dictionaries become accustomed quickly to this unique way of conveying information. It is only, perhaps, when we stop to think what a child might make of such a string of words as "any of various largely aquatic carnivorous mammals" that we realize that it is not particularly easy to understand.

Although the phrase does not contain any really very difficult words, its very compactness seems to aggravate the difficulty of the words that it does contain. It is like trying to swallow a very large mouthful all at once. The keyword, the noun, comes only at the end of the phrase and is plural (*mammals*), whereas an otter is singular, and we reach it only after negotiating the slightly obscure concepts *any of various* and *largely aquatic*. We soon realize that the former means that there are several different species or types of otter; and the latter, that otters spend a lot of their time in water, but do not live entirely in water. But would that be immediately obvious to a child? In this particular case, not until he or she was past the Latin terms in brackets would a child find any concrete information that is easy to visualize and relate to—assuming he or she knows what a mink and a weasel are.

But the point of this discussion is not to take issue with Merriam-Webster's defining style, but to see how such a style could be adapted to make it more suitable for children. It needs to be simplified without becoming simplistic or inaccurate. It also needs to be "de-compacted," so that the younger reader does not have to deduce the relationship between a series of terms listed one after the other.

There are dictionaries specifically designed for children already in existence. They work on these principles. *Collins New School Dictionary*, in its second edition, for instance, defines an otter like this:

a small furry animal with a long tail. Otters swim well and eat fish.

The *Oxford School Dictionary*, third edition, on the other hand, describes an otter as a fish-eating animal with webbed feet, a flat tail, and thick brown fur, living near water.

It would seem apparent from these definitions that Collins has a rather younger reader in mind than does Oxford. Collins's vocabulary and construction are about as simple as they can possibly be. The definition is divided up into two separate sentences to avoid the problems of compacted word strings. The problem is that Collins has perhaps gone too far in simplifying the language of the definition and left us with an image of an otter as, possibly, a kind of aquatic, fish-eating mouse. Was the compiler possibly overeager to enter into what he or she assumed to be a child's way of seeing the world? Did he or she suppose that children lump together mice, hamsters, koalas, squirrels, chipmunks, and otters as "small furry animals" seeing only their common cuddliness and disregarding their other distinguishing features?

Oxford's compiler does not make that mistake. He or she assumes that children will have no problem with the concept of a "fish-eating animal" and lists four defining characteristics in a businesslike way. (Oxford's otter, admittedly, must have interbred with a beaver to produce its "flat tail"!) Neither Oxford nor Collins, however, mentions the otter's body shape. An ideal definition would probably work on the same basic principles as those used in the two schools dictionaries cited but adding a little more of the information provided by Merriam-Webster, such as the following:

an animal with a long slender body, short legs, webbed feet, thick fur, and a long tail that lives near water and spends a lot of time in it, hunting for its usual food, fish.

Any readers who wish to try the same experiment for themselves might like to produce a child-oriented version of the following, Merriam-Webster's definition of the common colloquial verb phrase *have it out:*

to settle a matter of contention by discussion or a fight.

Compilers of dictionaries have special problems to contend with, but the same factors that sometimes make their definitions less than child-friendly could equally well appear in passages of ordinary writing:

To anxious watchers on the ground it must have seemed inevitable that the balloon would enmesh itself in the branches of one of the tall trees crowning the crest of the ridge. Despite the balloonist's best efforts—for he was firing his gas jet in increasingly long bursts at decreasingly short intervals—the result of the unequal contest between gravity and hot air seemed a foregone conclusion. The expressions on the faces of the people in the basket were clearly visible. They mirrored and magnified the anxiety of those below.

There is a case for saying that children who have reached a certain age and acquired some proficiency in reading enjoy coming to grips with an adult style, and they must, of course, at some stage make the transition to general, that is, adult-oriented, material. But a writer who was describing this same incident specifically for children would probably approach the task somewhat differently, avoiding, for instance, the slightly complex grammar of the first sentence with its "empty subject," *it*. Such a writer might also think about the point of view from which the passage is written. The verb phrase *it must have seemed* implies that somebody (the writer) is looking at the event from the outside and knows, in fact, what is going to happen. Concreteness is a virtue in most writing and particularly in writing for children. Since the people on the ground play an important part in the incident, it might make sense to describe it as they see it:

> *The people on the ground could see that the balloon was getting lower and lower and thought it could no longer avoid getting tangled in the branches of the tall trees along the top of the ridge. They saw the spurt of flame and heard the hissing roar as the balloonist fired his gas jet. He was firing it in longer and longer bursts at shorter and shorter intervals. They knew he was getting worried.*

Concentrating on one point of view puts the reader more directly into the situation. For children, and perhaps for many other readers, involvement in the situation through sharing the view of one particular character or set of characters is more important than an overall view. It is also a fact that children often see things with startling clarity and in very literal terms. Although children enjoy fantasy and often enjoy stories where fantasy elements intrude into real life, when the subject is real life, they want genuine reality. It is unlikely that children would be able to grasp what the writer meant in the final sentence of the extract:

> *They mirrored and magnified the anxiety of those below.*

The writer no doubt hoped that his or her readers would appreciate a neat and sophisticated way of saying that the riders in the balloon looked even more anxious than the watchers on the ground. But the phrase takes us a long way from real mirrors and real magnifying, and a child might well ask whether their faces were really magnified and how this could happen. As always, it is better to say what you mean rather than to translate your meaning into a fine phrase:

> *The expressions on the faces of the people in the basket were clearly visible. Those people were very anxious indeed.*

Alternatively, you could return to the viewpoint of the people on the ground:

> *They could clearly see the expressions on the faces of the people in the basket. Those people were terrified.*

As was said earlier, writing for children is a specialty. Books have been written on the subject. The purpose of this discussion has been to highlight some of the problems involved and to use these as an illustration of the general need for writers to think about their readers and to be prepared, when necessary, to enter sensitively into their readers' imaginative worlds. That does not mean you have to pretend to be a child in order to write for children. Unless you are very skillful and fully immersed in the thinking and language of childhood, children will quickly find you out. It does mean that you have to write clearly and simply and to be aware of possible restrictions on your readers' vocabulary and range of reference, but those are good rules for writing for any kind of reader.

CHOOSING A STYLE: AN OVERVIEW

- Tone is feeling or attitude embedded in text.
- Tone in writing is not the same as tone of voice, but it works in a similar way.
- Most writing will require a fairly restrained tone and a neutral style.
- The circumstances and the reader will usually dictate the tone of your writing.
- Know your reader. Knowing your reader will not only help you in your choice of tone but also make the whole writing process less impersonal.
- It makes a difference whether you regard your reader as a peer or nonpeer.
- Respecting your reader involves a certain, but not excessive formality of style.
- Respecting your reader also involves taking into account the reader's likely vocabulary and range of reference.
- Simplicity and clarity are qualities that will make most writing suitable for the vast majority of readers.

Expressing Tone
through Words

INTRODUCTION

In the previous chapter we discussed the nature of tone and the considerations on which writers should base their choice of a particular tone for a particular piece of writing. The task of this chapter is to outline the process of delivering tone in words and, in particular, to examine some of the broad categories of tone that were referred to earlier in the book but not fully defined or discussed. This chapter, therefore, deals with the concepts of formality and informality in language, tone, and style. It also introduces a concept that has not featured previously in these pages, but that is a very useful one for discussing certain aspects of style, namely the linguistic concept of "register." From there, the chapter moves on to consider the question of emotiveness and objectivity in the use of language, a topic with an ethical dimension, for it has to do with the power of language to arouse feelings in the people who hear it or read it.

It is with the power of language, in fact, and the ethical considerations that flow from this power that we begin. The study of language and of style is a serious study because both language and style are powerful tools. A book such as this one needs to acknowledge that fact, and such considerations aptly frame our discussions in this chapter.

THE POWER OF LANGUAGE

Language has power. It can be used directly as an instrument of power to give commands, to condemn, or to pardon. It can also be used to exercise power indirectly through the effect it can have on the feelings, attitudes, and opinions of other people.

It is with this indirect influence that we are mainly concerned here. The writer's relationship with his or her readers was dealt with explicitly in the previous chapter. But throughout this book, in examining the nature of effective writing and good style, it has been taken for granted that the writer's basic aim is to speak to the reader, to convey information, emotion, and opinion to the reader. The techniques that have been advocated are intended to make the conveyance of information, emotion, and opinion to the reader more effective. Inevitably, therefore, we have been talking about ways in which the writer can influence the reader, sometimes directly, sometimes indirectly.

Another way of putting that is to say that this book deals, at least in part, with the writer's use of the power of language to sway the reader. Yet, where there is an exercise of power, there ought also to be an exercise of responsibility—and that is where the ethical dimension comes in.

LANGUAGE AND PICTURES

The power of language is sometimes doubted, particularly in our own time, when the power of the image is a more frequent study of debate. It sometimes seems as if words and images are vying for the upper hand. The first stage of the technological revolution that took place in the final years of the 20th century and made computers, cell phones, and the Internet as integral to the lives of ordinary people as televisions, telephones, and the electricity grid had been for some decades before, took the written and the spoken word as its starting point. The wonder was that messages and documents could be flashed across the continent or between continents. The wonders of the second stage of that revolution seem to have more to do with the capture and transmission of images through digital photography and camera cell phones. Furthermore, we are often told that human beings are becoming increasingly visual creatures. Continually bombarded with images, we are becoming more and more used to responding to them and more and more reliant on taking in information in graphic form. Some people even suggest that communication via language is under threat from our dependence on our eyes and on moving pictures on screens.

This is nothing new. The power of iconic images has been known about from very early times, and pictures have been used to inform the people at least since the days when Bible stories were depicted in the stained glass of church windows. We have been told since newspapers began printing photographs that "One [or a] picture is worth a thousand words." Nobody would deny the potency of a well-taken or luckily captured photograph, but, with a thousand words at their disposal, writers worth their salt ought to be able to move or stir people as deeply as photographers can and, at the same time, outdo the photographers in the amount of descriptive and explanatory material they can provide. It is important to insist that, even in a visual-friendly age, words are not a dying medium and do retain their potency. It is not a waste of time to learn how to use a thousand words, or many fewer, to describe a situation or make a case as effectively as a photograph can.

Ethical Considerations

Another old media adage tells us that "The camera cannot [or does not] lie." While we may have become more dependent on having information presented to us in pictorial form, we have also become more sophisticated in our assessment of the images presented to us. We know that images can be manipulated; indeed, the computer software that goes with digital cameras enables us to do a certain amount of image manipulation for ourselves. It is possible to remove intrusive or inappropriate elements from the scene that we photographed in order to produce a more pleasing final image.

What the layperson with a digital camera can do today, the professionally skilled photographer has been able to do more or less since the camera was invented. A photograph of fairies dancing beside a brook in an English wood, taken in 1917, was declared to be genuine by Sir Arthur Conan Doyle, the creator of Sherlock Holmes, the astutest of all detectives. What many people suspected at the time has since been conclusively established: The picture was a clever fake. The camera can lie. Embarrassing incidents and persons can be airbrushed out of visual historical evidence, just as we can now enhance our digital photographs to make ourselves appear more skillful photographers than we really are.

When the camera learned to lie, it was, however, simply imitating its human operators who had perfected this ignoble art in words over the centuries. Words can represent the truth or distort it; they can provide an accurate account of situations or a false or biased one. It is in that sense that our present discussions are entering an area where questions of truth and falsehood, personal honesty and integrity, and their opposites are very relevant issues.

Power over the Reader

It was said in the previous chapter that words "sit firmly on the page" and that it is up to the writer to set the reader's imagination to work so that those words begin to "speak." But when we talk about setting the reader's imagination to work, are we not really implying that the writer has power over the reader and manipulates the reader's imagination or the reader himself or herself? Indeed we are. Words have power. Some of the power that they possess can, in fact, be illustrated by examining the different impressions conveyed by the two phrases that have just been used to describe this very process: "setting the reader's imagination to work" and "manipulating the reader."

If we say that we are "setting somebody's imagination to work," we surely suggest that the process we are initiating is essentially benign. To set children's imagination to work, for example, is a task for a teacher, a parent, or a book. Few people would argue that this was anything other than a legitimate and beneficial activity. An active imagination is, up to a point, a vital component of childhood; an active imagination, again up to a point and perhaps a slightly different point, is an asset to an adult as well.

But if we use the word *manipulating* in place of the phrase "setting the imagination to work," we convey a very different impression. If we talk about teachers, books, or parents "manipulating" the minds of children, we are unlikely to be thinking about a process that can safely be called benign. *Merriam-Webster's Collegiate Dictionary* (11th edition) informs us that *manipulate* can mean "to manage or utilize skillfully," on the one hand, and "to control or play upon by artful, unfair, or insidious means esp. to one's own advantage," on the other. It is difficult to keep that latter sense out of our minds entirely, even when the word is being used in the former sense. Whenever the word is used in connection with another person, or with another person's mental activity, the nonbenign connotations seem to make their presence especially strongly felt.

So when does setting the imagination to work become manipulation, and when does manipulation move from being skillful management to being artful, insidious, self-interested control? On which side of this rather subtle divide does the writer's activity fall?

Most writers, naturally enough, will assume that their intentions are innocent or honorable. If faced with this particular choice, they would probably opt for the phrase "setting the imagination to work." It describes accurately and truthfully what writers set out to do. Writers should, however, be aware that their activities could be described differently, that people can put "spin"— to use the modern political jargon—on almost any human action to make it appear more or less benign or admirable. Writers should also be honest enough to admit that they are among the people who use spin. Even if they do not actively spin for a particular party or cause, a lot of what they do manipulates their readers—at least in the first of the two senses cited from Merriam-Webster's dictionary. When we talk about "putting tone into words," we are essentially talking about influencing our readers in order to ensure that they receive the information we have to offer them in the correct spirit. We want them to understand the spirit of our message as well as the simple message.

In addition to the practical and aesthetic choices that writers have to make when they are creating or revising their work, there is sometimes an ethical choice or an ethical question confronting them. Do I attempt to influence the reader, or do I simply present the facts and leave the reader to make up his or her own mind? Have I presented the truth as it is—or at least as I see it—or have I, deliberately or accidentally, biased my account?

Telling the Truth

Most of us will have been raised to tell the truth and, when we write for other people, our aim is generally to tell them the truth—at least the truth as we see it. But how do we do this?

We return here to an issue that has concerned us at various points in this book: How much of ourselves do we put into our written work? As has been said before, it is virtually impossible to eliminate the personal element from style, nor in most instances should we wish to do so. But if we wish to tell the plain, unvarnished, and objective truth, can we afford to let any subjective elements in at all? Ought we not to aim at the kind of passive, unemotional recording famously evoked by the Anglo-American novelist Christopher Isherwood at the opening of his book *Goodbye to Berlin* (1939)?

> I am a camera with its shutter open, quite passive, recording not thinking. Recording the man shaving at the window opposite and the woman in the kimono washing her hair. Some day all of this will have to be developed, carefully printed, fixed.

Unfortunately, as we know, even the camera can lie. Furthermore, a human being usually has to choose which direction to point the camera in. It is probably impossible to perceive or record anything purely objectively, but at the same time there is a great deal that we can do to achieve at least relative objectivity. One of the main points to be discussed in this chapter will be how to keep what we write as objective as possible, how to write in a way that does not, either deliberately or inadvertently, prejudge the issue. This tricky and contentious subject will be dealt with later in the chapter (*see* EMOTIVENESS AND OBJECTIVITY, page 204).

It is not part of the purpose of this book to try to give moral lessons to writers. It is, however, very much part of its purpose to remind its readers of the power and potentialities of language and of the fact that writing, like most human activities, does not take place in a moral vacuum. You will be able to examine your own motives and will also know, depending on the kind of work you are doing, how much attention you have to pay to ethical considerations. In fiction, almost anything goes. If you are writing to inform, guide, or instruct others, however, then the onus is on you to be aware of your responsibilities toward both your readers and your subject matter.

Before we proceed any further with this discussion, however, there are other issues to be dealt with. Chief among them is the question of formality and informality.

FORMALITY AND INFORMALITY
The Hierarchy of Language

One of the many ways in which scholars attempt to organize language in order to understand better how it works is to classify words and senses of words according to the social context in which they are or ought to be used. As often as not, this form of classification results in what is in effect a language "hierarchy." Words and expressions are allocated to different levels in this hierarchy depending on their degree of acceptability and usefulness in various social situations and various kinds of writing.

When this form of classification is used, the bottom level of the hierarchy is usually made up of words that are considered vulgar or taboo, words that would cause shock or outrage if used in polite company or with children. In the next tier, usually, are slang words, words that people, especially young people, use within their own group and which may be unknown or incomprehensible to people outside that group. Slang words are generally colorful, frequently humorous, and sometimes racy. Their usefulness in most ordinary kinds of writing is limited.

As you go further up the hierarchy, so words become more widely and generally usable. In the middle reside those words that are the mainstay of Standard English, the words that none of us can do without and that form the bulk of all communication. As you move higher still, however, so the number of words in each category decreases, as does the range of applicability of each category. Literary words, which come close to the top of the hierarchy, have restrictions on their use similar to those that apply to slang. They tend to be either old-fashioned, if not actually archaic (*eventide*) or long, rare, and colorful in a way that can only really be appreciated by people who know languages and have read widely (*refulgent, sesquipedalian, callipygian*). As their name suggests, they occur mainly in literary works, and that means not in popular novels written in standard prose but in prose or poetry that aspires to a grander style. A collection of ordinary, respectable people would not be shocked by the use of a literary word, but they might not understand it, either.

The hierarchy of language, therefore, is roughly spindle shaped, with tapering ends and a very broad middle. Two points need to be made. First, the word *hierarchy* is not itself a technical term in language studies; it is merely a convenient way of describing this type of classification. Second, from a linguistic point of view, a word is not intrinsically a better word for being labeled *formal* or *literary* in a dictionary. As far as linguistics is concerned, all words are simply words and are equal. As far as modern lexicography is concerned, it is often the new words and vogue words, which start their lives at least in the category of slang, that excite the most interest.

But the style-conscious writer usually cannot afford to be as undiscriminating as the professional linguist. What he or she writes is almost inevitably going to have to fit into a social context. His or her interest will focus on the central area of the hierarchy of words, whether that are labeled *informal* or *formal* in dictionaries or have no label at all, because they belong to the standard vocabulary.

One word of warning: The boundaries between the different categories of English are fluid. Words move between categories as fashions change or as people change their view of what is and is not acceptable in ordinary discourse. Words such as *OK* and *guy* that were once thought of as daringly casual, if not a sign of definite linguistic indiscipline, are now acceptable in ordinary speech and in less formal varieties of writing. The adjective *no-frills* may have seemed rather slangy or frivolous when it first appeared but has since found a niche and become an almost indispensable term, particularly since budget airlines cut costs by reducing their services to passengers to a bare minimum. Writers need to try to keep up to date with what is happening to language in the wider world.

INFORMAL ENGLISH

Informal language is usually defined as the language of ordinary or casual conversation, that is, a conversation between people who know each other and feel relatively unconstrained so that they do not have to be on their best behavior, linguistically speaking. In such circumstances, it is perfectly natural and right to use colloquial words and expressions and contractions and to take occasional liberties with grammar. Let us briefly consider these, before we look at the place of informal English in writing.

Colloquialisms

Colloquial words and expressions are informal synonyms for terms in the standard language. If you say that someone is *stupid,* you are using a standard term. If you call that same person *dim, dopey, thick, chuckleheaded,* or even *dumb,* you are using a term that would usually be labeled *informal.* The same applies to *clever* and *intelligent* on the one hand and *brainy, bright,* or *cute* on the other. The formal *dollar* becomes an informal *buck;* a *darling* becomes a *sweetie; champagne, bubbly;* and so on. If you say that somebody *has no chance,* you are using a standard expression, if you say that person *doesn't have a prayer,* you are saying the same thing in a more vivid but also more informal way. Informally a person may *carry the can* or *pick up the tab;* more formally that person would *take the blame* or *pay the bill.*

Informal language—the same can also be said of slang—is often more colorful than standard language. It is often shorter, too. In conversation, people frequently want to put their ideas across in the shortest possible time, so longer words and phrases are abbreviated. A *telephone* becomes a *phone;* a *rhinoceros,* a *rhino;* and a *hippopotamus,* a *hippo. Pick up the telephone* becomes *pick up the phone,* which becomes simple *pick up.* In the case of the three nouns *phone, rhino,* and *hippo*—particularly the first of these—many people would argue that they no longer count as colloquialisms but are part of the standard language.

Shortened forms of words are known technically as "contractions." The contractions that are most typical of informal language, however, are not contractions of nouns but of verbs.

Contractions

Except when speaking formally, almost all users of English will say *I'm* more often than they say *I am* and *I don't* more often than they say *I do not.* We tend to use *he's, she'd, we're, you've, can't, won't, didn't, haven't,* and the rest as staples in ordinary conversation and only revert to the full forms when we wish to be especially emphatic:

> *You cannot be serious!*

> *I am going to marry her.*

> *They are not yours, they are mine.*

Most experts suggest that these contracted forms are the hallmark of informal English. We could as truthfully say that their use is the main factor that distinguishes spoken from written English. In written English you should, as a rule, use *I do not,* not *I don't; she has,* not *she's; we would go,* not *we'd go,* and so on. Only when the rest of your piece is written in an informal style should you use the contractions.

It should be noted, however, that there is a difference between the everyday contractions referred to above, which are characteristic of the speech of careful and educated speakers, and slang contractions such as *gotta, kinda, sorta, helluva.* These are expressions that people often say, but they have no place in writing, except on occasions when you are trying to reproduce what a person says in a quotation or in a dialogue.

Liberties with Grammar

The first point that must be made here is that informal English, whether spoken or written, is not non–Standard English. Nowadays *snuck,* used as the past tense of *sneak,* is accepted as standard in American (but not British) English by many people, and even those who do not consider it to be a proper equivalent of *sneaked* are unlikely to object to it in conversation. The same cannot be said, however, of *brung* for *brought* or *he don't* for *he doesn't* or *must of* for *must have.* Informal English uses essentially the same forms and follows the same grammatical rules as any other variety of the language.

That said, some liberties may be taken. The use of *never* as an emphatic negative may just about pass in spoken or informal English:

> *I never laid a finger on him.*

> *He never said that.*

Likewise, the use of adjectives in place of adverbs (*real sorry, mighty well*) is sometimes acceptable in informal English. With respect to the word *poor,* for example, the *American Heritage Dictionary,* third edition, says: "In informal speech *poor* is sometimes used as an adverb, as in *They never played poorer.* In formal usage *more poorly* would be required in this example." The same dictionary, however, does not sanction the use of *good* as an adverb in place of *well* and would classify *He did good* or *The engine runs pretty good* as nonstandard.

How Do You Distinguish between Informal and Standard Language?

Dictionaries and thesauri often label words and expressions that are considered to be informal. Even so, their labeling seems far from exhaustive, and you may often be less concerned to know whether a single word or phrase is informal than to judge whether a whole passage falls into that category.

As your awareness of and feeling for language develops, you will probably acquire an instinctive grasp of what is formal, informal, and so on. While you are waiting for that sense to mature, or in cases of doubt, probably the best test is to examine the verbs that you are using or, in the case of a particular word or phrase, to see what kind of verb form the term in question best suits.

The hallmarks of the informal style, remember, are contracted forms of common auxiliary verbs—*isn't, wouldn't,* etc. If what you are writing sounds more natural when you use the contracted forms, or if a particular word or phrase sounds more "at home" in combination with such a form, then the chances are that it belongs in the informal category. You might write down, for example,

> *I would say that he does not have a prayer.*

But if you said that sentence over to yourself, you would probably find that it sounds rather stilted, whereas

> *I'd say he doesn't have a prayer.*

sounds much more natural. On that basis, you can conclude, fairly safely, that *not to have a prayer* is an expression that is more at home in spoken or informal language.

Let us take another example. *Merriam-Webster's Collegiate Dictionary* (11th edition) does not label the verb *bust* in the sense of "to break or smash," thus leading the user to conclude that it is standard. *The American Heritage Dictionary* (third edition), on the other hand, labels the same word in the same sense as slang. If you had no personal opinion on the matter, how could you work out whereabouts in the hierarchy the word belongs except by considering it in context—either in contexts provided by other writers and speakers (an Internet search engine can be useful in this respect) or by trying the word out in contexts of your own creation?

I informed the manager that one of his salespeople had busted my watch while attempting to change the battery.

You can drop an extremely heavy weight on this watch, but you will not succeed in busting it.

Honey, can you lend me a watch? I just bust mine.

I'd busted my watch the day before and was looking around the store to find a new one.

In the more formal context of the first two examples, *break* would work better than *bust*. But the closer we get to what people normally say, rather than what you might normally find written, the more in place the word feels. The dictionaries can argue the point about where precisely the word belongs, but the ordinary writer would reserve it for informal use.

Other Aspects of Informality

Informality, like the other categories in the hierarchy of language, is not restricted to vocabulary. It extends to the other elements of writing as well. The test suggested above relies on your being able to construct an informal sentence in which to place the word you are investigating. Informal sentences tend to be short and simply constructed. They are preeminently the sort of sentences that people *say*, and when they speak, people generally start with the main clause and add on any subordinate clauses afterward. People do not tend to say,

Having finished this job, I'll now start on another one.

They say,

I've finished this job, so I'll start another.

Similarly, you might well write,

Because we had run out of milk and there was none in the refrigerator, I went down to the store to buy some more.

but you would probably say,

I went down to the store to get some milk, because we'd run out and there was none in the fridge.

Informal writing imitates speech in the patterns and rhythms of its sentences as well as in its vocabulary, and its punctuation, too, tends to be "lighter." People, by and large, do not talk in constructions that require semicolons and colons. But commas, periods, and question marks are indispensable however informally you are writing. The dash often features prominently too, along with the exclamation point, and sometimes other typographical devices, which can help to give the flavor of ordinary speech but are generally out of place in more formal writing:

And do you know what the man said? He said, I was too young to wear a hat like that! TOO YOUNG!!! I didn't know whether to kiss him or slap him—actually, I did. But I'm not going to start kissing strangers in the middle of the hat department at this point in my life!

The Place for Informal Language

Informal language, as was mentioned earlier, is usually defined as the language used between people who know each other well. Consequently, if you are writing for a person whom you do not know—or, indeed to anyone who could be classified as a nonpeer on the terms set out in the previous chapter (*see* WRITING FOR PEERS AND NONPEERS, page 175)—you should be wary about using an informal tone and style. To be informal in writing at the wrong time and in the wrong circumstances is like being too friendly toward someone before that person has, through words, gestures, and general behavior, invited you to treat him or her as a friend. This can apply even to such texts as chatty newsletters of a club or association. What may seem to you at the time of writing to be good-humored and a little waggish may come across as forcedly or even falsely cheerful and, if you happen to strike the wrong note, could offend someone who is particularly sensitive. The ability to write informally is a gift or a skill, like an ability to write in any other kind of style. Until you know that you possess it and that informality is welcome in the context in which you intend to deploy it, your best course is to keep to a neutral style.

This may seem unduly restrictive, as if you were being forced into a straitjacket of formality. But, as has been said before and will be explained in more detail below, this book does not advocate formal English as the norm. Instead, it suggests a writer's normal style should be a neutral one, neither formal nor informal and based on the standard vocabulary of English.

FORMAL ENGLISH

Different reference works mean different things when they speak of "formality" in language. Many seem to work on the assumption that if language and style are not informal, then they are formal. Most dictionaries, however, label as *formal* words that are more likely to be found in written texts than to be used by people speaking, except sometimes when they are making speeches. This book follows the same procedure as these dictionaries. For its purposes, formality means a conscious attempt to raise language above the level of everyday spoken or written discourse.

Like terms that are considered informal, formal terms generally have an equivalent in the standard vocabulary. Just as you might use the word *bust* instead of *break* if you were being informal, so you might replace *break*, albeit in a different sense, by a word such as *contravene* or *transgress* if you wished to give more formality to your writing. People do not normally say that they "request the pleasure" of something, nor for that matter would they usually write it, but it is usual practice when issuing an invitation for a formal occasion to have cards printed that read,

> *Mr. and Mrs. James B. Alexander*
> *request the pleasure of the company of*
>
> ————————————————
>
> *at the wedding of their daughter . . .*

The formality of the style suits the formality of the occasion. Likewise, during his inaugural address, President John F. Kennedy spoke these famous sentences:

> *And so, my fellow Americans: ask not what your country can do for you—ask what you can do for your country. My fellow citizens of the world: ask not what America will do for you, but what together we can do for the freedom of man.*

The way the president phrased his question would sound most peculiar in any other context. We would always, normally, form such a question using the auxiliary verb *do: Do not ask what . . .* A simple combination of an imperative form of the verb with *not* is more familiar to us from poetry, especially the poetry of an earlier age:

> *Go not, happy day, from the shining fields . . .* (Alfred, Lord Tennyson, *Maud* [1855]).

It is also found in the Bible, especially the King James Version:

> *Resist not evil: but whosoever shall smite thee on thy right cheek, turn to him the other also* (Matthew 5:39).

The president, conscious of the solemnity of the occasion and perhaps also of the fact that his inauguration was felt by many to mark the start of a new era, wished to make his utterance memorable and raise it above the level of ordinary speech. He did not choose at this point to make use of particularly formal vocabulary, but he did use this very formal and rather old-fashioned construction to achieve the same purpose.

In doing so Kennedy was following in a long and honorable tradition. The translators of the King James Version of the Bible, for instance, gave a great deal of thought to the style in which they should render the words of Scripture. Partly because they were basing their work on a translation made some 50 years before (the Bishops' Bible, 1568), but also in order to impart a fitting dignity to the text, they chose a style that was slightly out of date by the standards of their own day, so that "whosoever shall smite thee on thy right cheek, turn to him the other also" does not even necessarily represent the ordinary writing style of the first decade of the 17th century.

Other Aspects of Formal Language

Formal language, then, is studied and lofty, and it harks back to an earlier time. It does not have a close connection with the language of everyday speech—which is not to say that it can never be spoken, but it is not likely to be used in extempore speech, only in prepared speeches and then, usually, on important occasions. Formal language can accommodate complicated syntax; indeed, the use of more sophisticated constructions is one of its hallmarks. Whereas you might ordinarily say or write,

I tried as hard as I could, but I could not get rid of the stain.

you might more formally write,

For all my efforts, I was unable to remove the stain.

or

My strenuous efforts to remove the stain were entirely unavailing.

But formality does not appear to best advantage with homey subject matter.

There is, as can be seen from the examples below, a kind of long-breathed quality, too, about formal expression:

To prove the justice of this observation, one has only to contemplate the spectacle of a small nation making submissive overtures to a mightier neighbor.

The perspicacity of the man whom we are gathered here today to honor was equaled only by the breadth of his vision, the liberality of his views, and his profound reverence for the profession of which he was for so long a preeminent representative.

> *The crimes of which they stood accused were held in general abhor-*
> *rence, and, were their guilt to be proven, they could expect to pay no*
> *less than the ultimate penalty.*

Formal expression tends to be expansive and to need long sentences in which
to unfold itself. Consider the following pair of sentences. Which of them
seems more natural to you?

> *That child is an intelligent child. He knows what is what. One could ask*
> *that child any question one wanted to, and he would always give the*
> *correct answer.*

> *That kid's a brainy kid. He knows what's what. You can ask that kid any*
> *question you like, and he always comes up with the right answer.*

There are no prizes for guessing that the first version is a translation into formal language of the second. Although the first version uses a more formal
vocabulary, it retains the sentence structure and rhythm of the original, and
that structure and rhythm simply do not work in formal mode.

The point is worth making once again. Formality and informality are not
simply matters of vocabulary; they extend to every aspect of writing.

The Place for Formal Language

The place for formal language is in formal contexts. As has already been mentioned, the modern trend in most walks of life is away from formality (*see*
WRITING FOR PEERS AND NONPEERS, page 175). Only adopt a formal style if you
are certain the occasion warrants it and if you are certain that you can sustain the style. Because the formal style is lofty, because it consciously strives
to raise itself above the level of ordinary discourse, it can, on the one hand,
easily become inflated and empty, and, on the other hand, it can all too easily fall off its perch:

> *The perspicacity of the man whom we are gathered here today to honor*
> *was equaled only by the breadth of his vision, the liberality of his views,*
> *and his profound reverence for the insurance underwriting profession he*
> *was in.*

> *The crimes of which they stood accused were held in general abhor-*
> *rence, because of their seriousness.*

A writer should strive to preserve consistency in any tone or style, but lapses
from formality seem to stand out more prominently than most others.

NEUTRALITY

What this book refers to as the "neutral" style, tone, or register is the language of the middle ground, neither formal nor informal and based on the

standard vocabulary of English. It is the language that most people find most natural and easy to use for writing. It does not directly imitate speech, but it should be speakable without sounding stilted. To call it neutral may suggest that it is colorless or lifeless. But those are, in fact, merely connotations of the word *neutral*. It is possible to be witty, humorous, serious, dignified, businesslike, affectionate, passionate, critical, condemnatory, and downright rude without stepping over its boundaries. Its chief virtue is its scope and flexibility. On the one hand, it is usable for most ordinary writing purposes; on the other, it can be made more formal or more informal as the occasion demands without necessarily entailing a shift into outright formality or informality. And if you do wish to change your tone in the course of a piece of writing, it is easier to move up or down a category if you start from a roughly central position.

The text of this book is meant as an extended example of the neutral style, and most of its illustrative examples fall within that category. In this particular context, however, it is perhaps appropriate to give a specific example that helps to distinguish it from formality and informality:

> *The painting shows an elderly man and his wife standing in front of a building that might be a church. The man is holding a pitchfork. He has a rather suspicious expression on his face, while his wife looks distinctly disapproving.*

In an informal style, that text might read,

> *The picture shows an old guy and an old lady standing in front of a place that looks like a church. The old guy is holding a pitchfork, and they both look pretty sour.*

A more formal writer might, however, put it like this:

> *The painting depicts an elderly couple whose facial expressions are suspicious, in the case of the man, and severe, in the case of the woman. Behind them stands a building with certain ecclesiastical features. The man is holding a pitchfork.*

The neutral version is more precise than the informal one; it specifies that the object being described is a *painting* as opposed to a *picture* (which might mean a photograph), but it is quite content with the ordinary verb *show,* whereas the formal version prefers the less ordinary *depict*. Likewise, the neutral version avoids the complex construction in the first sentence of the formal one (*. . . an elderly couple whose facial expressions are suspicious, in the case of the man, and severe, in the case of the woman . . .*) in favor of describing the expressions of the elderly couple in a separate sentence that has an easier and more natural flow. At the same time, however, the casual humor of the informal version (*they both look pretty sour*) would be out of keeping with the neutral tone, so it has to suggest humor more gently (*his wife looks distinctly disapproving*).

Not surprisingly since it represents a middle state, the neutral style has some aspects in common with the informal and some in common with the formal style. It is, however, distinct from both, as these examples show, and is, when well handled, fully as colorful or as dignified as the one or the other.

REGISTER

Let us now turn our attention to a broader linguistic and stylistic topic, namely register. Up to this point, the terms *language* and *tone* have been used to discuss the different categories into which words and passages of text can be stylistically slotted. Instead of saying that the three examples given above use neutral, informal, and formal language, respectively, or are couched in a neutral, informal, or formal tone, we could equally well say that the first is an example of the neutral register and the others are examples of the formal and informal registers.

If we think back to two examples used previously,

> *That child is an intelligent child. He knows what is what. One could ask that child any question one wanted to, and he would always give the correct answer.*

> *That kid's a brainy kid. He knows what's what. You can ask that kid any question you like, and he always comes up with the right answer.*

we might suggest that the first passage sounds awkward because it is written in the wrong register for the kind of message it attempts to convey, or because it does not use the register in which it is written with complete consistency.

What Is Register?

Though most people may not be very familiar with it, *register,* in the sense in which we are now using the word, is not a particularly recondite term and is sufficiently nontechnical to appear in standard dictionaries. *Merriam-Webster's Collegiate Dictionary,* 11th edition, for example, defines it as,

> any of the varieties of language that a speaker uses in a particular social context.

The New Oxford Dictionary of English (1998), on the other hand, gives it a rather more elaborate definition:

> a variety of a language or a level of usage, as determined by degree of formality and choice of vocabulary, pronunciation, and syntax, according to the communicative purpose, social context, and standing of the user.

The definition offered by the *New Oxford* is probably more helpful to the person who already has a rough idea of what the word means than to the person who is entirely new to the concept. Nevertheless, it is immediately evident from the number of factors cited as determining its nature—vocabulary, pronunciation, and syntax, as well as the user's communicative purpose and personal standing—that it is a wide-ranging term. Given that most of these factors have already been subjects for discussion in this book, you might even come to the conclusion that *register* comes close to being a more technical synonym for *style*. That conclusion is basically correct.

Rather than attempting to explain or refine the dictionary definition further, let us consider an example, which may help bring home the meaning of the concept and its usefulness when language matters are discussed. Imagine a physician discussing a patient's case—first with another physician, then with the actual patient.

Even if we have never been privy to conversations between medical professionals in real life, we would probably guess from watching hospital dramas on TV that they often communicate among themselves in a kind of technical jargon laden with specialist terms, abbreviations, and the occasional word of phrase of Latin. Also, for professionals, a case is first and foremost a case, one among many. They have met with and treated many such cases before, and they have a job to do. We would therefore expect them to talk efficiently and dispassionately and, usually, to show few, if any, signs of emotional involvement.

The patient, on the other hand, has never been to medical school. Technical terms, however appropriate and however accurate, are likely to mean nothing to him or her. The doctors must choose a different kind of vocabulary to communicate the problem and explain the treatment. Not only that, but the patient's problem is not just any problem but his or her particular problem and, usually, a cause of considerable concern to him or her. The patient may not be helped and may even be distressed if doctors speak about his or her case matter-of-factly, without taking his or her feelings into account. The physician will probably, therefore, not only use a different vocabulary when addressing the patient but also choose a different tone, a more personal and, possibly, a more reassuring one.

This combination of vocabulary and tone, chosen to suit a particular set of circumstances, is precisely what is meant by the word *register*.

Different Registers

Now, there are as many different registers perhaps as there are situations in which humans communicate. We have encountered some, though without using this term to refer to them, at various points in this book. There is, for example, a particular register in which dictionary definitions are usually written, as they have to be clear and unambiguous but also have to fit into a relatively small space. People who write for children will likewise adopt a tone and vocabulary suited to their "communicative purpose" (*see* WRITING FOR CHILDREN, page 179). Writers for academic journals tend to employ an "academic register" not dissimilar to the one used by physicians discussing a patient's case among themselves. There is a register peculiar to commentators on sports events and reporters of sports news. If you open a copy of a newspaper and read through articles from its various sections, you will probably find that each section, each topic, has its own register.

Consider the following examples, all from the pages of the same newspaper:

> Never have the Cubs looked so alone. Already this season, the Cubs lost one key relief pitcher because of injury and traded another because of ineffectiveness. One of their pitching aces, Kerry Wood, has a strained shoulder, and another, Mark Prior, broke a bone in his elbow when he was hit by a line drive. Shortstop Nomar Garciaparra, who seemed to carry his misfortune from Boston to the Cubs last year in a midseason trade, tore his groin muscle running out of the batter's box and is on the 60-day disabled list (Lee Jenkins. "Now Cubs Have a Monopoly on Curses." *International Herald Tribune,* June 10, 2005, p. 23).

> The heavy weight has been lifted off José Pekerman, the Argentine coach. Having stepped up from youth team to national team trainer, he needed what every Argentine in the position needs to quiet the doubters and the critics, a victory in the big one. By daring to send out his team to attack Brazil, by throwing pace, power, and committed high-quality play at the world champion, Pekerman had his game won and his appointment consecrated by halftime (Rob Hughes. "A Somber Memory at the World Cup Parties." *International Herald Tribune,* June 10, 2005, p. 22).

> The bread was crusty and delicious, and the giant crock of local fromage fort—a fiery, spicy, devilish mixture of fresh cheese, black pepper and white wine—made the palate tingle. Here I discovered the winemaker Philippe Delarche's stunning 2002 white Burgundy, Pernand Vergelesses, deliciously priced at €31. . . . The wine was perfect, pure chardonnay, a brilliant balance of fruit, acid and alcohol, aromatic and soulfully satisfying (Patricia Wells. "Spring in Burgundy with a Full Wineglass." *International Herald Tribune*, June 10, 2005, p. 24).

> "The U.S. economy seems to be on a reasonably firm footing and underlying inflation remains contained," Greenspan said in remarks to the congressional Joint Economic Committee. . . . "Although a bubble in home prices for the nation as a whole does not appear likely . . . there do appear to be, at a minimum, signs of froth in some local markets" ("Greenspan at Ease." *International Herald Tribune,* June 10, 2005, p. 12).

It is not difficult to work out from which section of the newspaper each report actually comes and what the various writers are actually talking about. Register is not the same as specialist jargon, but a certain amount of jargon—or if *jargon* seems an unduly negative term to use, a certain amount of specialist vocabulary—is characteristic of each register: "traded," "pitching ace," "line drive," "batter's box," and "60-day disabled list" in the first example, for instance.

But establishing the register is not simply a matter of specialist vocabulary. Ordinary words are used in an unusual and distinctive way. Consider the way the writer on food and drink piles up the descriptive adjectives: "a fiery, spicy, devilish mixture" and "perfect, pure chardonnay, a brilliant balance of fruit, acid and alcohol, aromatic and soulfully satisfying," or from a little earlier in the same article, "a soothing warm creation of ultra-thinly sliced leeks that had been cooked long and slow to a melting tenderness." The writer's obvious intention is to evoke tastes and odors and the general pleasures of the table so vividly that the reader almost drools with anticipation.

The writer of the second example uses fairly ordinary words in a rather different fashion. A person who was unfamiliar with soccer and soccer writing might wonder what went on when the Argentine coach *threw* "pace, power, and high-quality committed play" *at* the world champion. Followers of this sport, or of any other competitive team contact sport, would realize that the Argentine team played offensively, that its players used their ability to run fast and their physical strength (pace and power) to overcome their opponents and showed not only skill but also "commitment," which in normal sports parlance means not simply a psychological will to win but also a fearless and often ruthless determination to obtain and retain the ball by tackling or fending off their opponents.

It would be impossible to describe almost any kind of sport without resorting to military terminology of some kind—*attack, defend, gain ground, aim, shoot,* etc. Metaphors and similes also contribute to different registers. An interesting example occurs in the fourth passage quoted above. Writers on economic matters borrow language from a variety of other spheres, such as the natural world (anything to do with *growth*), health and health care (an economy may be *healthy, sick, ailing,* or *moribund;* it may need *a shot in the arm* or *an injection of cash;* it may *strengthen* or *weaken*), and warfare and fighting (the dollar or the U.S. economy might be *under attack* or *fighting back* or, on a very bad day, *picking itself up off the floor*). In the extract quoted, Alan Greenspan, the Federal Reserve chairman, uses commonplaces of economic and financial discourse when he states that "The U.S. seems to be on a reasonably firm footing" (a metaphor from the general human experience of standing on surfaces of varying stability or solidity) and that "underlying inflation remains contained" (*underlying inflation* is an economic concept, while *contained,* in this context, is borrowed from law enforcement or peacekeeping, where a dangerous element has to be kept under control and within fixed boundaries). He then takes another standard economic metaphor, that of the "bubble" (a period when there is a great deal of economic activity and prices rise steeply, but the real value of the goods, shares, or property bought and sold is not equal to the value placed on them by speculators), but rather wittily adapts it and talks about "froth" (small bubbles, that is, a slight tendency for homes to be overpriced).

As we become familiar with discussions of a particular topic, we find it easier to tune in to the register that the speaker or writer is employing and have no difficulty in understanding what is being talked about. As we become more familiar still with a particular register, we may well find that the words and phrases in it enter our active vocabulary and that its general tone and style become part of our repertoire.

The same positive points can be made about register as were made about tone. To the extent that we are sensitive people, we tend automatically to try to find the right register, the right words, and the right tone of voice to fit any situation in which we find ourselves. A large part of this chapter of the book has been devoted to the need for such sensitivity with regard to our potential readers. When deciding whether to adopt the informal, formal, or neutral register, as we can now term them, we will be guided by our sense of what best suits our purpose and our relationship with our readers.

But the registers that apply to different types of subject matter are a somewhat different affair. The same reservations apply to them as to any other variety of specialized writing and also those that apply to any kind of "secondhand" language use.

Using Registers

In many respects, it is useful to be able to speak or write as if an insider. To use the language and the methods that most people use when dealing with a particular topic gives you a certain amount of credibility. You may imagine that if you fail to use the standard register for discussing fine wines, for instance, or a team's chance in the World Series, you will be suspected of not really knowing what you are talking about. It is often difficult to discuss a subject in language that studiously avoids the standard register of a particular discipline. If you do not say that a wine tastes of a certain combination of fruits, if you do not describe the progress of a particular company or a particular stock in terms of rise and fall, if you do not enthuse about a work of literature in terms of its effect on your emotions and inner life, how are you going to talk about them and be understood by people who have become accustomed to the standard way of discussing such matters?

This is a genuine problem that writers face if they take their craft seriously. On the one hand, you do not want to look like an ignoramus or an outsider; on the other hand, you do not want to parrot what everyone else is saying. A register is, to some extent, a ready-made mode of expression, and to that extent it resembles a cliché. A manner of writing can degenerate into a mannerism. For obvious reasons, this is something that the serious writer will wish to avoid.

A practiced writer can enter the register of his or her specialty and, perhaps without having to think too hard, produce a piece of prose that will fill a certain number of columns in a magazine or newspaper. Many beginners will envy this facility—and rightly so. It takes considerable talent and effort to achieve proficiency. But writers, especially writers who are not yet established, should remember that one aspect of progress, and indeed of success, in the writing profession is "finding your own voice" (*see* TO WHAT EXTENT IS STYLE PERSONAL? page 9). It may hamper your efforts to develop your personal style if you rely too much on an established register. Trust yourself, if you can, to put your own thoughts in your own words.

EMOTIVENESS AND OBJECTIVITY
Emotive and Emotional

Emotive language is not the same as emotional language. Words spoken or written are "emotional," if, essentially, they express the feelings of the person who utters them:

> *You are the dearest person in the world to me. I love you more than I could ever express.*

The above is an emotional statement, as are the following:

> *Your dog is a vicious, nasty, smelly creature, and it ought to be put down.*

> *That is simply the sweetest thing that anyone has ever said to me.*

> *Give me liberty, or give me death.*

Another way of defining emotional language is to say that its essential content is an emotion, and any information it provides is secondary to the feeling that it conveys.

What we call "emotive language," on the other hand, is language that is intended to arouse emotion in the reader or listener:

> *You are the dearest person in the world to me, and I cannot bear to see you throw your life away like this.*

The above is an emotive statement, as are the following:

> *There's no excuse for keeping a dog when he's vicious, nasty, and smelly and simply a trouble to himself and you.*

> *You never say sweet things to me now like you used to.*

> *Your country needs you.*

Whatever the content of an emotive statement, its main purpose is to appeal to the emotions of the person at whom it is directed.

It is difficult, however, to draw a hard-and-fast distinction between what is emotional and what is emotive. If you feel strongly about something, you will generally want other people to share your feelings. Wanting other people to share your feelings, in fact, will often be your motive for putting pen to paper or standing up to make a speech. Ordinary human experience, moreover, tells us that one of the best ways of arousing feeling in other people is to show feeling in yourself. If you can contemplate something unmoved, you are perhaps unlikely to be able to stir emotions for or against it in anybody else. Police officers know that to put victims of crime or members of a victim's family in front of a camera so that they can speak of their grief and suffering is usually a sure way of striking a chord with the public and producing information that will help their investigations. Hostage takers, however, share the same knowledge and use images of their victims' fear and suffering to put pressure on the authorities, or whomever they wish to extort money or concessions from, to make them comply with their wishes.

It is therefore highly likely that you will want to write material that is both emotional and emotive. You might also say that it is impossible to keep emotionality and emotiveness out of any kind of writing that is likely to be worth reading. This is true. On the other hand, both "emotional" and "emotive" but particularly the latter can be used as words of dispraise as well as praise. Politicians, for example, are sometimes accused of using "emotive language" when commentators wish to call their methods or their motives into question. There is, as was suggested at the beginning of this chapter, an ethical issue to be dealt with here. So let us first look briefly at the quality that we have evoked as the opposite to emotiveness—objectivity—and then consider the positive and negative aspects of emotiveness.

Objectivity

The word *objectivity* is used here to refer to an absence of emotional coloring or bias. The word *neutrality* would serve the purpose just as well and is often used in discussions of this topic, but since the word *neutral* has already been used in this book to denote a certain level of language and style, it seems best to avoid possible confusion by using *objective* and *objectivity* at this point.

We all know that it is often very difficult to be objective about issues in real life. We can never wholly escape from ourselves. At the same time, we are all endowed with the capacity to see things from another person's point of view. One of the faculties that enables us to do this is that most important tool in a writer's equipment, his or her imagination. It takes imagination to stand outside yourself and see things from another perspective. It has been said several times already that the imagination is in one respect a faculty that adds life and color; it is elaborative and expansive. But imagination can also be a critical faculty. To see things as they are, rather than as they seem to us, is often thought to be the business of reason rather than the imagination, and a large part of being objective is being rational, but reason can sometimes only take us so far.

Consider the following famous passage from Charles Dickens's *Hard Times* (1854):

> "Bitzer," said Thomas Gradgrind. "Your definition of a horse."
> "Quadruped. Graminivorous. Forty teeth, namely twenty-four grinders, four eye-teeth, and twelve incisive. Sheds coat in the spring; in marshy countries, sheds hoofs, too. Hoofs hard, but requiring to be shod with iron. Age known by marks in mouth." Thus (and much more) Bitzer.

"Now, girl number twenty," said Thomas Gradgrind. "You know what a horse is."

The irony in this passage, for those readers who have not read the novel, is that "girl number twenty," Sissy Jupe, is a child from the circus whose father is in charge of the horses that perform in the ring.

If you were asked to define a horse or, to return to the terms of our argument, to give an objective description of a horse, how would you do it? The deficiencies of the "Bitzer" approach, which is a caricature of the approach adopted by reference works such as dictionaries and encyclopedias in general—compare "a large solid-hoofed herbivorous ungulate mammal (*Equus caballus*, family Equidae, the horse family) . . ." (*Merriam-Webster's Collegiate Dictionary*, 11th edition)—are obvious.

But if you want to avoid a soulless list of facts and must also, in order to remain objective, avoid such approaches as personal experience:

My first experience of horses came when I was three years old. . . .

or personal opinion:

A horse is a handsome and noble creature, gifted with strength and swiftness, and an ally of humankind since earliest times in the struggle for both subsistence and progress.

then it requires a special effort both of your reason and knowledge and of your imagination to achieve that aim. Just as it takes imagination to use the neutral style effectively, so it takes knowledge to strip your vision of subjective elements and see things as they are or as they might appear to a disinterested observer.

A large four-legged creature with a brown coat, a tuft of long dark hairs sprouting from its rear end and hair of a similar color hanging down along its neck, stopped nibbling the grass at its feet and raised its head to look at me. It then put itself into motion on its slim, graceful legs, lifting horny feet that had narrow bands of metal attached, and made its way leisurely toward me.

It is not easy to describe a horse as a visitor from another planet might see it—nor, perhaps thankfully, is it a task that a writer is likely to be called upon to perform very often. But anyone who tries such an exercise will soon discover that it is quite a severe test of his or her powers of visualization and imagination, as well of his or her word power.

The general key to objectivity, as to so much else, is simplicity. When you are required to be objective, use the simplest words you can. The unvarnished truth may not always be simple, but if you try to describe it in simple terms, you can at least ensure that it remains unvarnished.

Now let us return to emotiveness.

Emotive Language—the Positive Aspects

Neither stark simplicity nor a dry recital of facts will suit every purpose. On many, if not most, occasions we will want our writing to have color and life and to produce a response in the reader.

The journalist quoted in a previous subsection could have described her dining experience thus:

> *a dish of local fromage fort—a mixture of fresh cheese, black pepper and white wine—had an enjoyably spicy taste.*

Instead she wrote:

> *"the giant crock of fromage fort—a fiery, spicy, devilish mixture of fresh cheese, black pepper and white wine—made the palate tingle."*

Her aim was to suggest to her readers that she had had a really pleasurable and exciting experience and that the food was truly special, and to make them share, vicariously, some of the excitement and pleasure she felt. Hence, the fromage fort comes in a "giant crock," which suggests both generous portions and, through the use of the word *crock*, a countrified setting. She also piles on the adjectives "fiery, spicy, devilish" to usher in and justify the final evocative phrase "made the palate tingle."

A word of any kind can be emotive. In the example just quoted, the adjectives do most of the work, and adjectives are usually the class of words to which we turn first in order to give atmosphere, color, or emotion to a passage. The bare sentence

> *A house stood on top of a hill.*

can be brought to various kinds of life by the addition of some adjectives and adjectival phrases:

> *A weather-beaten house stood on top of a bare, windswept hill.*

> *A fine house of imposing size and appearance stood resplendent on top of a stately hill.*

But, if our intention is to add flesh to the bones of a sentence, we should consider varying the nouns and verbs as well.

> *A flimsy dwelling teetered on top of a steep-sided crag.*

> *A splendid mansion looked out from a hilltop over the rich farmland spread at its feet.*

Some people might protest that what is being illustrated here is not "emotive language," properly speaking. It is simply "evocative language," the sort of lively descriptive language that no writer can possibly manage without. There is no sense in which describing a house as "weather-beaten" and standing on top of a "bare, windswept hill" constitutes an attempt to manipulate the reader any more than describing fromage fort as "fiery, spicy, and devilish" is an example of unscrupulous advertising. But that is only partly true. As has been said before, a crucial part of the writer's task is to set the reader's imagination to work, and it is through the reader's imagination that the writer reaches his or her feelings. Creating mood and atmosphere, imparting life and color, does involve a degree of manipulation, but—and it is a crucial but—the motive for that manipulation is essentially an innocent one, to increase the reader's pleasure.

Emotive Language—the Negative Aspects

It is now time to look at the other side of the coin. In order to show that the process is similar on both the negative and the positive side, let us use the same technique of building up a simple sentence into something more emotive:

> *A driver ran over my dog, Lucy.*

> *A hit-and-run driver mowed down my precious pet, Lucy.*

> *A drunken maniac in an automobile slaughtered my poor defenseless Lucy.*

In such instances, rather than adding adjectives and choosing more powerful verbs to add life and color to a report and give more pleasure to the reader, we are piling more and more emotional pressure on the reader to fuel his or her outrage against the driver and his or her sympathy with our sense of loss.

If we write,

> *More and more manufacturing jobs that used to be done in the United States are now being done overseas.*

we are making a sober statement of fact. If, on the other hand, we write,

> *Foreign workers are stealing American jobs.*

we have produced a much snappier headline, but at the same time, through using the emotive word *steal,* we have changed the way in which we want the reader to perceive the process that is taking place. Theft is, after all, a crime. If someone steals your job, you have a right to feel aggrieved. It would, we might say, be hypocritical of someone to write such a sentence and then protest innocence of any wish to arouse resentment among American workers against their foreign counterparts.

Now, there is plenty of wickedness at work in the world. There are callous hit-and-run drivers who kill animals and people and try to avoid responsibility for their actions. People do lose their jobs as a result of criminal or immoral behavior on the part of others. Writers should never be afraid of calling things by their proper names or arousing emotions in their readers for or against people or causes that they believe are either beneficial or detrimental to society. What writers ought not to do, however, is to whip up emotion purely for the sake of it.

When you write about an issue using emotive language, you are, in effect, prejudging it. You know how you view the issue and you know how you want others to view it. But there may be occasions where you genuinely wish to leave the reader free to make up his or her own mind or where you feel that the justice of your own cause is so transparently obvious that your best course is to present the facts of the case in a plain unemotive manner, for the reader cannot fail to come to what is, from your point of view, the right conclusion. Remember that a conclusion or a decision that a person reaches through his or her reasoning and insight is, on the whole, likely to be more firmly fixed than one that he or she has been persuaded into by somebody else. You should be able to recognize emotive language and be able to write objectively so as to be able to avoid that kind of language for that very reason.

If you find that you have written,

> *This policy will bring untold benefits to millions of people all around the world who are languishing in the direst poverty.*

consider whether it might not be more accurate, and more honest, to write,

> *This policy is intended to bring relief to poor people in many countries.*

Similarly, consider whether

> *The tyrant's fall was greeted with general rejoicing by the population he had so long oppressed and enslaved. They poured into the streets to welcome the liberators as they made their triumphal ride to the gates of the presidential palace.*

actually represents what tends to happen at the end of a war. A more restrained account, avoiding emotive clichés, rings considerably truer:

> *Large crowds turned out to greet the liberating forces as they rode through the capital to the presidential palace. Many seemed almost bewildered to find themselves free at last of a brutal and oppressive regime. There were tears amid the jubilation as the liberators passed by.*

Finally, with regard to the negative aspects of emotive language, the saying of Less is more applies to emotive language as much as to any other type of language use for special effect. If people feel that they are being badgered or bullied into a certain point of view, that you are trying to subject them to emotional blackmail, or that you are writing with excessive emotion, they may very well react against your views. Readers can be manipulated, for good purposes or ill, but they do not enjoy the feeling that they are being manipulated.

EXPRESSING TONE THROUGH WORDS: AN OVERVIEW

- An informal tone is characterized by its closeness to the spoken language; its use of contractions, such as *she's, we've, don't,* etc.; and its general casualness.
- A formal tone is mainly characterized by a conscious attempt to raise language above the level of ordinary spoken and written English.
- The opportunities for using a straightforward informal or formal tone in writing are limited.
- For most purposes, a neutral tone, neither formal nor informal, but definitely adjusted to writing rather than speaking, is the natural choice.
- *Register* is a useful technical term for a combination of tone and vocabulary characterizing a particular variety of speech or writing.
- Emotive language is language that is intended to arouse feeling in the reader or listener.
- Words that are in the broadest sense emotive are widely and properly used to give life and color to writing.
- Emotive language can also be used to give a subjective or biased slant to the discussion of a topic. There are many kinds of writing in which emotive language should be avoided, and writers should aim at objectivity.
- Words have power, and writers should be conscious of the fact that they are able to wield that power.
- Simplicity is often a powerful antidote to distortion of any kind.

Part II

STYLE IN PRACTICE

INTRODUCTION

The foundation promised in the introduction to part I of this book is now complete. We have considered the concept of style, the qualities required in stylish writing, and the skills required by stylish writers, from the ability to find the right word to the ability to use the right tone and register. If you, the reader, have absorbed all the information and advice contained in part I, then you should already be in a good position to put style into practice. A person who can write clearly, simply, elegantly, vigorously, and with variety, who is sensitive to the needs of his or her readers, and who can be more or less formal as the occasion demands possesses all the basic equipment needed to carry out any writing task that he or she may be called upon to tackle.

Nonetheless, there are special techniques that can usefully be applied when you face a particular assignment such as writing a letter or report. From this point onward, therefore, the book takes a new direction, turning its attention to specific types of document, the conventions associated with those documents, and the styles in which they are generally written. Chapter 10 deals with letters of various kinds, including cover letters and job applications. Chapter 11 deals with memoranda and résumés. Chapters 12 and 13 consider extended pieces of writing: essays, theses, business reports, and presentations. Promotional writing is examined in chapter 14. The final chapter, chapter 15, returns to the subject of style but considers it from another angle: Its concern is the stylistic conventions that publishers and institutions impose on written texts presented to them.

Part II is intended as a guide to practice, and consequently a considerable portion of its text is given over to providing examples of the types of document in question. The reader should be cautioned, however, that these are not all-purpose, schematic examples that can be copied straight from these pages and reused. They will, hopefully, assist readers in preparing their own documents, but their aim is rather to point readers in the right direction than to take them straight to their destination. As has been said before, you should already have a solid foundation for the confidence and skills that will make you a self-sufficient writer.

Letters and E-mails

INTRODUCTION

The personal letter is, in many respects, an endangered species. It may be difficult for people born after, say, 1975 to imagine how much time earlier generations spent writing letters to one another. Not just before there were telephones, but, in fact, for many years after the telephone was invented, before it became relatively cheap and easy to make long-distance and international calls, people who wanted to communicate but lived too far apart to speak face to face had no choice but to send letters to one another. Nowadays, in most countries of the world, everyday communications rely on electronics. Almost all of us have a cell phone in a purse or pocket, a telephone in our home, and access to a computer that enables us to send e-mails. When it comes to choosing a method of contacting friends and acquaintances, letter writing comes a long way down the list of options.

From the point of view of a writer, it is perhaps regrettable that the writing of personal letters is in decline. Sitting down to describe events, pass on your views and comments, or indeed open your heart in a letter to a friend or acquaintance was an everyday act that epitomized the whole writing process—the withdrawal from everyday goings-on, the concentration on a blank sheet of paper that had to be filled, the attempt to connect imaginatively across space with another person. In this way, writing letters provided an excellent opportunity for the budding writer to practice his or her skills. It may be possible to derive similar benefit from writing e-mails, but the electronic environment in which e-mail writing takes place and the very fact that e-mail is a medium designed for speed seem to militate against a writer's devoting the amount of time and care to the writing of a personal message that he or she would give to other writing tasks.

E-mail is still a relatively new form of modern communication, but since it is almost universally available, easy to use, cheap, and, above all, quick, it has caught on extremely rapidly. Millions of e-mails now shoot back and forth across the world. E-mail has, perhaps, shifted the balance back slightly in favor of written communications after a decade or two in which the telephone was the average person's medium of choice for fast contact. But those who see the advent of e-mail as heralding the rebirth of the personal letter are probably overoptimistic.

Nothing, probably, is going to bring back the personal letter. This does not mean that no letters are written or, to put it more broadly, that nothing is written in letter form. Nor does it mean that letter-writing skills have become irrelevant. Nor should the comment in the previous paragraph be taken as implying that e-mail is not or cannot be used for important communications. A great deal of the serious business of life is still transacted by means of the written word. Companies and similar organizations write to one another, to their customers or members, and to the general public. People in certain kinds of jobs must spend a large part of their workday preparing written communications. Such communications may be produced by word-processing software or e-mail programs and sent through cyberspace rather than by the mail, but, generally speaking, the same conventions apply to their writing, however they happen to be transmitted. For convenience, the first part of this chapter will generally refer to the documents it discusses as "letters," but it should be understood that what is said about a letter also applies to a formal e-mail used, for instance, to make an inquiry or place an order.

Because we no longer use letters for everyday communication with family and friends, a letter today is quite likely to be a relatively important document with, in the broadest sense, some businesslike purpose: applying for a job, complaining about a product or service, or expressing an opinion to a newspaper editor, for example. Furthermore, because we are unaccustomed to writing them, every letter we now have to write is more of an effort and a trial. Even people at work whose daily jobs do not involve producing large amounts of correspondence may find writing a letter something of a challenge. A lot may depend on a letter, and yet we may be altogether unprepared to meet the challenge of putting together such an important document.

The sections of this chapter are intended to help with any difficulties that writing letters or e-mails may present. For the reasons given above, the particular types of letter and e-mail dealt with are mainly of a business type—both the kind that a business writes to other businesses and the kind that private citizens write to organizations. Let us begin with an examination of the basic principles that apply to the writing of letters or formal (letter-type) e-mails.

The Basics

A letter or a letter-type e-mail is, essentially, no different from any other piece of writing. It requires planning, drafting, and revising. It may even require research. The same rules of style apply to it as to other texts. It should also be adapted in tone and style to the reader it is intended for.

Most letters should be kept short and to the point. An exception might be made for personal letters—a friend might perhaps love to hear you ramble on or follow you as you catch thoughts on the wing and develop them haphazardly, and perhaps we can never have enough from someone we love or enough of news from home. But, if we accept that personal letters are now a rarity, and that letters are mainly written in a business context, then they ought to be businesslike. The French philosopher and mathematician Blaise

Pascal wrote some 350 years ago: "I have made this letter longer than usual only because I have not had the time to make it shorter." This may sound paradoxical, but it will, hopefully, not seem so to readers who have taken to heart this book's comments on the need to revise work of whatever kind and its suggestions that revision often involves editing, shortening, and sharpening up an earlier draft.

Some letters are means of self-expression, such as letters written to newspapers or magazines to air our views on particular subjects or share our feelings with other readers. Some are means of self-presentation or even of self-advertisement. It is not uncommon for companies and institutions to request an application letter when seeking employment, sometimes handwritten, because it enables them to make a basic assessment of you, the applicant. In particular, it enables them to find out whether you are literate and whether you possess essential communications skills. Do not dash off a letter, or any kind of communication, that could be used as evidence, so to speak, for or against you. Treat the writing of a letter or a formal e-mail as a serious writing task, take time to plan and prepare, and allow yourself a reasonable amount of time to edit and correct. (This does not mean simply using the spell-checker after having written your document on the computer. Spell-checkers are not designed to distinguish sense from nonsense. If you write *Were are you going too?* your spell-checker will not object in the least.)

Whatever the purpose of your letter or e-mail, it will stand a better chance of being read carefully and given the proper attention if it is neatly presented. Make sure that it looks tidy on the page. The secret of tidy presentation is a skillful and generous use of space. Leave adequate margins around your text. Insert a line space between each paragraph. Use 1.5 or double spacing if the font you are using looks at all cramped with single line spacing. Further, choose a type of font and a point size that will ensure that your letter is easily legible. Fancy fonts, especially fonts that imitate handwriting, are not always immediately clear.

THE STRUCTURE AND CONVENTIONS OF A BUSINESS LETTER OR FORMAL E-MAIL

Structure

As with any other piece of writing, a principal key to success with the formal letter or e-mail is to know clearly the purpose for which you are writing. A business letter or formal e-mail should be short, businesslike, and to the point, and to enable it to be so, you have to know what the point is.

A standard business letter or formal e-mail has three main sections:

- the **introduction,** in which you state briefly the subject matter and purpose of the letter. This will usually consist of a single paragraph.
- the **body of the letter,** in which you discuss the subject matter or explain your purpose more fully. This may well take several paragraphs. The general rule of One idea, one paragraph applies here, as in other types of writing.

- the **conclusion,** in which you restate your purpose and, where appropriate, indicate what action you believe should be taken to put that purpose into effect.

It is possible to add a fourth section, a **postscript,** which comes at the end of the letter, after your signature and any supplementary information such as a list of attachments. It is sometimes suggested that a postscript is important and that many people tend to read the postscript first. That may be so in the case of promotional letters, where a postscript can be used to offer an additional inducement to a potential customer or to issue a reminder—for instance, that a particular offer is only available for a limited amount of time. In most cases, however, a postscript should be superfluous, because you will have planned your letter well enough to cover all the important points before you reach the end. Only use a postscript, then, if it is part of your plan and you wish to tease your reader slightly by withholding a valuable tidbit until the very end. It is probably not a good idea to attach a postscript such as this to the end of a cover letter when applying for a job:

> *P.S. I also speak excellent Spanish and have represented my state in table tennis at a senior level.*

If these abilities are immediately relevant to the position you are applying for, mention them in the body of your letter. If they are not, save them for your résumé.

Layout

Let us deal first with the layout of the beginning and the end of a letter. The layout of the body of the text, and indeed of the letter as a whole, will be dealt with and illustrated under FORMAT (page 219).

Before the salutation or greeting, in which you address the person for whom the letter is intended (*Dear Ms. Jones, Dear Dr. Ramirez,* etc.), the following items are presented in the order given below:

- your address, telephone number, and e-mail address
- the date
- the title, name, and address of the recipient
- the subject line

The top portion of a standard letter, therefore, usually looks something like this:

Department of Social Sciences
Alice B. Toklas College
3341 East 19th Street
Tulsa, Oklahoma 74120-8933
(918) 502-9977
gbbanks@abt.edu

December 15, 2005

Ms. Kathryn J. Jones
Subscriptions Manager
Whitewell Publishing
1025 Ocean Boulevard
Boston, Massachusetts 13000-4202

Subject: Cancellation of subscription

Dear Ms. Jones:

It is important that your contact details feature prominently at the top so that the recipient has no difficulty in replying to your letter and has a choice of means to do so. The date should also always be shown, as it is a standard point of reference, and if the correspondence continues for some period of time, it may be necessary to know who said what when—this is especially so when something is in dispute. Finally, the subject line (introduced, as above, by the word *Subject* followed by a colon) lets the recipient know immediately what the latter is principally about. (It also reminds you of your basic purpose in writing.)

At the bottom of the letter, beneath the closing (the conventional farewell and expression of regard *Sincerely, Sincerely yours,* etc.) and your signature, the following should appear in the order given below:

- your name, printed or typewritten
- your job title (if relevant)
- a supplement line (if relevant) giving a reference number for this particular piece of correspondence
- a list of any attachments
- the postscript (if necessary)

So the conclusion of a standard letter would look something like this:

Sincerely yours,

Gordon B. Banks

Gordon B. Banks
Professor of Sociology

Attachments (1)
P.S. I should be grateful if you would pass on my comments to the editors of the magazine.

Let us now look at the layout of a complete letter.

Format

There are three standard formats for laying out a business letter. The first is known as the "block format"; the second, as the "modified block format";

and the third, as the "semi-block format." As the names suggest, there is not a great deal of difference between them.

The block format gives a letter a slightly more formal appearance. In block format everything is aligned to the left. Here is an example of a letter in block format:

Department of Social Sciences
Alice B. Toklas College
3341 East 19th Street
Tulsa, Oklahoma 74120-8933
(918) 502-9977
gbbanks@abt.edu

December 15, 2005

Ms. Kathryn J. Jones
Subscriptions Manager
Whitewell Publishing
1025 Ocean Boulevard
Boston, Massachusetts 13000-4202

Subject: Cancellation of subscription

Dear Ms. Jones:

I wish to cancel the college's subscription to the *International Journal of Social and Institutional Affairs* once the current issue is complete, in other words, after delivery of volume 26, number 4, which was, may I point out, scheduled for publication last month.

As the college has been a subscriber to this journal since it began publication 28 years ago, I feel I owe a brief explanation of why we are now withdrawing our support. It will also give me a rather reluctant personal satisfaction to make my feelings known.

Not only has every single number of the last two years been published late, in some instances more than three months late, but the quality of the articles in the *Journal* has, in my view, declined markedly in both content and presentation. I do not feel that the present editorial board is being sufficiently strict in ensuring that the articles it accepts genuinely contribute to the advancement of knowledge and the promotion of scholarly debate on social science issues. I am quite certain that standards of copyediting and proofreading have deteriorated to the point where some articles are barely intelligible. To back up this final point, I am enclosing a copy of the last issue in which I have personally marked the spelling and grammatical errors.

May I say in conclusion, that it gives me no pleasure to bid farewell to a magazine that I used to look forward to with eager anticipation.

Sincerely yours,

Gordon B. Banks

Gordon B. Banks
Professor of Sociology

Attachments (1)
P.S. I should be grateful if you would pass on my comments to the editors of the magazine.

The modified block format arranges material slightly differently. It aims at a look that is closer to that of the traditional handwritten letter. It places some items (your address, telephone number, and e-mail address, and the date at the top of the letter; the closing and your signature and title at the end of the letter) in the center or on the right-hand margin. It is a little less formal than block format, so let us illustrate it with a less formal version of Professor Banks's letter to Ms. Jones.

Department of Social Sciences
Alice B. Toklas College
3341 East 19th Street
Tulsa, Oklahoma 74120-8933
(918) 502-9977
gbbanks@abt.edu

December 15, 2005

Ms. Kathryn J. Jones
Subscriptions Manager
Whitewell Publishing
1025 Ocean Boulevard
Boston, Massachusetts 13000-4202

Subject: Cancellation of subscription

Dear Kathryn Jones:

I'm sorry, but the college is going to have to cancel its subscription to the *IJSIA,* with the last number of this volume (26:4). By the way, wasn't that scheduled to be published last month?

It's the usual reason, I'm afraid. Our student numbers are falling, our funding is being cut back, and if we can save a few dollars on our publications budget, we have to do it. I have to say, though, that the *IJSIA* isn't quite what it was. One or two of the articles in recent issues have been, to be frank, shallow, poorly researched, and full of grammatical errors.

But it was a great magazine in its day, and I shall miss it.

Sincerely,

Gordon B. Banks

Gordon B. Banks
Professor of Sociology

The above letter in the semi-block format would be exactly the same except that the paragraphs would be indented.

Salutations and Closings

The rather quaintly titled "salutation" is, as has been mentioned earlier, the greeting with which a letter begins. Wherever possible, it is best to address your letter to a named person, using the addressee's title and surname, first name and surname, or first name, whichever is most appropriate to your relationship with that person:

Dear Ms. Jones:

Dear Kathryn Jones:

Dear Kathryn:

Note that the salutation in business correspondence ends with a colon, not a comma, in standard American usage (a comma is used in standard British, Australian, etc., usage).

It is slightly less formal to address someone as *Dear Kathryn Jones* than as *Dear Ms. Jones*. The combination of first name and surname is useful if you do not know the proper title of the person you are writing to. Kathryn Jones, for example, might be *Miss, Ms., Mrs., Dr., Prof., Rev.,* and so forth. Using only the addressee's first name implies a certain amount of acquaintance and is likely to usher in a less formal style of letter.

If you do not know the name of the person you are addressing, you have a choice between a reference to the job title or status

Dear Complaints Manager:

Dear Customer:

Dear Supporter:

or using a formula such as

Dear Sir:

Dear Madam:

Dear Sir or Madam:

Dear colleague:

To whom it may concern:

Writers on business correspondence suggest that if you are writing from a business or similar organization to a member of the public, you should try to identify the addressee in some way and only resort to *Dear Sir or Madam* when all else fails. If you are writing as a member of the public to an organization, however, it often makes sense to use that formula. You should not, of course, use *Dear Sir(s)* if there is a possibility that your letter might be dealt with by a woman.

Traditionally, certain types of salutation are paired with certain forms of closing. A letter beginning with *Dear Sir or Madam,* which would generally usher in a text written in a rather formal style, traditionally closes with *Sincerely* (American convention) or *Yours faithfully* (British convention). Letters beginning *Dear Ms. Jones* or *Dear Kathryn Jones* also usually end with *Sincerely yours or Sincerely.* More informal letters (*Dear Kathryn*) can have a variety of closes from *Yours truly* to *Cordially, With best wishes* or *Best wishes.*

LETTER-WRITING TACTICS

The basic tactics for letter writing have already been mentioned and relate to the basics of all good style. Plan and prepare carefully, keep it short, keep it simple, use a neutral style (using a more formal variant of neutral style where necessary and a more informal variant where circumstances warrant it), be as lively and vigorous as you can by avoiding the passive voice and addressing your comments directly to the reader, keep the reader and his or her interests in mind at all times, and revise and check what you have written carefully. Revise and double-check your spelling and your grammar, for, as has been said before, letters, especially those received by potential employers, are often used as tests of literacy.

There are certain other and more specific tactical maneuvers that are worth bearing in mind when writing a business letter or formal e-mail.

Beginning with a Bang

If you are "selling something," in the broadest sense, then it may be a good plan to dispense with the traditional form of introductory paragraph and to start with something that is calculated to grab the reader's attention immediately. Experts sometimes give estimates of how long a writer has to attract and hold the reader's attention, and these estimates almost invariably do not make for happy reading: The writer is usually given 20 seconds, at most. Perhaps this is a sign of how fed up the general public is with receiving sackfuls of junk mail and how ruthless businesspeople are with anything that might turn out to be a waste of their precious time. If you are sending a letter into a highly competitive environment, then it may be worth your while to try to think of an opening that will make your reader prick his or her ears.

However, though this is basically sound advice, the tactic is not exactly new. If, for example, you think of beginning your letter with a question—a tried-and-true attention-grabbing device—try to make it a question that your reader has not been asked a hundred times before. Therefore, you probably should avoid

> *Have you ever thought how much money you could save by changing your home insurance provider?* [The reader yawns, and the letter is crumpled and thrown into the wastepaper basket!]

or

> *Wouldn't you like a free vacation in a remote island paradise?* [Wouldn't we all? But just as there is no free lunch, there are usually no free vacations, either, when you look further into the matter.]

But you might consider

> *When did you last take a really good look at your fitted carpet? We don't mean standing up. We mean down on your knees, up close and personal—with a magnifying glass. . . .*

or

> *Do you have a mirror in the room? You do? Oblige me just for a moment. Take a look in it. . . .*

If you are going to grab your reader's attention, then you will need something reasonably imaginative and unexpected.

Again, if you are an ordinary member of the public trying to "sell" something, possibly yourself, to an organization, then before you try this tactic, you have to be very confident that it will work. Many ordinary folks think they have heard it all before; however, established businesspeople have heard it all so often that it is a wonder they can keep their eyes open at their desks. So, for example, if you are an aspirant writer who has just completed a first novel, it will probably cut little ice if you begin your cover letter to a potential publisher or agent (if you submit a manuscript, it should always be accompanied by a cover letter) like the following:

> *This novel is going to make you millions. This is a novel you simply cannot afford not to publish. My friends and family all say that it leaves* Harry Potter *in the shade. . . .* [Oh yes? And when did an author's friends and family ever tell him or her the truth?]

or

> *Can you imagine what it is like to be turned into a cockroach? That is
> what happens to my main character on page one. The novel is actually
> a psychological study of a person's inferiority complex. . . . [Nice try!
> But have you never heard of the writer Franz Kafka? And how exactly
> did you do the research?]*

or (beginning, not with a bang, but, as it were, with a whimper)

> *I know you must get hundreds of submissions like this from inexperi-
> enced novelists like me, but I am sure that this one is really special, and
> if you would only take the time to read it, I am confident that you would
> agree. . . .*

It is much easier, in this as in many other instances, to point out what is
unlikely to work than to offer a suggestion that is guaranteed to bring success. If anyone could devise such a beginning to a letter to a publisher and
patented it, he or she would stand to make a great deal of money.

If you are tempted to try this approach, then try to identify the "unique
selling point" of your book and make that your opening gambit. It might
be a very unusual situation in which your main character finds himself or
herself (as with the cockroach in the example above) or it might be a particular geographical or historical setting, or the point of view from which
the story is told:

> *My novel begins with the conception of my leading character and ends
> on her first birthday. The whole saga of her hilariously dysfunctional
> family is told from her point of view. . . .*

Generally speaking, however, the safer option is to begin with a more conventional opening paragraph:

> *I am sending you a synopsis and three sample chapters of my first novel
> in the hope that it will interest you sufficiently for you to consider it for
> publication. . . .*

Only "begin with a bang," if you feel very confident (or perhaps if you
have tried other approaches without success). You will soon find space for
your unique selling points (with respect to both your book and yourself) in
subsequent paragraphs.

Giving Prominence

Since a letter is a relatively short document, the opportunities for exploiting
the resources of your word-processing program to give special prominence to
particular items is usually limited. One of the most useful resources in letters,
and in longer documents, is blank space. The simplest way to give prominence to something is to isolate it:

There are four reasons why, in my opinion, the Dick Whittington Centre in London, England, is an unsuitable venue for next year's conference:

> the Dick Whittington Centre is a recently opened facility and has no track record of hosting conferences of this type;
> the dollar-sterling exchange rate is currently unfavorable to the dollar, which must add to the cost of holding a conference in the U.K.;
> the majority of the delegates to the conference are based in North America—it would be more cost-effective to fly the European delegates to America than to fly the American delegates to Europe;
> the Dean P. Sweetwater Facility in my home city, which does have a proven track record in providing conference services and hosted last year's event to the satisfaction of all delegates, is available for next year's dates.

There I might further add that . . .

You can add a little to the effect of separating out items by prefacing each of the listed points with a number or what printers call a bullet:

> There are four reasons why, in my opinion, the Dick Whittington Centre in London, England, is an unsuitable venue for next year's conference:
>
> - the Dick Whittington Centre is a recently opened facility and has no track record of hosting conferences of this type;
> - the dollar-sterling exchange rate is currently unfavorable to the dollar, which must add to the cost of holding a conference in the U.K.;
> - the majority of the delegates to the conference are based in North America—it would be more cost-effective to fly the European delegates to America than to fly the American delegates to Europe;
> - the Dean P. Sweetwater Facility in my home city, which does have a proven track record in providing conference services and hosted last year's event to the satisfaction of all delegates, is available for next year's dates.
>
> I might further add that . . .

Another method of achieving a similar effect is to use boldface to call attention to key words or concepts:

> We should not agree to an extension of the contract for one year only. I estimate that it would take us at least three years to make a reasonable return on the investment required if we are to meet the new specifications that Zorboyz are insisting on. I therefore propose that there should be a **minimum three-year extension of contract.**

Part of the purpose of using bold in a letter is to get the main thrust of your message across to someone who is skimming through your letter in order to extract the gist, as the person may be too busy (or too idle) to read the whole letter properly. You have to think of what you put into bold as a kind of "sound bite." You may need to exercise some degree of skill in constructing a sentence if you wish to highlight a particular phrase.

For instance, if the final sentence of the previous example ran

> . . . I therefore propose that we should refuse to agree to an extension unless it runs for a period of not less than three years.

it would be difficult to find a sound bite. You would be faced with the choice of either putting the whole sentence into bold—which would perhaps work if this were the only point in your letter that needed highlighting, but might look heavy-handed if there were other areas of bold elsewhere in the text— or of creating an effect such as

> . . . I therefore propose that we should **refuse** to agree to an **extension** unless it runs for a period of **not less than three years.**

which gives the impression that you have encoded your main message in a mass of less important material.

The same applies if you wanted to use bold with a list of points. Let us look again at the earlier example relating to the choice of a conference venue. It would work to put the opening words of the various objections into bold as they stand:

> **the Dick Whittington Centre** is a recently opened facility and has no track record of hosting conferences of this type;
>
> **the dollar-sterling exchange rate** is currently unfavorable to the dollar, which must add to the cost of holding a conference in the U.K.;
>
> **the majority of the delegates** to the conference are based in North America—it would be more cost-effective to fly the European delegates to America than to fly the American delegates to Europe;
>
> **the Dean P. Sweetwater Facility** in my home city, which does have a proven track record in providing conference services and hosted last year's event to the satisfaction of all delegates, is available for next year's dates.

The technique would be more effective if you introduced each of the listed points with a sound bite in bold that summed up the argument in a few words and then provided a brief explanation to back up your main point:

> There are four reasons why, in my opinion, the Dick Whittington Centre in London, England, is an unsuitable venue for this year's conference:
>
> **The Dick Whittington Centre is untried.** It is a recently opened facility and has no track record of hosting conferences of this type.
>
> **The dollar-sterling exchange rate is unfavorable.** This will inevitably add to the cost of holding a conference in the U.K.
>
> **The majority of the delegates are based in North America.** It would

therefore be more cost-effective to fly the European delegates to America than to fly the American delegates to Europe.

There is a venue available in the U.S. The Dean P. Sweetwater Facility in my home city does have a proven track record in providing conference services. It hosted last year's event to the satisfaction of all delegates and is available for next year's dates.

I might further add that . . .

Effective highlighting depends on your knowing the purpose for which you are writing and being able to distinguish between the more and less important elements in your sentences. (For more on methods of giving prominence to text, *see* FONTS [page 291] and LISTS AND TABLES [page 302].)

The Soft Soap Sandwich

This heading is intended to be memorable rather than cynical. It relates to a tactic that serves a very important secondary purpose of a great deal of letter writing, which is to retain good relations with the person to whom you are writing, even if your main purpose is to rebuke, refuse, or disappoint him or her. There are a great many business and personal situations in which you have to disoblige somebody, but you can never predict when you might need a favor from that person in future. Self-interest, consequently, dictates that you should not antagonize somebody unnecessarily, and common decency and politeness do the same. You should, therefore, endeavor to say something nice to a person, in order to mitigate his or her possible feelings of disappointment or humiliation.

The "soft soap" usually constitutes the bread in the sandwich; the bad news that you have to give forms the sandwich's filling. The informal letter from Professor Gordon Banks shown above is a case in point:

Dear Kathryn Jones:

I'm sorry, but the college is going to have to cancel its subscription to the IJSIA, with the last number of this volume (26:4). By the way, wasn't that scheduled to be published last month?

It's the usual reason, I'm afraid. Our student numbers are falling, our funding is being cut back, and if we can save a few dollars on our publications budget, we have to do it. I have to say, though, that the IJSIA isn't quite what it was. One or two of the articles in recent issues have been, to be frank, shallow, poorly researched, and full of grammatical errors. But it was a great magazine in its day, and I shall miss it.

Sincerely,

The letter begins with an apology and ends with a tribute to the magazine. The apology is intended to soften slightly the news that the college is canceling its subscription. You will notice also that the main paragraph suggests that the main reason for the cancellation is a failing on the part of the college, rather than a failing on the part of the magazine. Furthermore, the informal tone of the whole letter enables the writer to make light of the magazine's shortcomings to some degree.

The more formal version of this same letter is consistently harder on the magazine and, by extension, on Ms. Jones, but even it manages a slightly stiff, "more in sorrow than in anger" tribute at the end:

> . . . May I say in conclusion, that it gives me no pleasure to bid farewell to a magazine that I once used to look forward to with eager anticipation.

(For more on techniques for presenting bad news in a recipient-friendly manner, *see* DELIVERING BAD NEWS, page 231).

Answering Letters

It ought to be a truth generally acknowledged that any letter, e-mail, or other type of communication, unless it happens to be the one that closes a correspondence, deserves an answer. Everyday experience shows, however, that there are many people for whom this is not an obvious truth. They ignore everything that is sent to them and are apparently unconcerned about irritating or antagonizing the people who are trying to contact them, for there are few things more annoying than to send off a letter that seems to disappear straight down a big black hole.

If you are somebody whose job involves dealing with correspondence or if you are a person who regularly receives mail at home, then it is worth taking practical steps to ensure that you are not personally responsible for one of these black holes. These steps are simple:

* Look at your mail as it comes every day. Immediately discard anything that is junk mail. Sort the remaining mail into letters that require an answer and letters that do not require an answer but contain valuable information. File or store the latter.
* Sort the letters that require answers into those that are urgent and those that are less urgent.
* Set aside a period of time for dealing with correspondence. It need not be every day; it ought to be at least every week.
* Answer the urgent letters first, then move on to the less urgent ones. Make urgency your main criterion. It is tempting sometimes to write the pleasant answers first, which often leads to the unpleasant answers being repeatedly deferred with the result that any pain that, for example, a letter of rejection or refusal inflicts is increased by the recipient's having to wait to be rejected.

It is often easier to reply to a letter than to initiate a correspondence. You should always have the letter you received beside you when you reply to it for two reasons: First, your memory may fail you, and you may forget to deal with some point that your correspondent considers very important or may supply information or comments that are irrelevant to your correspondent's concerns; second, the original will almost certainly provide general assistance to you in framing your reply.

The assistance you receive from the original comes in two forms: tone and format. Regarding the former, your correspondent will have written to you with the degree of formality and/or friendliness that he or she thinks appropriate. In most instances you will take your cue from this and respond in the same vein. But you have the option of taking a different tone in your reply.

If you decide to adopt another tone, this will immediately send a signal to the other person, above and beyond any explicit signals contained in what you say. If, for example, somebody writes to you in an informal tone, and you write back more formally, your reply will most likely be interpreted as a "back off" signal, and any criticism will seem more severe for being delivered from a lofty height. If, on the other hand, a person writes to you in a fairly formal tone, and you adopt a more informal tone, this might be seen as an attempt to make friendly overtures, an invitation to "lighten up" a little, or as an ingratiating gesture, as if you were being friendly in order to make up for some wrong you have done and to divert wrath from you. The safest course, generally, is to reply in the same tone.

You can also often reply in the same format. If a person has made a certain number of points in a certain order, it will often make sense to deal with those same points one by one in the same order. Where the writer of the "Dick Whittington Centre" letter a few pages back listed four objections, you might, if you were replying and arguing against those objections, provide what could be called a counter-list of your own. To mirror your correspondent's format shows a considerable degree of attention and respect. It is as if you were saying to him or her: "As you see, I have taken your points seriously. I am giving them the respect they deserve by responding to them one by one." On the other hand, this approach may suggest finality, as if you were implying: "I am showing respect for your views; here are my answers; that is the end of the matter."

If you wish to open up the discussion or take it further, it may be a better tactic to move away from the format of the original. For example, you could deal with those four points in a continuous paragraph and then adding further paragraphs, or possibly a list of points of your own, to show your wish to engage in further discussion or to move the argument forward. (For an example, *see* page 232.)

Clichéd Formulas

Since the writing of business letters is for many people a routine task, a set of routine formulas has been developed over the years to assist managers, clerks, and secretaries with the sometimes tiresome business of answering letters. Many of these stock phrases now have a distinctly old-fashioned ring:

Pursuant to your request of . . .

Further to yours of April 15 . . .

Enclosed herewith, please find . . .

Your request will be taken under advisement.

It has come to my attention that . . .

In addition to sounding old-fashioned and being clichés, these phrases have an additional disadvantage in that they all belong in the formal register and will require you to continue in that register for the rest of your letter. The best thing to do is to treat them like any other kind of cliché and avoid them whenever possible.

Let us now move on to discuss specific types of letters and letter-writing situations.

DELIVERING BAD NEWS

At various points in this book, you have been urged to consider your readers. If ever there is a time when you need to be particularly sensitive to your readers' feelings, it is when you have to tell them something that they are hoping not to hear. Most of us have at some time or another applied for a job, which has in the end been offered to somebody else. Most of us have submitted an idea, plan, article, book proposal, and so forth and received a rejection letter in return. Most of us ought, therefore, to be able to empathize with any unfortunate people to whom we have to deliver bad news.

It seems to console people a little if they are at least given a plausible reason for having been passed over. Once again, you are showing basic respect. If you explain why somebody was not accepted, it indicates that you at least considered that person on his or her merits. And those merits should, if possible, be mentioned. Anything positive that you can say, you should say. It is here that the aforementioned "soft soap sandwich" comes into its own.

Let us suppose, for instance, that the letter from the person who objected to the Dick Whittington Centre in London as a conference venue reaches the vice president of the parent company. He or she might reply like this:

Bramstoker International
974 South Street
Edwardstown, Pennsylvania 44500-6801
(215) 387-0413

April 23, 2005

Mr. Peter Garfunkel
Director of Marketing
Bramstoker Western
West Aurora, Washington 97062-2444

Subject: Conference 2006

Dear Peter:

Thank you very much for your letter of April 12. I have now had a chance to think about the excellent points that you made and to discuss them with several other members of the conference-organizing committee. We see the merits of your arguments; nevertheless, we have decided to go ahead with our present plans, for the following reasons.

Although the Dick Whittington Centre is relatively new, we have received very positive reports from other organizations that have held similar conferences there. The facilities are state-of-the-art, apparently, and the staff is very helpful.

The dollar-sterling is certainly unfavorable now. Who knows what it will be in October 2006? However, even assuming that it is still unfavorable and granting your point about transatlantic traffic, there remain compelling reasons for choosing London.

Our European division has several times asked to host the annual conference, and, since a main plank of Bramstoker's strategy for the next five years is to open up new markets in the countries that have recently joined the European Union, this seems like the moment to show our commitment to our European operations and our Europe-based staff by granting them their wish.

I have very good memories of 2004 in West Aurora and would like to thank you once again for your personal contribution to making it such a successful event. I hope it will not be too long before we have another chance to enjoy your hospitality, but we are Bramstoker International and must try to live up to our name.

Sincerely yours,

Laura

Laura Y. Minto
Vice President, Human Resources
lym-pg:018

P.S. I look forward to seeing you this October in Honolulu, if not before.

This letter follows the classic pattern: a word of thanks and appreciation to the sender; a statement of the reasons for or against complying with his or her request or proposal; and a final reference to some positive factor, which is intended to reestablish or reinforce good relations.

There are a few other points about this letter that are relevant to points discussed in previous subsections. Although she addresses the recipient by his first name, the writer maintains a strictly neutral style; there are no signs of informality (she could, for instance, have made the postscript *See you in Honolulu . . .* but does not). She deals with Peter Garfunkel's letter more or less point by point, countering each on his first three arguments and using the fourth to provide her with a positive closing paragraph. We can infer from all this, that there would be little point in Mr. Garfunkel's trying to take the discussion any further. The vice president has spoken, and that is that.

Announcing the Failure of a Job Application

The same pattern should, in most cases, be applied to letters to unsuccessful applicants for jobs:

Dear Mr. Griffin:

Thank you very much for coming to be interviewed yesterday. The interviewing panel thought that you gave a very good account of yourself and was very interested to hear your views on using African motifs in textile design.

Unfortunately, you were up against strong competition from other applicants whose qualifications and experience were equal to your own. We were thus able to pick and choose and finally awarded the post to somebody whose specialty exactly matches the future direction in which we intend to take the company.

Thank you again for giving us the chance to meet you, and we wish you every success in your career search.

Sincerely yours,

In the interests of saving the unsuccessful applicant's face, it is usually better to emphasize the positive factors that influenced your decision in favor of somebody else, rather than the negative factors that weighed against him or her. A sensible interviewee will, nevertheless, read between the lines of this message and modify his or her interview technique.

COVER LETTERS

A cover (or covering) letter is one that is sent with another document (or other enclosed items) to provide further information about that document or to direct the recipient's attention to particular aspects or items that he or she might find interesting. A simple cover letter might look like this:

Outlandish Vacations
787 West 18th Street
Boothbay, Maine 77204-5406
(207) 963-7151

February 11, 2006

Ms. Angela Wu
101 Paul Revere Drive
Springfield, Massachusetts 01102-3989

Dear Ms. Wu:

Thank you very much for requesting our Winter 2006/07 brochure, which we have enclosed along with this letter.

Please note that the particular tour you inquired about no longer features in our program for 2006/07. We do, however, offer two alternative Nordic skiing expeditions to Sweden, where the skiing conditions and accommodation facilities are even better than they were in Norway, together with a brand-new Iceland tour, centered in the beautiful hot springs region and taking in trips to Iceland's two most active volcanoes.

We are sure that you will find something in our brochure that meets your requirements and look forward to hearing from you again very soon.

Sincerely yours,

Sven Karlsson

Sven Karlsson
Customer Service Manager
awu:001
Attachment (1) Outlandish Vacations Winter Wonderworld Brochure 2006/07

Personal cover letters can be more difficult to write, as you are providing further information about the sender—you. Let us imagine that you are sending a sample of your work to a magazine that will, you hope, publish it. Many novice writers find this a severe test. You expect, or at least you hope, that the quality of your writing will be what ultimately decides your success or failure in the writing business. You have, however, heard that publishers and editors receive hundreds of submissions, very few of which are accepted. You feel instinctively that a good cover letter will improve your work's chances of being read and taken seriously. Furthermore, you know that magazines—indeed, all publishers—want you to perform two difficult tasks at the same time: to produce work that suits their established readership and to be fresh, original, and excitingly new. You are also probably aware that most publishers prefer authors who are likely to be able to provide them with more than one contribution. This suits you fine—you would probably like nothing better than to become a regular contributor—but you have to write about yourself so that you appear as a credible writer for the long term. You have to sell yourself as well as your work, do it within the space of a single page, and avoid giving the impression that you are down on your knees begging the editor to give you a chance.

437 Hobbes Street
Boston, Massachusetts 02116-4538
(103) 424-8883
jaypile@dod.com

June 21, 2005

Ms. Robyn Robbins-Wilmot
Editor
June's Monthly
Arkansas Building
364 North Street
Chicago, Illinois 60637-2235

Dear Ms. Robbins-Wilmot:

I am sending you a copy of my story "Netting Hearts" in hope that you will consider it for publication in *June's Monthly* magazine.

My inspiration for this story came from two main sources. I have been very impressed by the stories written by Althea Ritchie that I have read in your magazine. I love her quirky characters and her humor. She showed me how to look at ordinary domestic life and see the flaky side of it. My second and more direct source is an account, given to me by a close friend, of a romantic encounter that began in an Internet chat room. I have changed the names of the people involved, obviously, and altered their characters, too, to some extent, but those real-life events form the basis of my plot.

As for myself, I trained and worked for several years as a teacher. I am now at home looking after two small children. I have always wanted to write but have only recently managed to get myself organized sufficiently to be able to write regularly and seriously. This is the third story I have completed, and I am sure that it is the best. So, feeling confident, I have collected material for two more stories and begun a first draft of one of them.

I hope very much that you will find time to read "Netting Hearts" and enjoy it. I would, needless to say, be very willing to make any changes to the text that would make it more suitable for the magazine.

Thank you for your time, and I look forward to hearing from you.

Sincerely yours,

Jean Pile

Jean Pile

The writer of this letter manages quite skillfully to say many of the things that a magazine editor is likely to want to hear, and to imply a few more.

The letter follows the standard pattern. A brief introductory paragraph sets out her purpose in writing. The two central paragraphs deal with the two essential issues in such a letter—the nature of the material submitted and the status of the person who is submitting it—and the fourth paragraph forms a conclusion. But note how the writer proceeds in the second paragraph. She does not say a great deal about her own story, in the sense that she does not seize on an aspect of the plot or characters and, as it were, dangle it in front of the editor in order to whet the editor's appetite. She realizes that her story will have to speak for itself, ultimately. Instead, she concentrates on the story's origins, which enables her to convey several ideas indirectly.

First, she lets the editor know that she reads the magazine (and so has some idea of the type of material the editor will be looking for). Second, she indicates that she enjoys the magazine, but by singling out one (presumably regular) contributor whose work she really likes, she avoids having to write something like *I always read your magazine from cover to cover and think the stories in it are so wonderful,* which reads like undiscriminating gush. By suggesting that she partly models her own work on Angela Ritchie's, she reinforces the point that she knows what *June's Monthly* requires. Third, she writes about matters that are reasonably close to her own life and about people she knows (her friend). This is usually considered to be a sounder basis for successful fiction writing than choosing exotic characters and locations.

In the third paragraph, the writer strengthens the impression that she is a level-headed person who is confident but not overconfident, and who has given some thought to the mechanics of pursuing a writing career. Finally, in her fourth paragraph, the writer suggests that she is willing to be guided by the editor. It is not usually a good idea to ask for advice or help from a person such as an editor or an agent (*I know this story is not quite right yet and would be most grateful for any advice you could give toward improving it and making it more sellable*). People in publishing are as busy as people in any other business and expect you to solve your own problems. On the other hand, however, it is generally worth indicating that you are not the sort of writer who regards every syllable and comma as sacred once it is written down, and that you would be willing to make changes, if necessary.

JOB APPLICATIONS

A letter of application for a job is oftentimes called a cover letter, for in many if not most instances, it is a specialized form of cover letter. You are, on the whole, unlikely to send an unaccompanied letter to a prospective employer unless you are asking for a first job or perhaps a simple manual job.

In most cases, the organization you are applying to will send you an application form to fill in or will ask you to submit a résumé. Your response to this will be, in part, a cover letter to accompany the other document.

Let us concentrate on the more common situation, in which the document your letter will be accompanying is a résumé. Your résumé is a distillation of your life and professional experience to date. It will say a lot about you, and you will to some extent be judged on what it says. But, by and large, résumés are not "speaking documents." They tell an employer what you have done, but they do not tell him or her what you are like. Your letter of application should speak of and for you as a person, and as a practitioner of a particular profession, sufficiently to give you a chance, at an interview, to show yourself in the flesh and enable the employer to form a rounded assessment of your personality and capabilities. (For more information about formulating a résumé, *see* chapter 11, page 247)

As has been said more than once already, letters can be tests, and this applies especially to letters of application. Most employers will welcome, if they do not insist on, good communications skills—of which good writing skills form a major part. Your letter is your chance to showcase the skills you possess—which is not to say that you should try to turn the letter into a virtuoso performance. This is not an opportunity to show off. It is, however, an opportunity to demonstrate that you can write in a competent and businesslike way, that you are able to spell and punctuate, that you prepare and revise your written work conscientiously (though it may still be advisable to ask somebody else to check your letter for you, since it is notoriously difficult to proofread your own work meticulously, especially when you set great store by it), and that you have a basic grasp of the proper tone to adopt.

A letter of application can also, incidentally, be a test of your understanding. Many applications fail because applicants have not read the advertisement for the job carefully, or have not studied any literature about the job or the employer. Before you begin your letter, therefore, you should gather as much information as you can about the job and about the organization that is offering it. Make sure that you frame your letter so that it relates precisely to this job with this organization. If the advertisement or the job description mentions specific duties or specific skills, you should respond by saying whether you have those skills and how you obtained them and what fits you to carry out those duties.

There are three basic areas that you have to cover in order to achieve all this: the training and experience that you have acquired, the sometimes less easily definable additional skills that you accumulated outside your formal training, and the personal qualities you possess that will make you an asset to this employer.

The first of these areas includes all your formal education, any additional training you have received or courses that you have taken, and all the jobs you have done to date. In order to cover the second area, you have to think hard about what you actually did when you were employed in particular jobs. You may have been officially employed in one role, but in addition to performing the duties of that particular position, you may have occasionally been called upon to deputize for another person, say, and so have learned the rudiments of a different job. This extra experience may be as relevant to the job you are now applying for as the experience you gained in your official post. If you are naturally modest or unaccustomed to analyzing yourself and your strong points, dealing with the third area may present a problem. Try to be as honest as you can, and if you really cannot think of ways to describe yourself, perhaps ask a friend or relative to suggest a few adjectives that sum up your character. Try to give an impression of confidence, but do not boast. Do not lie about yourself, for example, by claiming to be a wonderfully organized person when you generally muddle through. But it is quite legitimate to put the most positive gloss on something. A muddler-through, for instance, might claim that he or she "is not fazed when things do not go according to plan and is used to improvising solutions to unexpected problems."

You should make a note of everything that occurs to you. You may not be able to accommodate all of the material in the letter, which must be kept reasonably short, but these ideas are not necessarily wasted. You can also use them to construct or refresh your résumé, and they may come in handy if you are called for an interview.

Besides giving a positive impression of your own capabilities, you should also be positive about the job. Say what it is about the job that particularly appeals to you, and how you think it fits in to the career path you are planning for yourself. Likewise, if there is anything about the company you are applying to that makes you particularly eager to become an employee, mention it.

To sum up, a basic letter of application should contain

- an introduction stating which post you are applying for;
- a concise statement of the experience that fits you for the job;
- a concise statement of the aspects of the job that interest you;
- a concise statement of the personal qualities that you would bring to the job and the company; and
- a reference to any documents you enclose with the letter and a statement of your willingness to attend an interview.

Such a letter might look like this:

342 Pacific Drive
Santa Lucia, California 92595-7659
(805) 925-1515

May 3, 2006

Mr. George S. Breschini
Human Resources Manager
RUH International
45 Wills Avenue
Scott Valley, California 91083-2045

Subject: Position of Personal Assistant to Financial Director

Dear Mr. Breschini:

I am writing to apply for the above post, which was advertised in yesterday's issue of the *Santa Lucia Observer*.

You will see from the résumé enclosed with this letter that I have considerable experience as a secretary and personal assistant. At present I am employed with J. P. Tate & Co. in Santa Lucia as personal assistant to Mrs. Helga Brigg, the general manager. In addition to organizing Mrs. Brigg's schedule and performing general secretarial duties, I am also in charge of the company's payroll database. I am fully qualified as a secretary, am familiar with standard office software programs, and have attended two additional courses on the setting up and management of databases.

The position offered by RUH International interests me for two reasons. First, I should very much like to work for an executive in charge of finance, where the experience I have acquired while running J. P. Tate & Co.'s payroll could be useful and where I might have the opportunity to increase my knowledge of financial matters. Second, I would welcome the challenge presented by working for a large company with international connections. As you will also see from my résumé, I can speak Spanish well and have traveled a little in Central America.

The qualifications that I possess should, I think, suit me for this position. Mrs. Brigg will vouch for the fact that I am efficient and hard-working. I am also adaptable and, while I do not thrive on pressure, I am used to coping with pressure and remaining efficient.

I would welcome the chance to discuss this position further with you at an interview. If you require any further information, please contact me at my home address, given above.

Sincerely yours,

April Cantelo
April Cantelo

Attachments (1)

LETTERS OF RECOMMENDATION

When you are writing on your own behalf to apply for a job, it is, as has been said, important to be honest and yet, at the same time, to give the best account of yourself that you reasonably can. The same applies when you are writing on somebody else's behalf to recommend him or her to a new employer. You owe it to the applicant to do your best to further his or her ambitions, yet you owe it to the employer to give an accurate account of what the applicant can and cannot do. This can be a difficult balancing act. Most people will tend to favor the applicant and gloss over any minor shortcomings. But if you know, for example, that an applicant is suspected of dishonesty or has been the subject of complaints about sexual harassment, the new employer will have every right to feel aggrieved against you if you failed to mention this in your reference and the applicant subsequently shows the same bad propensities in the new situation.

It is an ordinary courtesy for an applicant to ask your permission before citing you as a reference. If you do not feel able to support a person's application positively, but, for whatever reason, you balk at providing a damning or half-hearted testimonial, then you should refuse to act as a reference.

Fortunately, the vast majority of people have much to recommend them. Where high praise is due, give it. Remember, however, that the reference you write has to establish your credibility as well as the applicant's. Unless the prospective employer knows you personally, he or she will rely, in the first instance, on what you write to establish that you are a responsible person who can be trusted to give an accurate assessment. If you seem to be exaggerating an applicant's strong points, the recipient of your reference may suspect that you secretly want to be rid of him or her.

If you are on good terms with the person for whom you are writing the reference, then it is usually helpful to ask him or her a few questions about what the new job entails and what he or she hopes to gain from it. You can then use that information to give support where it is most useful.

A specific letter of recommendation might read something like the following:

J. P. Tate & Co.
89 Cannery Row
Santa Lucia, California 92595-7659
(805) 925-0604
hbrigg@jptate.com

May 7, 2006

Mr. George S. Breschini
Human Resources Manager
RUH International
45 Wills Avenue
Scott Valley, California 91083-2045

Subject: Ms. April Cantelo
Confidential

Dear Mr. Breschini:

Thank you for your letter of May 5.

Ms. Cantelo has been my personal assistant for the past three years. I have to tell you that I am quite alarmed at the prospect of losing her, as she has run my office for me most efficiently throughout that time. I am particularly grateful to her for bringing order into our payroll system, which was, frankly, chaotic when I ran it myself.

We are a small company. We need people who are flexible and can turn their hands to many different tasks, which Ms. Cantelo has always been able to do. I know, however, that she has ambitions that we cannot fulfill and that there is limited scope with us for the financial knowledge and skills that she has acquired.

Personally, I have always found her to be very helpful, polite, and cooperative. She is not the most outgoing of women, but it has always suited me to have a cool, restrained presence about my office rather than a ball of emotional fire.

I have no hesitation, then, in recommending her for the position she has applied for and wish her every success in her future career.

Sincerely yours,

Helga Brigg
Helga Brigg, General Manager

It should be noted that Mrs. Brigg comments on the personality of the applicant as well as on her professional abilities. It is also worth noting that letters such as these do not have to be strictly impersonal in style. A few personal touches within a basically neutral style and a standard framework give additional credibility to a judgment by showing that it was made by a real human being.

A more general character reference, on the other hand, might be written like this:

342 Pacific Drive
Santa Lucia, California 92595-7659
(805) 925-1515

September 26, 2006

Subject: Mr. Peter Bothwell

To whom it may concern:

I have known Mr. Bothwell for the last two years, during which time he has frequently done odd jobs in my home and my yard. Mr. Bothwell is honest and reliable; if he promises to arrive at nine o'clock, he arrives at nine o'clock. I also particularly appreciate the fact that he clears up very thoroughly after he has finished his work. He erected a set of shelves in my study and relaid the lawn in my front yard; these are among the bigger jobs he has carried out for me. Recently he has also begun to walk my dog for me, since my new work schedule no longer allows me to walk the dog myself.

Mr. Bothwell has told me he is leaving this neighborhood. I am very willing to recommend him for the kinds of work I have mentioned.

Sincerely,

April Cantelo

April Cantelo
Assistant to the Financial Director, RUH International

As was said earlier, most of the letters exemplified in this chapter need not necessarily be sent using paper and envelopes. They could be sent as attachments to e-mails; they could also be sent as simple e-mails. At this point, let us move on to consider e-mail as a form of communication in its own right.

INFORMAL E-MAILS

Person-to-person e-mail, especially when the writers know each other well, is often conducted in a very casual manner. It is rare to receive an informal e-mail that is carefully thought out or laid out, or one in which much thought has been given to spelling, grammar, and punctuation. Plenty of people send newsy e-mails to friends, especially at the holidays, and they almost invariably make use of one of the main advantages of the medium, which is to send the same message to a very large number of people.

Though this is the way that many people use e-mail now, there is no reason to assume that this is the only way in which it can ever be used. Because e-mail is a relatively new medium, there is considerable scope for the present generation of writers or users to shape the way in which it will develop as a form of communication. It can be treated as a utilitarian device for a throwaway society, or it can be afforded the same respect as any other type of writing. As noted earlier, people are increasingly using e-mails in place of letters to transact serious business or convey important information. People who use e-mail in this way need to follow the same procedures, observe similar courtesies, and take as much care with matters such as style and tone as do people who write letters or other types of document.

Technical matters must be left to one side, as the software supplied by different e-mail service providers offers different facilities and, in any event, is being continually updated. So, the following will deal only with the basics of "netiquette," as applied to e-mail.

- Use the subject line to show the content or purpose of your e-mail. This allows the reader to see immediately why he or she is being contacted and, if the e-mail is stored, enables him or her to find it again among a number sent by the same person.
- Only send copies to people who really need them.
- E-mail is informal or "unstuffy" almost by nature, but the normal rule of respecting your readers still applies. If you do not know the recipient, be cautious about how you address him or her. (In other words, if you are e-mailing Dr. Jennifer Weiss for the first time, do not start with "Hi, Jenny" because you think that is the e-mail convention. Even "Hi, Dr. Weiss" sounds too familiar. "Dear Dr. Weiss" or simply "Dr. Weiss" is better.) By all means, however, include an appropriate greeting and close to your e-mail. Finally, do not SHOUT at people (that is, use capital letters), except in jokey e-mails to your friends.
- There is no reason why an e-mail should not be as carefully presented as an ordinary letter: well planned, clearly organized, and properly spelled and punctuated. An e-mail that is not clearly laid out and that does not express its message in a clear and interesting way is less likely to achieve its purpose than one that is. So, do spend some time thinking about and constructing your e-mail. It is usually better to do the work of composition offline so that you are not distracted by other Internet activity going on in the background. And do check and proofread the text after you have written it.
- Keep e-mails relatively short, and pay particular attention to the text first visible on the screen, which is what will persuade the recipient to scroll down further. If you have a lot of material to send, it is often better to put it into a separate file and send that as an attachment to your e-mail.
- Include other contact information, such as your mailing address and phone and fax numbers, with your e-mail signature.

Whatever the means of communication you choose—e-mail or letter—always remember that anything that goes under the heading of mail is directly addressed to another person or other people. In this form perhaps more than in any other, writing is a two-way process. So, here is where you should take everything this book has said in previous chapters about the relationship between writer and reader particularly to heart.

LETTERS AND E-MAILS: AN OVERVIEW

- The basic criteria for good style are as relevant to letters and e-mails that have a practical purpose as to texts written for self-expression or an aesthetic purpose.
- All letters and e-mails benefit from careful planning and presentation.

- Letters and e-mails should be clearly laid out, concise, and to the point.
- Use the appropriate formulas in salutation and closing.
- Always consider your reader. Remember that even in a letter of complaint, for example, part of your purpose may be to maintain basically good relations with the recipient.
- Remember too that, for some readers, a letter is treated as a demonstration of the writer's ability or lack of it.
- Be organized and prompt in responding to correspondence.

Memorandums and Résumés

In this chapter we shall briefly consider two types of document that have close connections with letter writing. A memorandum, or memo, is essentially a condensed letter. A résumé has a certain amount in common with a formal letter, albeit one that is designed to be sent to many different addresses on different occasions in essentially the same form. Nevertheless, as will be explained later, it is unwise to assume that once you have composed your résumé, it simply needs to be added to as your career develops and never needs to be adapted or revised.

MEMORANDUMS

The word *memorandum* literally means "something to be remembered." Memorandums (also sometimes appearing in plural form as *memoranda*) often still serve this original purpose. You might write a memorandum of what was said at an interview or meeting and file it in order to remind yourself of, or keep a record of, what was said or decided. More frequently, however, memorandums take the form of short messages to one or more people, informing or reminding them of something.

Most memorandums, then, are like very brief business letters without the usual formalities at the beginning and the end. These are replaced by a heading so formulaic and standard that stationers provide printed memo forms and most organizations use them. If you are not using printed forms, then you should type in the same heading:

MEMORANDUM [*or* MEMO]

TO:
FROM:
SUBJECT: [*or* RE:]
DATE:

The convention is that memorandums are not signed, but you may add your initials at the bottom. If another document is attached to the memorandum, then note the fact at the end, as you would in a business letter.

The hallmarks of most memorandums are brevity and a businesslike tone. They rarely cover more than one or two points and tend to be written in a rather impersonal style, especially if addressed to several people.

A typical memorandum might look like this:

MEMORANDUM

TO: Sales staff
FROM: Data entry manager
SUBJECT: Customer e-mail addresses
DATE: October 23, 2004

Would all sales staff please remember to obtain e-mail addresses for all new customers who have them and to ask existing customers to notify the company if they change their e-mail addresses. Company policy is to use e-mail for 75% of customer correspondence from January 2005, and there are still many gaps and errors in our database. Thanks.

T.P.S.

It is also possible to send more informal memorandums, especially to colleagues you know well:

MEMORANDUM

TO: Greg
FROM: Juanita
SUBJECT: Meeting on July 1
DATE: June 27, 2005

Here's the final agenda for Friday's meeting. A couple of points:

Item 3: Have you checked with the insurers whether we need extra coverage for the fragile goods in the shipment?

Item 5: I don't believe we should extend the contract with ACME Shipping when it runs out at the end of the year. I'm looking for a replacement. Let me know before Friday, if you have any suggestions.

Item 6: I'm expecting lots of questions on this. Be prepared!

J.V.

Attachment: Final agenda for board meeting July 1, 2005

Another way of describing a memorandum would be to say that it is like a brief note or set of notes for someone's attention. Brevity is the key, and, as always, the key to brevity is knowing precisely what you want to say. Short as they are then, even memorandums require a degree of preparation and forethought.

RÉSUMÉS

Résumés require a good deal of preparation and forethought. Your résumé is a vital document when you are applying for a job. It is a brief history of your education and working life up to the point at which you make your application. There is no standard form for a résumé, but the following points should be noted:

- A résumé should be brief. Its size will, of course, depend on the particular stage you have reached in your career, but it should not extend more than two pages.
- The information you give should be arranged in categories, for example, work experience, education, and activities and interests.
- The information you give in the main categories should be arranged in reverse chronological order. Start with your most recent job and work backward.
- In the interests of brevity only provide information that is relevant to the position you are applying for. You do not need to write in complete sentences. Information in note form is acceptable: for example, *Responsible for maintenance of customer database* or *Taught English to foreign students.*
- Make sure your résumé is up to date, and avoid leaving gaps in the chronological order. If you spent a period of time outside ordinary employment, for example, traveling abroad or raising children, mention this fact.
- Adapt your résumé to the particular position you are applying for by highlighting those aspects of previous jobs, or perhaps of your personal interests, that are most relevant to the available position. Do not think of your résumé as being forever the same, even though parts of it will not change from one use to the next. Check it and renew it—and, of course, update it—each time you have to produce it.
- You do not have to provide personal details apart from your name, address, telephone number, and fax number or e-mail address.

You may also include in the document a brief statement of your long-term career objectives, especially if you are at the beginning of your career.

A typical résumé might look like this:

Rebecca U. Maynard
1098 Long Street
Columbus, Ohio 43201-6623
(614) 299-7486
rmayn563@aol.com

Education
1996–1998   Ohio State University, Columbus, Ohio
            MLIS, Library and Information Science
1994–1996   Wayne State University, Detroit, Michigan
            B.A. English
            Major: English
            Minor: Fine Arts
1990–1994   Carl Sandburg High School, Detroit, Michigan
            Graduated with honors

Employment history
2001–present Publicity and Education Manager
              City Museum, 96 West Lane Avenue, Columbus, Ohio
              43201-7986
              Preparing and publishing advertising material for exhi-
              bitions and special events. Liaising with local and
              national media. Writing leaflets and guides to museum
              collections. Organizing visits and vacation courses for
              schools.

1998–2001   Publications and Acquisitions Officer
              G.H. Coutts Memorial Library, 345 Main Street,
              Couttsville, Illinois 56703-1124
              Preparing a guide to the collection for distribution to
              universities and other research facilities. Cataloging
              acquisitions to the library.

1996–1998   Visual Resources Assistant
              University Library, Ohio State University,
              1858 Neil Avenue Mall, Columbus, Ohio 43210-1286
              Cataloging visual resources, entering cataloging data,
              assisting research projects.

Publications and presentations
              "How to market museums," presented to the Annual
              Conference of Ohio Museums Association at the Sea-
              grave Center, Toledo, Ohio, on October 19, 2003.
              "Changes in the roles of catalogers in special col-
              lections," *The Reference Librarian* vol. 61, 2002,
              pp. 204–217.

Activities and interests
              Member of the Ohio State Museums Association
              Honorary Secretary of the Columbus Orpheus Choir
              Active tennis and squash player

To illustrate what is meant by "adjusting" your résumé to suit the post
you are applying for, let us assume that Rebecca Maynard is applying for a

post in a new museum in which the emphasis is on the educational rather than the publicity side. In that case, instead of writing:

Preparing and publishing advertising material for exhibitions and special events. Liaising with local and national media. Writing leaflets and guides to museum collections. Organizing visits and vacation courses for schools.

she might write:

Organizing an annual program of educational visits by schools, as well as lectures and vacation courses. Responsible for liaison with local educational institutions. Preparing publicity material for exhibitions and publishing guides to museum collections.

Your résumé should always, of course, be accompanied by a cover letter (*see* JOB APPLICATIONS, page 237).

MEMORANDUMS AND RÉSUMÉS: AN OVERVIEW

- A memorandum has a standard form, which you should follow.
- Memorandums are mainly for use in busy environments, and you should always be brief and businesslike.
- The key to brevity is knowing precisely what you want to say.
- Résumés should list your education, qualifications, work experience, and interests in separate sections under clear headings.
- The information in résumés should be presented in reverse chronological order.
- Remember not only to update your résumé but also to adapt it, as necessary, to suit the particular job you are applying for.

Essays and Theses

INTRODUCTION

This chapter deals with longer pieces of writing, texts that comprise several hundred to several thousand words. Among these, two kinds of document will be given special attention: essays and theses.

Such pieces of writing have a number of factors in common, the most obvious being their length. So let us begin with a general rule: the longer a document is, the greater the care required in planning it and in giving it a clear and solid structure. Even a short document such as a letter or a résumé benefits from being thought about, planned, and properly organized. Prior planning and organization are even more vital to a longer document. Without them, long documents are more difficult to write, and you may well waste precious time on matters that are not particularly relevant to your basic purpose. They can also be more difficult to read, because the reader has to find his or her way through them instead of being guided step by step by you, the writer.

Preparation and Planning

The process of planning and preparation for a piece of writing is a substantial subject in its own right. The following is a brief overview.

Give yourself time to think about the subject that you are going to write about before you begin your research. Roll it around your mind and see what ideas occur to you. Your own ideas, your own personal "take" on a topic, will be quite possibly the freshest and most interesting element in the piece you are writing. Pick out the aspects of the topic that mean most to you personally. If you have been given a very broad topic, you may need to narrow it down in order to make it viable for, say, an essay of 750 words. Narrow it down in accordance with your own knowledge, interests, and preferences.

As you start to collect ideas, and as you become clearer about the approach you wish to take to the topic, start looking for relevant backup material in outside sources. Begin with general reference works such as encyclopedias and dictionaries, then move on to books and articles that deal specifically with the topic or particular aspects of it.

Take careful notes of any information or ideas that you can use for your essay. Notes generally take the form of summaries, paraphrases, or quotations. Summaries and paraphrases will be in your own words and should, as far as possible, be distinct from the wording of the documents from which the information has been extracted. When you write down the precise words used in a source, put those words into quotation marks. It is vital that you should not use other people's words as if they were your own, either accidentally or deliberately. Always make a note of the publication details of the sources from which you take information as well (title of book, author's name, publisher's name, place and date of publication; name of Web site, address of Web site, date of download, etc.), and do not forget to make a note of the number of the page or pages where you found the information. Taking down the details of your sources during the research stage makes your task much easier if you have to go back at a later stage and consult them and when you put together your bibliography.

At some point either while you are collecting your material or once you have collected it, you will need to start to organize it. This means not only physically organizing it—for example, by making a card index—but also assigning it to a particular place in your work. In order to do this, you need at least a rough plan. Draw up a list of headings representing the main points you intend to put forward. Make a note under each heading of the material that belongs in that particular section because it supports the main point. Work away at this mass of headings and notes, until you have produced a complete list of headings and subheadings that constitute a kind of flowchart of your piece. You should aim at producing a plan that is sufficiently detailed that each subheading represents a paragraph in your finished work.

There are two things to remember at the planning stage. First, nothing is fixed in concrete when you are writing until such time as you have completed the final draft. Feel free to experiment. If you have an important piece of evidence or an important idea that does not fit well into your plan, try changing your plan. Second, although your plan may be fluid, any plan is better than no plan. For one thing, without a plan you are virtually obliged to start at the beginning—and the beginning is not always the best place to start. With a plan you can enter your piece of work at the easiest point and write about what you know best to give yourself confidence before you tackle the difficult sections, which usually include the introduction and the conclusion.

So, think, research, and plan—and only then begin to write. (For a fuller treatment of preparation and planning, see part I of *The Facts On File Guide to Good Writing*.)

ESSAYS

In academic contexts, extended writing is a measure of the writer's understanding of a subject. In other words, the essay is a test. There is no getting away from this fact. Everyone, naturally, feels somewhat nervous about being tested and may even resent, consciously or subconsciously, having to undergo a test. Consequently, few people actively relish the prospect of having to write an essay.

This is a pity. Obviously your attitude toward a task will affect your ability to perform it to some degree. If it were possible to put a more positive gloss on the nature of the essay and of essay writing, then perhaps more people would approach it in a positive spirit—not simply those who know already that essay writing is an area in which they can shine, but also those who are more diffident about their abilities.

An essay is, or ought to be, more than a test. It is an opportunity and a vehicle for you, your talents, and your ideas. An essay is a means of self-expression. Admittedly, it is not a medium as free as a poem, a dramatic improvisation, or a piece of graffiti, but if you are not expressing something of yourself in an academic exercise as much as in anything else you write, then you are probably approaching the task in the wrong way.

Most artists come to terms with, and many willingly confine themselves to, existing forms. As Wordsworth said in a sonnet in defense of sonnet writing: "In truth, the prison unto which we doom ourselves / No prison is" ("Nuns fret not at their convent's narrow room" [1806]). The conventions of the academic essay likewise should be regarded as a shape-giving agent and a challenge to your ability to discipline yourself and write succinctly. And, finally, remember again: Academic writing exercises are primarily for your benefit as a student; few instructors really need practice in grading.

The essay may also seem to be a form that exists in isolation, something that you have to write in high school or college and then never have to write again. That may be the case for many people, though anybody who is reading this book is presumably interested in writing in some form and ought to welcome an opportunity to practice the art. But it is not altogether true that the relevance of the essay ends when you graduate. You may never have to write another piece that you call an essay, but you may have to write an article, an editorial, or a review, all of which could be considered essays by another name. You may have to write an appraisal of somebody's character, abilities, or performance, which may seem like a very different exercise from writing an essay on the character of Macbeth but surely has something in common with it. The essay has many siblings and cousins, some of which you are almost bound to encounter in later life.

The notion that the essay is a vehicle for expressing yourself and a form with relevance to future endeavors will perhaps offset to some extent the disagreeable idea of the essay as a chore and a test. So let us begin our examination of it in a positive frame of mind.

Dealing with Practical Constraints

Most essays written for school or college are of between 500 and 1,500 words in length. Though this may seem a large number before you begin, it is not in fact a particularly generous allowance if you have to deal with a topic on which you have a lot to say. In addition, most essay assignments have to be carried out within a limited period. If you are taking an essay exam, you will be given at most two or three hours to plan and write your essay. If you are set to write a high school or college essay, you can expect to be given a week or two to research and write it. In either case, however, a time constraint is added to the space constraint. A high degree of organization is required if you are to operate successfully within these constraints. It seems that, in addition to being a test of your understanding of the subject, essay writing is also a test of your ability to marshal information and evidence and to discipline yourself.

But we are proceeding on the optimistic assumption that a test is also an opportunity. Self-discipline is an asset, as is organization. Before you begin to plan your essay as such, plan how you are going to divide up the time available to you. Outside the context of an examination, you should probably aim to spend roughly 50 percent of your time on thinking, research, and planning; roughly 25 percent on writing; and roughly 25 percent on revision and rewriting.

The large proportion of time allotted to the first stage of the process is partly an acknowledgment of how long it takes to read books and articles, search the Internet, and possibly conduct interviews and surveys, and partly based on the idea that time spent preparing and planning is time saved when writing. This does not suit everyone, for there are, as has been said before in this book, people who find it difficult to plan in the abstract, who get their best ideas while they are in the process of composition, and who are willing to pay the price of having to reorganize their material as they go along. You will discover the time division that best suits your working method as you gain experience in performing this writing task. Nonetheless, you will still need to allow yourself substantial amounts of time for research at one end of the process and for revision at the other.

Do not skimp on revision time. Avoidable spelling and grammatical errors spoil the effect of a piece of work. In addition—and once again emphasizing the positive aspects—the final stage of a project is the stage at which you are most "into" it, most familiar with the material and most practiced in writing about it. Your best ideas may come toward the end, and as many writers will tell you, it is after you have produced the first draft and while you are giving a piece its final shape and polish, that writing is most enjoyable.

The Subject

It is comparatively rare that students are given a free choice of essay subject. This may be a blessing in disguise, since this kind of freedom, in which you have the whole wide world to choose from, sometimes leads to paralysis. Being unable to think of a really good idea of your own may lead you to "borrow" a topic that a more decisive friend has already chosen or to opt for something ultra conventional, such as "What I did in my summer vacation" or "My favorite hobby."

Try not to get caught in this trap. Perhaps the most frequent hazard for writers is the feeling of being stuck, especially at the beginning of a writing task. There is no magic cure for "writer's block," or, as it should be more properly labeled in this instance, "ideas block." But, if you can be patient, and especially if you can disengage your mind from the problem of not having any ideas and go and do something else and think about something else, it is remarkable how often an idea will present itself.

Remember that academic exercises are primarily for your benefit, so look for a topic that will benefit you: for instance, something that will give you the chance to learn more about a subject you are interested in, something that will challenge you to think, something you feel strongly about, something that excites you but leaves many other people cold (one of the many possible functions of the essay is to persuade people or influence their opinion). If nothing gets your creative juices going, then consider at least the possibility of a little mild subversion: "What I did not do during my summer vacation" perhaps has more potential as an essay subject than its conventional counterpart.

More often than not, however, you will be given a set subject. In this case, the first test of your mettle centers on that subject: Do you understand what the instructor intends you to do? Can you use this topic as a springboard for a worthwhile essay?

Let us consider these two questions separately. Students sometimes come unstuck, particularly in essay exams, because they do not understand the nature of the task they have been given. We are not talking here about the student who when asked to discuss the foreign policy of President Roosevelt during the period 1905–1909 launches into a critique of the foreign policy of President Franklin Delano Roosevelt before World War II, but rather the student who simply describes the foreign policy of President Theodore Roosevelt without offering any assessment of its effects or its effectiveness, any opinion as to its rightness or wrongness.

Essay questions usually contain clues to the kind of response the instructor expects, and the main clue is often found in the verb used in framing the essay question. Look first at the verb, then at the rest of the wording, and try to decide what type of essay fits the subject as set.

Types of Essay

There are, broadly speaking, three different types of essay that instructors try to elicit from their students: the narrative, or descriptive, essay; the analytical, or interpretive, essay; and the discussion essay. Let us look briefly at each in turn.

The narrative essay, or descriptive essay, is the simplest type. If the verb in the essay question is *relate, outline, summarize, describe, give an account of,* or the like, then the instructor expects this first type of essay. If you are asked to outline the events leading up to the American Revolution, your task is to organize the historical facts you have collected, usually in chronological order, so that they tell the story of how the colonists became discontented with British rule and decided to declare their independence. This type of essay is primarily a test of your factual knowledge and secondarily a test of your ability to organize and present material; it offers little scope for you to show insight or put forward your opinion.

An analytical essay, or interpretive essay, is usually called for when the question prompts you to *analyze, investigate, examine, assess, evaluate, explain, give the meaning of, compare and contrast,* or something else along those lines. If you are asked to analyze the causes of the American Revolution, your task is not simply to list the factors and events that led the colonists to revolt; you have to show sufficient knowledge to be able to probe them a little—for example, were the reasons the colonists themselves gave for their actions the real reasons?—and to assess their relative importance—for example, Was American discontent or British obstinacy the primary cause? This type of essay is primarily a test of your ability to think. It requires factual knowledge and usually a more in-depth knowledge of the subject than is needed for a narrative essay, but instead of simply presenting the knowledge you have, you must also be able to break it down, weigh it, and relate the separate pieces to one another.

A discussion essay typically requires you to take a stand on a debatable or controversial issue: " 'The Americans did not win the Revolutionary War, the British lost it.' Please discuss." It is usually a test of your ability, first, to apply the knowledge you have of a subject to construct a defensible point of view; second, to select and marshal evidence in order to support that point of view; third, to write persuasively on behalf of your chosen side of the argument; and, fourth, to consider and deal with the arguments for the opposing side—that is, assuming that you either agree or disagree with the proposition. You could take a neutral stance, in which you would need to balance opposing arguments rather than pitting them against each other. Besides giving you a choice of point of view, the discussion essay also allows you a presentational or stylistic choice. You may discuss the question relatively dispassionately, weighing the pros and cons and eventually coming down on one side or the other as a jury member might after hearing a trial. Alternatively, you may embrace one side of the argument enthusiastically and try to refute the other. In either case, you will need to know the arguments for both sides. It is not a proper discussion if you give no space to arguments for the opposing point of view, even if you do so only to expose their weakness.

The categories are, of course, not absolute, and you will frequently find yourself, for instance, mixing explanation with discussion. But they should provide you with basic guidelines so that you can identify the kind of response the instructor is expecting.

Narrowing Down the Topic

All the experts agree that you are only creating trouble for yourself, if, when you are presented with a wide-ranging topic, you simply accept it as it stands and make no effort to focus on a significant aspect of it. A thousand words are obviously not enough to give an adequate account of "Women in contemporary society," "The Internet, a paradise for advertisers," "The influence of ancient Greek philosophy on modern thought," or "The nature of Shakespearean tragedy as embodied in *Hamlet*." When instructors set such topics, it is not because they delight in big themes and broad generalizations for their own sake, but because they want to allow you some freedom to select your own approach and also want to test your ability to use this freedom wisely.

If you were given the assignment of writing on, say, "Women in contemporary society," your first task would be to come up with a viable idea: one that could be turned into an essay of the desired length, would reflect your interests, and would shed some light on the topic as a whole. Probably the best way of tackling this task is to write down a list of the ideas that come to you when you think about this topic.

If your essay is an assignment for a particular course, then it is likely that you have class notes and books for required reading that you will be able to turn to. Check through any course-related material that you have, but be prepared to supplement that material from other sources and your own knowledge and experience.

Perhaps, however, "a list of ideas" is still too all-encompassing. Ideas such as "women in the workplace" or "the changed role of women in the home" represent little progress on the original grand topic. What you need is a specific subject, a focus, possibly something from your own experience. You might, for instance, focus your attention on a particular woman whose activities, career history, or fate may seem to you typical of the condition of modern women: "Condoleezza Rice/Martha Stewart, a Woman in Contemporary Society" might make a feasible essay title. You might know of a group of women in your neighborhood who have taken a stand on an issue, set up a business, or organized themselves in some form of self-help group. What they have done may speak volumes about the opportunities open to women nowadays or the special problems that they face.

Let us return to the opening theme of the preceding paragraph. Write down a list of ideas, but make sure that some of them at least are very focused or even localized ideas. Perhaps you will find that one of these ideas stands out, or that two or three have something in common. Puzzle away at those two or three until they coalesce into a viable subject. But always make sure your subject is manageable—that is, not too broad and generalized, able to be dealt with in a short space, and able to be backed up by specific evidence and examples.

The Thesis Statement

All essays, of whatever type, usually adhere to the standard three-part structure that we are already familiar with in other documents: introduction, body, conclusion. In pieces of writing such as essays, however, the intellectual structure, the coherent development of a central idea, is much more important than the basic physical structure—though teachers are still likely to take you to task if you omit or skimp on your introduction or conclusion. Once you have decided which type of essay you are expected to write, you then have to work out what the connecting thread is that will link your various ideas and pieces of information together. The central idea or linking thread is expressed in your thesis statement.

A thesis statement performs a similar function for an essay that a topic sentence performs for a paragraph (*see* THE TOPIC SENTENCE, page 133). It encapsulates the main theme. As LEO: Literacy Education Online puts it: "A thesis statement in an essay is a sentence that explicitly identifies the purpose of the paper or previews its main idea" (http://leo.stcloudstate.edu/acadwrite/thesistatement.html). The same online resource goes on to clarify that a thesis statement is "an assertion, not a statement of fact," that it "takes a stand rather than announcing a subject," that it "is the main idea, not the title," and that it is narrow and specific as opposed to broad and general.

According to Edward A. Dornan and Charles W. Dawe, who give an exhaustive account of the process of preparing and writing a college essay in *The Brief English Handbook: A Guide to Writing, Thinking, Grammar, and Research:* "If there is one moment in the composing process when an essay's final direction and shape become clear, it is when you write a thesis statement. A thesis statement stands as a college essay's intellectual center." They next elaborate on its purpose: "The thesis statement plays a significant role in the writer-reader relationship too. For writers, a thesis statement identifies and limits the subject, establishes a dominant purpose, and limits the discussion. . . . For readers, a thesis statement tells what the essay will cover and helps put discussion paragraphs into perspective" (New York: Pearson Longman, 2004, pp. 58–59).

A thesis statement is obviously a very important element in an essay, so let us just recapitulate what it is and is not. It is not the essay question, or a factual statement, or an announcement of your purpose in writing, or the title of your essay. It is an assertion.

If you were asked to write an essay on "Automobile use and the problem of pollution," a factual statement would be

Gas-powered automobiles produce pollutants.

An announcement of your purpose in writing might take the form,

I want to show that if Americans are serious about the problem of pollution, they must reduce their dependence on gasoline-powered automobiles.

And the title of your essay might, for instance, be

"Out of the Garage and into the Greenhouse."

None of these is a thesis statement. A thesis statement is an assertion and, moreover, one that can be incorporated in the text of your essay. So, the following are all viable as thesis statements:

Americans who are serious about the problem of pollution must reduce their dependence on gasoline-powered automobiles.

Until the U.S. government stops supporting oil companies, the automobile will continue to be a major source of pollution in our cities.

Pollution is an acceptable price to pay for the immeasurable benefits of motorized transportation.

We need to add that a thesis statement must be not only an assertion written in the style that you are going to use throughout your essay; it must also be a pregnant assertion from which you can develop a defensible case.

Now, obviously, the thesis statement is closely related to a title, to relevant factual statements, and, in particular, to a statement of purpose. Often the simplest way to reach at least a working thesis statement is to construct it from a statement of purpose. Another online resource, the University of Kansas Writing Center, suggests that you produce a rudimentary thesis statement by filling in the gaps in the following sentence:

> "I am writing about _____, and I intend to argue, show, or prove that _____." (http://www.writing.ku.edu/students/docs/thesis.shtml)

The topic of the essay fills the first blank space, and your basic assertion fills the second. From this you develop a usable thesis statement.

Note, that the terms *working thesis statement* and *rudimentary thesis statement* have been used in the foregoing paragraphs. Your essay ought to have a thesis statement, and that thesis ought to appear near the beginning, but you do not have to have a thesis statement in its final form before you start work. You need to know what you are arguing for or against, but a statement of purpose will suffice to get you started. A thesis statement naturally forms part of the introduction to the essay, and as has been mentioned elsewhere, the introduction is one of the hardest parts of any work to write and is often something that is best left to the end. (How can you inform the reader accurately about what you are going to say before you know what you have said—that is, made considerable progress with the body of your essay?) So do not be afraid to leave writing your definitive thesis statement until fairly late in the writing process or to write a tentative thesis statement and change it later. As long as the final version of your essay contains a proper thesis statement, all is well.

Essay-Writing Style

Essays should normally be written in a neutral style and with a fair degree of objectivity. Even if you are making a case for a point of view that you advocate enthusiastically, you should retain a sense of proportion in your advocacy and in your treatment of the opposition. You should not, for instance, seem to imply that anyone who supports an opposing view is automatically either foolish or acting in bad faith.

It is usual practice for essays to be written in straightforward paragraphs without graphics or the kind of highlighting (bullet points, numbered lists, and so on) that you might use in a letter or a report. It is important that the paragraphs should be logically ordered and linked together in such a way that your argument flows. It may be useful to look again at chapter 6, "Constructing Paragraphs," before embarking on an essay project (page 123).

An Example Essay

Let us assume that the assignment is to produce an essay of 750 to 1,000 words as part of a course on English literature. The essay topic that has been set is the following:

> *Theater director Marvin T. Bowdler said: "I left Fortinbras out of my recent production of Shakespeare's* Hamlet, *because* Hamlet *is essentially a private tragedy, and Fortinbras is an irrelevance." Give your opinion of Mr. Bowdler's directorial decision in an essay of between 750 and 1,000 words.*

Obviously, this is a discussion-type essay in which the student is expected to take a stand on the issue, as well as to demonstrate his or her knowledge of the play (and possibly of other Shakespeare plays as well). In this instance, there are two debatable parts to the statement: "*Hamlet* is essentially a private tragedy" and "Fortinbras is an irrelevance." The student perhaps looks at the first of these and wonders, What does "a private tragedy" mean? Is this a technical literary term? Isn't this a very broad question? The second part looks like the key to a much more manageable essay, especially since Fortinbras appears in only two scenes—act 4, scene 4, and act 5, scene 2—and is referred to only in three others—act 1, scenes 1 and 2, and act 2, scene 2.

As the student thinks and studies further, it may seem important that this character, though minor, figures at the beginning and the end of the play; indeed, he speaks the play's closing lines and is the highest-ranking character left alive on stage when the curtain falls. Moreover, though Fortinbras says very little in act 4, scene 4, most editions fill out the scene with a soliloquy by Hamlet that is prompted by Fortinbras's apparently senseless military expedition. The fact that this soliloquy was omitted from the text of the First Folio edition of Shakespeare's complete works in 1623 might suggest that Fortinbras is indeed an irrelevance. The student, however, takes the opposite view.

Moving on, the student tackles the thesis statement using the formula shown earlier:

> *I am writing about the role of Fortinbras in* Hamlet, *and I intend to show that Fortinbras is not irrelevant to the plot or meaning of the play.*

The eventual essay reads as follows (comments on the essay are interspersed):

Beaver 1

Anthony Beaver
Dr. Gervais
English 1
March 5, 2005

It is usual to put the writer's name, the instructor's name, the title of the course, and the date at the top of an essay. Pages should also be numbered, and the writer's surname should appear alongside the page number.

Unfair to Fortinbras

Capitalize all words in a title except definite and indefinite articles, prepositions, and conjunctions. Any of these should be capitalized, however, if they follow a colon. Do not underline your title or put it in quotation marks. You may, however, use quotation marks if your title contains a direct quotation, for example, "He has my dying voice": A Study of the Role of Fortinbras.

> Nobody could reasonably claim that Fortinbras is a major character in *Hamlet*. He appears in only two scenes and has less than a dozen speeches, none of them containing any particularly memorable lines. Mr. Marvin T. Bowdler has therefore decided that he is an irrelevance and has cut him out of his production. But although Shakespeare allowed Fortinbras into only two scenes, one of these is the final scene, and although he gave him few speeches, these include a brief eulogy for the dead prince and the closing lines of the play. In addition, Fortinbras is Hamlet's choice as the next ruler of Denmark and is effectively in charge of that country and of the stage as the curtain falls. Far from being an irrelevance, Fortinbras is an important element in a dimension of the play apparently ignored by Mr. Bowdler, the public and political dimension.

This is a rather long introductory paragraph, but it does two things quite effectively. It presents the basic facts relating to Fortinbras's role in the play; it also begins to make the case. It combines these two activities quite neatly by appearing to make a concession on the basis of Fortinbras's few appearances and small number of lines, but then stating what these appearances and lines are precisely in order to take the fight to Mr. Bowdler. These positive statements provide an effective lead-in to the thesis statement, contained in the final sentence. This puts the schematic statement of purpose, given above, into a form suitable for the finished essay.

> During the closing moments of the play, its public and private dimensions are interestingly juxtaposed. Shakespeare could have ended the work with the touching and intimate exchange between the dying prince and his faithful friend, Horatio. But he does not—because, so to speak, Hamlet himself will not let him.

Rather unusually, this first paragraph of the body of the essay is quite short. It picks up the word *public* from the final sentence of the introductory paragraph and places it together with the word *private,* derived from the original quotation of Mr. Bowdler. The two words form an obvious and useful contrasting pair, related to the main theme of the essay. The writer also continues with the tactic begun in the first paragraph of opposing one authority, Mr. Bowdler, to another and, in this case, a much greater one, Shakespeare himself: Mr. Bowdler did this; Shakespeare, however, did that.

> Hamlet is aware that the public perception of his actions must be very different from Horatio's perception. We, as readers of the play or members of the audience in the theater, have been privileged to watch Hamlet's private struggles and hear his private thoughts, and so we share Horatio's view. We may easily forget, as Hamlet does not, that the Danish public is completely ignorant of his real motives and more likely to assume that he killed the rightful king in a fit of madness or as part of a plot to seize the throne. Consequently, Hamlet prevents Horatio from committing suicide specifically so that Horatio can "go public" with the true story. "Report me and my cause aright / To the unsatisfied" (5.2.291–292), he commands him.

The writer quite cleverly weaves the keyword *public* into this paragraph. The phrase *go public* is put into quotation marks, because it belongs to a somewhat different register from the rest of the essay: It is rather informal and belongs more to the language of politics or business than that of literary criticism. It performs a useful function here, however, because it uses the keyword. Note the method of quoting lines of verse in the middle of a passage of continuous prose. The original capitalization is retained and the lines are separated by a slash. The act, scene, and line numbers are given afterward in parentheses.

> When Hamlet wrenches the poisoned cup from Horatio's grasp, however, there is no other named character alive on stage. Osric reenters at line 301 to announce the arrival of the ambassadors of England and Fortinbras. But Osric, "a chuff . . . but spacious in the possession of dirt," as Hamlet calls him (5.2.89–90), is hardly a worthy hearer of this story. Shakespeare, instead, brings virtually new characters, the ambassadors and Fortinbras, onto the stage at this moment, not to give an unexpected twist to the plot, but because they are needed as a fit audience for Horatio's tale. Logically, if Mr. Bowdler cuts out Fortinbras, he should also alter Hamlet's final speeches, because it is the arrival of Fortinbras that enables Hamlet's dying wishes to be appropriately fulfilled.

This paragraph is again linked to the one that precedes it. The penultimate sentence of the previous paragraph mentions Horatio's attempt to commit suicide, and this paragraph begins with a reference to that. Next Mr. Bowdler is mentioned, after two preceding paragraphs without reference to him. The writer now completes the first point he or she wanted to make, dealing with Fortinbras's role at the end of the play. As a clincher, the writer delivers another critical attack on the person he or she is arguing against. This helps to give shape and unity to the essay.

But the importance of Fortinbras does not rest solely on the role he plays in the final scene. He has a place, too, in the overall design of the play.

This is a classic transition paragraph. The first sentence sums up the argument of the previous paragraphs; the second introduces the main argument of the second half of the essay.

Shakespeare frequently bases his plays on a parallel structure: The fate of the leading character is mirrored by the fates of other characters. In *King Lear*, for example, Lear himself has one good daughter and two evil daughters, while Gloucester has one good son and one evil one. Lear has to go mad before he can reach understanding; Gloucester has to be blinded before he can see. In *Hamlet*, the mainspring of the plot is the fact that the hero has lost his beloved father by violence. Three other young characters are placed in the same situation. Ophelia and Laertes are orphaned by Hamlet's accidental murder of Polonius; the other fatherless character is Fortinbras.

In a literary essay—indeed, in any kind of essay—it is a good tactic to show that your knowledge extends beyond the topic you are currently dealing with. This paragraph begins with a general point about Shakespeare. This provides the writer with a good opportunity to show knowledge of another play. But there is no space in an essay of this size for a long discussion of general issues. The writer refocuses on Hamlet and then, in the final sentence, brings the discussion back to its main theme, Fortinbras.

We are told by Horatio in act 1, scene 1 (lines 81–106), that Fortinbras's father was slain by Hamlet's father in single combat and, as a result, the Danish crown acquired extra territories. Horatio suggests that old Hamlet's ghost is walking the battlements to warn of the danger posed by young Fortinbras, who is actively trying to get that territory back. Claudius certainly takes this threat seriously. In act 1, scene 2, he sends Valtemand and Cornelius on a mission to the king of Norway. In act 2, scene 1 (lines 59–85), we learn that the mission is successful and that Fortinbras will use the force he was raising to attack Denmark for an expedition against Poland instead.

This paragraph does not advance the argument greatly. It is like a paragraph from a narrative essay, inasmuch as it retells part of the plot. This is a perfectly legitimate procedure as long as the factual material presented provides evidence that backs up the argument. In this case, it does, for instance by explaining how Fortinbras comes to be fatherless. In this kind of paragraph it would be a waste of precious space to quote either of the two speeches mentioned. It is sufficient to refer the reader to them by means of line numbers.

Shakespeare's reason for including this material is surely not simply to show that Horatio's understanding of events is limited or that Claudius is an effective, if not particularly warlike, king. He includes it because Fortinbras's actions contrast with Hamlet's. Fortinbras literally "takes arms" in order to combat his troubles and does so apparently without question. There is no sense that he feels any doubts or scruples or engages in any soul-searching. The contrast with Hamlet himself could not be more marked.

This paragraph returns to the basic purpose of the essay: to argue for Fortinbras's relevance. In giving a suggestion as to why Shakespeare included this material (which can easily pass almost unnoticed in performance or even in reading), the writer justifies his own references to it in the previous paragraph. He refers indirectly to Hamlet's most famous soliloquy "To be or not to be" as a way of reinforcing the contrast between the active Fortinbras and the inactive Hamlet. (It is not a direct quotation, as the form of the verb has been changed—"or to take arms against a sea of troubles"—so a line reference is unnecessary, but the phrase is borrowed from Shakespeare, hence the quotation marks.)

And Hamlet himself is aware of this contrast. He compares himself to Fortinbras in the soliloquy "How all occasions do inform against me" and in other passages (see 4.4.23–57). If Shakespeare omitted this soliloquy in his final revision, I suggest that he did so because it delayed the winding up of the plot, not because Fortinbras was dispensable. Hamlet contemplates Fortinbras as a possible role model. Even if Shakespeare had second thoughts, it seems unlikely that he would at any stage have made his hero waste his time by thinking about a totally irrelevant character.

Wisely, the writer does not overlook the point—that Hamlet's soliloquy prompted by Fortinbras does not appear in the text of the First Folio—that could be used by the opposition. He does the correct thing by suggesting an alternative explanation to counter the opposing argument and then reintroduces the idea of relevance or irrelevance, contained in the topic and referred to in the opening paragraph, in order to launch the conclusion.

Fortinbras, as I have tried to show, is relevant to the play. Not only does he have an important role in its final scene, he is an integral part of its overall design by being in a parallel situation to the hero's. Moreover, he is part of the final tragic irony of the drama. Hamlet's private tragedy is that, like any other tragic hero, he is partly responsible for his own death. The public and political dimension to his tragedy is that, again partly as a result of his actions, the kingdom and people that he was born to rule fall into the hands of their ancestral enemy.

The basic purpose of a conclusion is to state finally what you have shown and to assure the reader that you have delivered on the thesis statement contained in your introduction. As a minimum it should deliver a summing up of the argument. But it is a good tactic, if you possibly can, to save something new for your conclusion, some telling anecdote, something that links the argument directly to the reader or to your own experience, or perhaps a particularly apt quotation. As Dornan and Dawe remark in *The Brief English Handbook,* "readers remember best what they read last" (p. 72). Anything you do reserve for an effective ending, however, must be brief, effective, and integral to the essay as a whole. It ought not to seem merely tacked on. In this instance, the writer introduces a shift in perspective, but one that remains within the ambit of the topic. The writer picks up the term *private tragedy* from the original quotation, reintroduces the contrasting phrase *public and political* from the introduction, and weaves them together with the standard definition of a tragic hero according to Aristotle—a person with a fatal flaw in his or her character that leads to disaster—to leave the reader thinking about other directions in which this line of thought might lead.

The essay is what we might call the "base form" for pieces of extended writing. Let us now look, in rather less detail, at some other extended forms.

THESES

If a student is called upon to write a thesis, usually as the culmination of his or her college major studies, it is likely to be the longest piece of work that he or she has to write in an academic context. (At a more extensive, elaborate, and specialized level, is the dissertation of graduate students.) Because of the length and importance of theses, most academic institutions provide guidance for the writing of them. The same or similar guidance is also available on the Web, and, obviously, it should be carefully followed. For the purposes of this book, we shall mainly be concerned with length, because managing length is perhaps the main skill that has to be mastered.

An Extended Essay?

A thesis has something in common with an essay in that it must have an introduction, a body, and a conclusion. But the similarities only go so far. If a thesis extends to, say, 10,000 words or more, then this is equivalent to roughly 10 essays, and if a thesis is divided into chapters, as it generally is, then it might be helpful to think of each chapter as being a separate essay. Each chapter must, of course, have the same kind of internal coherence that you will find in a good essay. But 10 internally coherent chapters do not necessarily make a good thesis. There must be some overall coherence; the reader must have the sense of the argument proceeding not simply from paragraph to paragraph but also from chapter to chapter. Each chapter will probably have its own introduction and conclusion, like an essay, but the conclusion of one chapter must contain a pointer to the next, and the introduction of the next should contain some kind of reference to the chapter that went before. A thesis should be a chain rather than a collection of essays.

A thesis also involves more in-depth research than an essay. On the one hand, a thesis should represent the writer's individual and original contribution to an ongoing academic debate on a subject. You will, therefore, need to know your subject well in order to find an area of it to which you can make a contribution. At the same time, you will also need to show that you understand and appreciate the contributions made by other writers in the same area. You will need to be able to review the literature, that is, to comment critically on the work of present and past scholars. Once you have found an area that you are knowledgeable and enthusiastic about, you will need to select a topic, narrow it down, and arrive at a thesis statement that your paper will set forth and defend. The procedures here are essentially the same as those you would use when preparing an essay topic and working out a thesis statement.

The style of a thesis should be somewhat more formal than that of an essay. Informality would be out of place in a work of this size and gravity. On the other hand, the prose of academe is often insufferably dull and turgid. Your aim should be to be suitably formal without becoming too heavy. Look again, perhaps, at chapter 3 of this book, "The Qualities of Style," (*see* especially the sections on VIGOR and VARIETY, pages 55 and 63, respectively). Also, use active verbs. For example, even when you are reviewing the literature, you do not have to say,

> *As was demonstrated by Smith and Jones (1995), based on the earlier work of Chadwin (1993), the availability of debt relief is often conditioned by the political relations between creditor countries and debtor countries.*

You could write,

> *Smith and Jones (1995), following Chadwin (1993), demonstrate that the political relations between creditor and debtor countries often decide whether debt relief is made available or not.*

Finally, the usual tense for writing theses is the present tense.

Managing Length

The reader should first be reminded of the principle set forth at the beginning of this section on extended writing: the longer a document is, the greater the care required in planning it and in giving it a clear and solid structure. A really long document such as a thesis requires very careful planning and organization. Even if you are in the habit of breezily setting off into an essay, relying on inspiration and your instinctive feel for form to shape the work for you, you would be well advised to change your habits when you have to write a whole series of essays organized as a chain.

But, as usual, you are not the only person who has to manage the length of the document. The reader has to do the same. To assist the reader you will need to provide additional direction-finding apparatus. You will need to write an abstract, or summary of your thesis, which is usually placed at the beginning and should not be more than two pages in length, and provide a table of contents. It may be useful to provide headings within your chapters. Finally, in order to preserve a reasonable degree of flow, it may be necessary to relegate additional information that does not fit easily into the body of the text into footnotes, endnotes, or appendices. Footnotes are preferable if the information tends to be short, because the reader does not have to look anywhere other than the bottom of the page for it. If the notes are longer than, say, four or five lines, it is probably better to gather them together at the end of the relevant chapter as endnotes. If you have additional material that is a page or more in length, it should be put into an appendix. You will, of course, have to provide a full list of the works that you have cited and those that you read in the course of your research but did not actually quote from. This goes in a bibliography at the back of the book.

Planning and Execution

The plan of any particular thesis will differ depending on the subject matter and the requirements of the institution to which it is being presented. A standard skeleton outline, however, might look like this:

Title

Abstract

Table of contents

I. Introduction

II. Review of the literature—a critical summary and discussion of relevant works on the topic

III. An account of how you planned and conducted your research

IV. A presentation of the findings from your research (this may take more than one chapter)

V. A discussion of your findings and their significance (this may also take more than one chapter)

VI. Conclusion

Reference list

Appendices

Most theses will contain all of these elements.

More than most documents, perhaps, theses tend to be written "from the inside out"; that is to say, it is unwise and sometimes impossible to attempt to start at the beginning and work your way through to the end. As *The Facts*

On File Guide to Good Writing explains, having a detailed plan frees you to begin work at a point of your choosing. The most important parts are the presentation and discussion of your own research. Many people start by writing those chapters or, possibly, by writing a review of the literature or an account of their methods. The abstract and introduction are usually only written after you have completed the body of the thesis, including your conclusions. When you are redrafting and revising the work, however, you should begin at the beginning in order to check that everything flows, hangs together, and is consistent.

ESSAYS AND THESES: AN OVERVIEW

- Academic writing exercises such as essays are intended for your benefit and should be approached in a positive spirit.
- Essay questions usually contain clues to the type of essay the instructor wants you to write.
- The longer an essay or dissertation, the greater the care required in planning it and in giving it a clear and solid structure.
- Narrow down a topic, using your own interests to guide you, until you make it into something specific that can be discussed in relation to concrete examples and is manageable within the length allowed.

Business Reports
and Presentations

BUSINESS REPORTS
Introduction

Business reports differ very widely in size and scope. An "occasional report" to pass on information to a colleague or update him or her on a situation may be scarcely distinguishable from a long memo (*see* MEMORANDUMS, page 245), and a report for colleagues on a meeting or seminar that you have attended may only run to a few pages. On the other hand, a formal report in which you investigate an issue on behalf of a large group or an organization and produce conclusions and recommendations may be as long as a thesis (*see* THESES, page 265) or even a small book. There are certain features that are common to the writing of all reports, however, so let us begin by considering those.

The basics of report writing, in fact, do not differ greatly from those of other types of writing. You should know the purpose for which you are writing and keep it clearly in mind. You should know the readers for whom you are writing and keep them clearly in mind as well. You should give considerable thought to the scope of the report, which will depend in part on its purpose and its intended readership. The terms of reference and the length may be determined for you—you should always get as much information as you can from whoever is commissioning the report before you begin—or you may set your own terms of reference. In the latter case especially, you may, as Suzanne D. Sparks says in *The Manager's Guide to Business Writing*, have to "balance the two parts of the information equation—what [you] want to give and what [your] readers want to receive" (New York: McGraw-Hill, 1999, p. 137). A compromise, she suggests, may be required in which either you provide less information than you have available in order to keep readers focused on the main issues and not take up too much of their time, or you extend your research because you know that your readers will want more factual detail than you have catered for at the outset (p. 138).

The essential purpose of a report is to report. This has certain consequences for the style in which a report should be written. You would normally be expected to embark on any kind of investigative report with an open mind. If you or whoever commissioned the report had already decided what decision or course of action you wanted to take, then the writing of the report would be an essentially pointless or insincere exercise. This does not mean that in the course of examining the situation and preparing the report you may not reach conclusions as to the advantages and disadvantages of particular choices or actions, because it is part of your task to do so, and it is quite legitimate for you to write persuasively for or against something in the relevant section of the report. But you should start out with an open mind and an intention to assess alternatives fairly and objectively. This intention should inform your writing, which should be plain and factual and avoid emotive language (*see* EMOTIVENESS AND OBJECTIVITY, page 204).

The Structure of a Report

The following is intended as a basic outline for a formal report. Obviously, not all reports will require all these sections.

Title

Executive summary

List of contents

List of tables and figures

Introduction—setting out the terms of reference and the background to the report

Presentation of factual material

Analysis of factual material

Conclusions

Recommendations

Appendices

References

It may suit your purpose better to combine the presentation and analysis of factual material together in a single section. Similarly, your conclusions may lead on so immediately to your recommendations that these both are best dealt with in a single section. On the other hand, to place something in a separate section gives it extra prominence. It might give extra force to your recommendations if you put them in a bulleted list. (On the use of appendices, see under MANAGING LENGTH, pages 266–267.)

Let us look briefly at certain features that are special to reports.

The Executive Summary

The executive summary is similar to the abstract of a thesis in that it condenses all the material in the report, including the conclusions and recommendations, into the space of a page or two. Its purpose is to enable a busy executive to assess whether he or she needs to read the whole report, only certain sections of it, or none of it. For general advice on the writing of summaries, see the companion volume to this one, *The Facts On File Guide to Good Writing,* chapter 1.)

The List of Contents

The executive who elects to read only certain sections of the report will need to refer to the table of contents. The list of contents should show not only the titles of the various sections, with the page numbers on which they occur, but also the various headings used within each section, likewise with page numbers:

3	Evaluation of the Intranet systems currently available	27
3.1	The Wondernet system	27
3.2	The Intraspace system	30

Headings

Even a short report will benefit from the use of headings. Headings mark off separate sections and enable the reader to navigate more easily through the page. They also break up the page and improve its appearance.

Both main sections and subsections should have headings in a formal report. You should use different fonts for different levels of heading. For instance, you might use CAPITAL LETTERS or Boldface for the headings of main sections and *italic* or *underlined italic* for subsections. It is usual to number headings in a report according to the decimal system in which the first figure stands for the number of main section and the second for the number of the subsection, as in the contents list example above. Headings should be consistent as regards the type of font used and their numbering. It may be counterproductive to introduce too many different levels of heading into a report. Two or three levels of heading will suffice in most instances.

PRESENTATIONS

Introduction

In all of the other writing contexts described and discussed in this book, the writer is essentially an invisible operator communicating indirectly with his or her "audience" via the words he or she has put down on paper. When you

are making a presentation, however, you are face to face with your audience
and have to deliver your text aloud to them, which is perhaps even more
daunting. This is a different situation, and you would expect rather different
rules to apply. In fact, however, many of the basic rules for good writing
remain valid; it is simply a matter of adapting them somewhat to suit the
circumstances.

Dealing with the Audience

As has been said before in this book, you should always pay attention to your
readers and their needs and expectations when writing. It becomes doubly
important to assess needs and expectations when readers become a listening
audience. The more you can find out in advance about your audience, the
easier it will be for you to communicate with them. If you are not addressing
a group that you already know, the easiest course is to ask the person organizing the presentation what sort of audience you can expect and, indeed, what
kind of address they will expect from you. Nevertheless, as actors will tell
you, no two audiences are ever the same. Actors can deliver the same performance to two different houses and meet with completely different recep-
tions. You may have the same experience if you deliver the same presentation
more than once. Actors are rarely able to find out in advance who is going to
be sitting in the auditorium at a particular performance, and there you, as a
speaker, may have an advantage. However, with a live audience nothing can
ever be foreseen absolutely, so one of the key qualities required of a successful presenter is flexibility.

We shall return to the question of flexibility later. For the moment, let us
concentrate on the factors that can influence the nature of your audience and
how those factors affect your preparations.

In the first place, size matters. Most speakers will find it reasonably easy
to adopt a friendly, informal tone when addressing a small gathering. It is
much more difficult to take the same tone convincingly with a larger audience. It takes a special kind of skill, not to mention special confidence, to be
able to reach out to a large crowd and speak to them with any kind of inti-
macy. Sound amplification systems do not help and in fact tend to hinder the
generation of a cozy atmosphere. As a rule of thumb, therefore, the larger the
audience, the more comparatively formal you should be in your approach.
(Formality is, however, very much a relative quality with regard to presentations, as will be suggested below.) Audience size, therefore, may affect the
tone of your presentation.

Audiences vary in size, but they also vary in what they expect you to
provide. Most will usually be hoping for a mixture of information and
entertainment, the term *entertainment* being used in its widest sense. It will
be up to you to assess what kind of mix is required. An audience of students
in a lecture hall or a group of work colleagues attending a briefing will usually expect solid information, leavened with a little humor or the occasional
anecdote; a club that has invited you to address its members on your special subject will probably expect you to keep the members interested and
amused and to impart a little useful information along the way. If you are

unsure about what the audience expects, it is generally safest to prepare a presentation consisting mainly of information interspersed with occasional moments of lighter fare. Audience expectations will affect both the content and the tone of your presentation.

It is comparatively rare to encounter an audience that is so entirely on the same wavelength as the speaker and so entirely concentrated on what he or she has to say that all its members can assimilate everything they hear in the course of an hour or more. The receptivity of audiences varies, along with their size and expectations. Some people will be rapt; some will be distracted. Some will come ready supplied with the background knowledge that they need in order to understand you fully; some will not. You have to try to assess the capacity of the average member of your audience to understand everything you have to say. Do not, on the one hand, pitch the level of your talk too high. Unless you are addressing an audience of your peers, many members of the audience will be far less familiar with the subject than you are. Do not, on the other hand, pitch your talk to what you take to be the lowest common denominator of your audience. Nothing is more boring than to hear simple information delivered at a slow pace and endlessly repeated. Make the same reasonable judgment of the receptive capacity of your listeners as you would if you were writing normally; that is, imagine yourself as a member of the audience and write your text with that in mind.

Your assessment of the receptivity of the audience will affect almost every aspect of your presentation: its content, its language, its tone, and its delivery.

Preparing Your Text

Before you begin your preparation, you will need to decide whether you are going to read a prepared text, memorize your prepared text, or work from a set of notes. Most experts advocate the third option.

If you read a text, your attention will necessarily be concentrated on the papers in front of you. This will make it less easy for you to make eye contact with the audience, which is often a great help in attracting and retaining its attention. It will also tie you to the lectern, when one simple method of varying your presentation is to move around a little on the platform.

If you memorize your text, you are free to roam and to make eye contact with the audience, but you are very much at the mercy of your memory. It is not simply that you might forget what you intended to say next. Something may happen in the audience, someone may, for instance, ask a question, you respond, and perhaps you become involved in a digression of some sort—and then you have to remember where you were and how you intended to continue.

Both reading and memorizing tend to reduce your flexibility, and flexibility, as has been said, is all important for presentations. Using notes generally gives you flexibility. Now, let us just be clear about what is meant by notes in this instance.

In preparing for a presentation, you will obviously, think, read, and research, as you would for any other piece of writing; take careful notes on the information you have gathered; and organize those notes into a coherent plan. You could use these outline notes as the basis for your talk; however, this may seem to leave too much to chance, especially if you are an inexperienced speaker. What happens if you look at these notes on the day and cannot think of a good way of developing them?

One way around this problem is to develop these notes on paper as you would normally—that is, to proceed to write out your talk in full—but then go one stage further and reduce your text to another set of notes or, perhaps more accurately, of headings and subheadings. This set of headings is what you take with you to the auditorium, either written on separate, numbered note cards or in the form of an outline:

I.   Introduce self—make contact with audience
      Glad to be with members of the Tallahassee Sports Cycling Club
      Personal reminiscence of Tallahassee in 1996

II. Introduce topic—Tour de France
      Greatest bicycle race in the world
      American involvement and American champions
      Joke: May be hard to find a "king of the mountains" in Florida

III. History of Tour de France
      A. French love affair with the bicycle
          First bicycles produced in France in 19th century
      B. Reasons for founding of race
      C. Personalities responsible for founding of race

IV. Conclusion
      May be looking at a future wearer of the yellow jersey right now

The notes or outline can take any form that you like and find helpful, and can include any aspect of the talk that you may need a prompt for, for example, a joke or anecdote. You should be much freer to react with your audience and to adjust to your time schedule if you work from notes. At the same time, the very fact that you have written the whole speech out before should give you a solid foundation. Although you have not deliberately tried to memorize every word of your text, you will probably find the act of writing them down has fixed certain formulations in your memory, and you will be able to reproduce them with comparative ease.

One final tip: If you take any sheets of paper or cards with you, make sure they are numbered so that you can put them back into order if you accidentally drop or shuffle them.

Time Constraints

You will usually have a set period of time to deliver your presentation, and even if no time limit has been set, you will not wish to go on too long and risk overtaxing your audience. You will need enough material to fill your time. It is embarrassing to run out of things to say after 40 minutes if you are scheduled to speak for an hour, and the audience may not help you with interesting questions. At the other extreme, it is frustrating to run out of time when you still have important points to make. To avoid either scenario, it can be very useful to speak out loud in your own private rehearsal, or in the presence of a trusted friend, to gauge how long your material lasts (*see* REHEARSING, page 276). Since you can never be sure of the pace at which things will proceed, even if you have rehearsed carefully and stick strictly to your prepared plan, you will again need to build some flexibility into your presentation.

The best plan is to provide yourself with too much material rather than too little. It is also useful to grade the material you have: things you have to say, things you want to say, and things you would like to say. Items in the final category should be able to be omitted if you are running short of time. This is one more complication when you are making your plan and writing out your script and notes, but it may be worthwhile.

Also, always make sure that you have a watch with you or can see a clock while you are giving the presentation.

Style, Tone, and Structure

A presentation is spoken and listened to: That fact determines its style, tone, and structure. If you write out your text, you will need to be more than usually aware of your inner voice to ensure that what you put down is easily speakable. Remember the basic hallmarks of good style: Be clear, be simple, and be as varied and vigorous as you can.

The tone will, as usual, depend on the occasion and the audience. A formal lecture will require a fairly formal style. Most presentations in an ordinary work or social environment, however, can be reasonably informal. Do not automatically assume, however, that you are going to be on very casual terms with your audience. If you establish a friendly rapport with your audience early on, you can adjust your style accordingly. Generally speaking, a style on the informal side of neutral will fit the bill; for example, write *I don't* rather than *I do not,* where appropriate, to signify to yourself that it is a spoken and relatively informal text, but do not include too many colloquial or slang expressions.

The style of your text may be informal, but its structure should not be. The structure will need to be more than usually clear because your listeners have to take it in through their ears without, necessarily, any visual aid. Organize your points in a simple, logical order and make the way your argument progresses abundantly clear. If you were writing an essay, you might pride yourself on moving smoothly from one point to the next and linking your paragraphs by various subtle means. Subtleties may be lost on a live audience, however. The basic rule for the overall structure of a presentation has already been mentioned elsewhere in this book: Say what you're going to say, say it, and say that you've said it. To this we may add another rule: Say what you're doing as you do it. Make your changes of subject and links explicit. In the Tour de France presentation outlined above, for example, you might say: "I've dealt with the history of the Tour de France; I'll now go on to say something about my personal experiences as a journalist covering the Tour." Or, in an entirely different example: "Those are the objectives of the planned sales drive, now let's look at the methods we can use to achieve those objectives."

You should not be afraid to repeat important points. If you make a point, provide evidence for it, or explain or develop it in some way, then make the basic point again before you proceed to something else. This makes it easier for the audience to follow your argument and also gives note takers an opportunity to jot down the essential information.

Rehearsing

If you have little or no public-speaking experience, or even acting experience, then you may find that you suffer from stage fright before you make your presentation. There is no cure for stage fright except to nerve yourself to go on and begin. Most actors find that as soon as they are actually on stage, they fall almost straight away into the routine they have rehearsed many times before, and their nervousness vanishes. If you rehearse your presentation, you may find the same relief. Even if you do not suffer from stage fright as such, it is still a good idea to rehearse in order to give yourself confidence. If you are at ease with your material, with your style of delivery, and, perhaps most important, with the sound of your own voice, you can be at ease with the audience as well.

You can rehearse by speaking or reading your text and tape-recording or videotaping yourself. It is, however, not uncommon for people to be somewhat disconcerted when they hear or see a recording of themselves speaking at length. Do not be distracted by the fact you may sound rather strange; there is nothing you can do about the basic sound of your voice, and the people around you are usually quite happy to live with it. Concentrate instead on whether you are pronouncing words clearly, whether you are putting the emphasis in the right places, whether you are going too fast, and whether anything that may have looked good on paper does not come over very well when you say it.

Also, if you have made a videotape, analyze your movements and gestures. If you do not have access to a video recorder, you can also rehearse in front of a mirror. This will give you a chance to practice any gestures you think may help to convey particular points. You can also check to see whether you have some automatic habitual gesture that may distract the audience. Some people scratch their noses, some people flap one hand or both hands every time they make a point. If you find yourself regularly or compulsively performing some small action over and over again, try to be aware of it and keep it in check.

Rehearsing with a tape or video recorder or in front of a mirror requires a fair degree of critical objectivity on your part. If you can find an audience or even a single auditor to rehearse with, this will be a great help. Ask your listener to check you for:

- audibility
- clarity and intelligibility
- speed of delivery
- the effectiveness and tastefulness of any humor
- irritating verbal habits or gestures

If you receive a good report on all those headings, you are ready to go.

Delivery

Do not rush. Speak at a steady pace, perhaps slightly slower than you would use in an ordinary conversation. Remember that your audience has to follow your argument. On the other hand, do not go too slowly. To ensure that your audience gets your point, repeat it rather than pronouncing it with unnatural slowness or leaving a long pause after it.

Visuals

Prepare any visual aids you intend to use beforehand. Make sure the apparatus works, make sure that you know how to work the apparatus, and practice using it. Most of all, make sure the visuals can be clearly seen by the audience.

Do not rely too heavily on visuals. A good visual can help you make a point, but a series of indifferent visuals can be just as boring as a lifeless speech. Try not to turn your back to your audience while you are using visuals, and especially, avoid making the audience wait while you manipulate the apparatus or write something on a board or overhead transparency.

BUSINESS REPORTS AND PRESENTATIONS: AN OVERVIEW

- Be clear about your audience and the purpose of your report or presentation.
- An objective use of language is generally required in the main sections of reports and presentations.
- Presentations are different from other types of document because they are designed to be heard, not read. The emphasis in preparing a text should be on making it speakable. The style should be quite informal, but the structure should be very tight and clear. Use repetition to drive home important points.
- Rehearse delivering your presentation much as an actor would rehearse delivering his or her lines.

Promotional Writing

INTRODUCTION

A writer of a manual on style may sometimes resemble a member of a temperance society standing in the doorway of a bar to pass on his or her message: Within are all sorts of tempting goodies, but outside is this spoilsport blocking the way and handing out texts advocating sobriety. The treasure chest of language is equally full of equally tempting goodies, but there is a dragon coiled around it roaring out the virtues of plainness, clarity, simplicity, objectivity, the neutral style, and various other essentially milk-and-water commodities. Surely, if there is ever a time to lift out a large handful of gems and let them sparkle, it is when your purpose is avowedly to promote something, to persuade people. What other tactic can you employ except to grab the reader's attention, fix it on whatever you are talking about, and fill him or her with excitement and enthusiasm? Is this not the occasion to bring out the linguistic equivalent of flashing lights and neon signs?

Admittedly, the first rule of promotional writing must be to attract and hold the reader's attention; however, this is not necessarily achieved by a big verbal splash. It is perfectly possible for people to walk down a street ignoring all the flashing lights and neon signs, especially if they have seen them all before. Furthermore, flashing lights and neon signs may simply generate a sense in people that something generally exciting is going on and that they are walking through a vibrant city without directing their attention toward your particular product or establishment. You want language that not only produces a response but also focuses attention on what you are trying to promote, and motivates people to take action. And when you are trying to find that kind of language, you need imagination, ingenuity, and quite possibly a certain amount of psychology and cunning. You may also find that some of the relatively mousy arts that ordinarily make for good writing start to come back into their own again.

EFFECTIVE PROMOTION

To be effective, promotional language should leave the reader with no choice but to respond to it; it should stick in the reader's memory so that the response, once produced, does not die away again; and it should put the reader into a frame of mind in which he or she wants to act in the way you, the promoter, would wish. In other words, promotional language should be direct, memorable, and above all positive. Let us try to illustrate this kind of language by way of a specific example.

Let us suppose that you belong to a club with its own clubhouse. Meetings are held and activities are staged in the house, and people sometimes make an effort to clean up after these events, but over the course of time the place gets dirtier and dowdier, and now it really needs to be spruced up. You are given, or volunteer for, the job of organizing the cleanup. You do not want to be the only one who turns up at the clubhouse with a mop and a scrub brush, so your first task is to generate some interest among the rest of the membership in participating in an event that is not in itself particularly enjoyable. In other words, you have to promote the cleanup. How might you go about this?

Any operation you want to promote will benefit from being given a snappy title or heading. Remember that you need to grab the attention of your readers from the beginning, especially in an instance like this one, because only the most altruistic of them will look forward to giving some of their precious free time to come and clear spiderwebs from the ceiling. "Cleanup Saturday" might perhaps suggest itself. But perhaps you can do better than that. Among the various resources of language that have been discussed in previous sections is the ability of words to mean more than one thing, in other words their pun potential. There are various senses of the verb *clean up* that you could play on, for example: "Clean Up Saturday" could introduce an extended joke comparing the operation to a moral crusade; "Your Team Needs Cleanup Hitters" might appeal to the male members; "Clean Up This Saturday" with a continuation such as "Make a million dollars worth of difference to yourself and your friends" could be attractive (you are entitled to exaggerate somewhat for a good cause!).

Now you have to turn to the matter at hand. When you are informing people of something, or asking them for something, be direct. Instead of saying,

Volunteers are needed for a cleanup of the clubhouse on Saturday.

or

We are having a cleanup of the clubhouse on Saturday.

ask,

Are you free next Saturday?

or

Can you help next Saturday?

Or, instead of using a question, use a statement but still aim it directly at the person you are speaking to:

We need you to help next Saturday.

or even

You have been specially selected to join an elite team of dynamic dirt busters next Saturday.

Addressing people directly is more likely to arouse their interest and make them feel involved.

What makes language memorable? This too is a question that has been discussed earlier (*see,* for example, THE ELUSIVENESS OF THE BEAUTIFUL, page 33). Language does not have to express a great thought or, indeed, be beautiful to be memorable. Slogans and advertising jingles, for example, are memorable, too. Generally speaking, they are memorable for the same reason that poetry or highly expressive prose is memorable: They exploit the possibilities of rhythm, rhyme, and alliteration. The human brain has a wonderful, or perhaps curious, susceptibility to musical combinations of words. If you say, *If a job is not completed on schedule, then it might as well not be done at all,* there is a chance that people may retain the message. But if you say, *If it ain't done in time, it ain't worth a dime,* people may wince at the trite folksiness of the expression, but there is a much better chance that, almost in spite of themselves, it will lodge in their memory. If you can coin a rhyme or an alliteration (*dynamic dirt busters*) or a rhythmic slogan (*Turn out, join in, clean up*), there is a better-than-even chance someone will remember it and repeat it to you before the operation is over.

So be direct, be memorable. Be clear and simple, too. But, above all, be positive.

EMPHASIZING THE POSITIVE

In order to achieve the final objective of all promotional writing, which is to make people take action, you need to make them feel upbeat about the prospect of doing or having something. If you are going to spark that feeling in them, that feeling must be in you, or at least in what you write. You must look at whatever it is that you are trying to "sell" and seize on its most attractive aspects, then find appropriate language in which to describe them.

If you are trying to promote a product that is a good-looking or beneficial product or one that performs its function well, the task should be fairly easy. If you are trying to promote something that is not obviously attractive, such as a cleanup at the clubhouse, more careful thought may be required.

Experts, such as Suzanne D. Sparks, author of *The Manager's Guide to Business Writing,* who write about the best ways to use language for purposes of persuasion generally suggest three important steps toward winning people over:

- Establish common ground
- Identify a problem and present a solution
- Stress rewards

Although you may not wish or need to use these three actions as steps in a process, they provide useful hints as to methods of showing things in a positive light. People need to feel that they are directly involved, that they are not being drawn into something that has nothing to do with them. People like tackling problems as long as they feel that the problems are soluble. They particularly like the feeling that they have solved a problem themselves. And, of course, everyone likes a reward. But none of these means will be fully effective unless you can present it in positive language.

Here is an example of an attempt to present something in positive terms from a few chapters back:

> *An essay is, or ought to be, more than a test. It is an opportunity and a vehicle for you, your talents, and your ideas. An essay is a means of self-expression.*

It uses the words *opportunity, talents, ideas,* and *self-expression* to try to press happy buttons in you, the reader, and stress the rewarding aspects of the task.

In the context of the club cleanup example, it might be accurate to say,

> *If we don't do something about the clubhouse soon, it will become totally unusable.*

but it would probably produce a better response to ask,

> *Wouldn't you like to see the clubhouse restored to its former glory?*

There is a problem, and you could make it seem like a real problem:

> *Nobody ever steps forward in this club when there is any real work to be done.*

That tactic, however, is unlikely to produce any volunteers, whereas the following just possibly might:

> *The members of this club are capable of fantastic efforts. All they need to do is to get over their shyness and volunteer.*

You could attempt to press people's guilt buttons:

> *Are you really going to stand by and let the clubhouse go to rack and ruin?*

But you might be better advised to take the persuaders' advice and stress the rewards:

> *Two weeks from now we shall be sitting in a sparkling clubhouse congratulating ourselves on what a good job we did.*

It is not difficult to distinguish upbeat, encouraging words, from down-beat, discouraging ones. The former are the words you want. Find them and use them.

PROMOTIONAL WRITING: AN OVERVIEW

- Effective promotional writing aims at giving readers no choice but to respond.
- Promotional writing should be direct, memorable, and above all, positive.

Keeping to Style

INTRODUCTION

This book began with an undertaking to cover several different senses of the word *style*. It has dealt with style in the abstract and with particular types of writing style, as well as with particular types of document and the stylistic conventions that they require. In order that its original promise should be completely fulfilled, however, it has still to cover one final meaning of the term. In this final chapter of the book, therefore, the word *style* will mainly be used in a sense different from the one in which it has been used up to this point.

Style, in the sense peculiar to this chapter, has little to do with the imagination, or with a person's feeling for language, or with his or her skill in choosing words or framing sentences. We have been accustomed up to now to thinking of style as being dependent on the writer's purpose or guiding idea—the best style is the one that encapsulates the writer's thought most clearly and expressively. As the title of this chapter implies, however, style here is something that is imposed from without rather than something that grows from within. It is essentially a matter of form. It consists of a set of rules or guidelines that determine precisely how a writer, publisher, or printer presents a text on the page. Writers who aim to be published ought to know what these rules are, and by and large, they observe them, it may help writers to get published.

The accent in the penultimate sentence of the last paragraph is on the word *precisely:* In most instances we shall be dealing with questions of detail. There are, in fact, so many details involved that they cannot all be covered here. This chapter will, therefore, first outline the general concept and offer suggestions as to where readers can look for fuller accounts. It will then deal with a number of specific issues relating to presentational style, such as fonts, numbers, lists and tables, and illustrations.

STYLE AND PUBLISHING
Another Definition of Style

Many good discussions start from a dictionary, so let us begin by seeing what the arbiters of meaning have to tell us. The sixth and final sense of the word *style* given in *Merriam-Webster's Collegiate Dictionary* (11th edition) is as follows:

> a convention with respect to spelling, punctuation, capitalization, and typographic arrangement and display followed in writing or in printing.

This definition is perfectly accurate, but it may be helpful to expand it a little for the benefit of those readers who have not actually had to adapt their writing to fit a particular style before.

It may, in the first place, seem slightly odd to talk about "a convention with respect to spelling, punctuation, [and] capitalization." It is hardly surprising that printers and publishers should choose to arrange and display the material on their pages in various different ways depending on their preferences and the type of book they are producing. But as far as spelling and punctuation are concerned, surely there are only two ways, the right way and the wrong way. A grammarian might say, "the normal convention is that a sentence should end with a period, a question mark, or an exclamation point," but the ordinary citizen takes this to be a rule not a convention. If a convention is, loosely, a rule or practice that the majority of people agree to observe, then most ordinary citizens cannot recall agreeing to observe the rule for ending a sentence. From their school days, they were taught how to do it properly, and if they ended a sentence in any other way, they were informed that they had made a mistake. The same applies to spelling. In American English, the word *vigor* is spelled as shown here, and that is all there is to it. If you spell it *vigour,* you are probably British, and if you spell it *vigur,* you are probably ignorant.

Now, as far as the basic principles of punctuation and the spellings of most ordinary words are concerned, there is no question of a choice of conventions. But, there are small areas of the language where a degree of flexibility exists or is allowed. For instance, if you look in *Merriam-Webster's Collegiate Dictionary,* you will find an entry for the word *cliff-hanger;* if you look in *The American Heritage Dictionary of the English Language,* however, you will find an entry for the word *cliffhanger.* Similarly, both dictionaries inform us that the same words can be spelled *lovable* or *loveable* and *sizable* or *sizeable,* yet they differ slightly on the standard word for a farewell: *Merriam-Webster's* offers *good-bye* or *good-by,* where *American Heritage* offers *good-bye, goodbye,* or *good-by,* both of which immediately follow entries for *good book* and *Good Book,* respectively. It is obvious that there is a some scope for variation within the tolerance limits of American English, as defined by two of the foremost authorities on the subject, as well as within those of the ordinary spell-checker.

In all the cases mentioned above the differences are minor: the presence or the absence of a hyphen, the letter *e,* and capital letters. None of these differences is likely to affect the average reader's understanding of a text, as exemplified in the two examples below:

> *In a powerful series cliff-hanger, lovable life-insurance adviser Johnny Delgado is seen handing his girlfriend a copy of the good book and kiss-*

ing her good-bye before running out into the street, apparently in front of a car driven by jealous schoolteacher Ruth Brooks.

In a powerful series cliffhanger, loveable life insurance advisor Johnny Delgado is seen handing his girl friend a copy of the Good Book and kissing her goodbye, before running out into the street apparently in front of a car driven by jealous school teacher, Ruth Brooks.

But the number of such small differences that can be worked into a single sentence might make us pause for a moment and wonder whether they are so minor after all.

Consistency

Minor or not, variations of this nature are what style, in the sense in which we are now using the term, is mainly concerned with. What concerns publishers and printers is not the question of whether it is more correct to write *lovable* than *loveable,* but the fact that it is bad practice to use two different spellings in the same text. If Johnny Delgado is described as a *lovable life-insurance adviser* on page 2, he ought not to be described as a *loveable life insurance advisor* on page 10 and as a *loveable life-insurance advisor* on page 110. It looks bad. The sharp-eyed reader who notices such discrepancies will quite rightly accuse the publisher of sloppy editing.

What style sets out to achieve, therefore, is consistency. Consistency is perhaps an underrated virtue, but it has been mentioned before in this book. Consistency of tone and register is important, because if you lurch wildly from, say, formality to informality, the reader may not know where he or she stands. If you are serious when you are formal, does that mean that what you write in informal mode is mean to be taken as a joke?

Presentational consistency is also important. Readers might not be confused or even irritated by the presence or absence of a hyphen in a word when that word is scattered more or less haphazardly throughout the text, but think of instances where the same word occurs several times in the space of a few paragraphs, or sections of a work in which many items containing similar information are placed together in a block. Think, for example, of the list of works cited at the end of an academic text. You do not have to be a publishing purist to feel that it is much easier on the eye, and on the mind, when all the entries present their information in the same way and in the same order, and when all the book titles are easily distinguishable from all the article titles, because the former are printed in italic and the latter in roman type.

Once you have conceded that much, you have begun to recognize the importance of consistency, and once you have recognized the importance of consistency, you have begun to appreciate the merits of style in the sense in which we are now using the word. Most publishers prize consistency of presentation so highly that they try not only to make separate publications internally consistent but to impose consistency through all the titles that appear under their imprint. To do this, they evolve what is usually known as a "house style."

House Styles

A house style, as far as writers are concerned, is a set of preferences with regard to the sort of minor issues discussed earlier, established by a particular publishing company or by some other organization that oversees the writing and publication of large numbers of books, periodicals, or other documents. The house style is usually set out in a book, pamphlet, or Web document, which is usually called a stylebook or stylesheet, a style manual or manual of style, or a style guide.

STANDARD STYLE GUIDES

If you are commissioned to write something by a publishing company or institution, then you will probably be sent a copy of its style guide or referred to one of the widely used manuals. The Associated Press (AP) publishes a stylebook that is used by most journalists; the American Psychological Association (APA) publishes a style guide and a publication manual that lay down guidelines for the presentation of written work in the social sciences; the Modern Languages Association (MLA) issues both the *MLA Handbook for Writers of Research Papers* and the *MLA Style Manual and Guide to Scholarly Publishing,* which set standards for a great deal of academic work and for articles in scholarly journals. Perhaps the most authoritative guide of all is *The Chicago Manual of Style,* published by the University of Chicago Press. Publishing companies frequently make a list of basic styles that they wish authors to observe and refer them to, for example, *The Chicago Manual of Style* for all outstanding issues. Another useful and commonly used reference is *Words into Type.*

Style guides commonly cover issues such as

- spelling variants
- punctuation
- abbreviations
- numbers
- the construction of tables and lists
- the selection of headings
- the citation of references
- the presentation of statistics

When you are referred to a particular style guide, you should obviously use it. Full or usefully condensed versions of many standard style guides are accessible via the Web.

If you are not a writer who is about to be published or who is writing for an institution that lays down particular standards for the presentation of written work, the question of house styles may seem to be of little relevance to you. But in the absence of someone else imposing a house style, you should adopt a house style of your own.

WRITERS AND HOUSE STYLE

While most writers and publishers treat reputable manuals of style as authoritative, the manuals themselves do not always make such high claims. John

Grossman, the managing editor of *The Chicago Manual of Style*, says in his preface to the 14th edition (Chicago: University of Chicago Press, 1993, vii):

> the renunciation . . . of an authoritarian position in favor of common sense and flexibility has always been a fundamental and abiding principle. At the heart of that principle is a respect for the author's individuality, purpose, and style, tempered though it is with a deeply felt responsibility to prune from the work whatever stylistic infelicities, inconsistencies, and ambiguities might have gained stealthy entrance.

Style manuals exist to serve authors and their work, in other words, not the other way around. e. e. cummings is one obvious example of an author who had his own style of presentation, and the British dramatist G. B. Shaw is another. Shaw willed that the greater portion of his estate should be devoted to the rationalization of English spelling and practiced what he preached in his plays and other writings, consistently using *dont* and *cant,* for instance, for *don't* and *can't,* respectively. No editor would have dared to cite a style manual, however authoritative or authoritarian, against writers of such distinction.

Writers who are, as yet, less distinguished may feel that they are in a weaker position vis-à-vis editors and publishers. Nonetheless, if your individuality and style are at stake, you do, as an author, have some rights in insisting on presenting your material in your own way. But this is not necessarily a matter for confrontation. Publishers, working in accordance with the principles set out in the *Chicago Manual* preface will frequently give instructions to copy editors and proofreaders to allow any reasonable style adopted by the author—usually, however, with the all-important rider, as long as it is consistent.

Consistency, again, is the operative factor. As a writer, you should adopt your own "house style," in the sense that once you have adopted one form, you should stick to it. If you write *Washington, D.C.,* on page 1, you should not write *Washington, DC,* on page 2. If you are writing a play or screenplay, do not use the speech prefix *Miss Blue:* in scene 1, and then indicate that the same character speaks again in scene 2 by using another, for example, *Miss B:* or *Betty:.* And if you start out giving your stage directions in italic—*Miss Blue enters in a rush*—do not suddenly change to capitals—MISS BLUE EXITS SLOWLY—further on. An awareness of style issues and maintaining consistency throughout the text will give your work a much more professional finish.

Copy Editors and Proofreaders

Copy editors and proofreaders are people employed by publishers to ensure that an author's text reaches the reader in a correct and orderly state. They have various functions; one among them is to act as a monitor of style.

COPYEDITING

The copy editor takes your manuscript (abbreviated as MS or ms.) or typescript (TS or ts.)—even a typewritten or computer-printed script is often referred to as a manuscript—and marks it up on the basis of guidelines provided by the editor in charge of the project and the book designer for the benefit of the keyboarders or typesetters. "Markup" is the usual name for detailed instructions as to how a piece of text is to be set, for example, the level of heading, if a line space should be inserted, where a table or illustration should appear, and if boldface or italics should be added or removed. The copy editor will also edit your text in accordance with the publisher's style, as well as for sense and grammar. However, a major part of the copy editor's job is to liaise with you, the author, and alterations that affect the wording or the basic look of your manuscript should be submitted to you first for your permission. A good copy editor will approach you in a courteous manner, making suggestions for improvements and corrections: It is generally wise to accept his or her advice.

Tight budgets often mean that publishers cannot afford to spend large amounts on copyediting standard texts that do not involve complicated typography. Often you, as author, will be expected to submit your manuscript in at least a semi-edited state. This is especially the case when your book is prepared with the aid of computer technology and submitted on disk. This is one more reason why it is good to cultivate habits of consistency and to evolve your own house style if the publisher does not impose one on you.

PROOFREADING

When your text has been keyboarded or typeset, copies are printed off so that they can be checked against the marked-up manuscript to ensure that no errors have crept in during the keyboarding or typesetting process. These first copies are known as "proof copies" or "proofs," or more specifically, galleys. A person whose job is to read, check, and correct the proofs is known as a proofreader.

At various points in this book, you have been advised to proofread your work. You will probably have interpreted this as meaning that you should look carefully through your work, correcting errors and making small improvements. This is, indeed, the essence of the task. But it is worth, at this point, considering the job in a little more detail.

Professional proofreaders generally work on paper. They have two sets of pages in front of them: the manuscript marked up by the copy editor and the newly printed proofs. They go through the two texts line by line, to check that the two match up and that any instructions given in the former have been carried out in the latter. Their job is primarily to monitor presentation and correctness, not to assess content.

Most writers nowadays work on screen. In addition, try as they may to concentrate on the purely presentational aspects of their work, it is usually very difficult for them to banish all awareness of what their work is saying and how it is saying it, all feelings of satisfaction when something is well expressed, all feelings of irritation when something has not come out quite right, and all desire to polish the text the little bit further. Alternatively, they are so weary of the text that they can hardly bear to look at it again and are longing to hand it over to somebody else to deal with. As a result, writers are often not the best people to proofread their own work. Yet it is a job they have to do. You will always be sent a set of proofs of a work of yours that is about to be published to examine and correct. If you have written an e-mail, a letter, or an essay on your own machine, you will probably have no choice but to do your own proofreading.

It is very hard to distance yourself from your own work, but this is something you have to try to do if you are to proofread it effectively. It is your intimate familiarity with the text, in fact, that militates against your looking at it searchingly and dispassionately with the trained proofreader's eye. It is amazing what obvious errors authors sometimes fail to spot, either because they have been involved with the text from the first draft, seem part and parcel of it, and the eye slips over errors, or because the errors result from a last-minute revision that authors have no time to revise further.

There is not a great deal that you can do to counteract this vulnerability. If your work is being published, you should be protected by the fact that an editor and proofreader will be working with you. If you are not being published, then you can at least do the following:

- If at all possible, ask somebody else to check or at least scan through the text.
- Allow some time to elapse between finishing the final draft and proofreading it.
- Change the medium; that is to say, if you have written your text on screen, print it out in order to proofread it.
- Try to forget content, and concentrate on spelling, grammar, punctuation, and general consistency of presentation.

FONTS

A "typeface" is a particular design of printing type; a "font" is a set of type, or a set of computer-generated characters, of the same design and style. Most computer word-processing programs contain a wide variety of different fonts. A great many of these are of little practical use for ordinary writing tasks. They are more likely to come into their own if you wish to make a document *look as if it is handwritten* or need a **special effect**, for example, if you are sending a greeting or preparing an advertisement or promotion. You should always use a simple, easily legible font for business correspondence, academic work, or text that you intend to submit to a publisher.

Even if you use relatively plain fonts, you still have a choice. Fonts and typefaces are of two basic kinds: "serif" and "sans serif." A serif is a tiny projection attached to the top or bottom of a straight stroke forming part of a letter. *Sans serif* means "without serif." A serif letter looks like this: R. A sans serif letter looks like this: R.

The differences between serif and sans serif appear slight, but a block of text in a sans serif font will easily stand out amidst a body of serif text, or vice versa:

I wrote her a poem for her birthday and attached it to the freezer door with a magnet. My poem read:

> These are cold thoughts for a cold cold place,
> The way you treat me's a disgrace,
> I've grown to hate your lovely face,
> So, goodbye, darlin'—oh, and happy birthday in any case.

It was not a very good poem, but I was not feeling very poetic just then. . . .

It is not, usually, a good idea to switch fonts frequently. Only use an alternative font to make a passage really stand out. There are other means of highlighting passages. It would suffice for an ordinary verse quotation to be "extracted," that is printed, as above, with a larger indent and a wider space above and below than ordinary text.

Roman

Ordinary upright characters in any font are known, technically, as "roman" (usually without an initial capital letter). Roman letters are used for the body text of almost all documents.

One special use of roman letters is worth pointing out. When you are using roman as your basic font, you will probably use italic for special emphasis or for the conventional presentation of, for example, book titles and foreign words (as explained in the subsections below). If you are, for any reason, using italic as the basic font for a passage, then you reverse the process and use roman for highlights:

> *Don Armado in Shakespeare's early comedy* Love's Labour's Lost *is another character afflicted with a curious* folie de grandeur.

Italic

Italic is generally used to highlight special features of the text, such as

- words that you wish to emphasize
- words shown as words, or letters shown as letters
- foreign words
- special terminology
- the titles of works
- headings

Let us look at these items briefly.

ITALIC USED FOR EMPHASIS

When documents were mostly handwritten, it was customary to underline words that would be given a particularly heavy stress if they were spoken aloud. Although word-processing programs make it easy to underline words, it is much neater to show stress by putting the affected word into italics:

> Such action should only be taken *on express instructions from the head of department.*

I do not believe there was any *conscious* intention to deceive.

The use of italic is roughly equivalent to raising your voice when speaking. Rarely should a whole sentence, let alone a whole paragraph, be put into italic simply for emphasis. If you find you are resorting to italic frequently to convey emphasis, then you should rather think of recasting some of your sentences so that the emphasis falls naturally on the words to be stressed:

Only on express instructions from the head of department should any such action be taken.

HIGHLIGHTED WORDS OR LETTERS
When you write a sentence such as

The word *latitudinarian* has seven syllables.

it is customary to put the word that is being singled out and held up for inspection, so to speak, into italics. The same applies when you do not use the formula "the word(s)" as an introduction, but that formula is nonetheless understood:

Both *argon* and *krypton* come from Greek.

Compare that sentence with the following:

Both argon and krypton are inert gaseous elements.

The latter sentence says something about argon and krypton as substances; the former is simply a comment on them as words.
Individual letters should likewise appear in italic when they are being highlighted:

Young children often write the letter *s* backward.

She spells her name with a (capital) *K*.

You don't spell *believe* with a double *e*.

If you have to pluralize a single letter shown in italic, show the *s* in roman:

There are only two *e*s in *separate*.

But it is usual to ask someone to "mind their p's and q's."

FOREIGN WORDS AND SPECIAL TERMS
Foreign words that have not been naturalized into English, or are not familiar to most English-speaking readers, are shown in italics.

> The French accused various other member states, especially the British,
> of being insufficiently *communautaire.*

> During the apartheid era, a member of the ruling National Party in South
> Africa who held more liberal views was commonly known as a *verligte.*

It is not always easy to know what is and what is not a familiar or naturalized term. If a foreign word is printed in a standard English dictionary, then
its use is recorded in a considerable number of English-language texts. In the
second example, the word *apartheid* appears in *Merriam-Webster's Collegiate
Dictionary* and would in any case be familiar to most politically aware
adults. The word *verligte* (meaning "enlightened person") does not appear in
the dictionary, however, and would only be known to people who had studied recent South African political history, so it appears in italics. Perhaps
more foreign words appear in standard dictionaries than are actually known
to the public—for example, *roman à clef, weltanschauung,* and *verismo*
(meaning "a novel that presents real persons or events in a fictional guise,"
"worldview," and "realism" [in opera], respectively). If you do not think that
your intended readers will know the term and you are forced to use it, put it
into italics. A better policy, however, is to find an English equivalent or provide an explanation.

If you provide a translation or explanation of a foreign term, place it
after the term in parentheses or quotation marks.

> The French accused various other member states, especially the British,
> of being insufficiently *communautaire* (community-minded).

It is also normal practice to put a technical term or any unfamiliar term that
is important for your argument into italics (or quotation marks) on its first
appearance:

> Among geographers this process is known as *glocalization.*

However, whereas foreign words should always be rendered in italics, special
English terms, once they have, as it were, registered themselves with the
reader, can then be shown in roman:

> Among geographers this process is known as *glocalization.* Glocalization
> is an unexpected offshoot of globalization and refers to an upsurge of pro-
> duction or community consciousness within a particular locality as multi-
> national firms move their operations away from their traditional centers.

TITLES OF WORKS

Italics are used to show the titles of books and plays:

> Scott Turow's *The Laws of Our Fathers*
> *Death of a Salesman* by Arthur Miller

the titles of long poems:

Homer's *Odyssey*

and of published collections of poems:

For the Union Dead by Robert Lowell.

The titles of individual shorter poems are set roman in quotation marks:

"I Know Why the Caged Bird Sings" by Maya Angelou
Robert Browning's "How We Brought the Good News from Ghent to Aix"

The titles of articles in journals, periodicals, and newspapers are shown in roman in quotation marks; the titles of journals, periodicals, and newspapers are shown in italics:

"FBI's No. 2 Was 'Deep Throat,'" written by David Von Drehler, staff
writer for the *Washington Post*
International Journal of Urban and Regional Research

HEADINGS

Italics are generally used for subheadings following a main heading that is shown in capitals or in boldface.

Boldface

The *Chicago Manual of Style* and other style guides are not, in general, favorably disposed toward the use of boldface in text. It is not good practice, generally, to intersperse words in bold in a body of text. Bold is, however, useful for higher-level headings in printed texts and for headings in letters. It can also be useful in highlighting points in a list.

NUMBERS

The basic style question with regard to numbers is whether they should be spelled out (*one, two, three* . . .) or shown as numerals (*1, 2, 3* . . .). Style guides frequently lay down specific rules in this respect. The following conventions should be followed in the absence of instructions to the contrary.

Spell out numbers when

- they are made up of no more than two words;
- a number is the first word in a sentence;
- you are expressing a simple quantity or fraction in a nonscientific work;
- you are writing about a particular century or giving the time without using A.M. or P.M.

Use numerals when

- it would take more than two words to spell out the number in question;
- a series of numbers are clustered together in a sentence;
- the number in question represents a date; a time of day, a percentage or a decimal, a numerical result such as a score in a game, an exact amount of money, or a division or page in a written work;
- you are expressing a quantity (including fractions) in a mathematical, scientific, technical, or statistical work.

Ordinal numbers follow the same rules as cardinal numbers (*first, twelfth, 101st*).

Let us briefly review these lists.

Spelled-Out Numbers

Two-word numbers are all the numbers from one through one hundred and whole numbers such as four hundred, two thousand, four billion, and so on. (It is also permissible to write very large numbers as combinations of numerals and words: *6 million, 4 billion.*) Any number in the twenties, thirties, and so forth to the nineties should be spelled with a hyphen (*twenty-one, forty-six, eighty-seven*).

> *There were twelve of us cooped up in a cell designed for two occupants.*

> *Of the twenty-six applications received, only nine were from people with suitable qualifications.*

> *More than five thousand members of the public responded to the advertisement.*

Even a number that would normally appear in numerals is spelled out when it occurs as the first word of a sentence:

> *Six hundred twenty-seven people attended the meeting.*

It is usually quite easy to recast such a sentence in such a way as to avoid having to write out the number:

> *The meeting was attended by 627 people.*

But if you wish to stress the number by putting it first (and, in this instance, avoid using the passive voice), spell the number out.

In work that is scientific, mathematical, or technical in nature, it is usual to express all quantities and fractions as numerals. In nontechnical writing the normal rules apply for numbers, and common fractions are spelled out:

According to the sign, we were sixty-seven kilometers from Paris.

She owes me forty-five dollars.

My weight in those days was about 120 pounds.

Approximately three-fifths of the population is living below the poverty line.

Christopher Columbus first sailed to the Americas more than five hundred years ago.

Although most dating is done using numerals, it is customary to use a written ordinal number with the word *century*:

During the second half of the sixteenth century . . .

What many European historians refer to as "the long nineteenth century" finally came to an end in 1914.

Times of day are usually written out when you are not giving a precise measurement of time or do not use the abbreviations A.M. and P.M.:

from half past twelve to a quarter of one

Let's meet up at three o'clock.

Numerals

Numbers that cannot be spelled out in one or two words should be shown in numeral form:

The child had already begun counting and knew that there were 351 days to go before next Christmas.

While words tend to be used for round numbers, approximations, and in nontechnical contexts, numerals tend to predominate when exact figures are given, when you use a figure with an abbreviation, and in scientific and technical contexts generally. For example, dates are given in figures:

November 12, 2002

the 1960s

A.D. 54 or 54 C.E.

(Note that abbreviations for eras, A.D. and B.C., or C.E. and B.C.E., are shown in SMALL CAPITALS. Also note that A.D. is always placed before the year.) Times that are followed by A.M. or P.M., designating a precise moment, are also set as numerals (and usually in SMALL CAPITALS, too):

12:54 P.M.

as are quantities using similar abbreviations:

90 lbs.

$45.23

and percentages and decimal fractions:

75 percent or *75%*

32.67 centimeters or *32.67 cm*

and scores in sports events, games, votes, and the like:

If you get a score of 500 you can go on to the next level.

In a 5-4 decision by the Supreme Court . . .

The divisions of a written work are usually shown in numerals:

in chapter 6 on page 127

lines 6–15

in act 2, scene 3

Volume 4 of this great work is to be published next year.

Scientific, mathematical, technical, and statistical work generally includes a lot of figures, and it is customary to use numerals throughout:

Of the 67 respondents, only 9, that is, less than 15%, achieved scores of 100 or above.

Consistency

Where possible, it is best not to mix spelled-out numbers and numbers given as numerals within the same passage of text. If you give a series of numbers, one of which should be expressed in numerals according to the basic rules, then you should put them all into numerals. Generally, where many numbers cluster together it is usually clearer and neater to use numerals, too:

> *The club president called out the numbers as the tickets were drawn from the hat. First came 76, then 5, then 133. I checked the numbers on my own tickets yet again.*

> *The ages of the members of the team are 22, 25, 27, 32, and 41.*

However, it may sometimes be an aid to clarity if you break the consistency rule in a case like the following, where one particular number refers to a different factor from the others:

> *The ages of the members of the team are 22, 25 (three members), 27, 32, and 41.*

If you begin a sentence with a number, which must be written out, then it is best to write out another number if one occurs within the same sentence:

> *Two hundred fifty guests were trying to sit down on one hundred fifty seats.*

But if the sentence involves several numbers, it would be much better to recast it.

QUOTATIONS

It is worth reminding readers here of the general rule that all borrowings from other sources must be acknowledged. When you repeat the actual words of another person, you should put them into quotation marks. (It is good practice to put them into quotation marks from the first time you make a note of them while doing research.) When you paraphrase the words of another person, you should show by means of an allusion or citation that the idea comes from another person:

> *Arnold Roberts insists that "no such undertaking was ever made."*

> *According to Arnold Roberts, his organization made no promises to the claimants.*

> *But another source suggests that no promise was made to the claimants (Roberts 2005, 24).*

It is good to use quotations in essays and similar pieces of work to show that you have read widely and to back up your own ideas with statements from other authorities. It is unwise, however, to use too many quotations, in case you give the impression of relying too heavily on other people's ideas. When you do quote, you should quote only as much of another person's text as is necessary to reinforce your point. This may sometimes require you to omit part of a text. You may also have to alter the exact wording of the quotation to make it fit grammatically into your own text. Let us look briefly at the rules for inserting quotations.

A short quotation can often be fitted into a sentence without additional punctuation, other than quotation marks:

> *When exactly is this "mother of all parties" you've been talking about actually going to take place?*

A longer and more formal quotation is usually introduced by a colon, and if it consists of a full sentence, it begins with a capital letter:

> *Smith's position on the question is quite clear: "There is simply no conclusive evidence that human activity is the principal clause of global warming."*

If you wish to insert a very long quotation, of say 60 words or more, it is best to insert it as a block separated by a space from the text above and below and indented:

> *Sandra B. Jones ingeniously relates the experience of eternity to a phenomenon that we all become aware of as we grow older:*

>> *As we reach middle age, we suddenly become conscious that the days, the months, and the years are passing much more rapidly than they did when we were younger. By the time we reach the age of eighty or ninety, we barely seem to have stood up from the breakfast table on one morning before we are sitting down to it again on the next. If people ask me how we could possibly bear the endless succession of days in eternity, I remind them of this fact and tell them that since time can accelerate for us like this when we are in the body, a whole age may pass in an eye blink once we are in the spirit.*

> *I find this thought immensely comforting. . . .*

A quotation set out as above is called a "block quotation," "extract," or "excerpt." Because it is separated from the main body of the text, it should not be put in quotation marks.

Quotations within Quotations

If you have put a passage into quotation marks, you should use single quotation marks for any quoted words that appear inside it:

> *"What Shakespeare actually wrote," Barnaby interrupted, "was 'All that glisters is not gold,' not 'All that glitters.' "*

The only exception is in a block quotation. The fact that a block quotation has no quotations marks around it enables double quotation marks to be used for quoted words that fall within it.

Adjusting Quotations

Let us assume that the original passage from which you wish to quote reads as follows:

> *Work in these factories is seasonal, with the bulk of production taking place between September and April, which results in many workers being laid off during the summer months and joining the throngs who seek to make a living from tourism.*

You might wish to quote some, but not all, of this rather long sentence. When you omit any words from a quoted passage, you should indicate the fact by inserting an ellipsis (. . .):

> *Cummings further notes that: "Work in these factories is seasonal, . . . which results in many workers being laid off during the summer months."*

You do not need to place an ellipsis at the end, however, simply because you have not written out the original sentence in full.

If you need to change any of the words within a quotation, for example, to make the quotation fit within the run of your own text, you should mark the change by enclosing it in brackets:

> *Because they cannot rely upon all-year employment in the factories, "workers [join] the throngs who seek to make a living from tourism."*

You should also use brackets if you wish to introduce your own explanation into a quotation:

> *Cummings informs us that "Work in the factories is seasonal, with the bulk of production taking place between September and April [the main growing season], which results in many workers being laid off during the summer months."*

Whatever you leave out or interpolate, make sure not to change the basic meaning of the passage you are quoting.

Italics in Quotations

Writers sometimes italicize certain words in a quotation in order to highlight them because they are especially important to the argument. However, it is perfectly possible that italics might have been used in the original script. In order that the reader should not be misled, whenever a quotation contains words in italics, you should always indicate whether they formed part of the original or have been added. If you add italics, put a note in parentheses after the quotation: (italics added) or (my italics). If they were in the original, the usual formula is (emphasis in original).

LISTS AND TABLES

Lists and tables are a useful means, in the right context, of presenting a large amount of information in a clear and user-friendly form. A good many paragraphs, a good deal of complicated syntax, as well as much tedious repetition would usually be involved if you attempted to provide the same amount of data in prose. There are few, essentially stylistic issues involved in the construction of tables; these will be dealt with briefly below. First, let us look at lists.

Lists

Consider the following fairly lengthy sentence:

> *The lessee of the hall is responsible for ensuring that the building is left in a clean and usable condition, that all electric lights and appliances are turned off, that no personal property belonging to the lessee is left inside the building, that people leaving the building do so in a quiet and orderly manner, that all windows and doors are left locked, and that the keys are returned to the church office on the following day.*

Though there is nothing intrinsically unclear about these instructions, they might perhaps have more impact if they were presented in the following manner:

> *The lessee of the hall is responsible for ensuring that*
>
> > *the building is left in a clean and usable condition;*
> > *all electric lights and appliances are turned off;*
> > *no personal property belonging to the lessee is left inside the building;*
> > *people leave the building in a quiet and orderly manner;*
> > *all windows and doors are left locked;*
> > *the keys are returned to the church office on the following day.*

This makes it much easier for the person or group renting the space to see precisely what is expected of them.

There is something at least crisp, if not positively imperative, about a list:

> *Every participant will be expected to arrive equipped with the following items:*
>
> *warm clothing*
> *a waterproof coat*

sturdy walking shoes
a backpack
emergency rations
a nonalcoholic drink
a map

If businesslike crispness is not part of your purpose, then it may perhaps be better to avoid using a vertical list. There is a place for lists in business letters, reports, certain types of essays, and indeed anywhere where it would assist the reader to give prominence to a number of distinct items or factors.

The standard forms of punctuation for lists are illustrated in the two examples above. When the items making up the list complete the sentence begun by the introductory words, no end-of-line punctuation and no final period are necessarily required. This format is, however, more suitable for lists in which the individual items consist of single words or only a few words. Where the listed items are longer, it is better to end each one with a semicolon (or a comma), and in that case the list must end with a period.

GRAMMATICAL CONTINUITY IN LISTS

Punctuation in most lists is, as the previous paragraph pointed out, dependent on the items in the list completing the sentence by the words that precede the colon. It is, therefore, important that each of the listed items matches up grammatically with the introduction:

The committee objected to the proposal on the grounds that

> *the schedule was unrealistic;*
> *it had not been properly costed;*
> *no assessment had been made of the strength of the competition;*
> *likely competition also with the company's existing product lines;*
> *the unavailability of a trained management team.*

For such a list to work properly, each separate item must follow grammatically the introductory words and be able to form a complete sentence. Too often when people are drawing up lists, they lose touch with the opening section and loosely attach a fresh item to the one that went before, as is the case above. The following is not a proper sentence:

The committee objected to the proposal on the grounds that likely competition also with the company's existing product lines

Nor is this:

The committee objected to the proposal on the grounds that the unavailability of a trained management team

In both these cases, the above list lost its grammatical coherence because there should have been a verb in the clauses that follow *that*, as there is in the earlier items. Obviously, the easiest way to maintain coherence is to give all the items in the list the same form. Therefore, if we recast those clauses so that they contain verbs, grammatical coherence will be restored (see below).

It is also important that you choose the introductory words with care in order to ensure that they provide a suitable springboard for what follows them. It is often, for example, easier to construct a series of clauses to follow *that* than it is to find nouns or noun phrases to follow a simple preposition. If, for instance, the writer had chosen to make the introductory words *The committee objected to,* some of the items shown above could be made to fit easily enough:

> *The committee objected to:*
> *the unrealistic schedule*
> *the lack of proper costing . . .*

But it would be difficult to attach the last three items in anything like their present form. For example,

> *The committee objected to the unavailability of a trained management team.*

seems like a proper sentence but does not actually make good sense because the committee are not objecting *to* there being no managers but *because* there are no managers.

There is one further question mark over the original example list given above. The second item forms a perfectly good sentence when attached to the introductory words:

> *The committee objected to the proposal on the grounds that it had not been properly costed.*

It is quite clear here that *it* refers to the proposal. In the actual list, however, where *it had not been properly costed* appears as the second item, the reader may not know whether *it* refers to *proposal* in the introduction or to *schedule* in the first item.

A list, therefore, needs to be thought of as a whole, as a series of branches emerging from the same stem. The correct relationship must be preserved between branches and stem on the one hand and between the various branches on the other. A revised version of the original example list should look like this:

> *The committee objected to the proposal on the grounds that:*
> *it had not been properly costed;*
> *the schedule was unrealistic;*
> *no assessment had been made of the strength of the competition;*
> *the new product might also compete with the company's existing lines;*
> *there was no trained management team available.*

Tables

Tables usually contain data in number form, often in percentages, that is arranged in vertical columns and horizontal rows.

Let us assume that you wish to construct a simple statistical table showing computer ownership among a sample of 500 people aged between 20 and 60, organized according to age ranges: 20–30, 31–40, 41–50 and 51–60.

This table requires four columns. The left-hand column, known technically as the "stub," lists the various categories of people or things to which the information given in the other columns refers. The second column shows the number of people or things in that particular category, and the other columns show the percentage of people or things that fit a particular description.

The topmost row of the table contains the column headings, which give the relevant descriptions. Our example table might, therefore, look like this:

Age	Number	Have computer (%)	Do not have computer (%)
20–30	185	82.3	17.7
31–40	140	71.4	28.6
41–50	170	70.5	29.5
51–60	105	61.9	38.1
Total	500		

A similar result can be achieved using the tables tool in a word-processing program:

Age	Number	Have computer (%)	Do not have computer (%)
20–30	185	82.3	17.7
31–40	140	71.4	28.6
41–50	170	70.5	29.5
51–60	105	61.9	38.1
Total	500		

Each table should be numbered and have a brief caption:

TABLE 1
COMPUTER OWNERSHIP BY AGE

If the table is reproduced from another source, the source should be acknowledged. (For more information, *see* CAPTIONS AND CREDIT LINES, page 307).

If the piece you are writing contains many tables, these should be listed, together with their title, at the beginning of the work after the table of contents and the list of illustrations (if there is one). A table should be positioned as close as possible to the correlating passage of text, which may contain an explicit reference to it. You should not leave a table to explain itself. You should relate it to your argument and show how it contributes to the point you are making. With respect to the example table shown above, you might comment in the text:

As Table 1 shows, the level of computer ownership is comparatively high among all age groups represented in the sample, but significantly higher among 20- to 30-year-olds than among 51- to 60-year-olds. These results are not unexpected and seem to confirm the principal idea proposed in this study that people who have not grown up with a particular technology may find it hard to adjust to that technology in later years.

Tables of much greater complexity than the one shown above can be created, but the same basic principles apply to all.

ILLUSTRATIONS

A discussion of the principles that should govern the choice of illustrations for a book or document and the technical processes by which photographs, drawings, and other types of artwork are reproduced lies beyond the scope of this text-oriented book. A few general pointers can, nonetheless, be given.

It is important to consult carefully with the person or organization that will be printing your work to ensure that you present your graphic material in a form suitable for reproduction and that the results will genuinely enhance your work. Modern color printers attached to home computers suggest that color printing has become easy, and the fact that newspapers frequently feature color photographs suggests that mass-producing colored artwork has become relatively cheap. Nevertheless, for the person who, for instance, intends to self-publish a book, color reproduction is still an expensive item. Any color printing is more expensive than black and white, and multicolor printing is most expensive of all.

If the main disadvantage of color printing is the cost, the main drawback with the printing of some black-and-white items is lack of clarity. Maps or diagrams with different kinds of shading or in which small-sized text is incorporated into the graphic material are particularly prone to indifferent legibility. So, if you are thinking of including an illustration of that type, you should take care that it can be reproduced with sufficient sharpness and is of sufficiently large size to convey its message clearly.

Like tables, illustrations—unless they are collected together in a separate section of the book—should be positioned as close as possible to the correlating passages of text, which also may contain a reference to them. Also, they should follow those passages, not precede them. When there are a large number of illustrations, the illustrations should be numbered (figure 1, figure 2) consecutively, either throughout the book or chapter by chapter. In the latter case, you might use a double numbering system: Figure 9.2, for example, would refer to the second illustration in chapter 9.

Again, when there are a large number of illustrations, a list of them should be provided at the beginning of the book or document after the table of contents:

Illustrations
1. View of the Houses of Parliament from the "London Eye"   21
2. Interior of the House of Commons   28

The figures are identified by their captions, if the captions are fairly short. If a caption is lengthy, it should be suitably shortened for the list.

When you submit a manuscript to a publisher or pass it to a printer, the artwork is kept separate from the text, nowadays usually on a separate computer file. It is quite easy for mistakes to occur when the illustrations are married to the text. It is very important, when you proofread your own work, to check that the illustrations appear in the correct order, are correctly positioned in relation to the text, and have the correct captions.

Captions and Credit Lines

Nearly every illustration, graph, and diagram needs a good clear caption. If an image is to be worth the traditional "thousand words," the reader must know what he or she is looking at.

A caption is, in effect, the title of the illustration. It should be kept factual and short:

Fig. 2. The kitchen in the victim's apartment

It is, however, perfectly legitimate to add additional material that may point to an item of particular interest in the illustration or explain some aspect of it. *The Chicago Manual of Style* distinguishes between the caption and any additional material and refers to the latter as the "legend." The legend follows the caption after a period:

Fig. 2. The kitchen in the victim's apartment. The police officer is pointing to the exact spot where the victim's body was found.

Like quoted words, visual material that is taken from another source must be provided with an acknowledgment. The acknowledgment is given in a "credit line." Written permission is often required to reproduce an image, graph, table, and the like, made by another person, so the credit line frequently takes the following form:

Reprinted, by permission, from [author's name and title of work]

If you ask somebody to prepare a map, photograph, etc., for inclusion in your text, you should likewise credit that person:

Map/photograph/drawing by [artist's name]

KEEPING TO STYLE: AN OVERVIEW

- Style, for the purposes of this chapter, is a set of rules governing choices to be made when there are several different legitimate ways of spelling, punctuating, or presenting the same piece of written material.
- The main purpose of rules of style is to ensure that consistency is maintained throughout a work or a series of work.
- Most publishers and institutions establish their own rules for style, which are set out in a style guide or manual of style.
- Even if you are not following a particular style guide, try to achieve consistency within your own work.
- Use a plain, easily readable font for the body of your text.
- Italic is the font chiefly used to highlight words or phrases to which a writer wishes to call special attention.
- Spell out numbers when they consist of no more than two words or occur as the first word in a sentence. In most other cases use numerals.
- Quotations should be chosen for their relevance and should fit comfortably into the context you provide for them.
- Quotations can be adjusted, if necessary, to fit the grammar of your sentence.
- All quotations should be acknowledged, as should all other borrowed material, such as reprinted pictures or graphs.
- Lists should be grammatically coherent: The items making up the list should naturally and correctly follow the words that introduce the list.
- Tables and illustrations should be positioned as close as possible to the correlating passage of text, especially if they are referred to in text; should usually be numbered; should have clear captions; and should be printed with an acknowledgment when they are taken from another source.

INDEX

Boldface page numbers denote the major treatment of a topic.

A

abbreviations 288
acknowledgments 308
adding and subtracting 16
adjectives, avoiding unnecessary 59–60
adjusting style 166–167
adverbs, avoiding unnecessary 59–60
aesthetic values 33–35
ambiguity, avoiding 50
analysis, use of 34–35
analysis of factual material 270
Anglo-Saxon versus Latin 75–76
announcing failure of job application 233
answering letters 229–230
appendices 270
applications
        announcing failure of 233
        for jobs 236–239
appropriate tone, finding 169–183
argument structure 44–45
Arnold, Matthew 49
artist's license 25–26
audibility 276
audience 277
        dealing with 272–273
authorial pronouns 47–48

aware, becoming 32–33
awareness, types of 30–31

B

bad news, delivering 231–233
beautiful, elusiveness of 33–34
beauty 5
boldface 295
Boswell, James 88
brevity 249
Browning, Robert 56
business letters, structure and conventions 217–223
business reports 269–271
        and presentations 269–277
        overview 277
Byron, Lord 25

C

captions 308
        and credit lines 307
changing point of view 130–131
Chaucer, Geoffrey 74
children, writing for 179–183
choosing a style 165–183
        overview 183
choosing words 71–91
        overview 91
Churchill, Winston 9
clarity 8, 19, 38–52, 69, 183, 276
        of expression 49–52

clarity *(continued)*
　　of organization　41–49
　　in the way you say
　　　　something　41–52
　　in what you want to say
　　　　39–41
clauses　95–97
　　main　121
　　subordinate　121
clear expression, bases of　49–50
clichéd formulas　230–231
closings
　　of letters and formal e-mails
　　　　223
　　salutations and　222–223
coherence　141–142, 152
colloquialisms　190–191
colloquial vigor　57–58
comic imagery　160–161
communication　23–24
comparison　163
completeness　93–94
complex, simple versus　76–82
composing and revising　133
composition, methods of　15
Conan Doyle, Sir Arthur　187
conclusions　270
connecting paragraphs　149–152
considerations, ethical　186–187
consistency　287, 298–299, 308
constraints, time　274–275
constructing paragraphs
　　123–152
　　from notes　135–138
　　overview　152
　　from text　138–141
constructing sentences　93–121
　　overview　121
contents, list of　270, 271
context　91, 153
continuity, grammatical in lists
　　303–304
contractions　191, 210
coordinating and subordinating
　　ideas　106–110
coordination　97–99, 121
　　and subordination　97–99

copyediting　289–290
copy editors and proofreaders
　　289–291
correctness, beyond　21–35
　　overview　35
cover letters　233–236
credit lines, captions and　307
criticism and self-criticism
　　16–17
crosswords　28–30
cues　151–152

D

dangling modifiers　114–115
dangling participles　114–115
dead metaphors　162–163
delivery　277
　　of bad news　231–233
　　speed of　276
devices, figurative　157–158
dialogue　131–133
Dickens, Charles　6, 7, 21, 76,
　　205
Donne, John　32
Dylan, Bob　26

E

effective promotion　279–281
elegance　5, 8, 19, 53–55, 69
Eliot, T. S.　32
e-mails
　　closings in formal 223
　　formal, structure and
　　　　conventions of 217–223
　　format of formal 219–222
　　informal 242–243
　　layout in formal 218–219
　　letters and 215–244
　　　　basics 216–217
　　　　overview 243–244
　　salutations in formal
　　　　222–223
emotive and emotional language
　　204–205

emotive language
  negative aspects 208–210
  positive aspects 207–208
emotiveness and objectivity
  204–210
emphasis, use of italics 292–293
emphasizing the positive
  281–283
English
  formal 195–197
  informal 190–194
  standard, distinguishing with
    informal language
    192–193
English vocabulary, origins
  74–76
essay example 260–265
essays 252–265
  and theses 251–268
    overview 268
  analytical 255
  descriptive 255
  discussion 256
  extended 265–266
  interpretive 255
  narrative 255
  subject in 254–255
  types 255–256
essay-writing style 259
ethical considerations 186–187
execution, planning and 267–268
executive summary 270, 271
expressing tone through words
  185–210
  overview 210

F

factual material
  analysis of 270
  presentation of 270
fewer nouns, use of 82–86
figurative devices 157–158
figurative language
  function of 155–156
  nature of 154–155
  perils of 161–163
  place for 158–160
  using 153–163, 156–157
  overview 163
Flaubert, Gustave 9
fonts 291–295, 308
forceful language 56–57
foreign words and special terms
  293–294
formal English 195–197
formality 183
  and informality 189–190
formal language
  other aspects 196–197
  place for 197
format 219–222
formulas, clichéd 230–231

G

grace 5
grammar 22–24, 93–97
  liberties with 192
  rules of 35
grammatical continuity in lists
  303–304
Greenspan, Alan 202
guidance formulas 48–49

H

hanging participles 114–115
headings 249, 271, 295
  selection of 288
hierarchy of language 189–190
Hemingway, Ernest 6, 7
highlighted words or letters 293
Homer 43
house styles 288–289
  writers and 288–289
humor 276

I

ideas
  coordinating and
    subordinating 106–110

ideas *(continued)*
distinguishing relative
importance of **110–112**
organizing and combining in
sentences **106–112**
ignorance of meaning **161**
illustrations **306–308**
imagery, comic **160–161**
informal e-mails **242–243**
informal English **190–194**
distinguishing with standard
English **192–193**
informality
formality and **189–190**
other aspects **193–194**
informal language, place for **194**
intelligibility **276**
introduction **270**
invisible reader **174–175**
Isherwood, Christopher **188**
italics **292–295, 308**
for emphasis **292–293**
in quotations **301–302**

J

James, Henry **21**
job applications **236–239**
announcing failure of **233**
Johnson, Samuel **16, 88**
joining **167–169**
Jonson, Ben **24**
Joyce, James **117**

K

Kennedy, John F. **195, 196**
key words, in paragraphs
142–143

L

language **12–14, 35**
and basic logic in sentences
105–106

and pictures **186–189**
distinguishing between
informal and standard
192–193
emotive **210**
negative aspects
208–210
positive aspects
207–208
emotive and emotional
204–205
feeling for **26–33**
acquiring **30–33**
figurative
perils of **161–163**
place for **158–160**
using **153–163,
156–157**
forceful **56–57**
hierarchy of **189–190**
power of **185–186**
spoken **210**
Latin, Anglo-Saxon versus
75–76
layout **218–219**
length, managing in theses
266–267
letters
and e-mails **215–244**
basics **216–217**
overview **243–244**
answering **229–230**
business, structure and
conventions **217–223**
closings in **223**
cover **233–236**
format of **219–222**
highlighted **293**
layout of **218–219**
of recommendation
239–242
salutations in **222–223**
letter-writing
beginning **223–225**
tactics **223–231**
linear organization **43–44**

linkers 145–146, 149–151, 152
   commonly used 146–148
linking in time and space
   148–149
lists 302–304, 308
   of contents 270, 271
   grammatical continuity in
      303–304
   and tables 302–306
   of tables and figures 270
logic 121
   basic, and language
      105–106
   of the sentence 105–115
lonely writer 173–174
longer words, careful use of
   87–88

M

major sentences 95
manuals of style 308
Marvell, Andrew 28
Marx, Groucho 27
meaning, ignorance of 161
Melville, Herman 21
memorandums 245–247
   and résumés 245–249
      overview 249
metaphors 163
   dead 153, 162–163
   extended 153
   mixed 153, 161–162
Miller, Arthur 135
Milton, John 21, 24, 85
minor sentences 95
mixed metaphors 161–162
modifiers, dangling 114–115

N

neutrality 197–199
nonpeers 183
   and peers, writing for
      175–177

notes, constructing paragraphs
   from 135–138
nouns 91
   use of fewer 82–86
numbers 288, 295–299, 308
   cardinal 296
   ordinal 296
   spelled-out 296–297
numerals 297–298, 308

O

objectivity 205–206, 210, 277
   emotiveness and 204–210
only, position of 115
ordering the body of the work
   43
organization 69
   linear 43–44
   structural 142–149, 152
organizing and combining ideas in
   sentences 106–112

P

Paine, Thomas 33, 34
pairings 72–73
paragraph breaks, when to insert
   130–133
paragraphs
   basics 124–133
   composing 133
   concluding 129
   connecting 149–152
   constructing 123–152
      from notes 135–138
      overview 152
      from text 138–141
   function of 124–125
   introductory 126–129
   length of 125–126
   making 133–141
   revising 133
   rounding off 144–145
   transition 130

paragraphs *(continued)*
    types of **126–130**
    unifying **141–149**
parallel structure **143–144**
Pascal, Blaise **216, 217**
peers **183**
    and nonpeers, writing for
        175–177
pictures, language and **186–189**
planning **41, 243, 268**
    and execution in theses
        267–268
    preparation and, in essays
        and theses **251–252**
point of view, changing **130–131**
Pope, Alexander **25, 116**
position, only get it right **115**
positioning **112–115**
    ambiguous **114**
    importance of **112–113**
    rhythm and **118**
positive, emphasizing **281–283**
Pound, Ezra **32**
power over readers **187–188**
practical constraints, dealing with
    253–254
preparation and planning in
    essays and theses **251–252**
preparing
    text **273–274**
    to write **39–41**
presentation **243**
    of factual material **270**
presentations **271–277**
    business reports and
        269–277
        overview **277**
prominence, giving **225–228**
promotion, effective **279–281**
promotional writing **279–283**
    overview **283**
pronouns, authorial **47–48**
proofreaders, copy editors and
    289–291
proofreading **290–291**
prose rhythm **115–117**

publishing, style and **285–291**
punctuation **288, 308**

Q

quotations **299–302, 308**
    adjusting **301**
    italics in **301–302**
    within quotations **300–301**

R

range of reference **179**
reader, invisible **174–175**
readers **183, 244, 283**
    power over **187–188**
    writers and **173–183**
recommendation, letters of
    239–242
recommendations **270**
recurrence **142**
reference, range of **179**
references **270**
    citation **288**
registers **199–203, 210**
    different **200–203**
    nature of **199–200**
    using **203**
rehearsing **276, 277**
relationship between writer and
    readers **175**
repetition **66–69, 69, 277**
report, structure of **270–271**
résumés **247–249**
    memorandums and **245–249**
        overview **249**
revising, composing and **133**
rhythm **121**
    and positioning **118**
    and sentence construction
        118–121
    of the sentence **115–121**
    prose **115–117**
    where to find **117–118**
roman **292**

Roosevelt, Theodore 117
rules 308

S

salutations 244
    and closings 222–223
Scott, Sir Walter 75
self-confidence 5
self-criticism, criticism and 16–17
sentences
    basics 93–105
    constructing 93–121
        overview 121
    construction, rhythm and
        118–121
    length of 99–105
    logic of 105–115
    long 102–103
        dividing up 103–105
    minor and major 95
    organizing and combining
        ideas in 106–112
    rhythm of 115–121
    short 100–101
        combining 101–102
    topic 133–135, 257
    verbs in 94–95
Shakespeare, William 21, 24,
    28, 33, 85, 87, 155, 260, 264
Shaw, George Bernard 33
signposting 45–47
similes 163
simple versus complex 76–82
simplicity 8, 19, 52–53, 69, 183,
    210
soft soap sandwich 228–229
speaking and writing 17–19
speed of delivery 276
spelling 288, 308
Sprachgefühl 26
standard English, distinguishing
    with informal language
    192–193
statistics, presentation of 288
Stevens, Wallace 32

structural organization 142–149,
    152
structure 217–218, 268
    of an argument 44–45
    of business letters and
        formal e-mails 217–223
    of reports 270–271
    parallel 143–144
    style, tone, and, in
        presentations 275–276
    traditional 42–43
style
    adjusting 166–167
    another definition 285–287
    choosing 165–183
        overview 183
    and content 12–14
    essay-writing 259
    and grammatical correctness
        22–26
        tools 24–25
    guides 308
        standard 288
    house 288–289
    keeping to 285–308
        overview 308
    learned 11–12
    manuals of 308
    nature of 5–19
        overview 19
    neutral 183
    personal 9–11
    in practice 211–308
    and publishing 285–291
    qualities of 37–69
        overview 69
    revising for 15–16
    tone, structure, and, in
        presentations 275–276
    treatment of 8–9
    in the writing process 15–17
    writing with 3–210
subject 254–255
subordination 99, 121
    coordination and 97–99
subtracting, adding and 16

T

tables 305–306, 308
  and figures, list of 270
  lists and 302–306
  and lists, construction of
    288
tactics, letter-writing 223–231
Tennyson, Alfred, Lord 195
terms, special and foreign words
  293–294
text
  constructing paragraphs
    from 138–141
  preparing, in presentations
    273–274
theses 265–268
  essays and 251–168
    overview 268
thesis statement 257–259
thought 12–14
time and space, linking in
  148–149
time constraints 274–275
title 270
titles of works 294–295
tone 183
  appropriate, finding
    169–183
  definition of 169–171
  expressing through words
    185–210
    overview 210
  formal 210
  informal 210
  neutral 210
  strong and neutral 171–173
  style, structure, and
    275–276
topic
  narrowing 256–257
topic sentence 133–135, 152,
  257
traditional structures 42–43
truth, telling the 188–189
Twain, Mark 58, 117
typefaces 291

U

unifying paragraphs 141–149
unnecessary adjectives and
  adverbs, avoiding 59–60
using figurative language,
  overview 163

V

vagueness, avoiding 50
variety 8, 19, 63–69
  creating 64–66
vary, what to 63–64
verbs
  active 69
  in sentences 94–95
  vigorous 60–63
vigor 8, 19, 55–63, 69
  colloquial 57–58
  for the long haul 58–59
vigorous verbs 60–63
visuals 277
vocabulary 35, 91, 183, 210
  enlarging 88–91
  origins of English 74–76
voice 10–11

W

way you say something (clarity in)
  41–52
Wesley, Samuel 12
what you want to say (clarity in)
  39–41
Wilde, Oscar 27, 117
wit 27–28
words
  careful use of longer 87–88
  choosing 71–91
    overview 91
  concrete 91
  expressing tone through
    185–210
    overview 210
  familiar 91

foreign and special terms
293–294
highlighted 293
key 142–143
use of those you know
71–73
Wordsworth, William 35
works, titles of 294–295
World Wide Web 29, 90

writer, lonely 173–174
writers and readers 173–183
writing
for children 179–183
preparing to write 39–40
promotional 279–283
styles 6–8
with style 3 –210